# STOP NUCLEAR WAR!
# A HANDBOOK

# STOP NUCLEAR WAR!

## A HANDBOOK

By David P. Barash, Ph.D.
and Judith Eve Lipton, M.D.

Foreword by Dr. Helen Caldicott

Grove Press, Inc./New York

Copyright © 1982 by David P. Barash and Judith Eve Lipton
Foreword copyright © 1982 by Helen Caldicott

First Edition 1982
First Printing 1982
ISBN: 0-394-52931-6
Library of Congress Catalog Card Number: 82-48162

First Evergreen Edition 1982
First Printing 1982
ISBN: 0-394-62433-5
Library of Congress Catalog Card Number: 82-48162


*Library of Congress Cataloging in Publication Data*

Barash, David P.
   Stop nuclear war!

   Bibliography: p. 386
   1. Atomic weapons and disarmament. I. Lipton,
Judith Eve. II. Title.
JX1974.7.B36 1982      327.1′74      82-48162
ISBN 0-394-52931-6
ISBN 0-394-62433-5 (pbk.)


Manufactured in the United States of America

GROVE PRESS, INC., 196 West Houston Street, New York, N.Y. 10014

To our children,
Ilona, Eva, Jacob, and Jenny,
and everyone else's children.

# ACKNOWLEDGMENTS

To make this book easily accessible to the nonspecialist, we have written it without footnotes or extensive referencing. However, we are very aware of our intellectual debts, especially to the following people. Their words and writings have become so integrated into our thinking that we are often unable to identify the origins of particular phrases, concepts, or viewpoints: Nathan Barash, Richard J. Barnet, Helen Caldicott, Roger Fisher, Randall Forsberg, Jerome Frank, Jack Geiger, Mark Hatfield, Fred Kaplan, Robert Jay Lifton, Morris A. Lipton, George Rathjens, Jonathan Schell, and Victor Sidel. Patrick Morgan and Valerie Trueblood made numerous helpful suggestions throughout the manuscript.

JEL gratefully wishes to acknowledge the pervasive influence of Helen Caldicott and Robert Jay Lifton on her personal transformation. The former is a Prophet; the latter a Sage. Their messages are complementary: If you love life, you must act to prevent nuclear war. If you work to prevent nuclear war, it is crucial to live fully, to love and feel deeply, and to celebrate life.

We also thank Fred Jordan and Barney Rosset for believing in this project, Gloria Stern our agent, and Joan Kohlenberg for cheerful and accurate typing. Most of all, we wish to thank the people of the peace movement, American and international, for giving us, and themselves, and all of our children renewed hope for a future.

# Contents

# Foreword

The world is moving rapidly toward the final medical epidemic: thermonuclear war. Over the last thirty-six years, both the U.S. and the U.S.S.R. have developed generations of ever more deadly nuclear weapons. Today these superpowers have between them some 50,000 such weapons. Weapons now being developed by both countries will add thousands of warheads, even though Russia and the United States now have enough nuclear weapons to target every town with a population of 10,000 or more. It is said that the Soviet Union has enough weapons to kill every American twenty times, and that America has enough to kill every Russian forty times. As a physician, I know that people can die only once.

This is the ultimate issue of our time. The earth is a delicate organism. It's like a single cell dependent upon intricate, little-understood mechanisms. If we don't protect it, it's going to die. If we all continue practicing psychic numbing and blotting out the reality of the nuclear arms race, it's possible that within ten years, or twenty, there will be a nuclear war, and we will destroy not only civilization, but history and the future as well. We're hostages on what might well be a terminally ill planet. This could become our global gas oven, with gravity as our barbed wire. And we can't escape. The only escape we have is to use our democracy to make sure the government does what we want it to do.

This book is an important aid in that work. Our current situation and how we got there are described in a concise, readable style, as are solutions and how to bring them about. Also discussed are ideas on how to personally cope with the despair that inevitably comes with facing the possible destruction of the planet. Barash and Lipton have succeeded in putting together the first "how-to" book for ending the arms race.

I urge you to use this book as a tool to save the world for our children. For it is the children who most clearly see what nuclear war will mean. The American Psychiatric Association recently studied 1,000 adolescents in Boston and Los Angeles and found, to their horror, that almost all of those children believe that they will never have jobs, that they will never get married or have children, because they are almost certainly going to be killed in a nuclear war. As these young people wrote: "In the event of a nuclear war, the youth of the world have the most to lose, having no legal power in decisions needed to help the arms race. We cry out for the right to live our lives in peace, without the fear of nuclear annihilation." (*Boston Globe*, May 10, 1982).

This is what it is all about. We must work like mad to make sure that all the children of the world survive. Nothing else really matters. It doesn't matter if we make sure our children clean their teeth or if we give them good food, if in fact they won't survive the next twenty years. Saving the planet is the ultimate form of preventive medicine. And the question to be asked now is not will *I* survive, but will I *be* survived.

—HELEN CALDICOTT, M.D.

# 1. Choose Life!

I believe that the problem of lessening the danger of annihilating humanity in a nuclear war carries an absolute priority over all other considerations.

—ANDREI SAKHAROV, 1980

I must study politics and war, that my . . . (children) . . . may study mathematics and philosophy, geography, natural history and naval architecture, navigation, commerce and agriculture, in order to give *their* children a right to study painting, poetry, music, architecture, statuary, tapestry and porcelain.

—JOHN ADAMS, 1790

This is probably the most important book you will ever read. It is the ultimate in self-help manuals: how to save the world. We have been sliding down the razorblade of possible nuclear war since 1945, but instead of jumping off, most of us have turned to psychic anesthesia, becoming numb to the pain and the peril. Now, in the last decades of the twentieth century, all of history stands balanced on the fine edge of survival or oblivion. We shall tip that balance, one way or the other.

If this sounds melodramatic, even corny, please be assured there is no way that we, or you, can be taking this issue too seriously. True, there are many other problems that beset our poor planet: overpopulation, pollution, the maldistribution of resources, and so on. However, imagine life on earth as water behind a dam. Each of these other problems are leaks in the dam. But nuclear war looms above all others—an enormous crack, running right down the center. If nuclear war occurs, the water of life will run out. All other problems will become meaningless, because life itself on this green planet may end. We Americans are a cheerful, optimistic people. We laugh at Chicken Little ("The sky is falling!) and the crazy, streetcorner prophets of doom ("The End is Near!"). But in fact, the end may really be near. Hence, this book.

How much time is left? On the cover of the *Bulletin of the*

*Atomic Scientists,* the hands of the doomsday clock read four minutes to midnight. Richard Garwin, brilliant physicist and longtime consultant to the Pentagon, estimates a 50-50 chance of all-out nuclear war by the year 2000. George Kistiakowsky, former head of the munitions division of the Manhattan Project and President Eisenhower's science adviser, estimates 50-50 by the year 1990.

Our message is as important as it is unpleasant: nuclear war is getting more likely. It is not only possible, but probable. Fortunately, however, it is not yet certain—and that also is our message: there is hope, if people like *you* begin to realize your peril and also your power. We are all under a death sentence, but one that we, together, can commute. Don't say you are not "political." If you are alive and want to keep on living, if you love others, if you have any feeling for this beautiful and varied planet, then this is *your* issue. It is not "just politics"; it is life and death.

We are addressing ourselves to that large group of hard-working, decent people who don't like what is happening in the world but who also don't try to do anything about it, either because they find politics and "activism" a messy business, or because they don't believe they can do any good. You are right—politics is a messy business. But not a fraction as messy as a nuclear war. And as for not doing any good, this is America, remember? Here, people do count. We *can* fight City Hall; in fact, we *are* City Hall!

We are talking about the most dangerous, uncertain, and anxious period in the history of civilization, the ill-begotten offspring of fear, mistrust, and the most destructive weapons the world has ever known. The pen, we have been told, is mightier than the sword. Perhaps so. Is there any hope that a book can be mightier than the bomb? Can the forces of life be stronger, smarter, more persistent than the forces of death? We hope so. This is a handbook, intended to aid those forces of life—to inform, to mobilize opinion, and to equip people with some of the tools that are needed if change is to come about. For "come about" we must, in the nautical sense—that is, we must change direction, by just about 180 degrees.

Under the banner of "realism," or for most Americans, under no banner at all except passive indifference, we are marching toward annihilation. Can things really be that bad? Sitting at our home in the suburbs of Seattle, Washington, watching our two horses chewing leisurely on their hay, hearing the birds sing as the clouds scud by, life seems very safe. It is hard, sometimes, even for us to believe our own warnings. The horses especially are reassuring—strong and serene, concerned only about their next meal and, possibly, whether they will go riding today or the disposition of the stallion next door. But in fact, they are in a precarious state—not these horses, of course, because we love them—but in fact we could send them off to become dog food and glue tomorrow, if we wished. Their security is illusory.

And so is ours.

Our animals would respond obediently if a truck drove up tomorrow and herded them inside for their final trip to a slaughterhouse, much as millions of thinking, intelligent people did in Nazi Germany less than forty years ago. They might be momentarily amazed, even perhaps resistent, as the sledge hammer bashed in their brains or the cunning knife silently slit their throats. But essentially, they would be helpless, capable only of a fit of anger, or more likely, bewilderment. We would all be in the same state if World War III began tomorrow: astonishment, perhaps a momentary confusion, maybe even a flash of anger or despair, dwarfed immediately by much larger flashes.

We deserve something better. It seems unworthy for us to go on simply chewing our cud, munching our mindless daily hay, awaiting our own liquidation as though we are mere bystanders instead of the lead characters in the only drama we will ever get to play. It is not only tragic, it is frustrating—"alarmists" like us won't even get to say "I told you so!" So now, before it is too late, we are telling you so: you, and everything you love and care about, are in mortal danger.

Other catastrophes have a warming-up period: overpopulation, famine, pollution, even plagues. But nuclear war can happen in thirty minutes, with no warning, no breathing space, no time to adjust. Civilization would be destroyed in a flash. In the pages to come, we shall explain the dangers, how we have been misled about our military strength and that of the Soviet Union, and what *we* can do as a nation as well as what *you* can do as an individual. Although things have always been dangerous in the world, especially since the invention of nuclear weapons, things are rapidly getting more dangerous yet, and this is why the American public must wake up, and quickly.

Fortunately, this is precisely what is happening. America is now experiencing the widest, deepest grassroots mass movement in many decades, perhaps in all of human history. Around the world, people are waking up to the mounting danger of nuclear war, determined to choose life over death, survival over annihilation. We have long been spectators at a parade, many of us looking the other way and pretending not to see while the preparations for our own destruction have been gaining momentum. Now, suddenly, the whisper has begun: "The Emperor has no clothes—nuclear weapons are wrong, dangerous, crazy, and must be stopped." That whisper is quickly becoming a roar, as from one end of the nation to the other, people are talking, reading, petitioning, meeting and demanding an end to nuclear madness. Garden clubs in Peoria, town meetings in Vermont, PTAs in Atlanta, and retired businessmen in California—America is getting busy. This is no fringe movement of radical peaceniks; it is people of all sorts, responding at last to the most important issue of our day, or any other. When Methodist ministers in Texas, with their ten gallon hats and cowboy boots, join with elegant, intellectual physicians from Harvard University and lumberjacks from southeast Alaska, something important is going on.

Don't search for the leadership of this movement, for there is none. Certainly, there are prominent individuals and groups, but by and large, the new anti-nuclear war movement is happening in a thousand different ways in a thousand different places, across America. The energy and direction of this movement comes from the people themselves. Included are antiabortion people and pro-abortion people, union members and corporate executives, blacks and whites, old and young, Republicans and Democrats, atheists and Archbishops. It has been moving so fast that its "leadership" is having a hard time keeping up. It is impossible to classify, too amorphous to describe and, most assuredly, it does not emanate from Moscow! It exists in so many shapes and sizes that you are guaranteed to find something that fits; if not, make something for yourself. We shall provide some blueprints and raw materials.

The peace movement of the 1980s has its roots in the Ban-the-

Bomb movements of the 1950s and 1960s. The Campaign for Nuclear Disarmament (CND), now the largest group supporting unilateral disarmament in the world, with over 250,000 members in the United Kingdom, was started by Bertrand Russell in 1958. Physicians for Social Responsibility, now numbering 14,000 doctors in the United States, started in 1960. However, the Ban-the-Bomb movement virtually ended with the Partial Test-Ban Treaty of 1963, which put nuclear weapons testing underground. Out of sight meant out of mind.

A few heroes, like the Berrigan brothers and Daniel Ellsberg, continued the struggle against nuclear weapons throughout the 1970s, but unfortunately, the majority of Americans turned a deaf ear. Vietnam, Watergate, the "Aquarian Conspiracy" preoccupied us, and we ignored the fact that three to ten nuclear bombs were made in the world every day. However, in 1979, our illusory security began to fall apart: SALT II was withdrawn, the Russians invaded Afghanistan, the Americans boycotted the Moscow Olympics, and the NATO generals decided to place a whole new generation of first-strike missiles in Europe. The hostage crisis in Iran seemed to frustrate the American people, and in 1980, right-wing hawk Ronald Reagan was elected President on a "Let's get tough" platform.

Almost simultaneously, in Europe, Japan, and the U.S., a new, determined peace movement began to grow. In Europe, it was spearheaded by the churches, particularly the Dutch Interchurch Peace Council, whose motto is "Let's rid the world of nuclear weapons, and let it begin in the Netherlands." By the fall of 1981, massive demonstrations were held all over Europe (400,000 people in Amsterdam; 300,000 in Bonn; over 200,000 in London, Paris, Madrid, and elsewhere) heralding a grassroots movement far greater than anything since World War II.

In the U.S., three separate forces began to build in 1980. American church leaders, both Catholic and Protestant, began to take an increasingly strong moral stand against the use or possession of nuclear weapons. The simple, elegant, and exciting concept of a bilateral nuclear freeze, first developed by Randall Forsberg, was printed and publicized as the "Call to Halt the Nuclear Arms Race," and ballot initiatives in Vermont and western Massachusetts were successful, even in those towns that supported Reagan. And finally, Physicians for Social Responsibility, lead by pediatrician Helen Caldicott, and the Council for a Livable World, began a series of symposia describing the medical consequences of nuclear war in graphic detail. In one city after another, the doctors' descriptions made banner headlines, and their message was clear: nuclear war would be the final epidemic. The only "cure" is prevention.

Organizers of the new movement felt like surfers waiting for a wave. By spring 1982, it was clear that the wave had arrived. The biggest splash was made by Jonathan Schell, whose magnificent book, *The Fate of the Earth*, ran as a three-part series in the February *New Yorker* magazines. Overnight, nuclear war became the talk of the town. Schell's book is a beautifully written, profound examination of the physical consequences of nuclear war, and the philosophical issues posed by extinction. It touched a barely concealed nerve in the American consciousness, and helped stimulate a new appreciation of our peril and new demands for what is after all a modest goal: the choice of survival over extinction.*

Then Roger and Earl Molander conceived and directed Ground Zero week, from April 18 to 25, 1982. Ground Zero was an attempt to educate the American people about the consequences of nuclear war and the technical aspects of the nuclear arms race, in a balanced and nonjudgmental manner. Hundreds of cities and towns all over the United States held rallies, debates, and discussions. The book, *Nuclear War: What's In It For You,* and the Ground Zero organization, attempt to present nuclear war in a "light and even entertaining" fashion, without advocating positions on policy questions. Their strategy is to involve and educate as many people as possible, permitting individuals to make up their own minds.

Our book is less shy.

"We have found it much easier to dig our own grave," writes Jonathan Schell, "than to think about the fact that we are doing so." Our book is for those who are ready to start thinking—and better yet, to start doing. In the chapters to come, we shall first describe some steps that the nation can take to start turning things

---

* Although we agree wholeheartedly with Schell that *anything* is better than the extinction of the human race, and possibly life on earth, this is *not* a revival of "better Red than dead." Rather, we advocate a movement that will help us remain both alive *and* free.

around. Then we will describe how you can contribute. Although we would like to have you, body and soul, lock, stock and barrel, totally committed to stopping nuclear war, we'll be happy with whatever you do. There are many ways to save the world: you can go whole hog, utterly committed and filled with righteous passion, or you can dabble a bit on the side, by joining an organization or two, and writing an occasional postcard. Whatever your decision, you *can* make a difference.

To be effective, however, you will also need information, and so the rest of this book will seek to inform as well as to motivate. We want to give you enough information to argue any general under the table and to give you the power to take your future into your own hands. We hope to frighten you, anger you, even entertain you in places, but most of all, we seek to *empower* you.

Why is this all happening now? Is it just the latest American fad, the hula hoop of the 1980s? Or is it the flailing, hopeless recognition of falling, doomed men, the final scream before we hit the pavement?

It is, instead, the greatest opportunity we shall ever have. Right now, in the 1980s, we are poised at the brink of the most dangerous escalations in the history of the nuclear arms race. Decisions made in the next few years—certainly within this decade—will determine whether you survive or not. That is why "the movement" exists, and that is why it needs you and you need it.

Right now, both sides are piling up bombs at a reckless pace, with other countries straining to join in. With onrushing technological "improvements" in bomb design and missile accuracy, each side (but especially the U.S.) is posing an ever-growing threat to the other, and therefore to itself. As a result, the dread "balance of terror," which has kept the precarious nuclear peace since 1945, is beginning to crumble. In addition, official government planners, wielding new strategic doctrines, are making nuclear war "thinkable," and hence, more likely than ever before. Add to this the growing risks of accidental war, nuclear terrorism, miscalculation between the superpowers, or the potential for escalation of local, conventional conflicts, and any thoughtful person should have trouble sleeping.

On the other hand, the worst is yet to come. *In other words, it can still be prevented.* Most of the really stupid, inexcusable, destabilizing developments in nuclear weapons are on the horizon—they have not yet been installed. We can still stop them. Even those in place can be dismantled. Do not misunderstand, however: we shall not be advocating unilateral disarmament. Too many people think that we have only two choices: pile up an ever more dangerous arsenal of weapons, or capitulate to the Russians. As we shall point out, there are many other roads open to us. In the course of this book, we shall discuss several of these—well-studied, risk-free, and entirely feasible strategies which would not only help secure our freedom and safety, but even benefit the economy as well.

The old cliché "eternal vigilance is the price of liberty" still holds true. We have been insufficiently vigilant and the price we may pay is not only our liberty but perhaps our lives and those of everyone else. We have let our vigilance slip, and not in letting the Russians get ahead: as we shall see, they have never been ahead, nor are they now. Rather, we have slipped in giving free reign to the hardline "bombs away" militarists, the professional cold warriors, the moral midgets who calculate "acceptable" deaths in the tens or hundreds of millions. We have let them push us into a deadly corner. It is time to push back; time to renew our vigilance. Time to get out of that corner. Time to admit that we have been duped and taken for fools, that we have failed ourselves and those we love, but—and here is the most difficult admission of all—time to admit that there is still hope, if we will only face the uncomfortable facts of our own responsibility.

Recently, we watched the delight in our daughter's four-year-old face as she read her first word. With tears in our eyes, we knew that we could not let her be incinerated in a nuclear war. That is our decision. We await yours.

And yet, you may wonder how to go on living and loving, if you accept that everything you treasure may vanish in a blinding flash, at any time. The answer lies in Robert Jay Lifton's work on "psychic numbing," the mental process that permitted the survivors of Hiroshima to walk amid the corpses and the dying, without collapsing hysterically in the debris. Dr. Lifton found that the survivors experienced a diminished ability to *feel*, not only the horror, but also grief, not only sadness, but also joy. He pointed out that we are, in a sense, all survivors of Hiroshima and Nagasaki. However, if we deny the problem, numbing ourselves to the reality of the nuclear threat, we also become numb to the positive aspects of our life. If you choose to be numb, you may experience less anxiety, but life loses its color and meaning as well.

But how can we learn about burned babies, charred children, all the true life horrors that have been and that may yet be, without becoming depressed? And how can we expect people to subject themselves to such a psychic ordeal, even if they can be re-sensitized after it is over? These are not easy questions, and we have no easy answers. And yet . . .

We have come to believe that the most complete and effective route is to immerse oneself in the awful reality, run the risk of transient, defensive numbness and despair, and then come out again on the other side, at peace with oneself and one's commitment. It is almost a ritual purification: to go through a personal purgatory, then to emerge devoid of illusion and ready to work. But it is painful and difficult, and many people—perhaps most—will shy away.

Fortunately, however, it is not the only way. Another option is to take an end run around the horror, by focusing on the goal, a celebration of life and of hope. The prevention of nuclear war is not, at its fount, a radical goal. It does not aim for a restructuring of society; rather, the *preservation* of society. Hence, it should appeal across a wide spectrum and moreover, it can and should focus on the beauty and wonder of that life which it seeks to preserve. One way around psychic numbing, then, is to emphasize the joy, beauty, family spirit and holy spirit of being alive. The new antinuclear war movement can legitimately wrap itself both in the flag of our country and in the pleasures of companionship, happiness, and love.

The Dutch, for example, are quite clear on what it takes to motivate people: they reject "Doomdanken" (doom thinking) and their huge demonstrations are joyous events, complete with children, students, church leaders, old people, even the military on parade. The police smile benevolently. You can buy hot dogs. Parade routes and indeed, entire cities are festooned with gay posters and elegant graffiti. Songs are everywhere: sad, defiant songs of Nazi oppression, satiric songs of mindless militarism, the Ban-the-Bomb boogie, happy songs about life and its precious joys. It is not necessary to be numb. Indeed, it is necessary to be just the opposite: sensitized—not only to nuclear war, which we are against, but also to life, which we are for.

Those who refuse to think about nuclear war, because it is "too depressing," show by their response that they have already thought about it. Nuclear war *is* depressing, but the cure is not to deny the problem or to repress the depression; the problem will not go away by your refusing to think about it. And your anxiety will simply show itself in other ways. So, to cure yourself, start curing the world: get busy. The best—perhaps the only—cure for the nuclear war blues is not denial, depression or numbing, but rather action. A final cure will come only when the threat is removed. In the meanwhile, treating the symptoms out there in the world—not in you—is the best possible therapy.

Actually, there can be real zest in saving the world. What bettar way to spend your time? It sure beats sitting around moping, feeling sorry for yourself, wrapped up in petty disputes or worries. If you want to tackle a really big problem,something truly and totally worthwhile, something that can take your best efforts and still offer a challenge, then try your hand at saving the world. (Either part or full time, anyone may apply.) If you want "relevance" in your life, if you want to work with some of the finest people in the very best and most important cause imaginable, if you want to fill your life with more meaning than you ever dreamed possible—then have we got a deal for you! Read on.

# 2. What *We* Can Do: The United States

We are confronted here, my friends, with two courses. At the end
of the one lies hope—faint hope, if you will—uncertain hope, hope
surrounded with dangers, if you insist. At the end of the other lies,
so far as I am able to see, no hope at all.

Can there be—in the light of our duty not just to ourselves (for
we are all going to die sooner or later) but of our duty to our own
kind, our duty to the continuity of generations, our duty to the
great experiment of civilized life on this rare and rich and mar-
vellous planet—can there be, in the light of these claims on our
loyalty, any question as to which course we should adopt?

—GEORGE F. KENNAN

After the final no there comes a yes,
And on that yes the future of the world depends.

—WALLACE STEVENS

There *is* hope, for there is much that the United States can do. We
are not helpless. We cannot afford indifference, inaction or false
optimism, but neither should we lose hope. Nuclear war is not
inevitable. It is our Frankenstein's monster; we made it and we can
stop it. As Wallace Stevens put it, there is a "yes," and as a nation
we must strive for it. The U.S. in particular has a unique obligation,
as the initiator and leader in the nuclear arms race. Moreover, we
also have unique and exciting opportunities. There can be no
greater challenge, no worthier quest. In this chapter, we shall out-
line twenty-seven different proposals—how our nation can help
save itself and the rest of the world. It is time to wage peace.

We shall propose (1) major policy initiatives which at a stroke
can reshape the world and make it safer, (2) subtle changes and
affirmations of attitude, and (3) certain warnings, words and deeds,
some of them limited in themselves, but which nonetheless can
help establish a bulwark of safety for us all and our descendants.
The various suggestions in this chapter are not all equally feasible,

or equally important. But each one *is* feasible and each one *is* important. Our situation will be improved every time one is adopted—the more, the better.

They are practical. They go beyond ringing declarations of universal brotherhood, or hand-wringing pronouncements of our peril. They can be implemented, both because they are within our power as a nation, and because they would be politically acceptable as well. They do not call for unilateral disarmament, but they do call, however, for imagination, courage, foresight, patience, a realization of our current danger, and a willingness to do something about it. Better to light one candle, it is said, than to curse the dark. Here are many such candles.

#### #1: Halt the arms race by immediately initiating a bilateral, U.S.-Soviet freeze on the testing, production and deployment of nuclear weapons and systems for delivering them.

We can and should immediately halt the nuclear arms race, thereby stopping things from getting worse and setting the stage for actual reductions. How? By joining with the U.S.S.R. in a "freeze," the fastest-growing and most exciting new development on the American scene in many years. It is desperately needed, feasible, understandable, verifiable, effective, and straightforward, and if we all work hard it could happen.

In one form or another, the idea of a freeze has been around for quite some time. It was proposed by Senator Mark Hatfield as an amendment to SALT II in 1979, and has been championed especially by Randall Forsberg, founder of the Institute for Defense and Disarmament Studies. Following a surge of grassroots enthusiasm, a nuclear freeze proposal was introduced into the U.S. Congress in 1982, co-sponsored by Senators Hatfield and Kennedy and 17 other senators, as well as 122 members of the House of Representatives. The proposal calls for a "mutual and verifiable freeze on the testing, production and further deployment of nuclear warheads, missiles and delivery systems."

Decades of failures in arms control have led to a widespread feeling of helplessness, hopelessness and despair, even cynicism. The nuclear freeze proposal can cut through all this—it may be the greatest chance we will ever have to turn things around. In many ways, the time is right—now in the 1980s—to take this first step.

The idea is breathtakingly simple. In a hot but conventional war, the freeze would mean a "cease-fire in place." In the current cold war arms race, it says "enough is enough"—or maybe, too much. There are some very good reasons why we can and should freeze the arms race at this time. For example:

*a) Prevent destabilizing developments.* The "window of vulnerability" that some military planners find so worrisome could be kept closed—for all time—if both sides agree not to deploy weapons currently scheduled for the 1980s. We claim to need ours because of their plans to deploy theirs, and *vice versa.* Why not agree to freeze both?

On the Soviet side, a freeze would mean a halt to production of their Backfire bomber and additional SS-20 missiles. It would also prevent the development of their newest generation, SS-21, SS-22, and SS-23 missiles. It would mean no additional MIRVing (for discussion of *MIR*Ving, see page 125ff.) of their single warhead missiles. It would prevent further production of the SS-19 ICBM and the submarine-launched SS-18, as well as development of a new generation of SS-17s, SS-18s, and SS-19s. It would also mean an end to additional Typhoon nuclear submarines—and anything else they may have planned that we don't know about yet.

On the U.S. side, a freeze would mean a halt to production of Trident submarines and Trident I missiles, and no Trident II. It would mean no Air-Launched Cruise Missiles for the B-52s, no Ground-Launched Cruise Missiles or Pershing IIs in Europe. It would mean no MX missile, no B-1 bomber and no Stealth. It would mean no Mark 12-A warheads for several hundred Minuteman IIIs, no new earth-penetrator warheads and no new-style gravity bombs. A freeze would mean an end to accuracy "improvements" on both sides.

By stopping these developments on both sides, each would be made immeasurably more secure. The history of the arms race has shown clearly that the most effective way for us to assure the growth of Soviet arsenals is to enlarge our own; the most effective way that we can stop the growth of Soviet arsenals is to stop the growth of our own. Even the worst "worst-case" projections speak to a "window of vulnerability" in the future—not now. That is, our ICBMs are said to be potentially vulnerable in several years, if the Soviets deploy additional missiles. Similarly, as we shall see, their ICBMs are more vulnerable than ours, and will become even more vulnerable yet, with the MX, Trident, and Navstar satellite system. Such vulnerability makes *both* sides *less* secure.

A freeze would also be welcome because it would prevent new systems, currently planned, that would be difficult to verify, and hence might be impossible to negotiate away once in place. In particular, continued deployment of cruise missiles and of Backfire bombers would greatly complicate any future arms control negotiations, simply because both systems contain unverifiable elements. Cruise missiles, for example, are so small that the Soviets might never be satisfied that they are all accounted for. They are easy to conceal and difficult to observe by satellite. It is only a matter of time before the Soviets have long-range, nuclear-tipped cruise missiles of their own—we would do well to freeze them now. For its part, the Soviet Backfire bomber seems to be a subject of unending controversy: it obviously was designed as a medium-range bomber, for use in Europe, China, or against ships. But it has limited intercontinental capacity as well—it could reach the U.S., but not return to the U.S.S.R. By stopping both cruise missiles and the Backfire, the options for eventual reductions would be enhanced. If unstopped, these escalations could propel both sides down a slippery slope; and once we reach bottom, it will be very difficult to climb out.

In short, the "window of vulnerability" is really a window of opportunity, giving both sides good reasons for a freeze.

*b) Maintain parity.* There seem to be two basic rules for negotiators: 1. don't negotiate when you are ahead, and 2. don't negotiate when you are behind. Hence, situations of rough equality, such as the present, are rare and precious opportunities. Nuclear arms negotiations were notably unsuccessful during the late 1940s and 1950s, because we were far ahead of the U.S.S.R., and we kept insisting on mutual and balanced reductions—which would have left us permanently ahead. It was only by the late 1960s, with the beginning of nuclear parity, that SALT talks began in earnest.

Now, in the 1980s, most experts agree that the U.S. and U.S.S.R. have finally achieved strategic parity (although as we shall see, the U.S. is actually ahead in every meaningful measure of strategic nuclear strength). In any event, disarming first strikes are currently impossible, by either side. As the Federation of American Scientists recently pointed out, a form of "saturation parity" has also been reached: the U.S. has only 2,000 cities of more than 10,000 people and the U.S.S.R. has more than 2,000 strategic warheads. A similar situation obtains on the other side. In fact, strategic "targeters" have long ago run out of targets. (And yet, we are now planning 17,000 additional warheads for the 1980s!)

U.S. warheads are more numerous and accurate, while the Soviets have more ICBMs with more megatonnage. They can't make missiles as small and accurate as ours, so they have settled for larger, clumsier ones. In fact, we will never reach precise add-em-up parity, simply because our two nations are different, with different resources, strengths, and weaknesses. To some extent, in comparing U.S.-Soviet military strength, we are comparing apples and oranges—although any way we look at it, it is a very dangerous fruit salad. The rough parity which now exists—discernible as it is to both sides—is therefore unique and possibly fleeting, a precious moment of balanced grace. There is a great opportunity to seize this moment, and it would be a great tragedy if we did not.

c) *Help stop the spread of nuclear arms to other nations.* World (and U.S.) security is reduced by nuclear proliferation; the more fingers on the Button, the less safe are we all. Hence, both the U.S. and the U.S.S.R. supported the Non-Proliferation Treaty, in which the world's non-nuclear nations agreed to forgo acquiring nuclear weapons. In return for this, the nuclear nations agreed, in Article VI of the Treaty, to "pursue negotiations in good faith on effective measures relating to cessation of the nuclear arms race at an early date and to nuclear disarmament and on a treaty on general and complete disarmament, under strict and effective international control." It is clear that the U.S. and U.S.S.R. have not met their side of the NPT bargain, thereby weakening the resolve of the non-nuclear signatories to keep *their* side. A U.S.-Soviet nuclear freeze would be a visible step in the right direction.

d) *A Comprehensive Test-Ban.* Many Americans believe that nuclear testing halted with the Partial Test-Ban Treaty of 1963. It did not. In fact, that treaty was really little more than an antipollution agreement; the nuclear arms race has continued after the treaty, the only difference being that tests were moved underground. In fact, there have been more nuclear test explosions, per year, after the Partial Test-Ban than before it! Negotiations for a Comprehensive Test-Ban Treaty (no testing of any sort, underground or anywhere else) have been under way for many years. The technical problems of verification have essentially been solved °—all that remains is the political will to reach an agreement. Little known to the American public, in July 1980, the U.S.S.R. dropped its longtime opposition to on-site inspection, thereby further enhancing the prospects for a CTBT. (In the revived cold war following the Afghanistan invasion, the boycott of the Moscow Olympics, and the U.S. presidential campaign, this potentially historic Soviet concession went virtually unnoticed in the American press.)

One virtue of a CTBT is that it would halt the development of new and ever more lethal warheads. The nuclear arms "race" is misnamed: it is not really a race, since no one can win. It is a *spiral,* with sprints by one side generating corresponding sprints by the other, and no end in sight unless we declare an end. Another virtue is that a CTBT would reduce each side's confidence in the reliability of its warheads. Periodically, military planners like to pluck a bomb from a missile nose cone or a bomber, and blow it up—just to make sure that they are still working. If such tests are banned, confidence will drop. Paradoxically, this reduced confidence will make us safer. Thus, planners on each side would be forced to abandon any thoughts of a surprise, first strike against the other side's missiles. This is because a "counterforce" attack, unlike mere deterrence, requires that virtually all of the attacker's warheads function correctly—otherwise, some of the victim's missiles will survive, and be available for a deadly retaliation.°° For an additional benefit, as planners on each side become less likely to design a first strike, they also become more secure—and hence, less

---

° At least for nuclear tests above one kiloton.
°° It would be embarrassing, to say the least, for one side to try a sneak attack against the other's missiles, only to have some of the attacking warheads go *Clunk* against the other side's missile silos!

likely to attack preemptively in a crisis—since they also know that their opponent is, like them, less likely to be planning a first strike itself.

There are additional benefits: since we do not have a SALT treaty, the U.S.S.R. is free, if it wishes, to put 20, 30, or even 40 MIRVed warheads on its large SS-18 missiles. This, in turn, would further add to anxiety about "Minuteman vulnerability." However, MIRVing of this sort would require that the Soviets conduct extensive testing of small, adequate-yield warheads. A comprehensive Test-Ban would prevent this. Finally, a ban on all nuclear weapons testing would provide additional support for non-profileration: in the Non-Proliferation Treaty, all sides agreed to seek "the discontinuance of all test explosions of nuclear weapons for all time." Moreover, if the military establishments of the U.S. and U.S.S.R. were prohibited from testing, they would probably be motivated as never before to discourage other countries from engaging in their own!

e) *Economic benefits.* Strategic weapons programs in the U.S., according to Reagan Administration projections, are in the neighborhood of $250 billion over the next five years. Soviet estimates are not available, but are probably comparable. The enormous savings from a nuclear freeze could be used for pressing domestic needs, to reduce taxes, to ease the North-South world economic disparity, and/or simply to help balance the budget and fight inflation. As we shall see in chapter 11, by shifting federal money from a military to a civilian economy, the nation's economy will be greatly strengthened.

f) *Verifiability.* A freeze would be highly verifiable. In fact, we would have even greater confidence that the Soviets are complying with a freeze than with SALT I or SALT II, simply because it is easier to verify that *no additional deployments* are taking place than to monitor a series of constantly changing numerical levels. It takes about two years to prepare a new missile launch site, during which time the evidence would be clear to spy satellites—referred to in SALT language as "national technical means" of verification.

The U.S. "Discoverer" satellite, followed by "Samos I" and "Samos II," replaced the ill-fated U-2 and ended the myth of the missile gap in 1961. More than twenty years ago, our satellites provided a clear count of the entire Soviet missile force. Our spy satellites at 100 miles elevation can achieve ground resolution of less than 1.5 feet—it is said that we can read a license plate in the Moscow streets! In addition, multispectral photography obtains simultaneous images at different wavelengths, thereby effectively penetrating cloud cover. The U.S. also maintains an extensive, worldwide array of radar tracking stations, including not only traditional "line of sight" systems, but also "over the horizon" radar, which receives signals bounced off the ionosphere. Stations in Taiwan, Japan, and the Philippines currently monitor all Soviet test firings in Asia—there is simply no way that new missiles could be tested without our knowing it. (And there is simply no way that a new missile could be deployed without first being tested—in fact many times.) All present weaponry, both U.S. and Soviet, have well-known "signatures": radar patterns, photographic electromagnetic characteristics, etc., such that any new ones would readily be detectable.

In theory, some concealed production and stockpiling could occur, but in practice, it is most unlikely, since major undertakings of this sort would almost certainly leave telltale signs of new construction, supply, even changes of worker patterns within a factory (which can be identified by infrared satellite photography!).

We could never be 100 percent certain that small-scale cheating wasn't going on. Either side would probably squirrel away several hundred additional bombs, undetected. However, for it to alter the current balance of terror, cheating would have to be massive—and it would then be readily detectable.

In addition, the really dangerous developments now scheduled involve not warheads but rather, new delivery systems—especially, new missiles. And the testing and deployment of new missiles would be the easiest part of a freeze to verify. What about some new secret weapon? It is simply impossible to conceive of any development, conducted in total secrecy from our eyes in the sky, which would render our 9,000 strategic warheads no longer effective as a deterrent.

g) *Popular appeal.* Unlike SALT II, which was too elaborate to be understood by the average citizen, the freeze proposal is simple, straightforward, mutual and just plain common sense: "stop where you are." After years of indifference and impotence, Americans are suddenly waking up to the facts of nuclear war and the nuclear arms race, and to the need and the possibilities of an immediate freeze. As of spring 1982, more than one million persons had signed freeze petitions, including over 700,000 in California alone, where a freeze resolution will appear on the November 1982 ballot. The freeze has been endorsed by 309 New England town meetings, 33 city councils across the nation, 10 county councils, and one or both houses in 11 state legislatures. And this is but the beginning. During the 1980 national election, the voters of western Massachusetts voted on a freeze resolution. The results? 59 percent yes—in an area of 33 towns and cities which voted for Ronald Reagan, of which 30 also voted for a freeze. Apparently, the 1980 election was not necessarily a vote for the nuclear arms race. A Gallup Poll, released in June 1981, showed that 72 percent of Americans favored a complete ban on the building of nuclear weapons, and a *Newsweek* poll, released April 26, 1982, showed that 68 percent either favored or strongly favored a nuclear freeze. An Associated Press-NBC News poll on May 10, 1982, showed that a freeze was favored by a whopping 83 percent of Americans.

Organized religion has been especially active, and the freeze has been endorsed by the Catholic archbishops of Seattle, San Francisco, and San Antonio, as well as supported by the national council of bishops. The United Presbyterian Church voted overwhelmingly for a freeze at its general assembly meeting, and the freeze has also been officially endorsed by the Unitarian-Universalist Association, the Greek Orthodox Archdiocese of North and South America, the Oregon-Idaho and Rocky Mountain Conferences of the United Methodist Church, the Rocky Mountain Synod of the United Presbyterian Church, and the Wisconsin-Upper Michigan Synod of the Lutheran Church in America.

h) *But wouldn't a freeze be risky?* President Eisenhower once commented that "the alternative is so terrible that any risks there might be in advancing to disarmament are as nothing." And the freeze is actually modest and virtually risk-free. There are presumably some risks with any prospect for arms control and disarmament. We must compare those risks, however, with the risks of *not* controlling our nuclear weapons—that is, of continuing and even increasing the arms race. For the alternative, we must push the hardline military argument as far as we can. Where does it lead? What does it offer, after all the expense, all the escalations, the tensions, the crises and the eternal racing? Is there a vision of stable, long-lasting security built upon the accumulation of more and more nuclear weapons? Doesn't it have to stop somewhere, either with mutual annihilation, or with mutual agreement to stop the arms race? And if we are agreed that the latter is preferable, is there a better time to start stopping than now?

President Reagan has proposed a new round of strategic arms talks, to be called START—Strategic Arms Reduction Talks. This sounds wonderful. Before we can "start" ending the arms race, however, we must stop the ongoing accumulation. In short, it's time to stop. Time for a freeze.

In fact, there would be no risk in freezing; or rather, no greater risk than already exists. Poseidon submarines on station at any given moment have the MIRVed ability to destroy all 218 Soviet cities with a population of 100,000 and above, *20 times over*. If that won't deter Soviet aggression, what will? In 1979, Secretary of Defense Harold Brown recommended that in order to guarantee ourselves the ability to deter a Soviet attack, we should have the ability to destroy 200 cities, kill 70 million people and destroy about two-thirds of their industry; this would require 300 to 400 warheads. We have about 9,300 strategic warheads, and another 20,000 tactical warheads. The "risk" of a freeze is insignificant compared to the risk of no freezing.

i) *Would the Soviet Union agree?* There is a good chance. All of the benefits that we would get from a freeze would also apply to them. In fact, since 1976, the U.S.S.R. has made numerous freeze-like proposals: 1) A September 1976 memorandum on "Questions of Ending the Arms Race and of Disarmament," submitted to the U.N. General Assembly, called for an end to all testing, reduction in nuclear stockpiles, and cessation of development and manufacture of all nuclear weapons. 2) In November 1977, Soviet President Brezhnev made a speech to the 25th Communist Party Congress in Moscow, saying

> The Soviet Union proposes a radical step: that agreement be reached
> on a simultaneous halt in the production of nuclear weapons. This

could apply to all such weapons—whether atomic, hydrogen or neutron bombs or missiles. At the same time, the nuclear powers could undertake to start the gradual reduction of existing stockpiles of such weapons and move towards their complete, total destruction.

3) In May 1978, "The Practical Measures for Ending the Arms Race" was submitted to the U.N. Special Session on Disarmament. It called for an end to the production of all nuclear weapons and the reduction of military budgets by a fixed amount. The Soviets also warned that

> The pace at which agreements on limiting the arms race are being achieved is slower than that at which the arms race itself is developing. Moreover, in some highly dangerous aspects of the arms race a point may be reached beyond which it will no longer be possible to conclude arms limitation agreements based on mutual verification. . . . It is the view of the Soviet Union that the time has come to give thought to ending completely any further quantitative and qualitative build-up of arms.

4) In February 1979, the U.S.S.R. proposed again in a letter to the U.N. that negotiations begin on an end to production of all nuclear weapons and the reduction of existing stockpiles.

5) In April 1981, Foreign Minister Andrei Gromyko submitted a letter to U.N. Secretary-General Waldheim proposing an end to nuclear weapons production, reduction of stockpiles, limitations and reductions of all missiles, a Comprehensive Test-Ban Treaty, and the reduction of all military budgets, either on an absolute or a percentage basis.

6) In May 1982, Brezhnev responded to Reagan's arms reduction proposal by recommending a bilateral freeze, before any further negotiations.

j) *Can we trust the Russians?* We wouldn't have to. We have superb verification procedures already available. In addition, we have already signed many nuclear weapons treaties with the U.S.S.R., and *they have kept every one:* 1959—demilitarizing of

Antarctica; 1963—Partial Test-Ban; 1967—ban on nuclear weapons in outer space; 1968—Non-Proliferation Treaty; 1971—ban on nuclear weapons on the seabed and ocean floor; and 1972—SALT I. In fact, thus far, they have even honored the terms of SALT II (as have we), despite the fact that the U.S. never ratified that treaty.

As part of SALT I, the U.S. and U.S.S.R. established a Standing Consultative Commission, to examine possible violations by either side. Ambassador Robert Buchheim, U.S. Commissioner to the SCC from 1977-1981, stated there had never been "a case of real . . . and substantial noncompliance with an existing agreement." We can assume that the U.S.S.R.—just like the U.S.—would keep any agreement that is in their interest to keep. And a freeze would be in their interest, just as it would be in ours.

k) *Will the U.S. ever call for a freeze?* Not unless the American people demand it. The forces arrayed against a freeze are impressive: decades of encrusted professional cold-warism, Pentagon officials whose personal advancement requires the development and procurement of new bombs and weapons systems; scientists and engineers who are in the same position; major industrial conglomerates which stand to make a lot of money from new weapons that would otherwise be halted by a freeze. To stand against the ruckus these groups will doubtless raise against any prospect of a freeze will require inspired statesmanship—or a clear message from the American people. Thus far, we have had precious little of the former. It is time, therefore, for the latter.

It could happen, however, even under the Reagan Administration. Thus, Defense Secretary Caspar Weinberger was quoted on April 13, 1981 as saying "I would endorse any future (arms control) agreement that could (1) be verifiable, (2) be balanced, and (3) promote stability between the two powers." If it ever became convinced of the merits of a freeze, the Reagan Administration could move effectively. Just as only a Tory like Churchill could preside over the dismantling of the British Empire with a minimum of recriminations, and perhaps only a professional anticommunist like Nixon could open the door to China, the Reagan Administration has the hardline credibility necessary to make a freeze acceptable to the right wing, and maybe even the Joint Chiefs of Staff if not the weapons builders themselves. Ronald Reagan could probably achieve arms agreement with the Soviets more readily than any other president in the past decade. If nothing else, he is the first president since Nixon who has not had to worry about Ronald Reagan!

Unfortunately, however, the Reagan Administration has rejected the freeze concept, dredging up phony claims that the Soviet Union is ahead, and that therefore, a freeze would leave us at a disadvantage (see Chapter 5, "The World According to Gap, Part II: Counterfeit Claims for the 1980s"). Indeed, the increasingly shrill opposition provides a good measure of the freeze campaign's remarkable success: in a March 22, 1982 editorial titled "Peddling Nuclear Fear," the *Wall Street Journal* equated the freeze movement with "hysteria" and an "apocalyptic ban-the-bomb mentality."

The amazing success of the freeze movement has induced many of the government's most dyed-in-the-wool hawks to scurry for some face-saving, freezelike initiative. One result was the Jackson-Warner resolution, endorsed quickly by a majority of the Senate, and by the Reagan Administration as well. It sounds superficially like a freeze, but it isn't; rather, it is an antifreeze. (You don't have to be a physician, or a military strategist, to know that swallowing antifreeze is hazardous to your health!) As opposed to the "freeze-now" proposal, the Jackson-Warner resolution calls for a "freeze-later"—after the Soviets have either reduced their arsenals or we have built up our own yet further. In short, the antifreeze is simply window dressing, to legitimize a new and perhaps final escalation of the nuclear arms race.

While it is important to distinguish the freeze-now from the misleading freeze-later campaigns, it is also important to recognize the powerful momentum now moving in this country, and to take heart from it. After all, who would have thought, a scarce year ago, that the nuclear freeze campaign would be front page news so soon, or that the President would be forced to respond specifically to its demands? No American government can remain indifferent to massive, sustained, and fervent public pressure. If the freeze campaign keeps building, then our government will either change its tune (and discover that it actually was for a freeze all along!), or we will change the government.

1) *Shouldn't we start arms negotiations with the Soviets first?* Arms negotiations are certainly desirable. However, it took three

years to negotiate the modest accomplishments of SALT I, and seven years for the never-ratified SALT II. During this time, weapons-building went on, on both sides. The next generation of strategic, first-strike weaponry would be so destabilizing that we simply cannot afford to spend several more years locked in talks, while pressures for new "bargaining chips" undoubtedly develop, and both sides reach an intolerable level of mutually threatening armaments. Rather, we must freeze *now*, and then begin negotiations for subsequent reductions.

m) *How could it be done?* The U.S. president could simply call up the Soviet president and offer "we'll stop if you'll stop," proposing a specific time—say, eight o'clock tomorrow morning. It literally could be done that easily. The effect would be electrifying.

Alternatively, a freeze could be proposed in a widely televised speech, with a specific proposal, in a signed letter, sent at the same time. If the Soviets didn't agree right away, the president could announce a variety of freeze options: for example, a three-month moratorium on all test explosions; the decision not to deploy some new system, such as the MX, Pershing II, or ground-launched cruise missiles; an indefinite delay in the deployment of additional Trident submarines. With each announcement, the pressure will mount on the Soviet leadership to accept the freeze, just as confidence will mount that the U.S., in fact, means what it is saying. Given the enormous overkill of our current deterrence posture, it is inconceivable that such initiatives, even if begun unilaterally, will in any way compromise our security.

n) *But does the freeze go far enough?* No. Things are bad now; a freeze would simply stop them from getting worse. It is a start, however. It would also help establish the right climate for arms reductions. For in the long run, arms reductions must be made. Stable deterrence, and its MAD principle—Mutually Assured Destruction—is preferable by far to an unstable and escalating arms race, bringing doctrines of counterforce and "limited nuclear warfighting" in its wake. But let's not kid ourselves: we simply cannot bank on our planet spinning off into eternity, poised to slit each other's throats and yet forever prevented from doing so by a rational calculation based on mutual fear. As Admiral George Miller put it: "As long as there is a button to push, somebody, someday is going to push it."

In a world of conventional arms, the argument can be made that more is better. In a world of nuclear arms, more is worse. Our own weapons make us *less* secure. This is a basic transformation of thought, difficult but necessary. Once accomplished, it leads smoothly on to arms reductions. Former ambassador and diplomatic historian George F. Kennan sees clearly, and so should we:

> I believe that until we consent to recognize that the nuclear weapons we hold in our hands are as much a danger to us as those that repose in the hands of our supposed adversaries there will be no escape from the confusions and dilemmas to which such weapons have now brought us, and must bring us increasingly as time goes on. For this reason, I see no solution to the problem other than the complete elimination of these and all other weapons of mass destruction from national arsenals; and the sooner we move toward that solution, and the greater courage we show in doing so, the safer we will be.

Hence, in his speech accepting the Albert Einstein Peace Prize, Kennan made a startling proposal, but one that is entirely feasible and eminently desirable—a 50 percent across-the-board reduction in all nuclear weapons and delivery systems, "to be implemented at once and without further wrangling among the experts." On this issue, the American people seem to be far ahead of their leaders; thus, a Gallup Poll released on December 13, 1981, showed that 76 percent of Americans would favor a 50 percent reduction in U.S. and Soviet nuclear stockpiles, if done equitably. Since the military forces of our two nations, although roughly equal in overall strength, are quite different in detail, the simplest procedure is for each side to reduce whatever it has by one-half. We would eliminate one-half of our ICBMs, one-half of our nuclear missile submarines, one-half of our bombers, etc. And the Soviet Union would do the same. As Kennan emphasizes:

> Whether the balance of reduction would be precisely even—whether it could be constructed to favor statistically one side or the other— would not be the question. Once we start thinking that way, we would be back on the same old fateful track that has brought us to where we

are today. Whatever the precise results of such a reduction, there would still be plenty of overkill left—so much so that if this first operation were successful, I would then like to see a second one put in hand to rid us of at least two-thirds of what would be left."

In fact, each side can hold the other's cities hostage with a minimal deterrent—perhaps a handful of submarines. Why not destroy the rest? The stronger power must take the initiative, and that is clearly us.

The scrapped weapons would pose an interesting problem: what should we do with them? George Kistiakowsky has one solution: "Let them rot!" Alternatively, perhaps we should literally hammer a few Minuteman missiles into ploughshares—it would be a great symbolic act, as well as a public relations triumph.

But gesture or not, something must be done, and soon. Arms reductions must be our long-term goal; the freeze is a start. A saved world is within our grasp, if we will but reach for it.

The freeze is important, maybe crucial, but there is more that we, as a nation, can do. For example:

#2: *Begin a series of unilateral initiatives, designed to reduce international tension.*

Fortunately for us—and the Russians—we need not thrash about blindly in our search for peace. There is a strategy for us both, a set of instructions that are well-researched, likely to work and virtually without risk. It was first developed by Charles Osgood, professor of psychology at the University of Illinois, who called it GRIT, for Graduated and Reciprocated Initiatives in Tension reduction. It is basically an international version of an old policy: tit-for-tat, *quid pro quo,* or "you scratch my back, I'll scratch yours."

The idea of GRIT is that tensions can be reduced by a series of graduated and reciprocated initiatives. When tensions rise, whether between individuals or between nations, it is usually the result of unilateral escalations by one side, followed by similar escalations on the part of the other. The essence of GRIT is that the process can also work the other way—with progressive de-escalations, both sides begin to march down the tension ladder. Husband and wife may begin fighting when either one says something nasty about the other ("You never clean up after yourself"). In response to this, the offended party may say something nasty as well ("Your parents are obnoxious"). Tensions rise. But personal experience tells us that these situations need not last for long. They can often be turned around if either party initiates a conciliatory, tension-*reducing* act—apologizing sincerely, cleaning up the bathroom, etc. What goes up can be brought down, but one side or the other must initiate the reduction.

When applied to international relations, there are certain useful rules for GRIT strategists:

1. Deterrence should be preserved at each step of the way. If we can at any time inflict unacceptable damage on the opponent, then unilateral peace initiatives cannot reduce our security. GRIT is not unilateral disarmament, although it may show us a safe route to *mutual* nuclear disarmament.

2. GRIT initiatives should not be accompanied by threats. Threatening the opponent is a sure way of maintaining the adversary relationship.

3. The initiative should be publicly announced prior to its action, and it should be made clear that the goal is to reduce tensions.

4. The initiator should explicitly invite reciprocity from the other side, but without specifying exactly what the other side "must" do. Otherwise, a peace initiative becomes a threat, and counterproductive. (Psychologists have found that the greatest impact in the tension-reducing process occurs when an opponent *voluntarily* reciprocates.)

5. Make a real initiative—that is, actually *do* something, don't just talk about it. And make it something that reduces tension, ideally by giving the other side something it wants or needs, especially if that can be done at relatively little cost to oneself.

6. Keep it up for a while, unilaterally if necessary. It might take some time for the other side to recognize the commitment and the logic of the process. In this sense, GRIT is an appropriate acronym, suggesting the characteristics of persistence and determination that will be required for success. (It also conjures up the rugged image of

John Wayne, which is probably more mollifying to the hardline militarists than a strategy that might be called, for example, SOFT—Strategic Offensive Force Terminations!) And finally,

7. The GRIT initiatives should be unambiguous; that is, they
should be things that we are clearly doing so as to reduce tensions,
rather than something we would be doing in any case. And they
should be clearly verifiable; that is, there should be no doubt when we
have actually done them.

GRIT has already been used, successfully, on an international
scale. For example, during the Berlin Crisis, when Soviet and
American tanks were facing each other—almost literally snout to
snout—a graduated and reciprocated pullback was accomplished
by both sides. In 1958, the Eisenhower administration announced
that the U.S. would stop atmospheric testing if the U.S.S.R. agreed
to do the same. They did. Regrettably, France then tested its first
atomic bomb shortly afterward, in 1960, and the U.S.S.R. resumed
its own testing in 1961. But fortunately, the process did not end
there. JFK apparently read Osgood's book *An Alternative to War or
Surrender*, in which the GRIT strategy was described for the first
time, and in June 1963 he made his celebrated "strategy of peace"
speech at The American University. In this speech, President Kennedy praised the Russians for their accomplishments and sacrifices,
expressed optimism about solving our mutual problems, and announced a *unilateral* act: the U.S. was stopping all atmospheric
tests, and would not resume them unless the U.S.S.R. did so first.

The speech was printed in full, on the first page of both *Pravda*
and *Izvestia*. It had a profound personal effect—many Russians carried the newspaper clippings in their wallets for months afterward—because for the first time in recent memory, an American
president had commented on their bravery and sacrifice during
World War II, and actually seemed to be reaching out to them. On
June 15, Nikita Khrushchev responded: he welcomed the U.S. initiative and further announced a halt to the plans for production of
strategic bombers. Further tit-for-tat followed. The U.S. had earlier
proposed a "hotline" to reduce the chances of misunderstandings.
An agreement on this was reached on June 20. Test-ban negotiations began for real in July and the Partial Test-Ban Treaty was
signed on August 5, 1963. GRIT was doing so well that the Russians

even coined their own phrase, calling it "the policy of mutual example." Tensions between the two superpowers had reached an all-time postwar low. On October 9, JFK announced a $250 million wheat sale to the U.S.S.R. and then, later that fall, he was assassinated in Dallas.

But GRIT didn't die altogether with President Kennedy, although it seems clear that a great opportunity for world peace was lost at the time. In 1969, President Nixon announced that the U.S. would *unilaterally* cease all production of biological weapons and would destroy any existing stocks. In 1972, we and the Soviets entered into the "Convention on the Prohibition of the Development, Production and Stockpiling of Bacteriological (Biological) and Toxin Weapons and on their Destruction."

GRIT has not always worked, however. In October 1979, Brezhnev announced a *unilateral* 15 percent military reduction in East Germany, withdrawing 20,000 troops and 1,000 tanks. He also offered a GRIT-like reduction in numbers of Soviet medium-range missiles, provided that NATO did not increase its missiles and achieved other reciprocations. To its great discredit, the Carter administration cold-shouldered this proposal—an opportunity lost. Two months later, Russian tanks and troops invaded Afghanistan and SALT II was declared officially dead.

With a little imagination, we could easily try GRIT once again. Each side can make concessions that have very little negative consequences for its own security but which would greatly increase that of the other side. (In so doing, of course, they would increase their own.) For example, let us try to see the world as the Soviets see it: what can we do that they might especially appreciate? For one thing, the U.S.S.R. has a long-standing and well-justified paranoia about Germany. We would relieve them enormously if we announced a unilateral decision to refrain from emplacing ground-launched cruise missiles on German soil—better yet, none anywhere in Europe. For another, we could announce publicly that despite our intent to develop improved and normal relations with China, our newly rediscovered friendship will not involve any form of military aid or alliance. What could the Soviets do for us? They might try reducing their tank force in central Europe and/or their SS-20 missiles. Given that they really have no strategic interests in the Western Hemisphere, whereas we clearly do, they might also consider renouncing any aid to leftist revolutions there, including perhaps the decision to force Castro to stand on his own feet. This would save them a lot of money, although it would cost them a good deal of face, since they still claim to be the champions of world revolution. In reality, however, their actions are dictated ultimately by perceptions of their own security, not the success of world communism, just as ours are presumably dictated by our security, not world capitalism. If both nations were more clear-headed about their own self-interest, and how this relates to each other's concerns, then both would be more secure!

There is more: we need Persian Gulf oil (at least we think we do, until we take our own effective conservation measures). The Soviets do not. But they need their buffer states in eastern Europe (at least they think they do, while they feel threatened from the west). It should be possible to work out mutual guarantees. In fact, Europe itself offers an interesting opportunity: since Germany is the great European bugaboo, especially from the Soviet viewpoint, what about two demilitarized and neutralized Germanies? NATO would lose a strong and loyal West Germany, but would probably gain European stability and a likely Soviet willingness for substantial military reductions. West Germany would lose a degree of prestige and the nationalistic pride of their current military-politico alignment, but in return would gain economically and morally. The world would unquestionably be a safer place with both Germanies joining Switzerland, Austria, and Sweden as a large demilitarized buffer zone separating east from west in Europe. Moreover, because they would have the luxury of a miniscule defense budget, the increasingly fat and happy German burghers would grow even fatter and happier than they are today, and would become the best possible advertisement for peace!

But the really exciting opportunities for GRIT-like reduction are in our nuclear arsenal. Here, the possibilities are as vast as our stockpile itself, which is saying quite a lot. The only thing good about having 30,000 nuclear weapons is that it provides great opportunities for creative, GRITty initiatives. We propose a freeze. If the Russians demur, then we go ahead anyhow and announce a unilateral, GRITty freeze of our own, either on all systems or just on certain identified ones. Following a mutual freeze, or even if the Soviets are still not reciprocating, we can afford to eliminate a wide variety of nuclear bombs, warheads, missiles, submarines and/

or bombers, in a most GRIT-like manner, without compromising our national security in the slightest. To appreciate the effect of such action on the Soviets, imagine they took the initiative instead: Pentagon officials would have a difficult time coaxing a hefty military budget out of Congress if the Kremlin unilaterally scrapped one-half of its ICBMs. Military hardliners and professional scaremongers on both sides need the provocative escalations of each other's government in order to justify and expand their own empires. When it comes to unilateral GRIT-like initiatives, we are probably safer in gradually dismantling our nuclear arsenal than virtually any other action we might take. But it will take true grit on the part of the president, and an informed and aroused electorate to keep his nose to the grindstone of peace.

### #3. Do not, under any circumstances, escalate the nuclear arms race.

The only sane use for nuclear weapons is to prevent their use: that is, deterrence. (And as we shall see, even deterrence is seriously flawed.)

There is an urgent need for reductions; it would be bad enough to remain at the current levels. It would be sheer madness to add more. The nuclear arms race follows its own special brand of Newton's Law: every action merely leads to an equal and opposite reaction—and often, to an overreaction as well. If it happens that the U.S.S.R. is stupid enough to continue adding to its nuclear arsenal, we should not even seek to match them; doing so would add nothing whatever to our security, and could only decrease it, while impoverishing ourselves at the same time. If they escalate the arms race, the best response we could make would be no response at all, despite the psychological temptation to match them, bomb for bomb. By reacting, we add fuel to the fire; by not reacting, we take away their motivation for escalating. And such inaction would in no way diminish our security, since we can only kill every Russian once, and we already have massive overkill even with a fraction of our current arsenal. Thus far, however, the major thrust for escalation of the arms race has come from the U.S., and this must cease—immediately.

It is especially important that we refrain from deploying the next generation of strategic missiles, the MX and Trident II. Because of their extreme accuracy, these missiles will be able to destroy Russian missiles, by direct hits on their silos. Thus far, in the absence of such weapons, both sides have been able to sit back, confident that the other side would never attack first, because if it did, it would be destroyed by the victim's remaining missiles. But once either side develops the ability (even the theoretical ability, whether real or not), to destroy a large part of the opponent's missiles, then in situations of international tension, that side just might be tempted to strike first. Even worse—because more likely— the side whose missiles are threatened might get so edgy that even a false alarm could start a nuclear war.

It is bad enough to threaten each other's cities, but at least there is some chance that such an arrangement can be stable—for a while. But it is inexcusable to go about intentionally destabilizing that precious balance. In short: Thou Shalt Not Threaten Thy Neighbor's Deterrence!

We must therefore cease the development of new, more accurate missiles, and of the satellite navigation aids that encourage such accuracy. In fact, the ideal deterrent is *inaccurate*—you don't need pinpoint precision to blow up Leningrad: nuclear warheads could do that job even if they landed a half mile off target. Inaccurate missiles of this sort would still deter attack upon the U.S., without making the U.S.S.R. nervous and hence, trigger-happy— which highly accurate missiles seem likely to do. In short, as long as a nuclear sword of Damocles hangs over all of us, our forces must be large enough to keep our opponent peaceful, but not so large as to make him nervous.

Thus, most of the controversy surrounding the MX missile has missed the point—the debate has focused on the various possible "basing modes," whether shuttled about in a shell game, placed in existing silos, etc., whereas the crucial issue is the MX itself: regardless of how it is based, the MX threatens the Soviet deterrence and hence, it endangers us as much as them. It should therefore never be deployed at all.

It is an unusual, but important concept: our security depends on *their* deterrence being secure. Richard Garwin has even proposed that we establish, by international treaty, certain open-ocean sanctuaries for the missile-firing submarines of each side. Antisubmarine warfare of any sort would be prohibited in these areas, which would be large enough to assure an absolutely invulnerable deterrent for each side.

### 4. We must not engage in a military build-up in the hopes of thereby securing arms control or disarmament.

A build-up on one side merely leads to a build-up on the other. We will have to wait a long time before Brezhnev or his successor in the Kremlin announces, "OK, Ronald, we give up—you win." As Paul Warnke, former director of the Arms Control and Disarmament Agency, has pointed out, trying to force the Russians to accept our terms by challenging them to an accelerated arms race is like "trying to cure an alcoholic by outdrinking him." It is both stupid and dangerous, and serves only the arms manufacturer, the military empire-builders, and those moral midgets who don't really seek arms control or disarmament in the first place, but rather, who hope to use the prospect of arms control as a carrot for more weapons that will become permanent fixtures.

Some people claim we must arm to disarm, recalling the Latin proverb: "If you want peace, prepare for war." The verdict of history, however, is otherwise. Over and over again, from the Pelleponesian War to the hostilities between Iran and Iraq, preparing for war leads to war. For our times, a more appropriate motto would read: "If you want peace, maintain a prudent and minimum deterrent (as long as this is absolutely necessary) and in the meantime, prepare for *peace*." You get what you prepare for.

### #5: We must recognize that our security is intimately tied to the security of our opponents; hence, our mutual security must be mutually arrived at.

In the good old days of conventional weapons, nations felt strong when they successfully threatened their opponents. Now that has changed, but the old habits die hard. We simply cannot achieve national security unless the Soviet Union also feels secure; this may be a difficult pill for some to swallow, perhaps even a bitter one. But it is a life-saving prescription. We cannot "win" in the sense of defeating "them." "We must all hang together," said Benjamin Franklin, discussing the peril of defying the British Empire. "Or most assuredly, we shall each hang separately." In defying the infinitely greater peril of nuclear war, we and the Russians must all live together, or most assuredly, we shall all die together.

"Spaceship earth" has long been a favorite metaphor of the environmental movement. As Harvard negotiator Roger Fisher points out, an apt metaphor for a nuclear-armed world might be "rowboat earth." We are in this little boat together, in stormy seas. We cannot make our end safer by making their end tippier. And yet, incredibly, that is the goal of hardline militarists. We cannot make nuclear war less dangerous or less likely for us by making it more dangerous or more likely for them. What happens to them, happens to us. In a literal sense, we are the Russians' keepers—and they are ours. If our boat capsizes, then we all drown together.

We need not wait for the dawn of universal brotherhood, however. All that is needed is a sobering dose of enlightened self-interest and the recognition of mutual dependence. We must make them (and everyone) *more* secure, not less, if we want to be more secure ourselves. This does not mean that we must love each other; the art of survival must become the art of getting along with others that you do *not* like, and/or with whom you disagree. The key is simple yet profound: recognizing that we are all in the same boat. This does not mean that competition will cease—the U.S. and U.S.S.R. have vastly different ideologies, and we cannot deny the likelihood of some forms of struggle. Indeed, we have no hesitation about ideological struggle—we would bet on Jefferson and Lincoln against Marx and Lenin, any day. But in any struggles between nuclear-armed superpowers, each side must recognize the essential interests of the other. Furthermore, each side must recognize that its own essential interests are served by supporting the other.

If we threaten Russia with new missiles, if we make military pacts with China, if we permit Germany and Japan to rearm, if we undermine the U.S.S.R's protective buffer in east Europe—then we are rocking the boat. And when the boat rocks, it rocks for thee.

### #6: We must not link negotiations on arms control or disarmament to "good behavior" by the Russians.

Arms control is in our interest, and in theirs. Agreements do not

require trust, only the ability to verify that the other side is complying with the agreements—and such means of verification now
exist—as well as the recognition that the security of each side is
enchanced by making these agreements and abiding by them.

Since we need arms control, just as the Russians do, then it is
not a *reward* to be granted them only if they behave themselves.
This would be stupidly spiteful. Any perceived threats to world
order, whether in Afghanistan, Poland, El Salvador, or the Middle
East, only make the need for arms control greater. Remember, we
do not need guarantees of their friendliness or even their honorable
intentions. Our need is for agreements which are in the interests of
both sides to achieve and to maintain, even if we disagree on other
things.

Hardliners hope to use "linkage" to manipulate Soviet behavior—that is, we refuse to negotiate arms control agreements unless
they behave as we wish. But in fact, when the Soviet Union is
threatened, it gets more repressive and harder to deal with, not
easier. For example, when Senator Henry Jackson attached the
Jackson-Vanik amendment to the 1974 Trade bill, requiring a
quota of Jewish emigrants in return for "most favored nation" trade
status, such emigration dropped to 10,000 in 1975—an all-time low.
At the height of détente, during 1978-1979, 51,000 were permitted
to emigrate, the all-time high. Similarly, Andrei Sakharov and the
other less celebrated Soviet dissidents were openly repressed only
after the U.S. response to the Afghanistan invasion signaled that
détente was ended.

For all practical purposes, the U.S. and the U.S.S.R. are military
equals. We cannot force concessions from them any more than they
can from us. When the subject is nuclear arms control, neither side
gains by such efforts, but both sides can lose.

### #7: We must not delay, hoping that inaction will improve the situation.

At present, military planners and their lobby are strong, persistent pressure groups in both the U.S. and Soviet governments,
much stronger than the forces of peace. Unless the nation moves
energetically to wage peace, the momentum of its well-organized

military establishment will continue pulling us inevitably toward war. "The stone age may return on the gleaming wings of Science," warned Winston Churchill, "and what might now shower immeasurable blessings upon mankind, may even bring its total destruction. Beware, I say; time may be short."

For several decades now, German parents have been telling their children that they didn't know what Hitler was really doing, that they had never heard of the concentrations camps or the crematoria. We, however, know full well what we have been doing since 1945: what are we planning to tell *our* children—that is, if they survive? That we did not know? That we did not care? That we were too busy? That it was not *our* job, or *our* problem, or *our* fault?

### #8: We must explicitly reject any doctrine of limited nuclear war.

As we shall see, the chances are very slim that nuclear war, once begun, could ever be limited. This means that any national strategy which makes limited war more likely, makes all-out nuclear war more likely. That cost is simply too great to be borne. Pentagon planners find scenarios of limited nuclear war attractive, because they feel that threats of all-out war would not be believable to the Soviets, and hence, might not deter their aggression. By contrast, they argue, the threat of limited war, using tactical weapons, might deter a conventional assault. But by lowering the nuclear threshold, doctrines of limited war are simply too dangerous to play with.

In late May, 1982, while the Reagan Administration was beginning its much ballyhooed "peace offensive," the government also revealed a remarkable and scary new "Defense Guidance" for the period 1984–1989. A blueprint for "protracted nuclear war" with the U.S.S.R., this document calls blithely for "decapitation" of Soviet leadership and shows such nonchalance about nuclear war as to be a new low point in high-level government responsibility.

The particular danger of "limited nuclear war" options is that in times of crisis, they could tempt the military into using such an option, which simply should not be available to them. It is the final option, for each of us—suicide. But suicide, nuclear or otherwise, is not an option that one person can ever properly prescribe for another.

As part of this recognition, we must stop manufacturing neutron bombs, and destroy those components already made.

The neutron bomb is not significantly different from other nuclear weapons; it is just more usable. Since using it would bring nuclear retaliation, its availability is a danger, since it may provide a temptation to national leaders—or even battlefield commanders—that should not exist. We must reject any doctrine and any weapon that lowers the threshold for nuclear conflict.

### #9: We must never adopt a policy of "launch on warning."

With a policy of "launch on warning," missiles will be fired after we receive *warning* that Soviet missiles have been launched. As missiles become more accurate, and MIRVed warheads become more abundant, each side is beginning to fear a surprise attack by the other, which—at least in theory—might destroy the victim's land-based missile force. One way to negate such an attack is to get your missiles out of their silos as soon as your radar warns of an attack ("Use 'em or lose 'em"). But launch on warning would be horribly dangerous, for several reasons: (1) Mistakes do happen, and often. If an erroneous "warning" leads to a launch by our side, then the Soviets will almost certainly retaliate, and nuclear war will have begun—by accident. (2) If either side adopts a launch on warning posture, and announces it—in the hope of deterring a surprise counterforce attack—then this may backfire as well. Thus, suppose the Soviets accidentally fired a single missile at the U.S.; if they believed that we had adopted launch on warning, then they would expect us to retaliate immediately with all of our missiles. So, the "best" thing for them to do under the circumstances might be to fire the rest of their missiles, in the hopes of somehow reducing our retaliation. Hence, not only should we never adopt launch on warning, but we should not even claim to have done so, even if we really didn't.

#### #10: We must not introduce Pershing II or ground-launched cruise missiles in Europe.

Cruise missiles are small, highly accurate jets that can fly as low as fifty feet above the ground, thus avoiding radar detection. Pershing IIs will take only six minutes to fly from Germany to Moscow. Not surprisingly, then, deploying these weapons will make the Russians edgy, possibly forcing them to launch on warning. It took nearly two weeks for the British fleet to reach the Falkland Islands, allowing time for efforts at resolving the crisis and correcting misunderstandings. We do not make ourselves safer by forcing the Russians to make life-or-death decisions in the space of several *minutes.* (And it is widely acknowledged that their radar and computer systems are inferior to ours, and thus, probably even more subject than ours to false alarms.)

#### #11: We should phase out all land-based ICBMs.

As we shall see, a counterforce attack against U.S. (or Soviet) ICBMs is not a realistic possibility. Nonetheless, there is good reason to eliminate any nuclear weapons systems that even *appear* to be vulnerable. Land-based missiles are sitting ducks, and even though they cannot be removed via a "surgical" strike, it may well be that strategic planners on both sides simply cannot resist the temptation to target each others missiles. In that sense, land-based ICBMs are "attractive nuisances," inviting trouble from the neighborhood children. Better to eliminate them altogether. Bombers and especially submarine-based missiles provide more than adequate deterrent in themselves. Although the land-based missile lobby will doubtless fight for their constituents, the larger constituency—the security of the nation—should prevail. After all, that is what the missiles are supposed to be all about.

**#12: *We should encourage peace overtures by our government, but should not be misled by them.***

Peace overtures are preferable to war overtures. However, we must beware the public relations smokescreen.

For example, in November 1981, President Reagan offered the "zero option" on European intermediate-range missiles: we would refrain from deploying Pershing IIs and GLCMs if the Soviets would dismantle their SS-4s, SS-5s and SS-20s now in place. It would be wonderful if they agreed, but we should not be surprised that they have not: after all, we have a commanding lead in both short- and long-range European nuclear weapons. A zero option for intermediate-range systems would eliminate the only area in which they are ahead.

Similarly, in May 1982 Reagan proposed reduction in the strategic weapons of both sides, limiting each to 2,500 land-based warheads. At present, they have about 5,500 such warheads and we have about 2,152—so they would have to remove about 3,000, whereas we could *add* another few hundred! The second stage of Reagan's proposals will reportedly be to equalize throw-weight (throw-weight is simply the weight that can be carried in the business end of a missile) on each side. These proposals single out specifically those few areas in which the U.S.S.R. is ahead, and insist on equality there, while ignoring other areas—submarine-launched missiles, bombers, cruise missiles—in which we lead.

There is no harm in such offers. In fact, they indicate how successful we have already been. But there are three dangers:

1. Proposals of this sort seem intended to take the wind out of the anti-nuclear war movement, the "zero option" targeted at the Europeans, and the proposed strategic cuts intended to silence domestic critics. We must not be deceived, and must keep up the pressure.

2. They are clearly unacceptable to the Soviets; indeed, they are so one-sided that they may even have been proposed with the hope and expectation that they would be rejected, thereby making the Russians seem intransigent and providing an excuse for additional escalations of the arms race. And finally,

3. Any complex agreement such as Reagan has proposed would require lengthy negotiations, during which both sides would continue to arm. Moreover, during such negotiations, we can expect pressure for additional weapons, as "bargaining chips," as well as claims that all criticism should be muted, so as not to undercut the government. The solution is simple: freeze immediately, then negotiate reductions, and reject any proposals that will permit or justify further build-ups.

**#13: We should negotiate, whenever, wherever and however possible, but we should not insist on negotiated treaties as the only possible form of agreement.**

Negotiations have their drawbacks: they are slow, cumbersome and often involve regrettable concessions to the military-minded at home. But as Winston Churchill pointed out, "Jaw, jaw, jaw is better than war, war, war." During his 1961 inaugural address, JFK announced that "we shall not negotiate out of fear, but we shall not fear to negotiate." The second part sounds just fine, but we ought to rethink the first: why not negotiate out of fear? As Harvard law professor Roger Fisher points out, if someone puts a gun to my head, I'll say "Let's negotiate!" The U.S. and U.S.S.R. are pointing guns at each other's heads. Let's negotiate.

We should also remember, however, that formal, negotiated agreements, complete with treaty ratification, are not the only way for two countries—even two unfriendly countries—to get something done. Two adults can live together amicably without a marriage license, and certainly, the license itself is no guarantee of wedded bliss. Given the drawbacks of formal negotiations, we must not insist that all agreements be formal treaties, signed, sealed, and ratified. There is enormous room for nonbinding, interactive decision-making: we cease a particular provocation (say, deploying the MX missile), then see what they do in return. If our action enhances their security, they will probably reciprocate with something that enhances ours.

As we have seen in the case of Grit-like moves toward a nuclear freeze, we can make giant strides toward peace by unilateral initiatives which are a far cry from disarmament, and which will in no way reduce our security. This is especially true since initiatives of this sort are not legally binding, so if they are not eventually reciprocated, they can always be rescinded. Nothing ventured, nothing gained; moreover, nothing ventured, and a world can be lost.

### #14: We should agree to a "no first use" pact.

A big source of world anxiety is the fear that in a conflict, one side or the other will use nuclear weapons—after which, quite literally, all hell breaks loose. Just the uncertainty that one side *might* escalate to nuclear weapons could lead the other to use them first. For some time, China has pledged not to be the first to use nuclear weapons. Between 1976 and 1980 alone, on three different occasions, the Soviet Union proposed a "no first use" pact between NATO and the Warsaw Pact. Each time, we refused. Then, in the opening days of the second U.N. Special Session on Disarmament, in June, 1982, Soviet Foreign Minister Gromyko announced a *unilateral* policy of no "first use." Once again, we spurned the overture. The reason? Official NATO strategy is that in the event of a conventional war in Europe, NATO may employ atomic bombs, whether the other side has done so or not. When he was Deputy Assistant Secretary of Defense, Morton Halperin said it clearly: "The NATO doctrine is that we will fight with conventional forces until we are losing, then we will fight with tactical nuclear weapons until we are losing, and then we will blow up the world."

There may actually be some merit in this sort of talk, if it deters conventional war in the first place. But there is no merit whatsoever in blowing up the world, or in the doctrine of first use, if it is meant seriously. Moreover, our present first use doctrine may have the paradoxical effect that if the Soviets find themselves *winning* a conventional war, *they* may be pressed to escalate to nuclear weapons, since according to our announced policy, we are going to do so ourselves! The world would be a safer place if we and the Soviets agreed that when it comes to blowing up the world, neither side would be the first.

We can see two possible negative effects of such an agreement: 1) it may require an increase in NATO's conventional strength, to offset whatever deterrent benefit is lost by explicitly rejecting first use, and 2) it might generate pressure for other NATO countries, especially West Germany, to obtain their own nuclear arsenals. Nothing seems likely to disturb the Soviet leadership more (and make a Soviet preemptive strike more likely) than an independent German nuclear force. Hence, German nuclear armament must always remain as unacceptable to our side as to theirs. The more tightly NATO countries cling to provocative U.S. nuclear weapons for their "defense," however, the more will they be threatened by comparable Soviet weapons.

It may be argued that by reserving a first strike option for ourselves, we deter war in the first place. Even if true, it is not worth the ultimate risk. Moreover, although a "no first use" pact would defuse tensions, some uncertainty regarding possible first use would always remain. They will never know whether we *really* mean it (even our own leaders will probably never know, until it comes time to decide), and we will never know whether they really mean it. So deterrence would still be available—and always will, as long as atom bombs exist in the arsenal of either country. But a "no first use" pact would be a step in the right direction; it would lower tensions, and raise the threshold for nuclear war.

In an article appearing in the April 1982 issue of *Foreign Affairs*, four of America's most credible and experienced national security experts—Robert McNamara, McGeorge Bundy, Gerald Smith, and George Kennan—urged that NATO consider a "no first use" policy, since any use of nuclear weapons "carries with it a high and inescapable risk of escalating into the general nuclear war which would bring ruin to all and victory to none." Secretary of State Alexander Haig responded that we could not rule out the use of nuclear weapons "to protect the essential values of Western civilization."

### #15: We should work vigorously to achieve a cutoff in production of weapons-grade, fissionable materials.

One way of reducing the likelihood of proliferation and also having partial arms control would be to cut off production of fissionable materials. To be weapons-grade, as opposed to reactor-grade (that is, suitable for use in bombs rather than reactors), the proportion of $U_{235}$ in the uranium fuel must be 90 percent or higher. Since it is very difficult and expensive to separate $U_{235}$ from the much more abundant form, $U_{238}$, a cutoff in the availability of highly enriched uranium could be a significant measure, especially if combined with an end to the reprocessing of plutonium from spent reactor fuel.

Eisenhower first proposed such a cutoff in 1953, during his "atoms for peace" speech at the U.N. He also suggested the transfer of military uranium stockpiles to an international agency. John Foster Dulles further developed this proposal in 1957; the Soviets refused, however. At that time, they were far behind the U.S. in nuclear stockpiles, and equal reduction of the stockpiles of both nations would have left them even worse off. In 1964, Lyndon Johnson announced a *unilateral* measure, a four-year, 20 percent reduction in plutonium production, and a 40 percent reduction in the separation of highly enriched uranium. The U.S.S.R. responded by canceling plans to construct two large plutonium-generating reactors, and reducing their stores of highly enriched uranium. The U.S. later proposed a complete cutoff, with the U.S. to transfer 60,000 kilograms of fissionable material to civilian purposes if the U.S.S.R would transfer 40,000. Here again the Soviets refused. The impending Non-Proliferation Treaty distracted further attention from a cutoff, and later, when Nixon listed a cutoff as a goal for the 1969 meeting of the Commission on Disarmament in Geneva, SALT I talks eclipsed interest in this proposal.

But the idea still has merit, now as it did then. Moreover, in the 1980s we may have a new opportunity: the U.S. and U.S.S.R. have essentially reached equity in their nuclear stockpiles. Hence, proposals that seemed one-sided to the Soviets during the 1950s and early 1960s may be received very differently now. There is, in fact, a real chance that an agreement, acceptable to both sides, could be reached—if we act quickly.

### #16: We should not poor-mouth U.S. nuclear strength.

The current U.S. nuclear arsenal is more than enough; in fact, it is dangerously excessive. Yet false claims of military gaps have regularly been used to alarm the public and build support for continuing escalations of the arms race. It is time for public officials to state publicly and categorically that we have great strength, so much that it threatens us, as well as any opponents. By poor-mouthing our nuclear strength, today's hawks, including President Reagan, actually do the country an enormous disservice: not only do they urge us to wasteful, unnecessary and dangerous escalations, but by sowing the seeds of doubt in the minds of Kremlin military planners, they may actually undermine deterrence itself. Deter-rence, more than anything else, is a state of mind; it is secure as long as the *perception* of our ability to destroy an attacker—to de-ter—is secure. As Richard J. Barnet has pointed out, our strategic military budget is actually an education effort designed to influence the perceptions of a half dozen or so old men in the Kremlin. As such, it is almost certainly the most expensive per-student school program in the world. Our security is not enhanced by undercut-ting that program.

### #17: We should keep our cool.

The story is told of how King Arthur's son Mordred led a revolt against his father. Two great armies met on the field of Camian while their leaders parlayed. Both sides were armed to the teeth, nervous and suspicious that the other would try something. Then, while the negotiations were making headway, an unnamed knight suddenly drew his sword to kill a snake. Warriors on the other side thought they were being attacked and a great battle immediately erupted, with slaughter on both sides. The moral should be clear: we should keep our cool, especially in times of tension, when a "false" move could be our last.

At the time of our worldwide nuclear alert in 1973, the head of the Strategic Air Command was playing golf. He kept playing. Perhaps he was just an ardent golfer, but in any event, cool behav-ior of this sort sends a clear message to one's underlings: "Don't get panicky; things aren't that dangerous." This is an important mes-sage, since a crisis situation in itself makes nuclear war more likely, and not only by executive decision: mid-ranking officials are much more inclined to overreact to a possible false alarm during a red alert than when they aren't nervously fingering the trigger. When does a flock of geese look like a salvo of missiles? During a missile crisis.

For the same reason, the worst thing we could do during an international crisis is to attempt "crisis relocation," that is, to attempt massive evacuations, cram our national leaders into blast shelters, or shuttle them off onto Doomsday planes. In fact, for the same reasons, we must be ever mindful of the need to keep international discourse as cool, courteous, and nonthreatening as possible, all the time, or else we will be threatening ourselves no less than our opponent.

**#18: We must never equate courage with willingness to wage nuclear war, or cowardice with arms control, disarmament, or reluctance to wage nuclear war.**

When Patrick Henry announced "Give me liberty or give me death," he gave himself immortality. Bellicose pronouncements in Henry's day were not suicidal, and hence, they may even have been laudable—when the sacrifice of a few lives could secure the liberty of many. Now, we are talking of the sacrifice of *all* lives, a willingness that is not even rational, certainly not stable. Some people died in the Revolutionary War, but our nation survived; indeed, it was born. But today, nuclear war is not survivable, and there is no conceivable end that can justify such means. Remembering the Cuban missile crisis, Khrushchev wrote:

> The Chinese say I was scared. Of course I was scared. I would have been insane not to have been scared. I was frightened about what could happen to my country—or your country and all other countries that would be devastated by a nuclear war. If being frightened meant that I helped avert such insanity then I'm glad I was frightened.

The real issue, then, is not hardliners versus softliners, but rather, the *bottom line,* which must be coexistence, because the only alternative is no existence.

We are long past the days of champions, when the best fighters from each side would slug it out, with the winner earning victory for his side, and the adulation of his comrades. Does any human being have the right to decide the fate of everyone else? Can political leaders legitimately commit suicide for all the world's children? Should we applaud such willingness? "To perpetuate this final act of malice seems somehow disproportionate, beyond endurance," wrote Loren Eiseley.

> It is like tampering with the secret purposes of the universe itself and involving not just men but life in the final holocaust—an act of petulant, deliberate blasphemy . . . The evil man may do . . . is not merely the evil of one tribe seeking to exterminate another. It is, instead, the thought-out willingness to make the air unbreathable to neighboring innocent nations, and to poison in one's death throes, the very springs of life itself.

We are threatened by warheads—a peculiarly apt word. In the 1960s, we had "pot heads" and "acid heads"; now we are surrounded by "war heads," and not just those perched atop missiles. We are, in fact, much more threatened by those war heads in the Pentagon and the Kremlin than by our worst fears of marauding dope fiends. We must identify war heads for what they are, and never do them homage.

**#19: We should educate our own politicians, as well as the leaders of other nations, about the liabilities of nuclear weapons, as well as the realities of nuclear war.**

One reason why the arms race has gotten so crazily out of hand is that nuclear weapons have been seen as symbols of national power and prestige, rather than the awful, excessive physical reality that they are. As symbols of national strength, there is no limit to how many bombs each nation will seek to have. But when we focus on their reality—what nuclear bombs *do*—then the absurdity of our present condition becomes clear. Hence, it would be useful if the leaders of the U.S. and the U.S.S.R. publicly acknowledge that nuclear weapons bring *insecurity*, not strength. They should also announce their heartfelt wish that their own weapons could be controlled, reduced, and eventually, abolished. We should admit that we have a tiger by the tail, and that we desperately need to let go.

We need, in short, a Declaration of National Shame. This would serve two useful purposes. For one, it would help create a climate more conducive to the control and reduction of nuclear weapons. And for another, it would become an active force countering today's dangerous trends toward nuclear proliferation, since the leaders of other nations can hardly be expected to forbear acquiring their own nuclear weapons as long as the U.S. and U.S.S.R. continue to revel in their own plutonium security blankets.

Amory and Hunter Lovins suggest that we form a "Bombaholics Anonymous," at which thoughtful officials and private citizens from current and aspiring weapons states meet privately to share insights on the difficulties of having—and kicking—the habit.

It would be healthy for world leaders, especially those possessing nuclear weapons, to understand—not just in their heads, but also in their guts—the consequence of a nuclear explosion. The responsibility, along with the physical power itself, is so awesome, that leaders tend to avoid thinking about it, preferring instead to deal in abstract numbers, concepts, theories and war games, not to mention posturing and boastfulness. It is nearly forty years since nuclear weapons were used in anger, and twenty years since the last atmospheric nuclear test; accordingly, it is quite possible that none of today's national leaders have even witnessed a nuclear explosion. Despite the danger of fallout from even a single blast, it might be a useful exercise if the world's leaders were assembled regularly for a demonstration—to impress them with the seriousness of their duties. The post-1945 generation did not live through the shock of Hiroshima and Nagasaki, and now they are beginning to assume the power of government. They have grown accustomed to nuclear weapons, at least in theory; a dose of reality might shake them into a new sensitivity. As Nigel Calder describes it, "they will stand in awe of its incomprehensible heat and force. Even at a safe distance of thirty miles or more they will feel it like the opening of an oven door, or the gates of hell."

It would also be useful if every American president made an annual pilgrimage to the holiest places on earth, the cities of Hiroshima and Nagasaki, Japan. This mission, part atonement, part personal education, and part public relations, should coincide with the bombings, on August 6 and August 9. It would remind Americans of what they have done and remind the world of what we could all do again, if we are not careful. It would also remind the president. Ideally, the leader of the Soviet Union should do the same; perhaps they could meet at the A-Bomb museum in Hiroshima. There, let them confront each other. Let them stand among the ashes, the twisted steel and the molten eyeballs, and try out their cold war rhetoric. Maybe they will be moved instead to follow the urgings of the Russell-Einstein Manifesto, issued in 1955 on the tenth anniversary of the bombing of Hiroshima: "We appeal, as human beings to human beings: Remember your humanity, and forget the rest."

### #20: We should make it clear that nuclear war will not be survivable.

The nation's energies and attention must be directed toward war-preventing, not war-fighting. Survival from a nuclear war is a cruel illusion, in two respects: for one, it directs efforts, energy and resources to a useless end. But that loss is trivial compared to the second, greater one, the loss of security that comes from making war more acceptable, thereby making it more likely. It is appropriate to plan for natural disasters—floods, volcanic eruptions, hurricanes—and to some extent, such planning may significantly reduce loss of lives and property. Certainly, planning for a natural disaster does not make the disaster any *more* likely. But the more we swallow the propaganda of "civil defense," the more we render nuclear war palatable and hence likely. In addition, we send a message to the U.S.S.R.: the U.S. is preparing for war, so you had better do the same.

Our eleven-year-old son came home from school one day singing this jingle:

> It doesn't take a military genius to see,
> We'll all be crispy critters after World War Three.

There's no place you can run to, there's no place you can hide.
For when they drop the big one, we all get fried.

Not a cheery message, but one that we all need to hear.

### #21: We should engage in a creative dialogue with the U.S.S.R., seeking a way to achieve "preventive arms control."

At present, we are endangered by today's weapons, and therefore our primary goal must be to control and, eventually, to eliminate them. But tomorrow's weapons will pose new problems for diplomats, who typically have more difficulty controlling something than the scientists do inventing it. The problem, however, is not simply runaway technology beyond human control. The invention of ever more sophisticated weapons takes time, money, and human resources, which are provided by governments. If governments stopped supporting the research that now undermines our mutual security, then such activity would cease. Each side worries, however, that perhaps the other would not stop, and unveil some new secret weapon. It will be a difficult problem to solve, but not impossible: after all, modern weapons are not created by some lonely genius, during a long weekend in his garage. They take armies of trained experts, working in major establishments. With suitable agreements, these weapons establishments could be shut down, with independent verification both by satellite and perhaps by a special U.N. agency.

### #22: We should not mistake nuclear weapons technology for "progress."

It is sometimes argued that as a nation we simply can't turn the clock back. Nonsense! Just because something is new does not mean that it should be embraced, or that it must always be with us. Imagine a new, lethal variety of influenza that kills many people and threatens to kill millions more: we would all agree to eradicate it. This is not unrealistic, new forms of influenza do in fact spring up almost annually, and recently we eradicated smallpox. No one argued that we should refrain because it turned the clock back to a time before smallpox existed! The moral is simply this: getting rid of an evil thing, whether that thing is new or old, is progress of the highest sort. Having "advanced" to the edge of the abyss, progress is stepping backward.

#### #23: We should eliminate nuclear power.

The real danger of nuclear power is not pollution, radioactive waste, or even the risk of accident, serious as these may be. Rather, it is the connection between nuclear power and nuclear weapons. There are not two atoms, one peaceful and the other warlike; rather, just one. In April 1945, shortly after Harry Truman had succeeded FDR as president, but before he knew about the Manhattan Project, Secretary of War Henry L. Stimson wrote a memo to the new president, telling of the atomic bomb project and also warning that

> it is extremely probable that the future will make it possible for atomic bombs to be constructed by smaller nations, or even groups. . . . The future may see a time when such a weapon may be constructed in secret and used suddenly and effectively with devastating power by a willful nation or group against an unsuspecting nation or group of much greater size and national power.

In September 1976, the Council for Economic Development (a sober, establishment group, neither "fringy" nor "antinuke") reported as follows: "In 20 years, 100 countries will possess the raw materials and the knowledge necessary to produce nuclear bombs. . . . By the year 2000, the total plutonium produced as a by-product of global nuclear power will be the equivalent of one million atomic bombs." The Council report continues:

> The many hazards associated with nuclear energy, especially with nuclear explosives, are enough to make any thoughtful person wonder

whether, despite the world's need for new sources of energy, it might be better for mankind if nuclear technology could be suppressed and forgotten. A world economy charging toward a fuel shortage . . . may be less frightening than a world economy powered by the fuel equivalent of millions of nuclear bombs. When the problem of radioactive wastes and the possibility of avoiding accidents are added, it is no wonder that concerned individuals are asking whether the world is obliged to imperil itself in this way.

In many nations today (Iraq, Pakistan, Argentina, Taiwan, South Korea, to name just a few) nuclear power serves as an acceptable smokescreen for nuclear weapons development. In a denuclearized world, plutonium or highly enriched uranium would not be regular items of commerce. Hence, their possession would be an unambiguous signal of intent.

A detailed treatment of energy policy is beyond the scope of this book, but we must note that the world most definitely is *not* obliged to imperil itself by nuclear power. Ironically, nuclear energy is not even needed to solve the energy crisis: for example, by using available technology, and simply increasing the heating efficiency of houses and the fuel efficiency of automobiles, all foreign oil imports into the U.S. could be ended. We would be "adding new energy" at six times the rate of the maximum nuclear power generating capacity estimated for the 1980s, at less cost and before a single new reactor, ordered today, could generate even a joule of energy. And this pattern does not apply only to the U.S.: a look at all new energy "supplied" to the nine Common Market countries from 1973–1978 shows that 95 percent came from more efficient use (i.e., conservation) and 5 percent from all other sources of increased supply, including nuclear power and North Sea oil.

For less developed, third world countries this picture is even clearer: nuclear generators require enormous capital investment and they provide not *energy*, but rather *electricity*, typically much more than a third world country needs or even can use. Developing countries need fuels and small, intermediate-technology generating plants. A wide range of these are already available and, not surprisingly, the earlier enthusiasm for nuclear power is now rapidly being replaced by a more realistic assessment of needs and how these can best be met. Let's face it, however: there is a certain sex appeal to a multimegawatt nuclear reactor (even if one doesn't yearn to build bombs with its effluent), that you can't find in a five-horsepower motor turning by the gas produced from cow farts. But there is no sex appeal in bankruptcy. If we put a fraction of the research and development efforts we now expend on new weapons into finding efficient substitutes for petroleum, and for inexpensive solar collectors, the worldwide appeal of nuclear energy will drop to zero, just as the worldwide need has already bottomed out.

In fact, the nuclear power industry even now is not economically viable—it survives only because of massive government subsidies. It cannot compete with other energy sources and it is time for the government to put it out of its misery. Amory Lovins suggests that we are now witnessing the most dramatic collapse of an industrial enterprise in modern times, adding that

> When the history of the nuclear controversy comes to be written, those who killed nuclear technology will be seen to have been its most ardent promoters, who systematically mistook hopes for facts, advocacy for analysis, commercial zeal for national interest, expertise for infallibility, engineering for politics, public relations for truth, and the people for fools.

### #24: We should increase the budget, size, and prominence of the Arms Control and Disarmament Agency, and see that it lives up to its name.

The ACDA is the only U.S. agency charged with arms control and disarmament. Yet even before the Reagan administration its total budget was less than the allotment for military bands! Its 1982 budget of $16.7 million is less than the cost of a single F-18 fighter. In summer 1981, the Reagan administration moved to disband the largest of the Agency's four subsections, the Bureau of Weapons Evaluation and Control. In the past, Congress got reports from the Bureau on the arms control implications of new weapons systems— that is, whether a proposed new system would make subsequent control or reduction difficult if it was deployed. Without the Bureau's advice, it will be even more difficult to resist escalations which are likely to become one-way streets.

At the same time, the Reagan administration moved to establish a new bureau for congressional and public affairs—that is, propaganda. Moreover, the propaganda doesn't even seem likely to favor arms control and disarmament. Thus, ACDA director Eugene Rostow told a Senate subcommittee that an "important part of ACDA's work must be to counter Soviet opposition to the neutron bomb." In short, the ACDA is to begin propagandizing in favor of nuclear weapons! (Insofar as this is true, perhaps we should rejoice in its small budget.)

The reality is that arms control and disarmament negotiations should have the highest government priority. Success will require a group of knowledgeable, highly skilled, dedicated professionals. Fortunately, we have the necessary framework in the ACDA. Properly staffed and supported, it can—and should—become one of the most important branches of government. In a sense, expecting any government that supports a large, well-entrenched military establishment to take the initiative in arms control and disarmament is like expecting a plantation master to take the lead in abolishing slavery. But slavery *was* abolished. We must do no less with nuclear war, and the ACDA is the only organized group of abolitionists in government.

#### #25: We should establish an Office of Economic Conversion, to initiate plans for converting from a military to a civilian economy.

As we shall see, a military economy employs fewer people, is weaker, less productive, and more inflationary than a civilian economy. In addition, budget priorities make it difficult for us to wage peace effectively. Careful planning is needed if we are ever to convert military industries into those producing civilian products. At present, there is not a single governmental agency doing this work; there should be. ·

An Office of Economic Conversion, probably located within the Department of Labor, could serve two major functions: 1) provide the planning needed to guarantee a smooth transition, if and when the nation comes to its senses and stops investing so much of its resources in death, and actually facilitate such a transition, by providing detailed studies showing how specific industries (Lockheed, Boeing, McDonnel-Douglas, Northrop) could redirect themselves toward productive, consumer, and service-oriented goals. 2) At present, members of Congress representing districts with a large military-industrial plant have a difficult time supporting arms control legislation, since a shift away from military priorities appears to endanger their constituents' jobs. It would therefore be helpful if a government agency could provide point-by-point accounts of how many jobs would be lost, how many new jobs would be created by conversion, how many people could directly apply their existing skills to civilian products, how many would have to be retrained, and how this could be accomplished. We cannot simply go "cold turkey" on our military addiction; we will need careful assistance and encouragement if we are ever to break the habit.

#### #26: We should recognize the interdependency of all nations, and exaggerate that interdependency whenever possible.

Following the Cuban missile crisis, physicist Leo Szilard gave Krushchev a safety razor (not widely available at the time in the Soviet Union) and added, "Every day that there is not a nuclear war, I shall send you a blade."

We should encourage educational, cultural, and scientific exchanges of all sorts, and in particular, we should maximize our trade with the U.S.S.R., since each side has something to offer the other, even aside from survival. Thus, the Soviets have 31 percent of the world's natural gas, 47 percent of the world's coal (twice the U.S. reserves), and 12 percent of the world's oil—in fact, it is a little-known fact that the U.S.S.R. is the world's largest producer of oil! So they have resources that could be useful to us, and we have much to offer them, especially agricultural products and computer technology. Maybe we can get them hooked on the latest instant breakfast cereal, which can only be made from corn grown in Iowa.

**#27: We should establish shared enemies, to help
unify the East and West.**

Perhaps the best thing that could happen for world peace
would be a threatening message from Mars. Threats from the outside do wonders to unify people who otherwise find reasons to
squabble among themselves. Throughout history, national leaders
have resorted to war and the villification of foreigners in order to
rally the troops at home. Modern-day Israel, for example, is made
up of a host of diverse, potentially feuding people, kept unified by
their shared fear of the Arabs. And for their part, the converse can
be said of the Arabs—insofar as they are unified at all. During the
early 1930s and again following World War II, Mao Tse-tung and
Chiang Kai-shek were bitter enemies; yet in between they joined
forces when pressed by a greater enemy: Japan. The U.S. and
U.S.S.R. have been allies united by a common threat from Nazi
Germany. Now we have another common enemy, much more
threatening even than Hitler—nuclear war.

We are not starry-eyed idealists. We recognize that *Homo sapiens* may well have a nasty streak, and require enemies. Para-
phrasing Leibnitz's observation about God, if our enemies didn't
already exist, we would probably have to make them up! But even
if we aren't so lucky as to be threatened by Martians, and even if
nuclear war does not seem adequate as an enemy in itself, here are
some enemies against which we and the Russians could join: hunger, disease, pollution, energy shortages, crime, illiteracy, even the
exploration of space—anything that joins "us" with "them," in cooperation rather than mutual annihilation.

# 3. What *You* Can Do:

## The Individual

Remember your humanity and forget the rest.
> —from the RUSSELL-EINSTEIN Manifesto

Nobody made a greater mistake than he who did nothing because
he could only do a little.
> —EDMUND BURKE

"But what can I do to prevent nuclear war?" You may be one of
the millions of basically good, honest, moral people who have asked
this question because you understood the peril and the stupidity of
the nuclear arms race, but who have answered for yourself, "Nothing, really." It's all too easy to think that you are small, or alone, or
don't know enough, or that you are too busy to challenge a global
question. More pernicious is the attitude that we should let the
"experts" handle it, because "it's none of my business." Of course
it's your business, and the expert's business, and everyone's business, because everyone will probably die, one way or another, if
there is a nuclear war. Nuclear war is nondiscriminatory. What,
then can *you* do, to take the future in your hands?

We have written this book to help rouse public opinion—your
opinion. We have already suggested some steps that the nation can
take to avert nuclear catastrophe. Your task then is to influence the
government, to take some or all of these steps, and soon. How? We
must use our democracy, for our own and our children's survival.
Our forefathers who founded the United States government, with
its marvelous Constitution and Bill of Rights, assumed that given
the opportunity and sufficient education, citizens of a democracy
would assert their privileges, become informed, vote, and take an
active role in the fate of the country. However, even in 1776, apathy was a problem. Thomas Jefferson wearily commented "The
bulk of mankind are schoolboys through life," as he strove to imple-
ment his grand ideals. Facing the peril of nuclear annihilation, it is
now imperative that we all grow up, become adults, and learn

to use this magnificent democracy which we are all anxious to preserve. We are not children, and the "experts" are not our benevolent parents who have our best interest at heart.

What happened to our democracy, such that only 28 percent of the eligible voters of America were able to put Ronald Reagan in the White House? In 1835, Alexis de Tocqueville issued a warning in his *Democracy in America*. It still applies today:

> It must not be forgotten that it is especially dangerous to enslave men in the minor details of life. . . .
>
> Subjection in minor affairs breaks out every day, and is felt by the whole community indiscriminately. It does not drive men to resistance, but crosses them at every turn, till they are lead to surrender the exercise of their will. Thus their spirit is gradually broken, and their character enervated . . . .

Perhaps American society today is merely exhibiting the decay that de Tocqueville predicted. With increasingly sophisticated technology, weapons so deadly that they make Hitler's gas chambers seem almost quaintly inefficient and messy, and computer-based systems that completely divorce the murdered victims from the cold eyes of those who would order their use, we have become numb to the total immorality of genocide.

In their comfortable living rooms, most Americans are unconscious of the "bomb of Damocles" hanging over their heads. While their children play computerized space war games, practicing destroying "enemy" aircraft with missiles of their own, parents dwell on the issues that seem closest: jobs, economic problems, family issues and disputes, or vacations. In times of economic scarcity, such as now, de Tocqueville's words have special meaning, because almost everyone becomes preoccupied with the details of daily life, and survival of the species seems distant compared with the challenge of paying the mortgage or having decent school clothes for the kids. Berthold Brecht put it succinctly: "First feed the face, and then tell right from wrong, for even saintly men may act like sinners, unless they've had their customary dinners."

Yet the facts are stark and terrifying. The world right now is at great and increasing risk of ending. As a European report states:

"The balance of terror is ending. As lambs to the slaughter, we are headed for nuclear war." If we are not to be sheep, we must stand up together, as men and women. It is time now to demand of our government the primary right, the first one mentioned in the Declaration of Independence: life.

It is easier not to know. It is more comfortable and pleasant to be ignorant of your peril, but it is no less deadly; indeed, it is an upholstered cushion on the guillotine. "The mind resists involvement with horror as in a normal person it resists preoccupation with death," wrote John Kenneth Galbraith. "And in consequence we leave the issue of nuclear arms, their control and their consequences to the men who make horror their everyday occupation. It is a reckless, even fatal, delegation of power." If this book informs you, even entertains you in a macabre sort of way, then it will be of some use, but not much. We want to move you, to reach you not just as readers but as potential *doers*. We want you to take back that power that you have so fatally delegated to the professional strategists of nuclear horror. If you simply put down this book and go back to "business as usual," then we have failed—and so have you. Reading this book, then, is not enough, it is only the beginning.

To those who claim that they are powerless, we answer: you are, most assuredly, if you think you are, and act as though you are—that is, if you do not act at all. Powerlessness is a self-fulfilling prophecy: it becomes true if you believe it. But fortunately, so is power.

If you answer that power or not, saving the world is not *your* job, we ask you: whose is it, then? The nuclear weapons industry, which makes money hand over fist from our present course? The military, itself dazzled by the latest in hardware and personally obsessed by the illusory security of career advancement, not real security for themselves or the nation? The politicians, whose thoughts rarely go beyond the next election? Shall we wait for Flash Gordon, The Lone Ranger, Superman, Popeye saving Olive Oyl, Rin-Tin-Tin running at the head of a troop of cavalry? The Messiah? No! We must do it ourselves, and that means you and me.

You ask: "Who am I, to save the world?" And we answer: *"You are the world."* Who else will save it? There is a compelling theme in western literature of the ordinary person suddenly called upon

to perform monumental tasks: the Biblical Job suddenly beset by
God, or Frodo the Hobbit suddenly called upon in Tolkien's *Lord
of the Rings* to save his world. But nuclear war is not for someone
else or in fantasy. It is for you and in the real world. We all have a
personal shell surrounding ourselves into which we admit very little: our personal needs, our loved ones, work, and maybe recrea-
tion. Here we dwell, within our private, intensely personal lives.
Other concerns—people we meet, books we read, movies we see—
generally pass around our little protective shell. Nuclear war, however, will easily penetrate that shell. Therefore, the determination
to stop nuclear war must also penetrate, and quickly.

Antiwar movements typically grow and mature while the war
they oppose is being fought. The Vietnam antiwar movement, for
example, became dramatically stronger as the war dragged on. The
anti-nuclear war movement is therefore faced with a dilemma: how
to organize opposition to a war that has not yet happened and will
be over before anyone can oppose it? During the Vietnam years,
the nation received a daily dose of violence and suffering, brought
into our living rooms with the evening news.

To become active in the 1980s, the "me generation" must overcome the human tendency to deny or avoid unpleasant truths and
to ignore dangers that we do not see on television or in the street,
and which therefore do not seem real. We must also overcome the
seductive lure that confuses personal growth with human progress,
the easy cop-out of substituting inner harmony for world peace.
Peace begins with me, you say? Don't kid yourself. War begins
with decisions in the Kremlin and Washington—and peace must
begin there too. No amount of organic food, loving thy neighbor, or
transcendental meditation will keep you and those you love from
the agony of nuclear war. By all means, go ahead and adopt peaceful, "centered," and harmonious personal lifestyles if you wish. But
let's not pretend that by doing so you are somehow saving the
world. The world—your only world—is now severely threatened,
and not by forces within you. The hard, unpleasant reality is that to
save that world, and yourself, you must act *outside yourself* to
counter that threat, regardless of how you choose to direct your
private, inner self. For those less associated with counterculture
ideals the message is no different: you can brush your teeth every
morning and evening, send your children to the right schools, jog

and/or pray religiously, but it will all come to nothing if the world blows up. Bumper stickers urge us all to be good parents—"Have you hugged your kids today?" Ask yourself instead "Did I do something to help prevent nuclear war today?" For that is the best way to hug your kids.

The poet Theodore Roethke wrote, "In a dark time, the eye begins to see." The time is indeed dark, but it can give us needed clarity. We have made a Faustian bargain with nuclear weapons, but we can still change our minds. Give me a lever and a place to stand, wrote Archimedes, and I shall move the world. We must move the world; nothing else will do. Fortunately, we have a place to stand: nuclear weapons are wholly evil and must be eliminated. In the short run, perhaps we must accept having some of them around, in the process of eliminating others. But in the end, there can be no more compromise. Life is full of shades of gray, without clear-cut black or white, but this we can see clearly; it is also a very definite place to stand. In fact, it is the only secure place.

The long enough lever will be public opinion. We need what Einstein called a "chain reaction of awareness," sweeping from all of you to those in government, working on the fulcrum of world survival through the elimination of nuclear weapons. We need a grassroots movement of unprecedented power to overcome a threat of unprecedented magnitude.

We must not be overwhelmed by the job ahead. If nothing else, at least it is "fighting the good fight." What can be more exhilarating or important than saving the world? What can match the egotistical glow of seeing oneself as so important that no less than the future of the world rides on one's actions? What greater satisfaction than doing something wholly and intrinsically good, and working against unalloyed evil? Moreover, you will not be working alone: there is the joy of fellowship with some of the world's finest souls, fighting the world's greatest battle ever, to save the world itself.

The real battle is not between communism and capitalism, or between tyranny and democracy. Rather, it is between nuclear-armed militarism and humanity, between the forces of death and of life. We do not seek to give aid and comfort to the Soviets—with their thousands of nuclear weapons and repressive dictatorship, they give neither aid nor comfort to us. Rather, we seek victory for humanity and life, regardless of political ideology.

Because of this goal, there is great hope for a massive popular movement, cutting across narrow political, social, and economic lines. After all, nuclear war would certainly be bad for real estate values—the realtors of America have every reason to join. Nuclear war would hurt investments—let's hear from the bankers. It would devastate the Social Security and pension system—where are the elderly and all those who hope to become old, someday. "War is bad for children and other living things," we were told during the Vietnam years. Nuclear war would be definitely worse than any other; we can enlist all the children as well as anyone who has children or hopes to have children. In short, the crusade against nuclear war must become the greatest mass movement in history.

As a guideline, "think globally, act locally." Even the most enormous task seems manageable when we break it down into small parts. As the trash can reminds us, most Americans really do try to "put litter in its place." We can do no less with nuclear war. Why do we put a candy wrapper in the trash can? Not because we expect personally to solve environmental pollution, but rather because we know that every bit counts, and because we can see the effect of our actions: drop it on the street and our eye is offended, drop it in the litterbox and we have done something to help. The moral is simple: people need something real and immediate, something they can do. And if they all do it, something gets done.

You may ask, "What about the Russians? It's all very well and good to use our democracy, but they don't have a democracy to use." Russia is a totalitarian state, governed by a select group of powermongers, and the people are not free to express themselves, or to join mass movements. How can a truly worldwide movement against nuclear war be generated, when many of the nuclear nations and soon-to-be nuclear nations (like China and Argentina) are not in the least democratic?

Our answers must be several. First, nuclear weapons don't make a country more secure, they simply make the country *feel* more powerful. This holds true for all countries. Any country that possesses nuclear weapons and threatens to use them becomes a target for nuclear war. Thus, it is in every country's interest to back away from the nuclear precipice.

Second, those who point accusingly to the absence of a vigorous peace movement in the U.S.S.R. seem to feel that, if our government has one influencing it, while theirs does not, then the result would somehow be one-sided and unfair to us. This is simply wrong. Many of our demands are for *bilateral* action: a freeze, no "first use," reductions. *Unilateral* actions, whether GRIT or renouncing first-strike weaponry, can only make us more secure regardless of what the Soviets do, and regardless of whether they have a peace movement.

In fact, there is evidence, at least from the Soviet Union, of official support for halting the nuclear arms race. We do not deny that the Soviet system is reprehensible. We are well aware of the Soviet treatment of dissidents, and the abhorrent restrictions on individual liberty that are intrinsic to a "closed society." Yet, on the issue of nuclear arms, the Soviet government has supported efforts by Soviet professionals both within the Soviet Union and when visiting other countries, to explain the risks of nuclear war and the benefits of halting the arms race. The Russian physicians who are members of the International Physicians for the Prevention of Nuclear War are not regarded as dissidents by the Soviet government. Billy Graham was allowed in May 1982 to preach to large Russian audiences on the subject of disarmament.

Should we then respond to Soviet repression by emulating them and repressing our own freedoms? The right-wing radicals who control American nuclear policy do so by grace of American democratic institutions. We can and must use those same institutions on behalf of nuclear sanity and survival.

Our first rule then, for those who wish to help stop nuclear war is USE YOUR DEMOCRACY. Your basic tool is your vote. VOTE EARLY AND OFTEN! Vote whenever you can, and use the nuclear issue as a litmus test, determining your attitude toward every candidate, from school board member to president. Participate in voter registration drives, and make democracy work. This is our basic right, and the key to our freedom and survival.

## Contacting Politicians

I like to believe that people in the long run are going to do more to promote peace than are governments. Indeed, I think that people want peace so much that one of these days governments had better get out of their way and let them have it.

—DWIGHT D. EISENHOWER

Our government can bring us peace, but it seems unlikely to do so unless we make it clear, over and over again, and as persuasively as possible, that peace is what we want. Whether it was civil rights, the Limited Test-Ban of 1963, or an end to the Vietnam War, politicians eventually responded to the demands of their constituents. Indeed, when the pressure is sufficient, politicians have the habit of suddenly discovering that, whatever the issue, they were actually in favor of it all along! We must make arms control, international tension reduction, and nuclear disarmament political necessities; we must make it political suicide to support the arms race, belligerence, and a cavalier attitude toward nuclear war.

Contact your politicians, especially Members of Congress, Senators, and the president. If you agree with his/her action or stance on an issue, indicate your support. All too often, politicians hear only criticism from the voters; it can be as helpful to reinforce a good stand as to take issue with a bad one. But by all means, don't hesitate to disagree when your politician has taken a pro-arms race, militaristic, dangerous, and shortsighted position. Your letters, cards, telegrams, and telephone calls *do* count. Ours is a representative democracy, and our elected representatives do not begrudge hearing from their constituencies—in most cases, they appreciate it. At minimum, your opinion will be tallied and used as a partial guide to the politician's subsequent behavior; few elected officials will vote for a measure when their mail is running ten to one against it! Most likely you will receive a reply, and you may even directly influence some opinions.

### Letters

Don't be fearful about contacting a politician, it's not that big a deal. A simple letter will do, even a postcard. Make it brief (if possible one page) and in your own words. Don't threaten. Where possible, congratulate the official on something, even if you must disagree with something much more important. Try to limit each letter to a single issue, or a related set of issues. Be reasonable—don't rant and rave—but don't be afraid of showing your emotion; after all, your life depends on the outcome. Don't be fearful and intimidated about not having "all the facts." If you have read this far, you already have more facts than many politicians. If possible, ask at least one specific, detailed question; this will increase the chance of a personal reply by making it harder to use a form letter in response. Your goal should be not only to show the politician what you think, but also to make him or her think. Type your letter if possible, but this is not essential. If you want a reply, be sure to include your home address on the letter itself—political mail is typically opened by staff members, and the envelope may be lost. Your letter can simply begin "Dear Congressman (Congresswoman) Smith," or "Dear Senator Jones," or "Dear President X." Mailing addresses are:

| Member of Congress | U.S. Senator | President |
|---|---|---|
| House Office Building | Senate Office Building | The White House |
| Washington, D.C. 20515 | Washington, D.C. 20510 | Washington, D.C. 20500 |

Write often. The higher the official, the more often you can write without losing any personal credibility. Thus, mail to the president is tabulated as "pro" or "con" particular issues, with individual identity usually lost. So, have no hesitation about writing once per day! You can usefully write a U.S. Senator several times per month before you become discounted as a "screwball," and Members of Congress perhaps a bit less often. The real danger is not that you will write too often, but rather, not often enough.

It is generally more effective to write elected officials than those who are appointed—that is, better to write the President than the Secretary of State; better a Senator than the Chairman of the Joint Chiefs of Staff. Also, you will have more impact with your own elected official than with someone who does not represent you; if you live in California, your letter to a Senator from New York will, at best, be forwarded to one of your California Senators.

We are here emphasizing contacts with the U.S. government, because we are addressing this book to Americans, because the U.S.

government is receptive to citizen pressure, and because there is much that the U.S. government can do to help us all. But don't be shy about contacting the U.S.S.R. as well. Write to: Embassy of U.S.S.R, 1125 16th St., Washington, D.C. 20036.

## Telephone Calls

You can also telephone. The switchboard at the White House can be reached at (202) 456-1441. Don't be nervous or flustered; you will speak to an operator, not the president! Say that you want to leave a "public opinion message," and you will be able to express yourself on three different issues. Your views will be tabulated; don't bother trying to persuade the operator. Such calls cost 50¢ per minute during the day, and 20¢ per minute at night; from the West Coast, calls before eight AM save money and reach Washington during the working day. The public opinion line for Senators and Members of Congress is (202) 224-3121.

You can send a telegram by calling Western Union. Call 1 (800) 555-1212. This is a toll-free line which can tell you the (toll-free) Western Union telegram phone number for your area code. When you dial that number, say that you want to send a public opinion message to the White House (Senate or House Office Building, etc.). It will cost $2.50 for the first 50 words, and then 50¢ for each extra 50 words. The cost will be charged to your telephone bill, so it is easy to pay; you need not write a special check.

Senators and Members of Congress all maintain local offices in their home districts. Look in the white pages of your telephone directory under "United States Government" for listings of the local office addresses and telephone numbers under "Congress" and "Senate." Federal politicians make regular trips to their home districts and typically they establish a round of public meetings to hear from their constituents. When you call their local office, find out the time and place of the next such meeting, and plan to attend. Express your views to the staffer who answers, and find out how you can best make your views known to the official. If possible, arrange to meet with him/her personally.

You can receive updated lists of Congresspersons by state and committee from the United Methodist Church, 100 Maryland Ave.

NE, Washington, D.C. 20002. You can receive "Action Alerts" on key military issues coming before Congress, from the Coalition for a New Foreign and Military Policy, 120 Maryland Ave. NE, Washington, D.C. 20002. You can also telephone for a weekly update of pending arms control and military legislation, by calling (202) 543-0006. Background information on legislators is available from *The Almanac of American Politics* (E. P. Dutton), updated every two years, and on the shelves of most libraries. Get voting records of Senators and Congresspeople from Friends Committee on National Legislation, 245 2nd St.NE, Washington, D.C. 20002. This same organization has also prepared pamphlets on "How to work in politics," "How to visit a member of Congress," and "How to work for the Congressional candidate of your choice," as well as guides on letter writing and local organizing.

We are all proud of our democracy, and yet most of us know nothing at all about how to make it work *for* us. We are generally content for government to go its way, while we go ours. But the way of our government will become the way of our lives, or our deaths—especially when it comes to nuclear war. You must learn to watch and influence your government in the same way that a diabetic watches and influences his insulin level. Write for the free "Citizen's Action Guide" from Common Cause; 2030 M St. NW, Washington, D.C. 20036. Also, a six-pamphlet "Action Course in Practical Politics" from the U.S. Chamber of Commerce, 1615 H St.NW; Washington, D.C. 20036, and a number of publications (such as "Public Action Pak") advising you how to be politically effective, available from the League of Women Voters, 1730 M St.NW; Washington, D.C. 20036. Request the guidebook on "How to Introduce a Resolution on The Arms Race Into Local Legislative Bodies," from Women Strike for Peace, 201 Mass. Ave. NE #102, Washington, D.C. 20002. Also, you can get Legislative and Organizing Packets ($5 each) from Traprock Peace Center, Woolman Hill, Keets Road, Deerfield, Mass. 01342. For information on organizing town meetings, New England style, write Connecticut Campaign/Arms Freeze, Box 494, Voluntown, Conn. 06384. And finally, for materials on "civil defense" and how to oppose and expose it, write: Civil Defense Awareness, 86 Wendell St. Cambridge, Mass. 02138.

Become an expert and share your expertise, regularly, with

your legislator. But even if you are not an expert, don't forget your stake in the political process, your right to speak out, and your need to be heard. And remember Edmund Burke's warning: "All that is needed for the triumph of evil is for good men to do nothing."

### Using the Media

People read the "letters to the editor" section of newspapers, and every newspaper has one. Write. Most newspapers require that all published letters be signed, and with return address. The briefer your letter, the more likely it is to be published. Avoid long, convoluted sentences. Don't be shy about disagreeing with your newspaper; in fact, letters to the editor are more likely to be published if they take issue with some editorial or news story. So read your newspaper carefully (as if your life depends on it—which it does) and when you see something that raises your blood pressure, write about it. You can also kill two birds with one stone by sending copies of your letter to local politicians, or copies of your letters to politicians, to the newspaper as well.

Many newspapers, also have weekly space for longer comments by the public, often called "Soapbox," "Forum," or something equivalent. These can usually be about 1,000 words—about three typed pages—and give the opportunity to develop an issue in more depth.

Contact local columnists with information that might be of interest to them. Remember, these people are constantly looking for publishable material; so don't be shy. If you have important and useful material for them, you will be doing them a favor as well. Local angles will be especially attractive to local columnists: the role of the community in military production or preparedness; the impact of military spending on the community; prominent local leaders (including religious figures) taking a stand on nuclear war; regional civil defense preparations; or the voting record of local politicians, for just a partial list. Most newspapers have editorial boards which set editorial policy on particular issues. Call your newspapers and suggest a meeting with its editorial board; there is a good chance you will get a hearing, especially if you can identify yourself as representing a respectable group or organization, and if you can claim some special reason for the meeting—a prominent visitor in town, some local development that warrants special attention (like the opening of a new military-industrial plant, new activity at a military base, etc.), or some national or international news upon which local individuals or groups want to be heard. Finally, watch the by-lines of news articles. In particular, communicate with reporters who cover related stories in a fair and sympathetic manner. Try to get to know them and interest them in other possible stories. Newspapers often respond favorably to "human interest" stories about the personal commitment of local citizens to preventing nuclear war.

Many radio stations have "call-in" talk shows. Call in and talk. Also, call the station and volunteer to appear yourself; it's a good way to publicize your activities and those of your group. Radio stations are also required by law to provide a certain number of "public service" announcements, free. You can use these to help publicize meetings and other antiwar activities. These announcements should be brief, and written out so that they can be read in about thirty seconds or so, and they must represent a nonprofit organization. Radio commentators generally have a good deal of discretion about the material appearing on their shows; find out who would be most sympathetic, and get to work on him/her.

Anti-nuclear war radio programming is also available from several sources, notably:

| | | |
|---|---|---|
| **In the Public Interest** | and | **"Consider the Alternative"** |
| 122 Maryland Ave.NE | | SANE |
| Washington, D.C. 20002 | | 1411 Walnut Street |
| | | Philadelphia, PA. 19102 |

Local radio stations can sometimes be persuaded to run material of this sort. Indeed, often they are eager for something new and controversial. You might want to contact some of the organizations in Appendix A first, so as to have literature in hand when you contact the Program Manager of your station.

Television stations are more distant than radio, but not unreachable. Although they typically show network programming, every station has local news. Contact the news director, and/or news reporters about possible stories that could help raise local consciousness. Most stations also organize local interview shows and other broadcasts highlighting regional events. These are all opportunities for wider exposure of meetings, protests, petition drives, etc.

### Local Group Activities

He who would do good to another must do it in Minute Particulars.

—WILLIAM BLAKE

Getting started yourself is both exhilarating and intimidating: exhilarating because you are finally beginning to *do something* about the most important thing in the world, and intimidating because the problem is so very big and you are so very small. But remember, just as a thousand-mile journey begins with a single step, the largest protest begins with a single voice—yours. Your voice will quickly become stronger and louder (and you will have more fun as well) if you get together with others. The best way to begin taking the world on your shoulders is to break it down into smaller chunks, beginning with your own state and your own community. In this way, the biggest problems become manageable, and your efforts can proceed on a comfortable, human scale.

You don't necessarily have to begin by forming your own group. If you live in a medium or large city, there are probably local chapters of various national organizations, such as those listed in Appendix A. They have the advantages of experience, good advice, and resources. Write to them, see what they have to offer, and which ones feel best to you. Some, like the freeze campaign, are focused on a single issue. Others, like the War Resisters League, oppose war in any form, with nuclear war considered just a special case. Others, like the AFSC, have numerous other social concerns as well, such as world hunger, environmental protection and human rights. If a particular national organization seems appealing but has no local chapter, see about starting one. Most of the larger groups have special information on establishing local affiliations, and will welcome your inquiry.

Whatever you decide, don't make the mistake of trying to "organize your community" right away, from the ground up; this can be an overwhelming and in fact, unnecessary task. Your community is already organized—into church groups, labor unions, garden clubs, professional and social societies of all sorts. Use your own personal network to get started. Talk to those you love and care about, your neighbors, your colleagues at work. You will be amazed how many contacts are already available to yourself and several friends. For example, it is said that any two people in the U.S. can be linked by a chain of no more than six or seven go-betweens—your doctor's brother-in-law writes for the newspaper and knows the local Member of Congress, who in turn knows . . .

Most organizations are looking for possible programs. To get people involved and start them thinking about nuclear war, and to establish a nucleus for subsequent organization, it is often more efficient to "plug into" one or more of these existing groups, even if they are not normally concerned with issues of war and peace. Because if they are not, they should be. Labor unions have a real interest in the economic effects of a military economy, as does the local PTA. Similarly, environmental groups should realize that nuclear war would be bad for birds, and the local LaLeche League might be interested in the effects of nuclear war upon nursing mothers as well as their infants. The list is endless. So you don't necessarily have to start off trying to get a group together—groups get together all the time. Use these meetings to focus attention on nuclear war. Then, get together with those individuals who have been most attentive, and take it from there.

*Some advice for initial meetings*

If you are uncomfortable speaking in front of others, a good way to start this sort of attention-focusing is with a film or videotape. You can rent one at a modest price, show it at a meeting, then spend some time discussing it afterward. Out of this can come a nucleus of people who want to do more; don't let the momentum drop at this point, and don't be discouraged by small numbers. Get together and decide on your next steps. One videotape that has been used with great success in all parts of the country is "The Last Epidemic," available from Physicians for Social Responsibility. This tape is thirty-six minutes long, and summarizes in graphic detail the medical effects of a single nuclear explosion on the city of San Francisco. You can show this tape to your neighbors, the editorial board of your local newspaper, your county or city Medical Society, or local elected officials. The effect of this particular videotape is to thaw "psychic numbing" in even the most frozen hearts.

An excellent movie is *War Without Winners,* produced by the Center for Defense Information and distributed by FILMS Inc., 733 Green Bay Road, Wilmette, Ill. 60091. Also, *Survival . . . or Suicide,* from the American Committee on East-West Accord, 227 Mass. Ave. NE, Washington, D. C. 20002. Further information on films is available from The Film Fund, 80 East 11th St., New York, N.Y. 10003; the Disarmament Film Bibliography, produced by the Riverside Church Disarmament Project, 490 Riverside Dr., New York, N.Y. 10027; and an extensive "War Peace Film Guide" available from World Without War Publications, 67 E. Madison, Suite 1417, Chicago, Ill. 60603.

Slide shows are somewhat less expensive and also effective. Good ones are available from

Packard Manse Media Project  
Box 450  
Stoughton, Mass. 02072

SANE  
514 C St.NE  
Washington, D.C. 20002

Coalition for a New Foreign  
and Military Policy  
120 Maryland Ave.NW  
Washington, D.C. 20002

AFSC/For Nuclear Weapons  
Facilities Project  
1432 Lafayette St.  
Denver, Colo. 80218

and especially,

Nuclear War Graphics Project  
100 Nevada St.  
Northfield, Minn. 55057

This latter organization can provide 1. an excellent set of 130 slides; 2. a slide show (60 slides) plus a narrative tape and guide book; and 3. a two-minute, 16mm film showing the effects of nuclear explosions on houses. Each is $15 and a bargain. The slides and film are valuable resources for developing your own talk, while the slide show can either stand alone or be a starter for subsequent discussions and presentations.

It can be very useful to have experienced, knowledgeable speakers address your meeting. In many cases, eminent experts are available through speakers bureaus, maintained by most national organizations. Inviting an outside speaker, especially one who is well-known and a recognized expert, can be invaluable for initiating community attention and activity. First, your new little group will gain cohesion and a sense of purpose as you plan the speaking engagement and the speaker's itinerary. Get all the mileage that you can from your speakers, by setting up TV and radio in-depth interviews, talk show appearances, and a press conference before the event. Many speakers will also allow you to have a reception or dinner to honor them, and this can provide you with an excellent opportunity to invite your local elected officials and dignitaries to become involved.

Use your speaker's natural "affinity group" to gain further exposure, and perhaps help to defray expenses. For example, if you wish to invite a doctor as a major speaker, be sure to talk to your local medical school, hospital staff office, or county medical society, to see if they might wish to co-sponsor the event or invite your speaker to an additional engagement at the hospital or medical school. Most colleges, universities, and professional schools have funds available for out-of-town speakers.

Remember that however committed to the prevention of nuclear war your speaker may be, he/she also must pay for living expenses. Traveling and speaking are strenuous, even for the most practiced speakers. Therefore, be prepared to offer both travel expenses and an honorarium to your potential guest. Honoraria vary with the prominence of the speaker, from a low of $50 to $100 to highs in the thousands of dollars. Don't be afraid to call any of the prominent people who have taken strong stands against nuclear war, but be prepared to make an offer, as best you can, and don't be surprised if your "target" haggles a little bit over the amount. It's not that he or she lacks conviction, it's usually a matter of personal survival and sustenance. In addition, most national level speakers will expect to stay in a pleasant hotel or motel, rather than a private home, so that they can relax and enjoy moments of privacy.

For information and lists of potential guest speakers, contact:

New Directions Speakers Bureau
305 Mass. Ave. NE
Washington, D.C. 20002

Institute for Policy Studies
Speakers Bureau
1901 Que St.NW
Washington, D.C. 20009

Council for a Livable World
Education Fund
11 Beacon St.
Boston, Mass. 02108

Physicians for Social Responsibility
Speakers Bureau
P.O. Box 144
Watertown, Mass. 02172

Public Affairs Director
Arms Control and Disarmament Agency,
Rm. 4936
320 21st St.NW
Washington, D.C. 20451

Mobilization for Survival
Speakers Bureau
3601 Locust Walk
Philadelphia, PA. 19104

Members of Congress for Peace Through Law
Rm 3538, House Annex #2
Washington, D.C. 20515

Photographs can be very effective in setting up tabletop displays. A full-fledged display on "The Effects and Dangers of Nuclear War" can be obtained from the U.N. Association, 152 St. Francis Blvd. Daly City, Calif. 94105. A wide range of military photos is provided by the Still Photo Section, A-V Division, Office of the Secretary of Defense for Public Affairs, Rm. 2E773, Department of Defense, Washington, D.C. 20301. For a general guide to "Pictorial Resources in the Washington, D.C. Area," write to the Information Office, Library of Congress, Washington, D.C. 20540.

One way to generate local involvement in preventing nuclear war is to point out how each local area is *already* involved, in the production and design of weapons, their deployment and transportation, as well as being targets if war ever happens. Civil defense is now being coordinated by the Federal Emergency Management Agency (FEMA). Write for a listing of "high risk areas," publication TR-82: FEMA, Public Affairs Section, Rm. 807, 1725 I St. NW, Washington, D.C. 20472. Also contact your local FEMA office (in the white pages under "U.S. Government") for information about regional civil defense planning. Draw media attention to the absurdity of the evacuation and sheltering plans for your community. Storage sites and underground bunkers for public officials—these are scattered throughout the country and their location should be available from FEMA offices—provide excellent targets for public meetings and demonstrations.

Maps and regional information concerning nuclear weapons research, production, transportation, and deployment are available from

| | | |
|---|---|---|
| Nuclear Mapping Kit | and | Military-Industrial Atlas of the U.S. |
| New Manhattan Project | | NARMIC |
| 15 Rutherford Place | | 1501 Cherry Street |
| New York, N.Y. 10003 | | Philadelphia, PA. 19102 |

The Arms Control and Disarmament Agency can provide detailed maps showing the estimated effects of various size nuclear bombs detonated over every U.S. city. This can be very effective in bringing the reality of nuclear war to every local street corner. Write to ACDA Public Affairs Office, 320 21st St. NW, Washington, D.C. 20451. Using these maps, it is easy to make transparencies which can be projected onto a screen as part of a talk describing the local impact of nuclear war. For additional sources of information, see Appendix B.

### Tips for Groups

Take a hard, objective look at your community, at the various national groups, and at your own inclinations. If you then decide to form your own group, go right ahead. If you are joining a local chapter of a national organization, then you can participate in (and influence) their activities. If you are forming your own chapter, or your own new group, then you are in for an exciting time. There are very few hard and fast rules; each group must be flexible, responsive to the needs of its members, and appropriate to the local community. To some extent, you will have to learn as you go. Here are some tips that might be helpful, however:

—Don't aim for a massive gathering of people, especially in the early going. A nucleus of five to ten committed, intelligent people is just fine.

—Set up a regular meeting time, and don't conclude any meeting without agreeing when and where you will meet next.

—You can meet in private homes, libraries, schools, grange halls, etc. Remember, there is nothing unpatriotic about preventing nuclear war, and you have as much right to public meeting places as anyone else.

Someone must lead the meeting, just as someone must lead the group (not necessarily the same person, by the way). No one wants to waste time, so be sure the meeting chairperson has a clear agenda, and keeps things on track.

—Make sure that the meeting ends with a clear feeling that something has been accomplished, and if possible, with each person knowing what he or she should do before the next meeting.

—Have brainstorming sessions to decide on goals for your group. Choose some easy and immediate goals (name of group, meeting times and places, basic rules of procedure, etc.), and others related to the long-term objectives. Start with some realistic and achievable projects, with no more than a few weeks' lead time. This will continue the feeling of momentum and success that is so crucial, especially in the early stages. These projects should also serve to widen the group's membership and community recognition: an invited speaker, debate, showing of a movie or slide-show, a public meeting to discuss local FEMA plan or military contracting, etc.

—You and your group must decide whether to focus on several different (but related) goals, such as human rights, energy policy, environmental protection, or just one: the prevention of nuclear war. We recommend the latter.

—To start, contact those people most likely to be sympathetic. Don't worry that you are simply preaching to the already converted; there are many millions of "already converted" Americans, who recognize the issue and its importance, and who are "with you" in spirit but not yet in deed. If these people can be converted into activists instead of just sympathizers, an enormous force for peace and survival will have been loosed.

—As your group grows, it will become increasingly important to have clear-cut decision-making procedures and some sort of executive process, with readily defined roles. A rotating chair is one possibility, since it eases the burden of leadership and gets more people involved. On the other hand, consistency of direction is also important. Your group must decide on its own governance, but remember that these decisions can always be undone if they are found to be wrong, and don't make the mistake of spending most of your efforts gazing at your own administrative navels.

—It might be useful to specialize, with at least one person (or possibly, a committee), concentrating on: fund-raising, membership recruitment, publicity and media contacts, education on technical issues, maintaining a speakers bureau (with regular efforts to encourage other groups to invite one of your speakers), etc.

—Raise money. Charge a modest admission to your film, lecture or debate. Put an ad in the local paper. Charge dues to your members. Try parties, newspaper ads, benefit concerts, raffles, bake sales, auctions, anything creative and not-too-outrageous. Check with local ordinances about canvasing, then consider organizing a telephone campaign, as well as good old fashioned pavement pounding and doorbell ringing. Divide your community—or the telephone book—into manageable sections, and assign different people to a section. For detailed suggestions on fund-raising, write for the booklet, "Dollars and Sense: the art of raising money," available for 75¢ from the League of Women Voters, 1730 M St., Washington, D. C. 20035. Do some brainstorming about possible large donors—remember, in most cases, 90 percent of an organization's money comes from 10 percent of its donors. Tax-exempt status, known to the IRS as "501(c) (3)," may be useful in attracting donors, but it is difficult to obtain; consult an attorney to see if it is worth your while. Also, with tax-exempt status, you cannot take a partisan position, or support legislation or specific political action. Nonetheless, some organizations, such as the Council for a Livable World, maintain a tax-exempt "education fund."

—Additional fund-raising techniques. If your group becomes ambitious, and decides to organize a large rally, symposium, or conference, you may be interested in how professional fund-raisers operate. First, you might locate a pro, and try to involve him or her in your group. Then, there are two basic strategies for raising big bucks: grants and direct mail campaigns. There are many nonprofit foundations which are interested in funding antiwar activities. Consult *The Grants Register,* or regional lists of granting agencies, for information on how to apply. These books can usually be found in local libraries or colleges. Most granting agencies prefer to donate money for specific projects, rather than ongoing expenses of setting up an office, salaries, or organizational maintenance.

Direct mail campaigns are used by politicians and private corporations to solicit funds from large numbers of donors. Local politicians who are sympathetic to your group may be willing to share their lists of donors. There are companies that specialize in obtaining mailing lists, and conducting direct mail campaigns. Even small organizations may want to obtain highly productive lists, to use when soliciting funds or advertising activities. While some mailing lists have to be purchased, you may be able to obtain others free, if you emphasize that you are working for survival.

—Communications within the group: The simplest and cheapest way is by a telephone tree, with each person delegated to call three or four others (a good example of using a chain reaction for our benefit!). Bulk mailings save some money, especially if you have 510(c) (3) status. But, only certain post offices will accept bulk mailings, and the packages must be sorted by zip codes and specially tied. Bulk mailings are also available for groups without tax-exempt status, but the saving is less; for groups of fewer than 100 or so, it may be that bulk mailing permits are not worth the trouble.

—Don't disparage the Johnny-come-latelies. You need them and they need you. The more of them, the better. Fit newcomers into existing committees, so that each new arrival is able to contribute promptly.

At the same time, be alert to new talents and ideas: if an artist joins, think about a poster exhibit or competition; if a carpenter, see if your office needs some work; if a musician, see about a benefit concert; your members are your greatest resource.

—Send out press releases before significant events. A press release is a news article, written by you (or your publicity person), which tells the news media about something and also gives them a potential ready-made news article. News media might use it directly; they might modify it; they might attend the event if you are announcing one and then write their own story, or they might ignore it altogether. Write the name of your organization at the top of a clean piece of paper. Then, either "For immediate release" or "For release eight AM, December 10, 1983," followed by "For additional information, contact Jane Smith, 322-1234." Next, the headline, and then the article itself. In general, send press releases a few days before the event. Address them to "city editor" at a newspaper, and to "assignment editor" at radio and TV stations.

—When the occasion warrants, hold press conferences, announced by press releases. It could be a visiting expert or dignitary (even a minor official or out-of-town speaker will do), or simply your organization or someone important in the community responding to something in the news: "Clergyman supports freeze actions by town council," "Local antinuclear group protests claim that defense spending makes jobs," etc. All you need is a place to hold the press conference, such as the meeting room at a church, school or library, and one or more articulate spokespeople. One person should be in charge; he or she should call the conference to order, identify the group behind it, and identify the speaker(s), who should be seated at a table at the front of the room. Typically, there is a brief opening statement of five minutes or so, followed by questions from the press. It shouldn't drag on much more than thirty minutes. TV and radio people may want to interview the principals, often separately, after the question period. If possible, prepare a brief "press pack," including relevant information, plus brief biographies of the participants. Don't hold too many press conferences, however, or news people may stop taking you seriously. On the other hand, don't be shy: nuclear war is the top issue of the 1980s, and newspeople are beginning to recognize it.

—To avoid having your home besieged with mail, you might want to establish a P.O. Box as a mailing address. Later, if things go well, consider renting a small office, in some convenient part of town.

—If personality clashes, ego-trips or other minor irritants threaten to throw your activities off track (as they almost certainly will), don't be shy about reminding everyone of the reason for your group and its activities: to prevent nuclear war. That will usually suffice.

—In public meetings and pronouncements, avoid despair, whatever you might be feeling inside. Nothing depresses a group so much as a leader who is "down," so put on an optimistic face, if not a happy one. Remember, despair is like masturbation—okay if you must, but best done in private; certainly, don't expect it to generate followers.

—Look and act respectable. Much of the promise of the new anti-nuclear war movement lies in its wide base of real and potential support. When speaking to business people or doctors, for example, look and act in a way that shows respect for yourself, for them, and for your cause.

—If someone argues vigorously with you, especially at a well-attended meeting, try to remain reasonable. Remember that you are unlikely to persuade your opponent (especially not in public); your real goal, therefore, should be to win the others in the audience. Be calm, don't be strident and remember that people will be attuned at least partly to your manner, as well as the logic and cogency of your viewpoint.

—Develop a good piece of literature, ideally no more than one piece of paper (both sides), that can be reproduced cheaply and distributed wherever possible. Check with local regulations and consider setting up literature tables wherever people gather: at various public events (concerts, ballgames, picnics), and in shopping centers or parking lots. Be sure to check with local officials about legality first.

—Civil disobedience: You must act according to your own courage, convictions and conscience. For example, in September 1980, Philip and Daniel Berrigan, along with six others (the "Plowshares Eight") entered the General Electric plant at King of Prussia, Pa., hammered on two Mark 12A warheads and then poured blood on them and on nearby desks and documents. They were found guilty of burglary, criminal conspiracy and criminal mischief, and they received prison sentences. The Plowshares Eight did not really expect to beat the warheads into plowshares and they knew they were breaking the civil law. They were following their sense of a higher law, their own intense conviction about truth, morality and the rightness of personal action and responsibility in the face of greater dangers than a prison sentence. A wasted act? Perhaps. And yet, imagine if two million Americans, or twenty million, hammers in hand, descended on our nuclear facilities, intent on beating swords into plowshares. One way or another, they would probably make quite a dent.

On the other hand, many people are frightened by the prospect of civil disobedience. They equate joining an anti-nuclear war group with lying down in front of a missile base, and being arrested. We must stress that this is a decision of individuals and their groups, and that an enormous amount of very effective work can be done entirely within the civil laws. Indeed, depending upon the local situation, civil disobedience may be drastically counterproductive. You must tailor your actions to the membership of your group, the opportunities and standards of your community. Saul Alinsky has pointed out that when Ghandi organized mass civil disobedience in India, he was employing the ammunition available to him: he had a vast population that was largely inert, sitting around, so he told them where to sit. In the U.S. we have a very different population, and each individual and each group will have to decide where to sit, and how.

—Also, don't forget the impact and value of public demonstrations, carefully planned and well-publicized. In this, we can take some lessons from the European peace movement: it is possible—even desirable—to maintain a sense of joyous, crusading enthusiasm, complete with bright banners, humorous as well as serious posters, buttons, and songs. Don't count on 500,000 demonstrators the first time, but also don't forget that the time is right; this is the issue of the 1980s. After all, more than 750,000 people gathered in New York City on June 12, 1982, to protest the nuclear arms race in a mood of enthusiasm, determination, and hope. Be patient, work hard, and your crowds will grow. Important dates provide good opportunities. For example, don't let Hiroshima and Nagasaki days go by in your community without some public event. Traditionally, Easter has been a time for demonstrations, and in general, the months of April and October. However, don't feel constrained by these traditions. A Christmas candlelight service for peace, or caroling for peace, makes for a fine and spiritually uplifting ceremony. Thanksgiving and Passover feasts are excellent times to celebrate life, and the bountiful earth. Each birthday that we celebrate reminds us that we have survived another year, and wish for many more. In other words, take every opportunity both to celebrate life and survival, and to renounce nuclear war, with friends, family, and your community.

## Community Activism

> Our representatives depend ultimately on decisions made in the village square . . . to the village square we must carry the facts (of nuclear war). From these must come America's voice.
> —ALBERT EINSTEIN

Whether you choose to work as an individual, or as a member of a national or a local group, your goal is to prevent nuclear war, and to do this, you must make yourself heard at the local level—in "the village square," as Einstein put it. Indeed, some of the most effective work, both in Europe and in the U.S, has been done at the neighborhood level.

There are many advantages to this approach. For one, it is relatively easy and comfortable. Your family, neighbors, friends, your colleagues at work are known to you and are not intimidating. Raise the issues at local neighborhood coffees, picnics, and other familiar gatherings. These settings offer both intimacy and autonomy, and the good feeling of getting started, being heard, and surrounding yourself with those you know and trust.

Get active in your local political process. Find out what precinct you are in, and how your party machinery works: when the caucuses are held (usually, very few people show up, so if you do, you might well find yourself a delegate by default!), and how you can become a county or statewide delegate. Local chapters of the League of Women Voters typically prepare brochures describing the political structure in each city. Make an appointment with the mayor, members of the town council or board of aldermen, etc. Dress up in your most respectable clothes and, if possible, accompanied by some friends, explain your concerns. You may find it useful to have something to show: a film, slide presentation, or perhaps a visiting expert to introduce.

Local petitions are a good excuse for such a meeting. Petitions are a powerful way of influencing the government, triply effective because they 1. indicate widespread public sentiment, 2. inform the public about the issue and also generate some commitment, if only by the signing of one's name, and 3. are attention-getting in themselves, especially when presented to an elected official. Knock on your neighbor's door with a peace petition; pass it around at work; set up a table at shopping centers, movie theaters or outside city hall. The nuclear freeze campaign has been coordinating a widespread petition drive, which can be directed both nationally (to the president) and locally (to members of Congress, local mayors and town councils, etc.). Americans rightly cherish their democratic political process, and no elected official can disdain the written demands of his or her constituency. Petition in hand, you cannot be ignored.

Be absolutely insistent that nuclear war is relevant to every aspect of public life. Each candidate for office, whether for dog-catcher or school board, is influenced not only personally but also in the conduct of his or her job by preparations for war, and certainly, by the reality of nuclear war, if it ever happens. So make sure that every candidate takes a stand on military spending, on the local "civil defense" plans, etc. Lobby everyone you can reach. Urge that local school boards and town councils hold hearings on one aspect of the issue or another, and let the press know about it. A new, exciting organization has become increasingly active on the West Coast. Known as CLEO (Concerned Local Elected Officials), it provides an opportunity for mayors, council members, town managers, etc., to join with others and make themselves heard. For more information, write to

**CLEO**
**P.O. Box 13528**
**Seattle, Wash. 98130**

Don't be discouraged, by the way, just because you may live in a small town. Admittedly, the smaller your community, the less impact it can have on preventing nuclear war. But on the other hand, the smaller your community, the more influence *your* views can have. And often some of the most influential politicians come from rural, small-town districts.

Look into the possibility of initiating some form of referendum—good targets include recommending the nuclear freeze, rejecting FEMA plans, calling for serious efforts at economic conversion, etc. In most states, the Secretary of State is charged with overseeing the electoral process; contact him or her at the state capitol, and find out about requirements for statewide initiatives or referenda. The following states have provisions for some kind of statewide voting process of this sort:

Alaska, Arizona, Arkansas, California, Colorado, Delaware, Florida, Idaho, Illinois, Maine, Massachusetts, Michigan, Missouri, Montana, Nebraska, Nevada, North Dakota, Ohio, Oklahoma, Oregon, South Dakota, Utah, Washington, Wyoming.

The following states have provisions for some kind of local referendum or initiative process (i.e., counties, cities, towns, state representative or senatorial districts, etc.):

Alaska, Arizona, Arkansas, California, Colorado, Florida, Georgia, Idaho, Illinois, Kentucky, Louisiana, Maine, Massachusetts, Michigan, Minnesota, Missouri, Montana, Nebraska, New Jersey, Nevada, North Dakota, Ohio, Oklahoma, Oregon, Pennsylvania, South Carolina, South Dakota, Texas, Utah, Vermont, Virginia, Washington, West Virginia, Wyoming.

Even if your state has not established such a procedure, don't give up. In many cases local towns, villages, and cities have the option of conducting their own votes.

If you are a neophyte at the political process (and even in this democracy, most of us are), perhaps the best way to get started and be effective is to contact local politicians who you know or suspect to be sympathetic on this issue. They can advise you on making good use of your energy and enthusiasm. Express your feelings and your desire to work. Then do so.

You may wonder about forming a Political Action Committee (PAC). These are rather new on the political scene, required because of various federal and state financial disclosure laws. Essentially, PACs are formed to facilitate the channeling of large campaign contributions to selected candidates. Each state has its own laws and its own apparatus for overseeing financial contributions to candidates for state office. In some states, there is virtually no such oversight; in the majority of states, however, control is exercised by the Secretary of State's office, or a Fair Political Practices Committee, a Public Disclosure Commission, Ethics Commissioner, etc. Find out how things work in your state. In many states, if you choose to pool resources in support of any candidate, you are obligated to register with the appropriate state agency.

The Federal Elections Commission oversees campaign practices for all federally elected officials. Recent laws have made it illegal for corporations to give money to Federal candidates, or for individuals to give more than $1,000 per election per candidate. Hence, the advantage of forming PACs. The crucial thing about a PAC for the Federal Election Commission is that it establishes a "Separate Segregated Fund," in which money for political use is placed, and which is carefully watched. Although corporations, labor unions, etc., cannot give money directly to PACs (and thereby to candidates), they can legally support the "establishment, administration and solicitation costs" of running a PAC. The PAC can then solicit money from its members, which can then be channeled to specific candidates. In this regard, PACs provide another advantage: once your PAC has been established (that is, once it has fifty or more members, has contributed to five or more candidates, and after it has been in existence for six months), individuals can donate up to $5,000 per year to the PAC, which can then donate up to $5,000 per year to each candidate that it chooses. By forming a PAC, therefore, people with a common interest can unite, and in so doing give more than they could separately.

Forming a PAC is relatively easy, much easier than becoming incorporated. Basically, you must file a registration statement, establish a bank account, identify a treasurer and other responsible officers, and keep careful records of contributions and expenses.

Periodic reports are also required. There is no expense directly incurred in forming a PAC, but there is a fair amount of administrative work and a requirement of careful record-keeping. Organizations with tax-exempt status can generally form separate PACs, but it is wise to check with IRS for details in any particular case. As you have probably gathered by now, PACs are generally unnecessary and more trouble than they are worth for small organizations and/or small to average sized contributors. For large groups and wealthy individuals, the advantages of a PAC can be considerable, however. The Federal Elections Commission has the following toll-free number for additional information: 1(800)424-9530.

Finally, no matter how you choose to become active in your community, don't worry about being branded a "radical." Point out, if it seems useful, that you are actually being profoundly conservative. Community organizing has a radical flavor to it, for better or worse. But by seeking to prevent nuclear war, the community activist is seeking to *conserve* society by preventing the most radical of all possible changes.

## Working Within Your Church *

Ultimately, many would consider the issue of nuclear weapons to be a moral, ethical, and spiritual one. In times past, it was the role of religion to reconcile the fact of individual death with a human need to find transcendence or meaning in life. Now, faced with the possibility of grotesque and meaningless mass suicide and the possibility of the extinction of the human race, organized religion must make a quantum leap in moral and ethical scope, to the consideration of social, as well as personal, death.

This is not merely empty rhetoric. Rather, it is fundamental to dealing with nuclear issues, and religion may provide a scaffolding upon which to hang a new, life-loving morality that turns a cold shoulder to the nuclear demon. On an individual basis, only a relative few will resolve the despair and fear generated by nuclear weapons with a completely existential position: to oppose nuclear

---

* We thank Dr. Charles Meconis for his helpful suggestions in preparing this section.

weapons not out of faith, or hope, but rather simply because they are evil and because the job of human beings is to oppose evil. Many more people will turn to God, whether Allah, Jesus, the Dharma, or the Tao, for spiritual answers and solace.

Then it is for good reason that churches and other religious organizations are increasingly important in the anti-nuclear war movement. On one level the churches are unlikely allies, since organized religion traditionally has been a safe, unchanging haven from the vicissitudes of the temporal world. Hence, many church people are reluctant to become involved in something as potentially controversial and divisive as nuclear war. But once recruited they are enormously powerful, since they have great staying power, excellent organization and a very high degree of credibility. People trust their churches; it is not easy to accuse them of being communist-inspired or weak-kneed Russian sympathizers, unwilling to stand up for God and country. The growing involvement of America's churches is therefore a cause for celebration, encouragement, and hope.

Furthermore, it is in the church's benefit to grapple with real issues that trouble people, rather than performing empty and mechanical rituals that enhance "psychic numbing." It is said that in Europe, since religion's deep involvement in the European peace movement, church credibility has gone up, and membership has increased! The brave stands of the U.S. Catholic bishops (Hunthausen, Matthiesen, and Quinn) have caused some shudders in their parishes, but on the whole have been productive for the church.

Appendix C is a partial list of some of the many organizations now active within the national religious community. Let them know of your support and interest; see how you can join their work.

If your local church is active in the anti-nuclear war movement, so much the better. Get involved yourself. But what if it is not?

Most churches are organized on three levels: local, regional, and national. Find out what resources are available; most likely, the national level will be the most helpful, especially if there is a "peace followship" office such as those listed. The chances are that your church has a "social concerns" committee, or something equivalent by another name. If it doesn't, speak to your clergyman about starting one. If there is such a committee, and it isn't addressing your number one social concern, get it to do so. Find out when it meets, attend the meeting, and make your case. If the meetings are closed, find out how you can join. If at all possible, speak to the other members privately both before and after the meeting.

As an initial goal, you might want to aim at getting nuclear war included as a topic for the "study forum" or equivalent, that typically precedes or follows Sunday worship services. Again, showing a film like *The Last Epidemic* may be useful. Another modest aim is one of the typical mid-week discussion groups—if either of these go well, members of the congregation may want to repeat the exercise, perhaps with wider participation and greater advance planning. Especially in the early stage, there may be strong feeling for a "balanced presentation." If so, try initially to get another member of the congregation to speak out for the other side (presumably, not in favor of nuclear war, but rather, supporting Peace Through Strength or some other, comparable slogan). Alternatively, you can invite speakers from the local Veterans of Foreign Wars, National Guard, ROTC, American Legion, etc. Often such speakers will have audience credibility because of their affiliation, but will not be well-versed or very persuasive, especially if they degenerate into telling war stories or wrapping themselves in the flag.

If your clergyman is unsympathetic, then you have a real problem, but don't give up. Meet with other members of your congregation, privately in your own home first. Discuss your concerns and plan your strategy. Arrange to visit your clergyman as a group, and tell him that you consider nuclear war to be not only *the* pressing human issue, but also the ultimate moral and religious one as well, one that your church should address. It might be helpful if you can bring along relevant literature (herein lies one value in contacting some of the religious organizations listed earlier). It may be counterproductive, however, to present Baptists, for example, with the antiwar teachings of Catholics, or to try to persuade Methodists with the writings of Lutherans. If possible, use literature and arguments from your own denomination, but if necessary, use anything.

Many clergymen who are reluctant to get involved with the issue of nuclear war see it as potentially divisive within their congregation, and they may be right. It might be useful, therefore, to point out that a similar crisis of conscience arose last century, on the issue of slavery. During the twenty-first century, religious groups that refused to take a stand on nuclear war during the twentieth may seem just as amoral as those that ducked the issue of slavery during the nineteenth. A timorous clergyman can also be helped along by evidence of strong support from other members of the congregation. Hence, the importance of meeting with him as a group.

Sometimes a frontal assault is not the best way to get started. Try sidling up to your minister, priest, or rabbi at a picnic, or during the socializing after worship services. If you are a newcomer to the congregation, you won't get very far demanding anything, especially if the clergyman is afraid of adverse response from others. Similarly if you are a longtime member, but one who attends services only rarely. In either case, you would do well to get to know some of the "pillars of the congregation," oldtimers whose opinions are valued. It may take a while, especially since first you must determine who are most likely to be sympathetic, then get together with them before approaching the clergyman. But it will probably be worth it.

What are your goals in working within your church or synagogue? For one, as already mentioned, aim to get the subject aired at one or several of the non-worship activities. Make nuclear war a major, announced social concern of your congregation. Sponsor symposia, visiting speakers, film series. Try to get use of an office, telephone, a piece of the existing organizational structure, all the while solidifying your position in the community. Catholic churches have study series, especially during Advent (before Christmas) and Lent (before Easter); see about getting this period devoted to nuclear war. Aim also at making it the explicit focus of one or more worship services: there is nothing radical about praying for peace, and indeed, worship services concerned with nuclear war can range from the utterly innocuous to the powerfully moving. Some clergymen will relinquish their pulpit for special occasions, but don't press too hard for this; you might offer to obtain a speaker, or perhaps to be one yourself, but don't persist if the response is cool. You won't make friends and influence people by competing for a jealously guarded prerogative.

If things go well, consider holding a worship service or a vigil at some prominent place—the local FEMA headquarters, SAC or missile base, or a nearby industrial plant. You can also aim to have your church or synagogue endorse some particular action, say, the nuclear freeze or a reduced military budget; or to oppose something such as the production of bombs, bombers or missiles nearby, or the local FEMA plans. Most congregations have some sort of democratic process, through which the organization can take a stand on such issues. To those who argue that nuclear war is not a legitimate local issue, you should have an easy response. To those who worry that even bringing it up will "tear the church apart," you might point out that some issues are simply too important to duck, and moreover, by working within the existing channels, you are trying to address this issue in a wholly responsible manner, precisely to minimize potential divisiveness.

Insofar as you succeed, you will have mobilized one of the most important forces in the country. Insofar as you fail, you might want to ask yourself whether your chosen religious organization is responsive to your needs. Alternatively, you might want to stick with it, fighting the good fight. The Bible makes it clear that love of God divorced from love of man is meaningless. Thus, Christ says:

> If thou bring thy gift to the altar, and there rememberest that thy brother hath aught against thee, leave there thy gift before the altar, and go thy way; first be reconciled to thy brother, and then come and offer thy gift.

Commenting on this, Jonathan Schell has pointed out that "we who have planned out the deaths of hundreds of millions of our brothers plainly have a great deal of work to do before we return to the altar. Clearly, the corpse of mankind would be the least acceptable of all conceivable offerings on the altar of this God." By working within our religious organizations, we become reconciled to our brothers, and at the same time fulfill a spiritual commitment to God.

### Tax Resistance

Like death camp inmates forced to stoke the fires of their own crematoria, we provide the money that fuels our nation's nuclear madness. Catholic Archbishop Raymond Hunthausen of Seattle called the Trident submarine base recently completed in the Pacific northwest, the "Auschwitz of Puget Sound." He also had a practical and courageous suggestion for those of us who are uncomfortable emulating those patriotic, law-abiding Germans of the 1930s who primly looked the other way when the smoke of that other Auschwitz blew in their faces: "I think the teaching of Jesus tells us to render to a nuclear-armed Caesar what that Ceasar deserves—tax resistance."

Ask yourself: do you feel at ease knowing that more than 50¢ of your tax dollar goes to the military? "If you're not part of the solution," wrote Eldridge Cleaver, "you're part of the problem." Although Cleaver was concerned with civil rights at the time, his words are even more true when applied to federal income taxes and nuclear weapons. You can look the other way, even vote the other way and also vigorously criticize our military policies, but when you abjectly and unceremoniously fill out your income tax form and send in your check, you are voting directly with your pocketbook, one of the electoral mechanisms to which our government is most acutely responsive. To pay uncomplainingly is to be an accessory to premeditated genocide—more accurately, an accomplice. To refuse is civil disobedience. Which is worse? Thoreau had no doubt, although he wrote long before nuclear weapons:

> If a thousand men were not to pay their tax-bills this year, that would not be a violent and bloody measure, as it would be to pay them, and enable the State to commit violence and shed innocent blood.

Tax resistance has an ancient and honorable history, especially among the Quakers. Responding to the French and Indian Wars, John Woolman and twenty Friends wrote in 1755:

> And being painfuly apprehensive that the large sum granted by the late Act of Assembly for the King's use is principally intended for purposes inconsistent with our peaceable testimony, we therefore think that as we cannot be concerned in wars and fightings, so neither ought we to contribute thereto by paying the tax directed by the said act, though suffering be the consequence of our refusal, which we hope to be enabled to bear with patience.

Similarly, in 1756, Joshua Evans commented:

I found it best for me to refuse paying the demands on my estate which went to pay the expenses of war; and although my part might appear at best as a drop in the ocean, yet the ocean, I considered, was made of many drops.

There seems little doubt that the arms race would quickly run out of steam tomorrow if all those who lament it would just stop paying for it! It's largely a matter of putting your money where your mouth is. Not that simple, you say? Perhaps not, but it is not that difficult, or that dangerous, either. Certainly, tax resistance goes against the inclinations of most Americans—aside from a fundamental patriotism, we generally treat the IRS the same as we do local draft boards or grizzly bears: keep as much distance as possible between them and us. But we are a nation of laws, and there are ways to make our protest known, and felt, without being mauled in the process. Indeed, the Internal Revenue Service is not nearly as fierce as we are led to believe, and it relies almost entirely on voluntary compliance. "If the taxpayers of this country ever discover that the IRS operates on 90% bluff," an official once wrote to Senator Henry Bellmon, "the entire system will collapse."

*Paths of resistance*
   If you are an employee and your tax is withheld, then you have the fewest options, but some, nonetheless:
   1. You can file a W-4 form, declaring more dependents than you actually have, and/or
   2. You can file a form 843, requesting a refund.
   If you file independently, you can
   1. Simply refuse to file at all,
   2. File a blank 1040 form, including a letter explaining your actions.
   3. Intentionally earn less than the taxable income, perhaps by giving away the excess, to tax-exempt causes, or
   4. File a "normal" tax form, but deduct whatever you choose. This is the most complex option for tax resisters, offering many different possible paths. It also seems likely to be the most effective as well as the least risky for the individual resister.
   You can elect to refuse a token amount ($1, $5, $50), or the amount that goes to the military (about 50 percent) or the amount

that goes for nuclear weapons and their delivery (about 10 percent). Or, considering that the military will get its percentage from whatever you pay, you can take deductions equaling the total "balance due." Regardless of how much you choose to deduct, you have two basic options: one is to deduct the amount directly from the balance due, at the end of the form. Although this is simplest to do, it offers you the least flexibility—the IRS will likely just disallow your return as a mathematical error and can then move directly to collect the money. On the other hand, you can take a "war tax deduction" on Schedule A, under "miscellaneous deductions." This deduction is then subtracted from your gross income before you actually calculate the *taxable* income and from this, the amount due. Therefore, a "war tax deduction" requires a tedious procedure—but not a difficult one—to figure out how much to deduct from your gross income in order to wind up with a final tax resistance that feels like the right amount. Trial and error with a tax schedule will give you a good figure after just a few tries, however.

The advantage of this technique is that it opens the door to a series of appeals, all perfectly legal, before your tax resistance goes to collection. In short, the IRS must give you due legal process in evaluating your requested deduction, just as it must give a fair hearing to someone requesting a business expense deduction that may ultimately be disallowed. In the process, you clog the system by your resistance, you deprive the government (if only temporarily) of your support, you draw attention to your resistance and its reasons, and you provide yourself with a dragged-out process from which you can "bail out" by paying the amount due (plus interest) at any step of the way.

## What the government will do

Possibly, nothing. Some people have been openly practicing tax resistance for decades, with no response whatever from the IRS. For resisters with small earnings, enforcement costs the government more than it would to collect! Assuming that your resistance is noted, however, the next step is an audit—a face-to-face meeting with an IRS employee. Such people are neither cruel nor wicked; they are generally quite polite and will hear you out. Assuming your requested deduction is denied after the audit, you can request an appeal within the IRS system (a "conference"). The request is often denied, but once again, it takes bureaucratic time and more paper-shuffling. If your conference appeal is denied or simply not granted in the first place, you will then get a "statuary notice of deficiency," giving you ninety days to appeal to the U.S. Tax Court. If you don't appeal, the IRS can then begin collection after this ninety days has elapsed. In appealing to the Tax Court, if the amount in dispute is less than $1,500, you can use the "small tax case" forms, a do-it-yourself procedure which does not require a lawyer. Assuming that you lose once again, the IRS will ask you to pay voluntarily. Finally, if you do not comply, they can attach your income, seize assets such as bank accounts or property. But once again, recall that at any point along this route of resistance, you can call off the government's hounds by simply paying the disputed amount. No matter how far you carry your resistance, you will have made a significant statement, which if made by enough people, cannot be ignored.

You should note, however, that a $500 penalty is possible, under a rarely used law aimed at discouraging "frivolous" suits designed merely to delay payment of taxes. One person's frivolity is another's conscience, and as tax resistance spreads, we can expect the government to react more severely. Thus, Congress has already raised the Tax Court filing fee from $10 to $50, to discourage such "meritless" cases as those protesting the nuclear arms race. There is also legislation afoot that would raise the penalty to $5,000. Perhaps soon, only the wealthy will be able to afford tax resistance!

It seems likely that the government's response will depend on the number of tax resisters, and the amount of money involved. As long as only a relative handful of people claim war tax deductions, their actions are not especially threatening, and the IRS can therefore afford to be relatively indifferent and rather lenient. If the numbers ever become massive, then once again the government's response will probably be limited—this time because it will not have the resources to cope with large-scale citizen resistance. If the tax resistance movement really gets started, however, it is in the middle range that we can expect a more vigorous response, when the movement is large enough to be threatening but not so large as to be unmanageable. One goal, then, is to make it unmanageable.

### Some advice for tax resisters

Tax resistance can be civil disobedience, but it need not involve the commiting of any crime. Thus, avoid possible prosecution for

tax fraud by being scrupulously honest and above-board with the
IRS. There is nothing fraudulent about claiming a deduction to
which you feel entitled, as long as you are open about it, and not
seeking to deceive. It may therefore be a good idea to accompany
your tax resistance with a letter to your elected officials, newspapers, etc., and keep copies for yourself, to show the IRS auditor.
Given that you are drawing attention to your financial records, you
might also want to protect yourself against accusations that your
tax resistance is just a smokescreen for personal stinginess, and/or
that by resisting military taxes you deprive the government of
funds needed for worthwhile purposes as well, such as health care,
education, and other social services. A good strategy is to join one
of many tax resistance funds, set up for just this purpose. The idea
is simple and elegant: money which you withhold from the government is given instead to a fund, which invests the money and uses
the interest earned to finance various worthwhile community projects, such as day care centers, medical care for the needy, etc. At
any point, contributors are permitted to withdraw the amount they
initially put in, thereby permitting them to settle affairs with IRS
whenever they choose to do so. This way, you cannot be accused of
using tax resistance to line your own pockets, the money goes to
good causes, and you make a public statement of your intention.
For addresses of some local tax resistance groups, see Appendix D.

For detailed legal advice regarding tax resistance, write: The
Center on Law and Pacifism, P.O. Box 1584, Colorado Springs,
Colo. 80901. Some people are not ready to resist now, but may feel
differently if others do likewise. You can register with the following
organization, agreeing to withhold some portion of your taxes
when notified that 100,000 such registrants are on file: Conscience
and Military Tax Campaign; 411 Bellhaven Road, Bellport, N.Y.
11713. You can also support a World Peace Tax Fund Bill, S. 880;
H.R. 4897, which would permit taxpayers to designate that their
money should be used for nonmilitary purposes. For more information, contact the National Council for a World Peace Tax Fund,
2111 Florida Ave. NW, Washington, D.C., 20008.

Before World War I—the war to end all wars, you may recall—
William James wrote that "the war against war is going to be no
holiday excursion or camping party." Now, seventy years later, it is
no easier than James imagined, and certainly much more urgent.
Since most of us pay taxes, or are expected to, we also cannot hide

behind the comfortable illusion that the war against war is simply too big for us to fight.

## Taking Care of Yourself While You're Taking Care of the World

While you are doing all this, don't forget to be nice to yourself. Don't underestimate the problem—saving the world is a big job, bigger than anything you have ever taken on before. Moreover, nuclear war is the stuff nightmares are made of, and the more you are personally converted to the "cause," the more you must live with it. In a sense, then, the safer you try to make everyone else, the more vulnerable you may feel.

You may develop the same relationship to nuclear war that a Hebrew prayer enjoins us to have with God: present in your thoughts when you wake up in the morning, and when you go to sleep at night—and most of the time in between as well. If so, you will actually be one of the lucky ones whose life will be filled with a unique glow of meaning and worth, overwhelming all other worries, outshining all other joys. You may find yourself impatient of those who look frantically and unsuccessfully for "meaning" in their relatively empty lives, whether in drugs, sex, personal advancement or even the more traditional, humanitarian "good works." By reaching through the anxiety that pervades all people in the nuclear age—whether they are conscious of their burden or not—you will have broken through that unmentioned, isolating numbness which surrounds and imprisons so many of your fellow citizens. You will have finally identified that fear that lurks behind us all, and *doing something about it* will feel indescribably good. Even aside from your real accomplishments in making the world safer, you will know the unbounded joy of finally growing up (whatever your age), of finally working toward something that is wholly good, of devoting yourself unreservedly to the most important issue of all times, and of doing something about it.

But don't forget the darker side; it can be very trying to work as hard and as singlemindedly as we are hoping that you will. "Burnout" is real; guard against it. Pentagon officials, strategic planners, and industry representatives don't have this problem, for they are motivated by the more traditional, venal goals: salary, personal advancement, profits, and prestige. They can usually "turn off" their profession on the weekends to play golf, go to a movie, etc. The anti-nuclear war activist, on the other hard, often finds this more difficult: he or she is moved by a near-religious commitment, by a sense of profound urgency that becomes a hard taskmaster. Saving the world is a more-than-full-time job, and its demands are never satisfied.

This makes it all the more important that you retain a little margin of selfishness. Keep in touch with your own needs. Remember, at least part of the reason why you are trying to save the world is because it is a beautiful, marvelous and fascinating place. Give yourself permission to enjoy it. If you like to run, do just that. Maybe you find a hot bath relaxing; if so, don't deny it to yourself just because you also have other, more important things to do. If nothing else, you will find yourself *more* effective in saving the world, if you save a little part of yourself along the way. Some activists find it useful to declare a "nuclear freeze" every evening, say around nine P.M.—no talk about nuclear war (possibly, even no reading about it), after that.

If you find that you are feeling despair, or intolerably immersed in death, or afraid all of the time, remember that the opposite of death is life. The antidote for despair is love, so love your children, your spouse, your lover, your God, your planet, any and all. Don't neglect the relationships that make your life meaningful. We relish the story of the highly respected, dignified, orthodox British rabbi, renowned for his skill and sensitivity in ministering to the terminally ill. When asked how he managed the personal, emotional strain of dealing with pained, dying people on a daily basis, he leaned over and whispered confidentially, "I fuck a lot."

People need rewards, both large and small, to keep them going. So, set small goals—meaningful ones, to be sure, but *achievable* ones as well—and bask in the warmth of your own burgeoning self-esteem. Stop and congratulate yourself when you have given a good talk, when your letter to the editor is printed, when you receive good news coverage for some particular antiwar event, when you make progress converting a politician, when the local volunteer firemen take a stand against FEMA, when the town council finally comes out in favor of the nuclear freeze. We may never be able to sit back and announce with relief and satisfaction:

"At last, I have done it; the world has been saved. " But you can get a whole world of satisfactions along the way.

What about your children? People worry about how to tell their kids about nuclear war, and that by becoming active themselves, they will make their children more anxious. For many parents, talking about the facts of death may be more frightening than telling a child about sex, "the facts of life." Obviously, every parent has had some experience with sex. Not so with nuclear war. But as with sex, the more comfortable the adult, the easier the conversation and the more comfortable the child. Personal death is inevitable, and we all realize this, increasingly as we grow. But nuclear war is not inevitable. We don't have to accept it, and neither do our children. Tell your children that nuclear war is a big problem, but that you are working as hard as you can to prevent it, and express confidence that you'll succeed. The children of America are already anxious, just as their parents are. But remember, the treatment for nuclear anxiety is action. And the real danger to our children is not that they may think about nuclear war, but rather, that they may die in one. They will no longer be anxious when they are no longer threatened.

Remember also that what you are doing is heroic, so don't be shy about being a hero. It will feel good, and it should. You should accept your family's praise; indeed, you can demand it.

Recently, a friend told us that his son's second grade class had discussed nuclear war. Of the eighteen students, seventeen thought there would be a nuclear war, and they were frightened. Only one was confident about the future—our friend's child. When asked why, the boy replied "I know there won't be a nuclear war because my Daddy goes to meetings all the time to prevent it." We hope he will. If nothing else, his efforts have given his son a very precious gift: hope. Those of you who join him deserve all the thanks, congratulations and tender loving care that a grateful world can bestow. And if the world is too ignorant, selfish or preoccupied to notice, then *you* notice.

## The Ten Percent Solution

Overwhelmed by all these suggestions? Many people have been inhibited in getting started because of fear that once begun, their involvement will get out of hand, at the cost of their normal, day-to-day lives.

For them, we propose *The Ten Percent Solution*. When you finish reading this book, set a limit on your commitment, and stick with it. Resolve to spend ten percent of your time, money, creativity and energy saving the world, but reserve ninety percent for your own needs. Refrain from martyrdom, or instant and heroic sacrifices that you may quickly come to resent. The peace movement will benefit most from the steady, persistent efforts of reasonable people, who will not "burn out" in a flash, but who will not rest until every last nuclear weapon has been dismantled.

Find your own level—ten percent, ninety percent, five percent, or whatever fits. And then stick with it, as long as it takes.

## A Final Pep Talk

Don't be bamboozled by those who claim that nuclear war is just part of the greater problem—our penchant for violence—and that even without nuclear war we would just find some other way to menace each other. We cannot afford the luxury of such philosophical debate, any more than someone trapped inside a burning house can afford to contemplate the process of oxidation, or take comfort in the fact that several billion years from now, the sun will go super-nova and destroy the earth anyhow. It is time for action: informed action, to be sure, but determined action nonetheless. Decisions made within this decade, perhaps within the next few years, will literally be life or death decisions for us all. If, partly through your action, we make the right decisions, then we shall have time to address the underlying problems of humanity, and perhaps, to organize the world in a humane and peaceful manner. But first things first.

Above all, and whatever your personal decisions, don't forget your own importance. Divide responsibility so you will not become overwhelmed and dispirited. But accept responsibility as well. Reject the claim that you are being "unrealistic." After all, who are the "realists"? Those who play computer games of nuclear warfighting? Those who mindlessly pile bomb upon bomb with no thought for the future, no concept of where it will lead? Those who think that nuclear war can be won? Those who don't think at all? Is it realistic to live on the edge of an abyss and never look down, never try moving us all to a safer place? We recommend, instead, the ultimate in realism: look nuclear war straight in the eye, confront your peril, and get busy.

Remember, however, this is a marathon, not a sprint; it will take time to turn the world around, so pace yourself for a prolonged and steady effort. Take yourself, your ideas, and your world seriously. As the old "Talking Union" song of the 1930s put it: "Take it easy, but *take it.*"

# 4. The World According to Gap

## Part I: History and Some Explanations

*In the beginning was the Gap. The Manhattan Project had said "Let there be nuclear weapons," and there were nuclear weapons. And President Truman saw that the Gap was good, for it separated the light from the darkness. Following the Second World War, the earth was without form and void, and Stalinism was upon the face of Eastern Europe. The spirit of the Cold War was moving over the waters. And there was evening and there was morning of the first new day.*

No sabbath has marked the end of this nuclear genesis. Never have we ceased our labors, looked back, and been glad. Instead, we have worked unceasingly to maintain and expand our precious Gap; in so doing we have only exhausted ourselves and spurred our opponent to similar efforts, so that our peril has, if anything, increased. And it is still increasing. We hear the insatiable demands of Gap-maintenance, mixed with the frightening cries of imminent Gap-reversal: the U.S.S.R., we are told—and have forever been told—is about to pull ahead. So the high priests of our nuclear world call for unending creation, of warheads, bombers, missiles and guidance systems. True to their instructions, they have been fruitful and have multiplied—beyond all reason and almost beyond counting, until they have achieved dominion over all other things. They also threaten our survival as never before.

Although there have been a variety of measurable Gaps since 1945 (virtually all of them, as we shall see, favoring the U.S.), in the past thirty years there has never really been any sort of U.S.-U.S.S.R. Gap that mattered. Each side has been capable of destroying the other for the past few decades. But at the same time, alarmist cries about Gaps have kept us from widening that one crucial Gap—between survival and oblivion. Moreover, the Gap-yappers are now causing us to respond to imagined Gaps in ways that make nuclear war *more* likely. Our peril is probably greater now than ever before—not because of strategic Gaps between the

Soviet Union and the United States, but because our misperception of these gaps is leading us toward a military posture of almost unbelievable danger and stupidity.

The supposed Gaps have persisted for more than a Thirty Years' Cold War, now about to enter its fourth decade. They have not been static, however: from a handful of atomic bombs in the kiloton range by 1946, we now have about 30,000, many of them weighing in by the megaton. The Soviet Union, not to be outdone— at least, not by much or for long—has about 20,000. In the late 1940s, neither side had any intercontinental bombers; now, even the supersonic variety is accused of being obsolete, and both sides sport an arsenal of missiles that could annihilate the other within thirty minutes. One of the biggest ironies of modern times is that after acquiring the greatest destructive power ever assembled, all in the name of security, our security today is less than at any time in history—certainly less than at the end of World War II, when the initial Gap was proclaimed and enthroned as our salvation. Incredibly, while we huddle on our side of the Gap, the average American (and Russian) is clearly less safe than the average resident of Sri Lanka or Sierra Leone, "weak" countries that haven't competed in the nuclear arms race and hence are not prime targets.

Another irony is that during the course of our nuclear rivalry with the Soviet Union, the Gap has repeatedly been misrepresented as favoring them while in fact it has always favored us. Moreover, each new round of scare tactics, as a new and seemingly ominous Gap has been announced, has led to further escalation of the arms race, followed by further Soviet efforts to keep pace, which in turn have then been cited by the Cold Warriors responsible for it all as evidence of their acumen and the need to redouble our efforts!

A final irony is that throughout the sorry history of mythic reverse Gap-making, the United States appears never to have learned from the experience. We are as Gap-happy as ever. The purveyors of Gap-pap have never truly been held accountable for their misdeeds. They have not even lost credibility; indeed, some of the most prominent—men like Eugene Rostow and Paul Nitze—are now directing "arms control" strategy for the Reagan Administration. It is worse than having the fox guard the henhouse, more like installing Peter as chief of a Wolf Early Warning System. And predictably, the old tired war drums are once again sounding. They proclaim, not for the first time, that our beloved Gap has been reversed and that we are on the short end. They demand a vast expenditure of national treasure and—what is even more dangerous—they preclude serious negotiations with the Soviets until that Gap is closed and once again reestablished in our favor. Since the stakes are so high, it seems appropriate to review the history of the postwar nuclear Gaps, since by ignoring history we may be doomed to repeat it. In the next chapter, we shall take a hard-nosed look at *current* claims of Soviet-U.S. Gaps, claims which, like those of the past, are in fact much closer to the Apocrypha than to Gospel.

Significantly, the nuclear arms race began with the misperception of a Gap, just as it has been fueled by descendant Gaps ever since. In a now-famous letter to Roosevelt, which launched the Manhattan Project, Einstein warned that Nazi Germany might well be seeking to unleash nuclear energy for military purposes. The resulting crash program sought to close this possible Gap. Even after German research facilities had been overrun, Nazi physicists interrogated, and we knew that Germany was not even close to developing nuclear weapons, work on the Manhattan Project continued feverishly, for use now against Japan. Looking back, we find that virtually no one at the time seems to have seriously questioned whether the project should have been continued at all, once fears of a Nazi atomic bomb were known to be groundless.° But such has always been the nature of Gaps—once announced they acquire a reality of their own, which quickly moves them beyond any external need. Once we begin responding to a Gap we keep at it, long after the Gap itself has been proven groundless, and heedless that our greatest danger lies not in the purported Gap but in our response to it.

When he witnessed the first atomic explosion, Robert Oppenheimer, scientific director of the Manhattan Project, recalled a line from the Hindu Bhagavad-Gita: "I am become Death, the shatterer of worlds." He might also have recalled an earlier segment:

---

° Actually, one physicist, Joseph Rotblat, left the Project after it was clear that Hitler was far from developing an atomic bomb, and a group, led by James Franck, argued that the bomb should not be used on Japan.

> If the radiance of a thousand suns,
> Were to burst at once into the sky,
> That would be like the splendor of the Mighty One . . ."

The power of that Mighty One, however, was not lost on U.S. politicians anticipating a cold war with the Soviet Union.

Historians still debate American motives in bombing Hiroshima and Nagasaki—whether it was a military necessity or whether Japan was on the verge of surrender anyhow. In any event, some of the urgency for those acts clearly came from the desire to establish a Gap between the U.S. and the U.S.S.R. Moreover, Stalin had agreed earlier at Potsdam that he would declare war on Japan within three months after Germany surrendered. Since that happened on May 8, 1945, there wasn't much time to lose before Russia would join the Asiatic fray and we might have to share the postwar spoils on that continent as well. As Nobel Prize-winning physicist P.M.S. Blackett has commented: "The dropping of the atomic bombs was not so much the last military act of the Second World War, as the first act of the cold diplomatic war with Russia."

When Britain still ruled her empire, Hilaire Belloc recognized a technologic Gap that helped keep things that way: "whatever happens we have got/ the Maxim gun, and they have not." It was equally certain that in the aftermath of World War II, we had the Bomb and they (the Russians) did not. Nonetheless, most scientists agreed that the A-bomb secret would not remain secret for long: the Russians were bound to close the Gap. If so, then it might have made sense to establish a postwar world through attempted even-handedness, equality and trust, rather than hiding behind, and reinforcing, our nuclear Gap. On September 12, 1945, Secretary of War Stimson wrote in a memo to president Truman:

> If the atomic bomb were merely another though more devastating military weapon to be assimilated into our pattern of international relations it would be one thing. We could then follow the old custom of secrecy and nationalistic military superiority. . . . But I think the bomb instead constitutes a first step in a new control by man over the forces of nature too revolutionary and dangerous to fit into the old concepts. I think it really caps the climax of the race between man's growing technical power for destructiveness and his psychological

power of self-control and group control—his moral power. If so, our method of approach to the Russians is a question of the most vital importance in the evolution of human progress.

But "old concepts" die hard. After all, the A-bomb had given Truman new confidence and assertiveness at Potsdam, and the fateful decision was made: to rely on a nuclear Gap for U.S. security. Curiously, there was virtually no public debate in the late 1940s over whether U.S. policy toward the U.S.S.R. should emphasize and seek to exploit our nuclear monopoly. A notable exception was Henry Wallace, then Secretary of Commerce, who suggested publicly that we try to see ourselves as others see us. He concluded that we would be forced to identify ourselves as either preparing to win a forthcoming war, or at least, hoping to intimidate the rest of mankind. He was fired.

Actually, we did make one well-publicized effort to bridge this Gap, to share our nuclear Maxim gun with the Soviets: the Baruch Plan, first sketched out by Secretary of State Dean Acheson and AEC Chairman David Lilienthal. We may never know if this was a sincere effort at bridging a Gap, or a cynical propaganda maneuver. In any event, the U.S.S.R. rejected the Baruch Plan, which had called for internationalizing the atom. This confirmed many Americans in their view that the U.S.S.R. was aiming for world dominion; hence, a morality Gap, also known as "you can't trust the Russians," which has persisted to this day. The Russians, however, had some good reasons to reject the Plan, morality Gap or no.

The Baruch Plan had called for the Soviet Union to turn over control of its uranium mines and production facilities *immediately* to an international authority, while the U.S. would go on making bombs and researching new ones until such time as we were satisfied with the international procedures of inspection and control. Then, and only then, would we relinquish our nuclear warheads to the proposed International Atomic Development Council. Moreover, failure to abide by the agreement would subject any violator nation to "condign punishment" at the behest of the U.N. Security Council, which at that time was dominated by the United States. Under the Baruch Plan, the U.S.S.R. would have to give up its veto, as well. Not surprisingly, the Russians smelled something fishy in the Baruch plan: Kool-Aid laced with cyanide; i.e., sanction for a "preventive" nuclear war against them.

Soviet paranoia on this should not be surprising; after all, American political climate following the war was almost as anti-communist as it was anti-Nazi. In 1946, for example, a memo was circulated among the upper echelons of the Office of Strategic Services —precursor of the CIA—proposing that Stalin be given an ultimatum: democratize your society or we obliterate your cities with nuclear weapons. (The author of that cheery missive was a bright young man named Eugene Rostow, currently director of the Arms Control and Disarmament Agency. Which shows how far we have come.) So the Baruch Plan failed, as many believe it was intended to do. And we found ourselves on the "safe" side of the postwar nuclear Gap, more than ever convinced of the need to keep that Gap between ourselves and the Russian bear.

But that Gap favoring us, led to another, favoring them: although the Red Army was significantly reduced after the war (down from 11 million at its height to 2.8 million in 1948), the conventional forces of the U.S.S.R. were kept high, in contrast to U.S. military manpower, which declined under our nuclear umbrella. In addition to our overwhelming nuclear superiority, we had ringed the U.S.S.R. with airbases in Greenland, Iceland, Okinawa, Japan, and Alaska, adding Spain, Saudi Arabia, Tunisia, Morocco, and Turkey by 1951. The swollen Red Army provided the Soviet Union with a counterweight to our strategic strength; Stalin held western Europe hostage against any nuclear attack on the Russian homeland. To the U.S. hardliners, the size of the Red Army (almost 6 million men by 1955) constituted a threat that required a large and expanding nuclear arsenal on our part. Of course, our great advantage in nuclear weaponry doubtless seemed threatening to them. Gap-makers on each side had ample fodder for domestic propaganda.

Just after the war, Senator Arthur Vandenburg had advised President Truman that to keep up a strong military, it would be necessary to "scare hell out of the country." No time was lost in doing just that. One of the most vigorous postwar debates centered for a while around the military's demand for Universal Military Training (UMT), a compulsory draft for all citizens. But the nation was weary of war, and resisted. When, in 1946, a specially equipped B-29 flew nonstop over the Pole, UMT advocates breathlessly warned against "hordes of airborne troops" airlifted onto U.S. soil by this route. For once, the public didn't buy this one, the airlift Gap, and UMT foundered.

But 1949 was a bad year. A Czechoslovak coup had just installed a communist government, the Berlin Crisis still simmered, we "lost" China to Mao, and, worse yet, we lost our nuclear monopoly when the Russians exploded their own atomic bomb. Anxiety increased, McCarthyism flourished, and the fur flew over "internal security" Gaps, as we pushed ahead to develop the "super" or hydrogen bomb, so as to recapture our lost nuclear Gap.

The decision was not easily reached however. The General Advisory Committee had met in that difficult year of 1949, chaired by Oppenheimer and charged with recommending nuclear strategy, including whether to build a hydrogen bomb. It is worth noting that the Committee's final package of recommendations were far from pacifist, including strong support for expanding A-bomb research and development, and urging that tactical nuclear forces be stationed in Europe. But on the hydrogen bomb, the majority concluded

> We believe a super bomb should never be produced. . . . In determining not to proceed to develop the super bomb, we see a unique opportunity of providing by example some limitations on the totality of war and thus of limiting the fear and arousing the hopes of mankind.

The Committee was well aware that the Russians might beat us to the hydrogen bomb:

> To the argument that the Russians may succeed in developing this weapon, we would reply that our undertaking it will not prove a deterrent to them. Should they use the weapon against us, reprisals by our large stock of atomic bombs would be comparably effective to the use of a Super.

Moreover, the majority report emphasized that H-bombs would be weapons of mass civilian destruction, of no real military significance.

There was also a minority addendum, by physicists Fermi and Rabi. It was even stronger in its condemnation:

> The fact that no limits exist to the destructiveness of this weapon makes its very existence and the knowledge of its construction a danger to humanity as a whole. It is necessarily an evil thing considered in any light.

David Lilienthal, the first AEC chairman and early architect of the Baruch Plan, concurred with the Committee's recommendation. But Truman decided on a crash H-bomb program anyhow. We exploded the first H-bomb at Eniwetok in 1951. An improved model was detonated successfully at Bikini in 1954, using an outer shell of uranium that made the bomb small enough to be deliverable by airplane. However, the Soviets were hot on our heels, having exploded their own clumsy H-bomb in 1953. In 1957, they touched off the largest ever: 57 megatons, more than 4,000 times the strength of "Little Boy," which had snuffed out Hiroshima. We had more bombs, and greatly superior technology, but the Gap was not nearly as reassuring as it had seemed in the late 1940s.

Actually, by 1953 we already had an arsenal of several thousand bombs, obtained at about $1 million apiece, whereas the U.S.S.R. had "only" about 300. In those days, we were largely running the arms race with ourselves, but by running so hard and so fast, we forced the Soviets to run competitively. Soon both sides were really sweating.

On the diplomatic/political front, the Berlin Blockade of 1948 had followed the decision by the U.S., Great Britain, and France to consolidate their occupation zones into a single country, known to us now as West Germany. Through two World Wars, Germany has been a Soviet nemesis, and the Russians were less than enthusiastic about even this partial reunification. But even as the Berlin Blockade ended, we formed NATO. In 1955, we pushed for admitting West Germany into NATO; two months later, the U.S.S.R. announced formation of the Warsaw Pact.

The infamous Bomber Gap made its debut following the Soviet Air Show in July 1955. The Eisenhower Administration had just unveiled its "New Look" for the U.S. military, emphasizing reliance on nuclear weaponry, to save money and mollify right-wing

Republicans. Unlike today's "conservatives," whose fiscal restraint rarely extends to the Pentagon budget, during the Eisenhower years fiscal conservatives felt otherwise. For example, Treasury Secretary George Humphrey actually maintained that Stalin had a secret plan to bankrupt the U.S. by tricking us into excessive military spending. The right wing of the Republican Party, led by Ohio's redoubtable Robert A. Taft, even opposed the stationing of U.S. troops in Europe and the build-up of NATO. Nuclear weapons were seen as the cheap way out, certainly cheaper than matching Russian conventional forces. Accordingly, the military worried that it might not receive its share of the budgetary pie. While the Pentagon fretted that Ike's New Look would make them paupers, Soviet generals worried that the U.S.S.R. was already dangerously weak. So the stage was set in 1955 for a great deception that served the military on both sides, and just about no one else.

At the Soviet Air Show, the U.S.S.R. unveiled its first intercontinental bombers, a squadron of ten Bears, which flew repeatedly past the reviewing stand. The effect was dramatic. Our military estimated that their military *could* produce 600 such airplanes within two years, and then Air Force General Curtis LeMay declaimed that such a huge Soviet bomber build-up would give them a two to one advantage. *Voila:* The bomber Gap. Although the U.S. Air Force had been receiving the brunt of the Eisenhower Administration's military appropriations, they had received no small amount of flak as well: the B-36 had been obsolete almost as soon as it was deployed; it was then replaced by the even more costly B-47, and shortly thereafter, the first generation B-52s. In response to the announced bomber Gap, the U.S. expanded its strategic bomber forces to about 500 B-52s and more than 1,500 B-47s. In fact, at the time of the Air Show, the U.S.S.R. was displaying its entire long-range bomber force, and even after, the Soviet Union has never possessed more than 300 long-range bombers. The bomber Gap, then, *never existed,* at least never as reported in our press. At its height, there was a different Gap, however: about five to one, favoring the U.S.

The pattern revealed in the bomber Gap saga has been repeated ever since—we identify a Russian *capability* and immediately expand this into an *intention*. We then respond to these bear-scares by trying to close the imagined Gap. In so doing, we pull ahead further, thereby also pulling the rug out from under any moderate elements within the Kremlin, and insuring that they will also run hard to keep up.

In testimony before Congress, John S. Foster, director of Research and Engineering at the Department of Defense under Jimmy Carter, reported:

> We are moving ahead to make sure that, whatever they do, or the possible things we imagine that they might do, we will respond . . . we see possible threats on the horizon, usually not something the enemy has done, but something we may have thought of ourselves that he might do, and that we must therefore be prepared for.

Anticipatory Gap-phobia of this sort has been extraordinarily successful in fattening up the military budget; from 1949 until 1968, not a single military appropriations bill was cut on the floor of either the House or the Senate. In his memoirs, Nikita Khrushchev recalled a conversation with President Eisenhower at Camp David in 1959. The subject was how the U.S. sets its military budget. Eisenhower recounted to Khrushchev:

> My military leaders say "Mr. President, we need such and such a sum for such and such a program." I say, "sorry, we don't have the funds." They say, "we have reliable information that the Soviet Union has already allocated funds for their own such program." So I give in.

Khrushchev commented that it was just the same in the Soviet Union. The United States once invested more than a billion dollars in the absurd Buck Rogers-sounding atomic airplane, "Weapons System 125-A," simply because of the (incorrect) report that the Soviet Union was doing the same thing.

General Douglas MacArthur—clearly no shrinking violet or Soviet sympathizer—sensed the absurdity and duplicity of Gap-mongering. "Our government has kept us in a perpetual state of fear—kept us in a continuous stampede of patriotic fervor—with the cry of a grave national emergency," he wrote in the mid-1950s. "Always there has been some terrible evil at home or some monstrous foreign power that was going to gobble us up if we did not blindly rally behind it by furnishing the exhorbitant funds demanded."

We never did learn from the bomber Gap, perhaps in part because events moved too quickly. The Russians apparently had felt hoplessly outclassed in bomber competition and had elected instead to invest in missiles. They tested their first ICBM on August 26, 1957 and then shocked the world two months later by launching the first orbiting satellite, Sputnik, using the same new SS-4 rocket. President Eisenhower appointed an intelligence investigative group, the Gaither Committee, to assess the new, confounding Soviet missile capability. The Committee reported that by 1959, 100 Soviet ICBMs *could* attack the U.S. So out of the ashes of the bomber Gap there emerged a new one, the missile Gap. It was a Gap with gape.

Actually, by 1959 it was already becoming apparent that the U.S.S.R. was *not* embarking on a crash program of ICBM construction, although some first generation launchers were implanted along the Trans-Siberian railroad. Also in 1959, Defense Secretary McElroy said that the missile Gap arose out of the difference between what the U.S. actually planned to build and what the U.S.S.R. *could* build, if they went all-out. Nonetheless, in 1960, McElroy suggested that the Soviets *could* have a 3:1 lead in ICBMs within a few years. Also in 1960, SAC commander Thomas S. Power announced that with "only some 300 ballistic missiles, the Soviet Union could virtually wipe out our entire nuclear strike capability within a span of 30 minutes." He called for more bombers, a brand new bomber—the B-70—and additional hardware to close the latest Gap. Amid the near-panic of the missile Gap, we almost lost sight of the fact that the Soviets actually had at most about 10 ICBMs and 150 bombers, against our 600 B-52s and 1,200 B-47s (capable of intercontinental missions via in-flight refueling). By 1962 the missile Gap revelation had provoked us into spending $146 billion (1979 dollars) on 50 ICBMs, 80 Polaris missiles, about 90 Thor and Jupiter missiles positioned in Europe, 1,700 long-range bombers, 300 carrier-based and about 1,000 supersonic land-based fighters, all with nuclear weapons. In contrast, the U.S.S.R. had 50 to 100 ICBMs and less than 200 long-range bombers. Some Gap.

John F. Kennedy had made the missile Gap a major focus of his 1960 presidential campaign, and Francis Gary Powers had been shot down in his U-2 trying to clarify the widely conflicting intelligence reports concerning the Soviet missile arsenal. But the missile Gap slid quietly into oblivion shortly after Kennedy's victory. In fact, Khrushchev tried to use the Gap to win U.S. concessions on Berlin during their meeting in Vienna during June 1961, but the bluff failed since JFK knew that the Gap was nonexistent, or rather, that it favored the U.S. by a substantial margin. (The missile Gap even led in part to the Sino-Soviet split, since Mao too had swallowed the Gap and was disillusioned when Russia failed to push the U.S. around as he thought they could.)

Kennedy and McNamara learned early in 1961—from accurate first-generation spy satellites, which replaced the ill-fated U-2s—that the U.S.S.R. had not chosen to invest heavily in first-generation ICBMs, just as they had gone lightly on strategic bombers. Nonetheless, even after the missile Gap was proven phony, we continued to escalate our missile program. By 1963, Defense Department plans called for 1,000 new missiles, to be called Minutemen, over 650 submarine-launched Polaris missiles, and over 1,000 long-range bombers, even though the Soviets had only about 300 ICBMs and fewer than 300 bombers. The general pattern has been repeated ever since. In the deadly serious game of nuclear poker, the Russians have played their cards close to their chests, making wagers that ultimately turned out to involve only minimal deterrence on their part, matching our escalations often with a fair amount of bluff. Certainly, they rarely made the all-out efforts we regularly assumed of them. Our response, on the other hand, was to up the ante: "we'll see you, and raise you 500 more."

For example, we introduced our first Polaris nuclear missile submarine in 1960; by the time the U.S.S.R launched its first comparable subs, in 1965, we had already gone through the Polaris A-1 and A-2 missiles, and had deployed the A-3, with the innovation of the three warheads per missile (MIRVs). And so it has gone: whenever the Soviets made a tentative step in strategic arms (usually seeking to match us), we proclaimed a new Gap, thereby "scaring the hell out of the country" and leaving the Soviets far behind, panting to catch up, only to scare the pants off us once again whenever they tried to close the Gap at last. By 1964, Khrushchev had been deposed and the missile Gap was comfortably forgotten— with our missiles outnumbering theirs by ten to one!

In the history of Gaps, the Cuban missile crisis is particularly noteworthy, since it can teach us several important lessons, none of them cheery. Unfortunately, the moral most Americans seem to have drawn from the experience is that we can get the Russians to back down if we are stronger than they—in other words, if the Gap is wide enough. After all, as Dean Rusk put it, "we were eyeball-to-eyeball, and the other fellow blinked." It is possible that Khrushchev backed down because he was aware that the Soviet nuclear forces at the time were greatly inferior to our own. But for better or worse, a Gap like that can never occur again. Following the Cuban missile crisis, and because of it, the U.S.S.R. began a vigorous and continuing program of missile development. At present, neither side is so clearly ahead that the other can be expected to blink.

In 1959, we had installed Jupiter missiles in Turkey and Thors in Britain; these intermediate-range missiles posed a direct threat to the U.S.S.R., but we satisfied ourselves that they were "defensive." When the Soviets responded by implanting missiles in Cuba, we called it unacceptable and risked war to have them removed. At the time, we enjoyed an enormous strategic advantage and Khrushchev almost certainly was trying to maintain the balance of terror that our lead threatened to disrupt. The major lesson of the Cuban missile crisis was never learned: it is not that the Soviets will back down if we rattle our weapons, but rather, that when they perceive a strategic imbalance, they will seek to correct it. This has important implications for any Reagan Administration goals of a "margin of safety" for the 1980s.

Another lesson from 1962 is that once two opponents are armed with nuclear weapons, any serious confrontation between them can be assumed to escalate almost automatically to all-out nuclear war, regardless of the size of the Gap separating them. Thus, nothing in the details of the Cuban missile crisis necessarily called for possible nuclear war. John F. Kennedy had demanded that Khrushchev withdraw his missiles from Cuba, and he initiated a naval blockade. A confrontation between the U.S. fleet and Soviet blockade crashers was drawing close, but on the face of it, there was no reason why such an affair should become a nuclear war. And yet, military strategists on both sides immediately assumed that such would be the outcome, if the crisis was not resolved quickly and peacefully. And in fact, they were probably right, although fortunately we will never know for sure.

Following the crisis, JFK estimated that the chances of nuclear war had been somewhere "between 1 in 3 and 50/50." In his book, *Thirteen Days: A Memoir of the Cuban Missile Crisis,* Robert Kennedy had this to say of his brother's frame of mind: "The great tragedy was that, if we erred, we erred not only for ourselves, our futures, our hopes, and our country, but for the lives, futures, hopes and countries of those who had never been given an opportunity to play a role. . . . It was this that troubled him the most." Well might it have troubled him. And thinking of our own future, well might it trouble us all today.

The final lesson of the Cuban missile crisis, and perhaps the most worrisome one of all, concerns the attitude of high-ranking military leaders toward nuclear war. Robert Kennedy had this to say about his brother, the President:

> But he was distressed that the representatives with whom he met, with the notable exception of General (Maxwell) Taylor, seemed to give so little consideration to the implications of steps they suggested. They seemed always to assume that if the Russians and the Cubans would not respond or, if they did, that a war was in our national interest. One of the Joint Chiefs of Staff once said to me he believed in a preventive attack against the Soviet Union. On that fateful Sunday morning when the Russians answered that they were withdrawing their missiles, it was suggested by one high military advisor that we attack Monday in any case. Another felt that we had in some way been betrayed.

Military minds are trained to be aggressive, "can do" people. They chafe at battles unfought, at wars unwon. In a world bristling with bombs and bloated with overkill, when such minds have a role in national policy, the already fragile Gap between our survival and our incineration becomes even more endangered. Such "minds" have their own private Gaps—between their ears.

During his 1964 presidential campaign, Barry Goldwater tried to sell a reliability Gap. Although by that time no one doubted our numerical superiority in missiles, Goldwater charged that they were unreliable and that more bombers were therefore needed. However, this Gap failed to rouse a following. In fact, military analysts have been and continue to be convinced that the reliability and readiness of U.S. missiles exceeds that of the U.S.S.R.

Although subsequent claims have rarely been as straightforward as the earlier bomber and missile Gap, the American military has continued to pave the way for new weapons by sowing doubts about possible future Gaps, which might render current systems obsolete. In 1969, Defense Secretary Melvin Laird argued for a massive ABM system, claiming that our Polaris and their replacements, the Poseidon submarines, would soon be detectable by Soviet antisubmarine warfare. Even the Navy agreed that by the mid-1970s all of their Polaris subs *could* be vulnerable. By 1978, this "detection Gap" had successfully spawned the Trident submarine, whereupon the Navy revealed that since 1960, 41 Polaris-Trident submarines had conducted about 1,500 patrols of 60 days each, and not one sub had been detected!

The Russians' new Delta-class missile submarines were also used to justify our Trident subs, since the Delta's missiles had a lethality rating of 1.56 as opposed to the Poseidon's 1.3. Unmentioned, however, was the fact that there were more than 13 times as many warheads on a Poseidon sub as on a Delta. Moreover, the new Trident I missiles have individual lethality ratings of 3.34, and there will be 12 to 16 times as many warheads as on Soviet Deltas.

Back in 1969, the Army had also joined the clamor for ABMs, to defend their Minutemen against Soviet MIRVs which at that time didn't even exist. Meanwhile, the Navy and Air Force began deploying their own MIRVs (Multiple Independently-targeted Reentry Vehicles) to penetrate a massive Soviet ABM system—which still does not exist! The "ABM Gap" had first appeared in the American press in 1963 when Sen. Strom Thurmond (then still a Democrat) announced that the U.S.S.R. "had a lead of at least several years in the development of an active defense against ballistic missiles," and moreover, they were supposedly already building such an ABM system around Leningrad, the so-called Tallinn Line. In this latest adventure in Gapism, the predictable Dr. Edward Teller warned "the Soviet Union is at present ahead of us."

First under Lyndon Johnson and then Richard Nixon, we rushed to plug the ABM Gap, proposing a succession of hare-brained schemes, of which not one could offer any defense against the attacks of skeptical scientists, not to mention Soviet missiles. (JFK had likened an ABM system to "trying to hit a bullet with a bullet.") Nonetheless, first came the Nike-X program, consisting of two parts; Spartan missiles, large, megaton-carrying monsters intended to explode incoming rockets above the atmosphere, and then the faster, smaller, shorter-range Sprints, designed to knock heads with any intruders that escaped the Spartans. Despite the Army's enthusiasm for the $15-50 billion program, Robert McNamara turned it down, reasoning that the Soviet Union could easily degrade the system with decoys, and/or overwhelm it by simply increasing the number of incoming warheads. An expensive military system dies hard, however, and the Nike-X was resurrected as the Sentinel in 1967, three years after China tested its first atomic bomb—this time as an admittedly "thin" system, to defend us from a nuclear "yellow peril," anticipated when they deployed their "primitive" ICBMs in the 1970s. Finally, it emerged once more under the Nixon administration as Safeguard, to defend ICBM silos and as a "bargaining chip" in the forthcoming SALT I talks. A small version was actually built, at $6 billion. Inaugurated on April Fool's Day, 1975, it was unceremoniously abandoned ten months later, and its silos are now filling with rainwater on the North Dakota plains. (Look for the latest installment to defend the MX missile.) Fear of the Tallinn Line ABM in the mid-1960s also led to the fitting of multiple warheads onto submarine missiles, the deployment of supersonic F-111 fighter-bombers, Poseidon submarines and missiles, the Minuteman III, and most importantly, full speed ahead with MIRVs. We continued each of these escalations even after it was shown that the U.S.S.R. was *not* proceeding with the ABM system that was the main argument for building them in the first place.

MIRVing was probably the most crucial and ominous of these U.S. innovations. By MIRVing, a single missile could be outfitted with numerous warheads, each of which can be independently aimed once the missile is in flight. It enables one missile to destroy many, widely separated targets. It also figures prominently in one of the most ironic stories of nuclear Gapism. As we have seen, MIRVs were justified by the presence of the Soviet Tallinn Line, purportedly an ABM system. However, our first MIRVs were deployed in 1970, even though two years before, it had been confirmed that the Tallinn-ABM Gap, like its ill-begotten predecessors, the bomber and missile Gaps, simply did not exist! Moreover, it never had. In fact, the Tallinn Line was exclusively an anti-*bomber* defense, never intended to counter missiles and posing no threat whatever to our ICBM deterrence. (The Tallinn Line was nothing more than the U.S.S.R.'s defensive response to our overwhelming bomber superiority, which itself had been stimulated by our response to the phony bomber Gap the decade before.) So there was absolutely no strategic need for our MIRVing. But by the time the Tallinn Line's true purpose was revealed to the American public, we already had our usual five year lead in a strategic system, so we decided to push ahead, refusing to consider any restriction on MIRVs in the SALT I treaty, then nearing fruition. After all, the phony ABM Gap had given the impetus for a new Gap in our favor—the MIRV Gap. There was little motivation to negotiate away an advantage, especially when its original justification had conveniently been forgotten. (So much for the facilitating effect of bargaining from strength.) In fact, the Soviets did install a very modest and almost certainly ineffective ABM system of 64 rockets surrounding Moscow.

The irony is that ten years ago, by clinging to our MIRV Gap, we set the stage for new alarmist cries about another Gap. Thus, hawkish strategic analysts now claim to be worried by a newfound "counterforce Gap" in which Soviet ICBMs—MIRVed at last and unfettered by SALT treaty restrictions—are seen to threaten our land-based ICBMs during the supposedly forthcoming, "window of vulnerability" sometime in our harried future. The Soviets, not surprisingly, had been eager to include a limitation on MIRVing in the SALT I treaty; we had stood firm. Once again, not surprisingly, the Soviets moved during the 1970s to close the MIRV Gap, deploying their first MIRVs in 1975. And once again, those same Gap-yappers on our side who brought us the bomber, missile and ABM Gaps, and who zealously guarded our short-lived MIRV Gap, thereby assuring its eventual disappearance, are now telling hair-raising stories about a new series of Gaps for the 1980s.

Although MIRVs are clearly important in toting up a balance sheet of who sits on what side of which Gap, they cannot really change the outcome of a nuclear war, since either side can destroy the other even without MIRVs, and regardless of whether one side makes a surprise attack. The real significance of MIRVs is in raising fears about the other side's intentions, and thus making nuclear war more likely. The U.S. has always been far ahead in MIRV technology and yet, when the U.S.S.R. finally tested its first MIRV in August 1973, Defense Secretary James Schlesinger announced that the Russians "are seeking a strategic advantage." Such a statement would be simply incredible to anyone not familiar with the history of the world according to Gap, although it was readily accepted by those who have unquestionably swallowed every alarmist pronouncement about U.S.-Soviet relationships.

George Rathjens of MIT, one of our most astute analysts, has pointed out that the whole, sad history of U.S.-Soviet strategic relationships has been one of action followed by reaction. Often, the reaction has been overreaction, and in response to the identification—frequently, misidentification—of a Gap. In nearly all cases, the U.S. has been the initiator. Here is a summarized chronology, the Struggles of Red Gap:

| Action | Initiated By | Date | Reaction by | Date |
|---|---|---|---|---|
| Sustained nuclear chain reaction | U.S. | 1942 | U.S.S.R. | 1946 |
| Atomic bomb | U.S. | 1945 | U.S.S.R. | 1949 |
| Intercontinental bomber | U.S. | 1948 | U.S.S.R. | 1955 |
| International military pact (U.S. NATO: U.S.S.R. Warsaw Pact) | U.S. | 1949 | U.S.S.R. | 1955 |
| Tactical nuclear weapons deployed in Europe | U.S. | 1954 | U.S.S.R. | 1957 |
| Nuclear powered submarine | U.S. | 1955 | U.S.S.R. | 1959 |
| ICBM | U.S.S.R. | 1957 | U.S. | 1958 |
| Satellite launching | U.S.S.R. | 1957 | U.S. | 1958 |
| Supersonic bomber | U.S. | 1960 | U.S.S.R. | 1975 |
| Submarine-launched ballistic missile | U.S. | 1960 | U.S.S.R. | 1968 |
| Solid fuel missiles | U.S. | 1960 | U.S.S.R. | 1968 |
| Accelerated ICBM build-up | U.S. | 1961 | U.S.S.R. | 1966 |
| Multiple reentry vehicles (MRVs) | U.S. | 1964 | U.S.S.R. | 1968 |
| Penetration aids on missiles | U.S. | 1964 | U.S.S.R. | none yet |
| ABM system | U.S.S.R. | 1968 | U.S. | 1972 |
| High-speed warheads | U.S. | 1970 | U.S.S.R. | 1975 |
| MIRVs | U.S. | 1970 | U.S.S.R. | 1975 |
| Computerized missile guidance | U.S. | 1970 | U.S.S.R. | 1975 |
| Neutron bombs | U.S. | 1981 | U.S.S.R. | none yet |
| Long-range cruise missiles | U.S. | 198? | U.S.S.R. | none yet |

Reviewing this sorry history, we cannot help asking "Why?" The answers, however, are as complex as the predicament in which we find ourselves. For one thing, the very nature of "worst-case" analyses, standard operating procedure for Pentagon (and presumably, Kremlin) bureaucrats, insures an escalated arms race. For example, let us assume that U.S. military officials are anxious about the reliability or survivability of our missiles; accordingly, they order 100 new bombers, capable of penetrating Soviet air defenses—call it the B-1. To Soviet planners, these 100 bombers constitute a Gap. Like most military strategists, they make a conservative, worst-case assumption, namely that all 100 of our new B-1s could function flawlessly and penetrate their border defenses. Accordingly, they order development of a new anti-B-1 missile. Moreover, they assume that some of their own defensive missiles will malfunction, leaving them with, let us say, only 85 percent of their original number. As a result, and because of their worst-case figuring, they order 125 missiles (giving them an assured 100). On the other side, Pentagon officials view the 125 Soviet missiles with alarm, and proclaim a new Gap, made even larger by their worst-case assumption that in fact *fewer* than our fleet of 100 B-1s will actually arrive within the U.S.S.R. In fact, they had been assuming that perhaps only 85 percent of our bombers would make it to Soviet targets. Given the new missile/B-1 Gap, they increase U.S. production to 150 bombers. (Note that it would not even suffice to match the Soviets and make 125 bombers, since under worst-case assumptions, all of their missiles will work as designed, but only some of our bombers.) And so it goes, not so much a race as a never ending spiral.

The MX missile, incidentally, is a classic case of a potentially spiral-producing weapon: however deployed, it requires only that the other side build enough warheads to threaten each silo. Our response, then, would be to build more silos. And theirs? More warheads. And on and on, a race neither side can win.

In general, we overreact more to Soviet military decisions than they do to ours, perhaps because we keep them better informed, so they are less likely to overestimate our strength. The U.S. Secretary of Defense is required to submit an annual report to Congress, detailing the current state of American defenses. If Soviet strategists were smart, they would provide us with comparable information about their military posture, regularly updated, since without reliable data, analysts are permitted—even encouraged—to let their worst-case imaginations run wild.

Well-meaning but misguided people may be led to proclaim illusory Gaps for other reasons. They may honestly fear that the Soviets are bent on world domination, a worry that certainly was not lessened by Khrushchev's well-publicized "We will bury you." ° Even if such persons privately acknowledged that the U.S. leads in all identifiable Gaps, their anxiety may lead them to exaggerate. Moreover, some people proclaim Gap in the hope of spurring us on to "victory," whatever that may be.

We have a peculiar, Jeckyll-and-Hyde view of communism. Thus, the Soviets are often pictured as on the one hand laboring under a faulty economic and social system that barely provides the necessities of life and must therefore maintain its hold by tyrannical oppression, and yet on the other, demonically competent and efficient when they set about building strategic weapons. When Khrushchev claimed (both innacurately and unwisely) that Soviet missiles could "hit a fly in outer space," Americans actually seemed to believe him. A strange and unadmitted partnership has evolved, linking the military of both countries; it is difficult to maintain national enthusiasm for expensive military programs whose only purpose is to ensure that they will never be used. Hence, each side points to the aggressive statements of the other, to justify continuing and expanding its own programs.

Douglas MacArthur recognized this in 1952: "It is part of the general pattern of misguided policy that our country is now geared to an arms industry which was bred in an artificially induced psychosis of war hysteria and nurtured upon an incessant propaganda of fear."

"There are fears, resentments, national pride, personal pride," as diplomat-historian George F. Kennan has pointed out.

> There are misreadings of the adversary's intentions—sometimes even the refusal to consider them at all. There is the tendency of national communities to idealize themselves and to dehumanize the opponent. There is the blinkered, narrow vision of the professional

---

° Which could equally have been translated "We will *outlive* you"!

military planner, and his tendency to make war inevitable by assuming its inevitability. Tossed together, these components form a powerful brew. They guide the fears and the ambitions of men. They seize the policies of governments and whip them around like trees before the tempest.

For some people, Gap-yapping is pure selfishness. In his farewell address, on January 17, 1961, Dwight Eisenhower had this to say:

> We have been compelled to create a permanent armaments industry of vast proportions. Added to this, three and a half million men and women are directly engaged in the defense establishment. We annually spend on military security more than the net income of all United States corporations. This conjunction of an immense military establishment and a large arms industry is new in the American experience. The total influence—economic, political, even spiritual—is felt in every city, every State house, every office of the Federal government. . . . In the councils of government, we must guard against the acquisition of unwarranted influence, whether sought or unsought, by the military-industrial complex. The potential for the disastrous rise of misplaced power exists and will persist.

Unfortunately, Ike's message has almost been forgotten, even as his words have become a cliché. Yes, Virginia, there is a military-industrial complex, and for many, it is Santa Claus. Pentagon generals, admirals, and civilian procurement officials regularly play musical chairs between government and the defense industry. For example, while Thomas Morris was spending his last year as Assistant Secretary of Defense—the Pentagon's chief procurement official—the defense contracts of Litton Industries went from $180 million to $466 million; the following year, Morris became a highly paid executive for Litton. The fires of military preparedness have been stoked at least as much by personal greed as by patriotism.

There is something indelicate about pointing to financial gain as a motivator in the American defense community. But the reality is that military officials and big business are very cosily entwined, and most of our largest corporations make many hundreds of millions of

dollars whenever a Gap is identified. Moreover, government officials who proclaim Gaps have typically just come from those industries which are about to profit from their proclamation—more often
yet, they can count on joining their beneficiaries when they leave
government service. Old soldiers never die, they just fade away—to
General Dynamics, Lockheed, or United Technologies. As John
Kenneth Galbraith put it: "A curtain is lowered over the future.
Sufficient is the dollar today; let there be no thought that it means
death for one's self and one's children tomorrow."

In the same speech in which he decried the military-industrial
complex, Eisenhower issued another warning as well, one that has
received considerably less attention, but which is no less cogent
today: "We must also be alert to the . . . danger that public policy
could itself become the captive of a scientific-technological elite."
Robert Oppenheimer once commented that when they built the
atomic bomb, physicists for the first time had "known sin." Although some recoiled at the knowledge, the vast majority have
found the experience quite pleasant indeed. Thus, there are more
than 500,000 scientists and engineers employed by the military-
industrial complex. And from Edward Teller on, these scientists
have done their share to influence policy, often by ringing false
alarms about impending Soviet superiority. Herbert D. York, on
the other hand, is a repentant sinner: former Assistant Secretary of
Defense for research and engineering and also the first director of
the Livermore Laboratory, established by Teller as competition to
the Los Alamos nuclear weapons lab. In his book *Race to Oblivion:
A Participant's View of the Arms Race,* York described the personal
motivation of his colleagues in the scientific-technological elite:
"They desire either their incomes, their profits, or their consultant
fees from it. But much more important than money as a motivating
force are the individuals' own psychic and spiritual needs; the majority of the key individual promoters of the arms race derive a
very large part of their self-esteem from their participation. . . ."
When it seemed possible that a Comprehensive Test-Ban Treaty
might be signed during the early days of the Carter Administration,
scientists at both the Livermore and Los Alamos laboratories lob-
bied heavily against it, just as Teller and others had vigorously
opposed the 1963 Partial Test-Ban Treaty.

For many scientists and engineers, there is an irresistible allure to the solving of difficult problems, especially if the solution uses the newest in high technology. As Oppenheimer put it:

> It is my judgment in these things that when you see something that is technically sweet, you go ahead and do it, and you argue about what to do about it only after you have had your technical success. That is the way it was with the atomic bomb. I don't think anybody opposed making it. . . ."

The technical sweet tooth is almost irresistible, and the first rule of advanced weaponry seems to be that if it can be done, then it will be done—and only in part because, otherwise, the Soviets might do it first. (Of course, once done, this assures that the Soviets will do it too—as they always have.) In this respect military officers are the ardent cheerleaders for the scientific-technological elite: Pentagon brass hats seem particularly entranced by the newest, shiniest innovation; what a new, sexy, overpowered and overpriced automobile is to the American public, a new improved warhead or missile guidance system is to the military. In the end, even Robert McNamara deplored the "kind of mad momentum intrinsic to the development of all nuclear weaponry."

Part of that "mad momentum" obviously comes from the scientists themselves. As individuals, they are rewarded for innovations in weaponry, typically with money as well as prestige. And given the tortuous pace at which arms control negotiations usually proceed, it is a classic case of the hare (bright, motivated scientists) outrunning the tortoise (ponderously negotiating bureaucrats). By the time the politician get around to banning or even controlling a weapons system, the system is often already obsolete, replaced by a whole new generation of devices—more lethal and even more uncontrollable.

Many scientists and engineers are also in it simply for the joy of the chase, the gut-level satisfaction that comes from solving a challenging problem even if the problem is how "best" to commit suicide. For a good example of this intellectual tunnel vision, consider the following joke, told in the defense community about a particular, very prominent physicist: the physicist had been condemned to die by the guillotine, along with two other prisoners. As the blade descended toward the first prisoner, it unaccountably screeched to a halt inches before his neck. The executioner assumed that divine intervention must be responsible, so the prisoner was set free. The same thing happened to the second prisoner. Then it was the physicist's turn. As the executioner was cranking up the blade, the physicist, who had been studying its progress, suddenly cried out "Wait! I see your problem!"

Finally, the American people themselves have made Gap-yapping politically expedient. The public has a remarkably short memory and does not seem to learn from past false alarms. Moreover, there is great charismatic appeal in sounding the bugles of alarm and posing as the ever-vigilant watchdog of the nation's defense. By contrast, "sufficiency" or "parity" have very little sex appeal, and careful, reasoned reassurance can be made to seem tantamount to apologizing for "inferiority," which is a turn-off indeed. After all, what greater service can a government provide than security? And how better to appear security-minded than to point out a Gap? Beyond this, we are easily stampeded by fear, and most of us would really prefer to believe government spokesmen anyhow, especially on matters of defense, in which they are presumably the experts. We don't like to think that we have been lied to—but the truth is, we *have* been lied to, again and again. And the biggest, costliest, and most dangerous lies concern the Gaps of the 1980s.

# 5. The World According to Gap*

## Part II: Counterfeit Claims of the 1980s

The history of spurious Gaps and of U.S.-Soviet action-reactions should cause us to view claims of present or future Gaps with a jaundiced eye (or, one might add, a grain of SALT). But on the other hand, the issue now before us is too grave to risk error by simply assuming that the future will repeat the past; the stakes are too high for us to relax our guard. We must be wary, however, not only of the Soviet Union, but also of the Gappers on our own side. Erring on the side of excess, as we have done so often in the past, may at first glance seem at least to be erring on the side of caution: better safe than sorry. But overreaction in the nuclear age carries with it an enormous possible cost, even more than wasted dollars, unmet social needs, and heightened inflation. By overreacting to Gaps—real or imagined—we make ourselves dangerously *less* safe, so much so, in fact, that we might never have the chance to be sorry.

The strategic balance has actually been rather stable over the past several decades—not because of Gaps and action-reaction, but rather, in spite of them. This is because nuclear weapons are so destructive and the advantage of offense over defense is so great, that even a modest nuclear arsenal spells deterrence. The great danger today is that if we allow ourselves to be stampeded by claims of fictitious or exaggerated Gaps, we may then go ahead with a new generation of nuclear weaponry, with horribly dangerous prospects of counterforce first strikes, missile launches on warning of attack, and doctrines of "limited" nuclear war.

Moreover, the latest Gap-flaps are almost invariably coupled with the insistence that negotiations must be postponed until each

* We gratefully thank Rear Admiral Eugene Carroll USN (ret.), now deputy director of the Center for Defense Information, for reviewing this chapter and correcting the data as of June, 1982.

Gap is closed. "There could be serious arms control negotiations," said Reagan's chief arms negotiator, Paul Nitze, "but only after we have built up our forces." Given the action-reaction history of the nuclear arms race, such an insistence can lead only to a never ending arms spiral, since what is seen by one side as Gap-closing is seen by the other as Gap-Widening. Let us therefore take a hard-eyed look at the latest round of Gap-crap.

The bomber, missile and ABM Gaps were simple by contrast. Although the 1980s version is no less wrongheaded than the earlier models, it is more difficult to refute, simply because it is multi-dimensional and hence, rather slippery. Its purveyors claim that we suffer from a wide range of sometimes unrelated military weaknesses vis-a-vis the U.S.S.R., and their credibility is buttressed by the pervasive frustration and anger that seems to characterize America in this new decade. To do these claims justice, we must take them one at a time.

### The Spending Gap

In February 1981, President Reagan stated that "since 1970, the Soviet Union has invested $300 billion more in its military force than we have." Mr. Reagan may honestly believe this, but it is certainly not true. In fact, the supposed spending Gap is one of the most transparent pieces of flimflammery in the history of "scaring hell out of the country." Unfortunately, the U.S.S.R. does not announce its military budget as we do. As a result, the CIA prepares regular estimates of Soviet military spending. There are many ways such estimates could be made, and the CIA uses one technique which makes the estimate as large as possible—so distorted in fact, as to be almost useless at best, grossly misleading at worst. The technique is this: take everything the Soviet military buys each year, and then calculate how much they would be spending if they were buying comparable items and services in the U.S. at U.S. prices.

The results are bizarre. For example, the Russians pay their conscripts the ruble equivalent of $6.50 per month; U.S. base pay is about 80 times higher. As a result, the salary of the Red Army alone costs the U.S.S.R., according to the CIA estimators, about $50 million. At *their* actual pay scales, however, it is closer to $5 billion. With the 17 percent pay raise we recently granted to our own military in autumn 1981, we can therefore look for a sudden increase in our official estimates of Soviet military spending! Les Aspin (D-Wis.), a former Pentagon analyst and now a Congressman, described the result of this sleight-of-hand: "By computing Soviet manpower costs at American rates, one discovers a huge Soviet defense manpower budget of over $50 billion that exists only in American documents." The cost of Soviet weapons is estimated similarly: for example, the CIA totes up the number of new tanks produced in a given year, then pretends that each one costs them as much as our best and newest tank, the XM-1 Abrams Main Battle Tank, costs us ($3 million each). In fact, this almost certainly overestimates the Soviet expenditures on tanks by at least a factor of two or three. Small wonder that the prestigious Stockholm International Peace Research Institute (SIPRI) concluded that the CIA's estimating procedure for Soviet military expenditures is "wholly worthless for virtually any purpose." In all fairness to the Agency, it should be pointed out that our sleuths are quite candid about the technique and its limitations—but such fine print is almost invariably overlooked in the paranoia that follows.

The crowning idiocy of the spending Gap occurred in 1976, just before the Carter Administration took office. Gerald Ford's CIA director (George Bush) had commissioned a review of our estimates of Soviet military spending, and had accepted the views of "Team B," a group of avowedly right-wing hardliners including Richard Pipes and Paul Nitze. Here is Richard Nixon's account of their findings, from his book *The Real War:* "In 1976, the CIA estimates of Russian military spending for 1970-1975 were doubled overnight as errors were discovered and corrected. . . . Thanks in part to this intelligence blunder we will find ourselves looking down the nuclear barrel in the mid-1980s." But here is the actual CIA report: "The new estimate of the share of defense in the Soviet (GNP) is almost twice as high as the 6 to 8 percent previously estimated. This does not mean that the import of defense programs on the Soviet economy has increased—only that our appreciation of this input has changed. It also implies that Soviet defense industries are far less efficient than formerly believed." What happened was simply this: the CIA decided that Soviet military procurement and production were only about one-half as efficient as previously thought—*ipso facto,* they must have been spending twice as much, 11-13 percent of their GNP instead of the previously estimated 6-8 percent! In other words, this much ballyhooed near-doubling of our estimate did not imply that the Russians were actually obtaining anything more whatsoever, only that they were twice as clumsy at getting it.

When Soviet military spending is estimated by exchanging their cost in rubles into equivalent dollar amounts, we find that the U.S. outspent the U.S.S.R. by 67 percent in 1979 and by 80 percent in 1980. Moreover, during 1979, our NATO allies (excluding ourselves) had combined military budgets of $76 billion; by contrast, the U.S.S.R.'s Warsaw Pact allies (excluding the U.S.S.R.) spent $17 billion, less than one-fifth as much. And this doesn't count France, which spent an additional $20 billion. In fact, even using the government's own figures, with its inflated estimates of Soviet expenditures, we find that NATO (including the U.S.) has outspent the Warsaw Pact (including the U.S.S.R.) *in every year* of the 1970s, for a total NATO "advantage" of $207 billion, based on former secretary of Defense Harold Brown's final report to Congress, 1981.

Finally, even our own DoD spending estimates are clearly too low. For example, they do not include the approximately $4 billion spent on nuclear warheads (part of the Energy Department's budget) or the $4.7 billion spent on military uses of space (NASA).

It would be erroneous to conclude, however, that there has not been a large Soviet military build-up. They ended War War II in a shambles and now they are the second strongest military power on earth; clearly, they have built up. Especially since the mid-1960s, that build-up has been steady and almost relentless. However, like the sudden "discovery" of a Soviet brigade in Cuba, which in fact had been there for nearly twenty years, the "discovery" of a sudden, dramatic Gap-producing Soviet leap in military effort is equally phony political grandstanding with no basis in reality, strategy, or national security. In summary, and like it or not, the booby prize for spending profligacy belongs to us. We are indeed on the wrong side of a spending Gap, but because we spend *more* than the Soviets, not less.

## Conventional Forces Gap

One of the most pervasive myths about East-West military Gaps concerns the balance of conventional forces, especially in Europe. The early NATO plan, adopted at U.S. insistence during the Lisbon conference of 1952, called for nearly 100 divisions in Europe by 1954. This was not achieved, and NATO began to rely increasingly upon tactical nuclear weapons, first deployed in 1954. (The Soviets responded with tactical nuclear weapons of their own in 1957.) NATO's refusal to live up to the ambitious U.S. goals of the early 1950s has spawned a continuing impression that western conventional forces are inferior to the Warsaw Pact. In fact, this is simply not true. Scare stories emphasizing Soviet power often point to the large "military manpower" of the U.S.S.R.—over four million men. But it is irresponsible to equate this with an army, since the U.S.S.R. uses its "military" for a variety of non-army chores. For example, about 500,000 men are concerned with internal security, 550,000 are relegated to air defense, and more than 700,000 deal with such typically American civilian functions as railroad construction and maintenance, engineering projects, and especially, agricultural harvest.

Comparing armies *sensu strictu*, we find that the U.S. has 775,-000 men and the U.S.S.R., 1,825,000. Even this is misleading, however, since the Soviets have nearly one million men deployed along the 4,500 mile border with China. We have no comparable drain on our military attention. This leaves the Russians with about 900,-000 men facing NATO in Europe, and of these, fully 25 percent "are there to maintain the reliability of Warsaw Pact Forces," by the admission of Bernard W. Rogers, NATO Commander-in-Chief. A military configuration of this sort hardly lends itself to a massive, coordinated attack against the West. Thus, four Soviet divisions are stationed in Hungary (part of their presence since the 1956 uprising) and five are in Czechoslovakia (since 1968), so that only 21 divisions are left for deployment against NATO. NATO has 64 active divisions and the Warsaw Pact, 68—is this, then, an imbalance? No, because each NATO division is larger. In fact, NATO has a standing ground force of 2,700,000 men and the WP, 2,600,-

000. Clearly, no Soviet tactician can be counting on the offensive reliability of satellite troops, such as Poland's. Counting available reserves, NATO forces swell to 4,933,000 and WP, 4,788,000. Moreover, these figures do not even count the French Army of 321,000. NATO has 150 percent the population of the WP, and three times the GNP.

The Soviet Air Force has 475,000 men; the USAF, 558,000. The Soviet Navy has 443,000 men; the USN, 528,000. The Soviet Naval Infantry totals 12,000 men; the U.S. Marine Corps is 188,000. Not surprisingly, a recent RAND Corporation report concluded that "gross Soviet capabilities to project power abroad do not remotely equal the U.S.'s"—i.e., they could not sustain an invasion beyond their immediate borders. In 1979, the Chairman of the Joint Chiefs of Staff concluded similarly that the U.S. was the only nation capable of projecting and maintaining global power, since the U.S.S.R. lacks a large Marine Corps, Air Force transports, naval carriers (we have 14 giants and they have 2 small ones), and they have insufficient air and ground support, logistic systems and amphibious assault ships. In addition, we have about 200 bases and military facilities worldwide; the U.S.S.R. has nothing comparable.

NATO has 454 surface combatant vessels; the WP, 269. In gross tonnage, NATO has a nearly 3:1 lead. NATO has 191 attack submarines; WP, 158. NATO has 12,000 helicopters; WP, 4,000. Admittedly, WP forces have a total of 7,500 military aircraft as against 6,850 for NATO. But this ignores the more than 500 French military aircraft and the 807 forthcoming British Tornados to be added to the air forces of Britain, Italy, and West Germany. Moreover, western training and technology is acknowledged to be superior in virtually all weapons systems. There is one well-known area, however, in which NATO does seem to be overmatched: tanks. The WP has 26,300 against NATO's 17,053. Even disregarding the technologic superiority of western models, this seems to be a Gap worth noting, and indeed, it is the great bogeyman of NATO conventional war-gamers. But there are very effective non-nuclear weapons for use against tanks, and NATO has invested heavily in them. NATO currently maintains an arsenal of about 250,000 antitank weapons, most of them precision-guided devices such as the Maverick, Dragon, and TOW missile, Copperhead laser-guided 155mm shell and the Walleye television guided bomb. (By contrast, WP forces have many fewer and their models are relatively primitive.) The development of precision-guided "smart" weaponry has revolutionized conventional warfare, since cheap, fast, small, highly accurate missiles can effectively destroy expensive, slow, large targets such as tanks. The Falklands War, for example, has emphasized the importance of "smart" conventional weapons, as when the British destroyer H.M.S. Sheffield was itself destroyed by a single French-made Exocet missile, fired from more than twenty miles away. Indeed, the day of the blitzkrieg is now clearly over, as evidenced during the 1973 Yom Kippur War, in which Egyptian antitank missiles demolished whole brigades of seemingly invincible Israeli armor. The conclusion is undeniable: the Soviets have more tanks, but the military answer to a tank threat is neither more NATO tanks nor nuclear weapons, but, rather, more and better antitank systems. NATO already has this advantage and is wisely adding to it.

In his Annual Report for 1981, Defense Secretary Brown concluded that "a rough numerical balance exists between the immediately available non-nuclear forces of NATO (including France) and those of the Warsaw Pact."

### Tactical Nuclear Forces Gap

What about nuclear forces in Europe? If tanks are the bogeymen, then the SS-20 is a three-headed Frankenstein. It is a MIRVed missile, of intermediate range and carrying three warheads. The U.S.S.R. began deploying its SS-20s in 1976, as a newer version of their SS-5 single-warhead missiles. In reaction to this deployment— which, we claimed, unbalanced the tactical nuclear forces in Europe, thereby threatening a new gap—we pressured our NATO allies to accept 108 Pershing II missiles and 464 ground-launched cruise missiles by December 1983. Our European allies, however, have not taken kindly to our concern. Are they insensitive to their own Gap, one that imperils the stability of Europe and cries out to be addressed? Or is this another phony? Judge for yourself.

The U.S.S.R. currently has 300 SS-4 and SS-5 missiles in Europe, along with about 290 SS-20s (of which approximately one third are aimed at China). Nonetheless, NATO currently has *sev-*

*eral thousand more* nuclear weapons in Europe, largely because of superior numbers of short-range weapons, as well as French and British submarine-launched long-range missiles plus U.S. Poseidon subs assigned to NATO. If we focus only on the SS-20s and their counterparts, we find that indeed there is an intermediate-range ballistic missile Gap. But there is also a borsht Gap, a vodka Gap, and a caviar Gap. If the Russians introduced dogsleds for delivering nuclear weapons, there would be a dogsled Gap—but not one that we would necessarily have to fill. Serious gaps could be dangerous; spurious Gaps are dangerous only if they lead either side to escalate the danger by overreacting. Now and for the forseeable future, the fact remains that even with their SS-20s, the U.S.S.R. is playing a nuclear second fiddle in Europe.

When confronted with the undeniable facts of NATO nuclear superiority, advocates of closing the "SS-20 Gap" point to the new threat these missiles ostensibly pose to European capitals. In fact, the threat is nothing new. Western Europe has been targeted by the SS-4s and SS-5s for more than twenty years. And NATO's submarines, Jupiter and Thor missiles have similarly threatened western Russia for the same time period. This not to excuse or apologize for the SS-20—it is an ugly, monstrous weapon and should be dismantled. The same applies to NATO's more-than-comparable weapons. It is nothing short of duplicity, however, to represent the SS-20 as giving the Soviets any form of tactical advantage. They never had such an advantage; they do not have it now; and they cannot have it in the forseeable future.

Another Gapper's favorite is the Soviet "Backfire" bomber, the TU-22M. These supersonic bombers, like the SS-20 missiles, are intermediate-range, for use in China or Europe. About 135 are currently deployed. Comparable NATO aircraft already exist as well: the F-111s (156 of them) and the British Vulcans (48). Backfires are being produced at about 30 per year; at that rate, it would not be until the year 2005 that the Soviets would even equal the 807 British Tornados which are scheduled to enter NATO by 1986.

The NATO high command has rushed to close the imaginary tactical nuclear Gap by introducing 464 ground-launched cruise missiles and 108 Pershing IIs; the former are small and fly low enough to evade radar detection, and the latter fly too fast for ABM defenses and can reach Moscow from West Germany in about *six minutes,* allowing almost no time for verifying a possible computer or radar error. Their deployment would undoubtedly make the Kremlin jumpy and, not surprisingly, the prospect is making the rest of Europe jumpy as well. Our misperception of a tactical European nuclear Gap is straining Western unity and increasing East-West tensions. Moreover, our proposed solution to the non-problem may well make accidental nuclear war more likely, by driving the Soviets to a "launch on warning" policy. Even if there was a Gap, such a solution hardly commends itself. Given that NATO nuclear forces are actually far ahead of the Warsaw Pact, our current European nuclear policy seems even more insane than the rest of the arms race. Which is saying quite a lot.

### The Missile Gap Revisited

#### a. The Numbers Game Gap

By contrast with tactical forces, intended for use on a battlefield, strategic forces are those directed at the opposing country. For time out of mind, people have "gone to war"; now, that seems unnecessary—war can come to us, courtesy of both sides' strategic weapons. From the early days of the missile Gap, we had undeniable superiority in numbers of strategic delivery vehicles. However, a steady Soviet build-up since the mid-1960s has brought them slightly ahead in certain measures. As a result, alarmists have slapped us with another series of worrisome Gaps. Some of the material to follow is admittedly "obscene," concerned as it is with reducing death and misery to numbers. However, since our government leaders claim that Soviet "superiority" precludes an immediate freeze followed by balanced reductions, it is important to answer them in their own terms. Here are the numbers:

|  | Intercontinental Ballistic Missiles (ICBMs) | | Submarine-Launched Ballistic Missiles (SLBMs) | | Bombers | |
|---|---|---|---|---|---|---|
|  | missiles | warheads | missiles | warheads | planes | weapons |
| U.S. | 1052 | 2152 | 520 | 5000 | 316° | 2300 |
| U.S.S.R. | 1398 | 5500 | 960 | 2000 | 145°° | 290 |

° Not counting 31 additional B-52s on active inventory and 60 F-111s.
°° Not counting 70 medium-range Backfire bombers.

The question is, do these numbers mean anything? As Henry Kissinger pointed out during debate over SALT II, missiles don't kill anyone, warheads do. And we have about 9,400 strategic warheads to the U.S.S.R.'s 7,800. Not surprisingly, this Gap is only rarely noted by those who otherwise like to play the nuclear numbers game. Because of our lead in MIRV technology, we are able to place a larger number of warheads on a smaller number of missiles. Indeed, this is why the U.S. military agreed in the first place to a SALT I restriction in which the U.S.S.R. was permitted more ICBMs than we. Under SALT I, in fact, we went from 4,600 strategic warheads to over 9,000, while the U.S.S.R. went from 2,011 to about 4,000. During the 1970s, when, we are told, the Soviets pursued their unconscionable Gap-producing build-up, they added 4,560 warheads. We added 5,250. The Soviet Union has, in fact, been modernizing and expanding its strategic forces more vigorously than we had expected, and much more than is conducive to world peace. But this does not mean that our strategic mission of deterrence has in any way been compromised, especially since we are still far ahead in the "stuff" of deterrence—deliverable warheads. (This does not even consider another fact that U.S. Gap-publicists and the American public typically ignore, but which is painfully real to Soviet military planners: whereas the U.S. need only worry about Soviet warheads, the U.S.S.R. is targeted by missiles from Great Britain, France and China, in addition to the U.S. For example, France alone has about 100 strategic bombers, 5 nuclear submarines with 16 missiles each, and is busily MIRVing her land-based missiles.)

Other factors are relevant to the numbers game Gap, even looking only at the U.S. and the U.S.S.R.: although the Soviets have more submarine-launched missiles, they can only maintain about 15 percent of their vessels on station at any one time, largely because they lack mid-ocean stations and an extensive coastline, so that they must rely on long transit time from their very few all-year ports. By contrast, the U.S. has two long, uninterrupted coastlines plus an additional submarine base in Scotland. As a result, 55 percent of U.S. subs are cruising at all times, so that we have *more*, not fewer SLBMs effectively available. In addition, analysts estimate the "readiness" of U.S. strategic missiles at 95 percent, the U.S.S.R's at about 75 percent. The "reliability" of U.S. missiles is 75-80 percent; for Soviet missiles, it is 65-75 percent. The former measures the probability that a missile, once fired, will actually perform as expected, and the latter measures the percentage of existing missiles actually ready to be fired on command. In practice, a larger number of unready, unreliable missiles actually gives the U.S.S.R. a much weaker force than our slightly smaller number of missiles, which are more ready, more reliable, and much less vulnerable. On balance, we have a much larger number of deliverable weapons.

Pentagon officials have played a classic game of having their cake and eating it too: intentionally keeping a lid on the actual number of our own ICBMs while increasing strategic forces by MIRVing those same ICBMs as well as SLBMs. At the same time, they have bewailed the fact that we have fewer missiles than the U.S.S.R., and used these comparisons as an argument for augmenting our strategic forces yet further.

Strategic bombers deserve some mention, if only because many Americans, incredibly, seem convinced that ours are inferior to theirs. Nothing could be more untrue. The 150 Soviet bombers are basically unchanged from the mid-1950s. Indeed, more than two-thirds of their strategic bomber force are "Bears," still propeller-driven! By contrast, our 316 B-52s have been constantly upgraded, with new engines and armaments, millions of dollars in antiradar and missile-baffling devices, as well as the forthcoming addition of Air-Launched Cruise Missiles. For years, it has been almost obligatory to preface any journalistic account of our B-52s with the adjectives "obsolete," "ancient," or "1950s vintage," whereas in reality they stand unchallenged as the premier bomber fleet in the world. During the Vietnam War, B-52s flying over Hanoi—probably the most heavily defended region in the world—suffered an attrition rate of about 3 percent. In other words, 97 percent of the airplanes successfully reached their targets. It seems likely that since the Soviet border is so vast, it will be less well defended than North Vietnam, and if anything, the effectiveness of B-52s should be even greater.°

For some reason, numbers have cogency in evaluating purported Gaps, and therefore the analysis you are now reading is well-stocked with numbers. However, we should all realize that in

° Moreover, bomber effectiveness would be further enhanced since in the event of nuclear war, they would not arrive at their targets until after heavy U.S. missile attacks have destroyed Soviet air defense bases, radars, and communication systems.

fact, these numbers are simply irrelevant. Thus, both sides have passed far beyond the strength needed for deterrence—a single Poseidon submarine, for example, can deliver 160 to 224 independently targeted warheads. Sixty percent of these warheads are 40 kiloton weapons (three times the Hiroshima bomb) and the remaining 40 percent are now Trident I weapons with 100 kilotons each (seven times the Hiroshima bomb). In all the U.S.S.R., there are only 218 cities with a population of 100,000 or more. And we have 31 Poseidon submarines of which 12 have just been back-fitted with Trident missiles. Moreover, we are moving toward a projected fleet of 12 Trident submarines, of which a single vessel will carry 24 missiles, each MIRVed with up to 17 maneuverable warheads—resulting in 408 deliverable nuclear bombs per submarine, each bomb with several times the blast power of the Hiroshima bomb. Both the U.S. and U.S.S.R. clearly have massive overkill, exceeding any needs for deterrence. Overkill was defined, non-numerically, by James Real as "throwing another bucket of gasoline on a baby who is already burning nicely." The overkill capacity of both sides is such that counting the number of full, available buckets hardly seems important—although, to be sure, if we choose to count, we find once again that our side is far ahead.

## b. The Size Gap—Throw-weight and Megatonnage

There is a strategic megatonnage Gap: Soviet strategic warheads carry the destructive power of about 7,000 megatons (million tons of TNT), whereas U.S. strategic warheads total about 4,000 megatons. (Overkill fans may want to note that our arsenal alone computes to more than one ton of TNT for every man, woman and child on earth; counting the tactical arsenal as well, the figure is more than doubled.) But this Soviet "lead" was intentional on our part. We are quite capable of making enormous, multimegaton bombs; the fact that theirs are generally larger than ours is no indication that they are somehow "ahead." During the 1960s, American strategic planners intentionally opted for smaller, more numerous warheads, because of the great technological advantage we had (and still have) in *accuracy*. In strategic planning, accuracy is much more important than brute megatonnage. Analysts compute a value known as "lethality," by considering both megatonnage (the size of the bang) and "Circular Error Probable" (a measure related to accuracy). According to the physics of bombs, a large increase in megatonnage results in a less than proportional increase in lethality. At the same time, an increase in accuracy results in a much greater than proportional increase in lethality: multiply accuracy by ten, and you increase lethality by 100. The upshot of all this—well known to strategic planners on both sides— is that a favorable trade-off can be·made, increasing lethality by improving accuracy, while sacrificing megatonnage. Soviet planners would love to have our smaller, more accurate missiles. Lacking the necessary technology, they have had to settle for larger, clumsier ones.

For a practical example of this seemingly arcane principle, as close as today's headlines, consider the new Pershing II missile. With its 1,500-mile range, it can reach Moscow from West Germany, causing consternation to the Soviet Union and to many Europeans as well. The greatly improved navigation system installed on the Pershing II made it possible to reduce the megatonnage in the warhead, thereby saving weight. In turn, this reduction in weight permitted extra fuel and the capability to reach Moscow from long range.

Making a bomb twice as accurate is equivalent to making it eight times as powerful. We could easily have big bombs too, just like the U.S.S.R.; we chose not to do so, because we could make ours more lethal by going for accuracy instead. For example, the Minuteman II missile, with a single warhead of one megaton and CEP of .3 miles, had a lethality of 11. Its replacement, the Minuteman III, has individual warheads of 170 kilotons (about one-sixth that of the older model), but a CEP of .2 miles, giving a lethality per warhead of 7.6, more than one-half that of the older model. But in addition, the Minuteman III is MIRVed, with three separate warheads, giving a total lethality of 23. So, by MIRVing and increasing accuracy by one-third, the U.S. more than doubled its Minuteman lethality, even though the total megatonnage has been *reduced* from one to .54. Even this increase in lethality is now being overtaken by technology as the Minuteman IIIs are being upgraded with Mark 12-A warheads. This new system has a yield of 340 kilotons and a CEP of merely .1 for a lethality that is greater yet. Progress indeed!

For similar reasons, our projected strategic arsenal for 1985 will have grown to about 15,000 warheads, while the total megatonnage will actually *decline*. So here is a familiar Gap tactic, back again: introduce more accurate warheads, which permit a reduction in the strength of each warhead—and then point to this lowering in megatonnage as evidence that we have been unilaterally disarming!

The throw-weight Gap is perhaps the epitome of throwaway Gaps, closely related to the megatonnage Gap, both in origin and in absurdity. Thus, larger warheads (more megatonnage) generally weigh more, and hence, they require a missile of greater throw-weight. Proponents of the throw-weight Gap point out that the U.S. has nothing to compare with the throw-weight of the Soviet SS-18. And they are right: the SS-18 can transport 16,000 pounds, and our Minuteman IIIs, "only" 2,000 lbs. The proposed MX, which will be our largest missile (if deployed), has a throw-weight of 8,000 pounds. Yet, both the MX and the SS-18 carry 10 warheads; for that matter, so can the much smaller Trident missile. As we have seen, the Soviets have elected to invest in large missiles not because they are ahead of us in rocket technology, but rather, because they are *behind*. (Note, for example, that the Minuteman missiles are smaller than the Atlas and Titans, which they replaced.) Specifically, the U.S.S.R. is behind in microminiaturization and the technology required for pinpoint accuracy. The large, particularly scary Soviet missiles therefore result from a *weakness* in their strategic posture, not a strength; hence, it is both absurd and irresponsible to point to the throw-weight Gap as evidence of a Russian lead.

## c. The Missile Replacement Gap

A glance at Soviet missile deployment during the past fifteen years can give the impression that they have greatly outpaced us in the introduction of new models. Thus, their strategic arsenal reads like an ever-increasing pyramid of numbers: SS-9, SS-11, SS-13, SS-17, SS-18 and SS-19, plus five new models of submarine-launched ballistics missiles, the SS-N-5, 6, 8, 17, and 18. By contrast, we have just been sitting around, it seems, with our absolete Titan IIs and rusty old Minutemen.°

° The following discussion will leave aside the question of what obsolescence even means in the case of the Titan II, for example, ready to "deliver" its nine megaton warhead—700 times more powerful than the Hiroshima bomb—at more than ten times the speed of sound.

In fact, U.S. strategic missiles have regularly been upgraded and modernized. The Minuteman I and Titan II were deployed in a crash program during the early 1960s, as part of our response to the mythic missile Gap. The second generation Minuteman, the Minuteman II, was introduced in 1966, replacing 450 of the MM Is. The other 550 were replaced by a yet newer model, the Minuteman III, in 1970; the MM III was the world's first MIRVed ICBM, carrying three 170 kiloton warheads, each of which is three times more accurate than the Minuteman II, and seven times more accurate than the Titan II. In 1979, the Mark 12-A warheads were introduced, this time doubling the accuracy and increasing the yield per warhead from 170 to 335 kilotons.

During our period of supposed inactivity in the 1970s, we also finished development of the Trident submarine and Trident missiles, further developed the satellite global positioning program, the MX missile and the B-1 bomber. We have now developed and deployed 79 nuclear attack submarines, as compared to the U.S.S.R.'s 52, and none of theirs even approaches ours in the ability to detect opponents at long range. President Reagan's call for "rearming" America suggests that we have been disarming up to now. This is simply untrue, just like his claim that the U.S.S.R. has achieved strategic "superiority."

The U.S. style has been to modify existing missiles; by contrast, the U.S.S.R. introduces entire new models to do the same thing. Hence, a catalogue of their new missiles makes it sound as though the U.S.S.R. is leaving us far behind, whereas in fact, nothing of the sort is happening. Their style—replacement instead of modernization—also costs more money. Thus, for example, the Mark 12-A modification cost the U.S. about $155 *million* whereas the U.S.S.R. deployed three new models (SS-17, SS-18 and SS-19) toward the same end, at an approximate cost of $28.5 *billion*. Although no one has ever accused Pentagon procurement officers of being tight-fisted, they have long sought to get the most "bang for the buck." Soviet counterparts may have their own equivalent goal ("more rubble for the ruble"?), but they are clearly less adroit at achieving it. Ironically, however, their *failures* provide fuel to those who like to point to both missile replacement and spending gaps. (This lower Soviet efficiency also further gives the lie to proponents of the throw-weight Gap, since the Mark 12-A modification, converting 170 kiloton warheads into 335 kilotons, added a total of only 35 pounds to the existing 2,000 pounds of throw-weight.)

### d. The Counterforce Gap

A favorite Gapper's claim is that we are facing a potential "window of vulnerability" sometime in the mid-1980s, when increased numbers and accuracy of Soviet missiles will make our land-based ICBM force vulnerable to attack. Of course, our *cities* have always been vulnerable to attack, just as theirs have. The new wrinkle is that an attack against U.S. missiles—a counter*force* attack as opposed to a counter*city* or counter*value* strike—would supposedly render us powerless to retaliate. The particular worst-case planner's nightmare goes as follows: the Soviets attack and destroy our Minuteman and Titan missiles, holding the remainder of their forces in reserve. They then announce that any retaliation on our part would be met with massive destruction of our cities, which are as yet untouched. Faced by such an ultimatum, the only rational response by the U.S. president would be to surrender, rather than launch our missiles to destroy millions of Russians, only to have millions of Americans incinerated in return. In support of this possible scenario, Secretary of Defense James Schlesinger testified before Congress in 1974 that a Soviet counterforce attack would produce "only" 800,000 American casualties. Hence, a "surgical" strike by Russian missiles could, in theory, deprive us of our ICBMs, while still leaving enough of the country intact to make surrender preferable to Armageddon.

There are several ways to analyze this claim. First, would U.S. civilian losses in a counterforce strike be so low as to make inaction a feasible response? Second, can such a counterforce strike be successfully executed? Third, if executed, would a counterforce strike leave us unable to respond? Fourth, are we more vulnerable than they—that is, does a counterforce Gap exist? And finally, what response should we make to the possibility of counterforce attacks?

It is now widely acknowledged—even by Schlesinger himself—that a Soviet counterforce attack would produce many more than 800,000 casualties. That original estimate had been based on many unrealistic assumptions, now discredited. For example, it was assumed that we would have thirty days warning to shelter the civilian population. Yet the whole idea of counterforce rests on *surprise*—if there was sufficient warning for the population to begin scurrying into shelters, then clearly the international situation would have become so tense that both sides would be prepared to launch their missiles on warning of attack, rather than waiting for an actual strike.

In addition, the low estimate assumed only one warhead per missile silo; this is absurd, since military worst-case analyses must assume occasional missile failure. Therefore, in order to have a high probability of destroying a silo, at least two warheads must be exploded against it. Moreover, since ICBM silos are "hardened" with steel-reinforced concrete to withstand several thousand pounds of blast pressure per square inch, counterforce warheads must be groundbursts, rather than airbursts, so as to scoop out the targeted missile. But groundbursts also produce massive fallout. Current estimates from the U.S. Congress Office of Technology Assessment are that such an attack would cause two to twenty million civilian fatalities. For example, given the prevailing westerly winds, an attack on Whiteman Air Force Base in western Missouri would deposit lethal fallout on St. Louis, Louisville, Charleston, and quite possibly even Richmond and Washington, D.C. Agricultural losses would be staggering, since most ICBM bases are located near prime farmland. In short, the country would be devastated; any such attack that had any military significance would necessarily cause enormous civilian casualties. A "surgical" counterforce strike would be much closer to butchery, and no rational Soviet leader could plan that the U.S. leadership would not respond to it. (The possibility of irrational leadership cannot ever be discounted, but then again, the whole structure of nuclear deterrence assumes rationality—presumably, no rational leader would order an attack which would result in destruction of his own country. The germ of counterforce Gapism is that a counterforce attack might be attractive to a *rational* decision-maker; hence, it is appropriate for us to examine the rational bases for such a claim.)

The second question is: regardless of its likely effects, can such a strike be successfully executed? There are many reasons to doubt it. For example, the necessity of using at least two warheads per silo introduces a new imponderable: fratricide. The first exploding warhead will generate thousands of tons of flying matter, plus enormous heat, shock waves and electromagnetic pulse. Neither we nor

Soviet planners can know the effect of one exploding warhead on the next incoming one, but it seems likely that its accuracy and reliability will be decreased.

In addition to fratricide, there is the imponderable of missile accuracy: in an actual attack, missiles must be fired over the North Pole, something never yet attempted—simply because neither side would tolerate a "test" that might actually turn out to be the real thing! Both the U.S. and U.S.S.R. have well-established missile testing zones in the Pacific and Siberia. In the event of World War III, we know that we could blow up Kwajalein Island, since we have been shooting missiles at it for years. But neither we nor the Soviets can know whether our missiles would perform as expected when fired at each other, over the North Pole. A polar route would pass through regions of novel geo-magnetic patterns, whose effects on missile guidance systems cannot be predicted. This uncertainty is important, because to be effective (and hence attractive to planners), a counterforce attack must be virtually 100 percent successful. Imagine an initial surprise barrage, that leaves the victim with even a small number of operational missiles, MIRVed to the hilt, and very angry!

Finally, there is an enormous difference between theoretical calculations of success in a counterforce strike and the reality of actually pulling one off successfully. Theoreticians live in a dream world of probability calculations and computer printouts, somewhat removed from the actual world of breakdowns, misunderstanding, a whole range of snafus that are individually unpredictable but absolutely certain in the aggregate. Analysts calculate a "probability of kill" for hard targets such as silos by first calculating the lethality, then adding a fudge factor for reliability and readiness. The appropriate numbers can then be read from a circular slide rule, available to anyone from the RAND Corporation (1700 Main St., Santa Monica, Calif. 90406). Just set the megatonnage and CEP, and you can read out such useful information as the number of warheads required to achieve 99 percent probability of kill, the crater radius and depth, the amount of blast overpressure generated at various distances from the point of impact, and so forth. Then, multiply by the number of land-based ICBMs and *presto*, you have a "window of vulnerability." These are the sort of unreal, theoretical calculations upon which counterforce Gaps are based. But a national leader would have to be literally insane to think that such numbers could be translated directly into reality.

Executing a successful simultaneous attack on more than 1,000 target silos would require unheard-of coordination, secrecy, and the total absence of failures. Even a simple computer program almost invariably reveals numerous "bugs" once it is tested; a counterforce strike would be like installing a massive, totally new computer network, requiring literally thousands of relays, new programs, storage, transfer, communications and action systems, and then betting your life that it would work perfectly the first time. Even without the traditional conservatism of military worst-case planning, we must conclude that neither side can be planning a counterforce attack.

Let us now make an extraordinarily worst-case assumption: a successful counterforce attack has occurred. Are we unable to respond? First, consider the B-52 fleet. During operation "Global Shield" in February 1981, several hundred B-52s were successfully launched in less than ten minutes. Although in a real attack some would doubtless be caught on the ground, a formidable arsenal would be airborne, and since they could all be recalled if the attack was a false alarm, there would be little U.S. hesitancy in getting them into the air if need be. Furthermore, about 50 percent of our submarines are on ocean patrol at any given time, and these are invulnerable to any counterforce attack. Just one such vessel could devastate the U.S.S.R. in retaliation, and we always have more than 15 available, not even counting the forthcoming Trident submarines. The U.S. strategic deterrence rests on a "triad," three legs which are about equal in strength, although not in vulnerability. The land-based ICBMs are clearly the most vulnerable (although as we have seen, not nearly as vulnerable as some have claimed). But the bombers are much less vulnerable and the submarines are totally safe once at sea and submerged. Indeed, when it comes to antisubmarine warfare, former navy secretary Graham Clayton concluded that "the qualitative edge that we hold over the Soviets in both equipment and personnel is awesome." Carl Levin, of the Senate Armed Services Committee, adds that "Soviet open ocean ASW (antisubmarine warfare) capabilities are extremely limited if not non-existent. . . . This technological advantage carries into every facet of acoustic ASW, including surface ship, submarine and aircraft sensors and weapons."

As a mental exercise, let us assume the most extreme case, a "perfect" Soviet counterforce attack—possible in theory only: all U.S. land-based ICBMs are gone, 70 percent of the B-52s and 45 percent of the submarines (all those in port at any one time). The U.S. is still left with 3,500 strategic warheads.

Finally, American capacity to respond to a counterforce attack is not limited to our designated strategic weapons; there are also 10,000 or so forward-based tactical nuclear weapons, including thousands aboard aircraft carriers and missile cruisers, 700 land-based in Korea and at least another 1,000 elsewhere in Asia. Even a small fraction of these could easily destroy any aggressor. We could in fact unilaterally destroy more than 90 percent of our nuclear weaponry, then absorb an absolutely perfect worst-case attack, exceeding a counterforce Gapper's worst imagining, and still retain enough firepower to devastate the U.S.S.R. several times over. The worst imaginable counterforce attack still leaves us with more than enough to deter such an attack, simply because land-based ICBMs are only a small part of the U.S. nuclear deterrence. It is worth noting, however, that there *is* a real counterforce Gap. It is not the U.S., but rather the *Soviet* deterrence force which is more vulnerable. There are two reasons for this: for one, unlike the balanced American strategic triad, the Soviet Union relies disproportionately upon its land-based ICBMs; these comprise about 75 percent of their deterrence. By contrast, 24 percent of the U.S. strategic warheads are on ICBMs, 26 percent in B-52 bombers and 50 percent submarine-based. At any one time, only 15 to 20 percent of the Soviet Union's submarine-launched ballistics missiles are at sea, comprising 3 to 5 percent of their strategic warheads; by contrast, 26 to 30 percent of U.S. warheads are submerged at all times and hence safe against any surprise attack. For another, the American arsenal is both more abundant and more accurate. The cruise missile, MX and new generation Trident missiles are each more accurate than any Soviet counterparts, and it is accuracy that makes counterforce even a theoretical possibility. For example, the MX (model 2) will have a "probability of kill" of 99 percent; the most effective potential Soviet counterforce weapon, the SS-19, scores much less. Accuracy of U.S. sea-launched missiles is currently maintained by the Transit system, 6 satellites 500 miles above the earth, which can position a submarine to within 50 yards. The Navstar satellite system is currently being installed, with 12 satellites to be established in 12,500-mile polar orbits in 1981; when 12 more are added by 1985, this system will be able to update a missile's path in flight, achieving three-dimensional precision within 30 feet of a target. Although ostensibly slated as a navigation aid, the military significance of Navstar is clear to anyone who looks. If (when?) Trident II missiles are linked to this system, the result would be a counterforce capability that greatly exceeds anything that the U.S.S.R. seems likely to achieve during this century.

But there is no reason to take comfort in our "counterforce advantage," because the ability to threaten the other side's deterrence is dangerous to both sides, and offers security to neither side. In fact, it makes both sides less safe. You don't need a Ph.D. in military strategy to see why: if the U.S. develops weaponry that has a high probability of destroying Soviet missiles while still in their silos, then in times of crisis or panic, the Soviets will be more likely to launch their missiles preemptively. They would be forced to "use 'em or lose 'em."

Perhaps the crowning lunacy is the claim that weapons such as the MX, Trident II, or cruise missile need their great accuracy so as to be credible "second-strike counterforce weapons"—that is, following a hypothetical Soviet surprise counterforce attack, we should have the ability to eliminate their remaining missiles. But imagine that the Soviets have just launched such an attack: surely, they would expect retaliation and would place their remaining missiles on alert, to be launched on the slightest warning of our attack. Hence, having a second-strike counterforce ability is a sure way to guarantee that if deterrence fails, *all* of the U.S.S.R.'s missiles will come hurtling against the U.S. A more self-defeating "defense" can hardly be imagined. And yet, at the urging of today's counterforce Gappers, we are now busily designing and deploying systems which are themselves counterforce weapons.

As we have seen, it is very unlikely that either side could execute a successful counterforce strike, and equally unlikely that either side is planning to do so. But by scaring us into belief in a nonexistent window of vulnerability and—worse yet—inducing us to respond by deploying a counterforce threat of our own, the Gappers do us all an immense disservice.

There is no more dangerous situation than having both sides armed to the teeth bellowing threats at each other, and also scared as hell that the other side might strike first. It makes even the nervous decades of the 1950s, 1960s and 1970s seem utterly serene by contrast, since as long as each side retained the ability to obliterate the other's cities—no matter who struck first—each was deterred. But in the 1980s each side is becoming anxious that the other may eliminate its deterrence by a counterforce first strike. The more both sides worry about it, and the more each promote fears of a counterforce Gap, the more likely it becomes that in times of crisis, someone *will* strike first. Counterforce strikes are most likely *not* when the attacker is strong but rather, when it is weak—that is, when it fears for the survivability of its missiles. Hence, the last thing we should do is threaten their missiles. And yet, this is precisely what we are planning to do. There is perhaps no more urgent problem in the world today.

### The "Civil Defense" Gap

When it comes to "civil defense," the only thing more absurd than our own ridiculous efforts is our worry that the Soviets are ahead of us—with theirs! If there was an effective defense against nuclear war (which there isn't), then in fact, a civil defense Gap—if real—would be a legitimate worry. One possible U.S. strategic planner's nightmare was spelled out by General Daniel O. Graham, former director of the Defense Intelligence Agency, and a professional Gapper:

> The Soviets evacuate their cities and hunker down. Then they move against NATO or Yugoslavia or China or the Middle East with superior conventional forces. The US is faced with the demand to stay out or risk nuclear exchange in which 100 million Americans would die, as opposed to 10 million Russians.

On the surface, this seems plausible—all Gap-pap seems plausible on the surface. It is generally acknowledged, for example, that the

U.S.S.R. spends more money on "civil defense" than does the U.S. Moreover, they are said to have 100,000 full-time "civil defense" employees and extensive evacuation plans in which each urban resident is assigned a specific evacuation area or an identified collective farm. In turn, each collective farmer supposedly has a list of those city-dwellers assigned to him. American officials also hint darkly of the "dispersal" of Soviet industry, even the possible establishment of entire underground cities. The image is of a dug-in, armor-plated society, ready to absorb our Sunday punch, to be contrasted with our own feeble level of soft-bellied preparedness.

Former Secretary of Defense Harold Brown commented on the possibility that the Soviets might beef up their civilian shelter program and that if so, we should do the same: "There is little reason to believe that this will confer a significant advantage in the event of a nuclear war. The way to counter a relatively ineffective system is not to replicate it. . . ." Worry about a "civil defense" Gap is bad enough. If either side comes to believe that it can survive a nuclear war, this would be immeasurably worse, since it could undermine deterrence, make prudence less likely, and war more likely.

Aside from the fact that nuclear war simply cannot be "defensed," the reality is that the U.S.S.R. is no less vulnerable than we, and probably more so. Indeed, they have done somewhat more "civil defense" planning than we, much of this attributable to their history of being invaded, which has produced an obsession with defense. But all other factors operate against an effective Soviet "civil defense" posture.

For example, the U.S.S.R. is a highly centralized society. As a result, their nation can easily be destroyed by only a small number of warheads. Although the U.S. is smaller in total area, the nation as a whole is actually more dispersed. Transportation in the U.S.S.R. is largely by electrified rail; destruction of a relatively small number of fixed, easily-targeted power plants would paralyze the entire country. U.S. transportation, by contrast, is more individualized, relying primarily on trucks. Soviet roads are much worse than in the U.S.; would-be evacuees would probably have to walk.

The latest Russian Five Year Plan allocates two-thirds of revenues for modernizing existing plants, not for building new ones. In the U.S.S.R. all chemical plants are concentrated in 25 cities, 60 percent of all steel is made in just 25 plants, there are only 34 major oil refineries, 8 copper refineries, 6 turbine manufacturing plants, 8 major shipbuilding works, 16 heavy machine plants, 15 manufacturers of major agricultural equipment, and only 5 power plants for the entire central and Volga regions. Materials for the crucial Siberian powerplant transmission line are all made in just 4 cities: Moscow, Leningrad, Kharkov and Riga. The gigantic Karma River truck and auto complex, about the size of Manhattan, makes over one-fifth of all Soviet motor vehicles. In short, the Soviet economic style has favored "gigantomania," yielding a small number of vulnerable targets in the event of war. The list could go on, but the point should by now be clear.

In fact, because the Soviet economy is weaker than ours it has substantially less "fat," so that any major losses would be truly devastating. Their centralized system already suffers from numerous "choke points" which impede development. These bottlenecks are particularly vulnerable to nuclear attack. The CIA noted in 1978 that Soviet civil defense efforts "would not prevent massive damage from an attack designed to destroy Soviet economic facilities." Moreover, they concluded: "We do not believe that the Soviets' present civil defenses will embolden them deliberately to expose the U.S.S.R. to a higher risk of nuclear attack." All other intelligence agencies agreed with this.

Granted that the Soviet economy could not survive a nuclear war, what about "defense" of the Soviet population? Russian cities are more concentrated than ours. In fact, they are typically about one-half the area of comparable American cities. A higher proportion of Russians live in apartment houses (as opposed to the American passion for dispersed, private dwellings); as a result, the Russians are more subject to blast effects and the demolition of buildings. Because of the relatively poor transportation system, a higher proportion of Soviet citizens live near their work rather than in the suburbs, once again making them easier targets. In fact, if the U.S. lost all of its bombers, all of its ICBMs and fully one-half of its submarines in a Soviet surprise attack, we could still destroy 3 percent of the Soviet land area. The major Soviet cities occupy about one-quarter of 1 percent.

A CIA report released in July 1978 concluded that about 12-24 percent of the total Soviet work force could be accomodated in shelters, and possibly about 10-20 percent of the total urban population. Looked at another way, this means that 88-76 percent of the work force could *not* even theoretically be accomodated in shelters; similarly, 80-90 percent of the urban population would be out in the cold. (And it is also worth noting that Russian winters are indeed cold, much colder and longer than anything U.S. survivors would encounter.) The U.S. Arms Control and Disarmament Agency estimated in December 1978 that blast shelters for the Soviet population *might* reduce fatalities by one-fifth, but that by targeting evacuation areas and using groundbursts to produce large amounts of lethal fallout, the population of the U.S.S.R. would be decimated no less than our own.

Former CIA director Stansfield Turner concluded there was "little evidence today of serious efforts at mass indoctrination of the population." In fact, there is every sign that the average Russian takes his government's civil defense propaganda about as seriously as we do ours. In Russian, civil defense in *grazhdanskaya oborona.* Take the first two letters from each word and you get the makings of a widespread Russian joke: they call their civil defense *grob,* which in Russian means coffin. Another joke goes as follows— Ivan: "Do you know what to do when the Bomb drops?" Yuri: "Sure, take your belongings and walk quietly to the cemetry." Ivan: "Why quietly?" Yuri: "We don't want to get people worried, do we?"

Just as Americans can readily be scared by tales of theoretical Russian "civil defense" planning and preparedness, it may well be that the Soviets take ours seriously as well. And *on paper,* our plans seem impressive. Thus, the Federal Emergency Management Agency, currently charged with U.S. civil defense, has officially identified shelter for 230 million Americans and plans to protect 80 percent of the population from attack. Unknown to most Americans, the Federal Reserve Bank maintains emergency headquarters 650 feet under Hutchinson, Kansas, in the warehouse of an abandoned salt mine. There, microfiche copies of the nation's bank records are updated daily. Civil Defense manuals exist for virtually all industries. The 1978 U.S. Government "Disaster Planning Guide for Business and Industry" urges that the private sector do its civic duty to protect financial records, establish alternate headquarters and make lists of succession for top management. Some firms have been doing just that: from the early 1960s until 1975, Shell Oil maintained a three-story alternate company headquarters, complete with clinic, laundry and kitchen, buried inside a mountain in upstate New York. Section I, Article I of the Exxon Corporation's bylaws provide that the firm can operate on a reduced quorum "during an emergency . . . resulting from an attack on the United States or any nuclear or atomic disaster/or from an imminent threat of such an attack or disaster."

Not to be outdone, AT&T has established an underground emergency center, chiseled through 40 feet of solid granite in Netcong, New Jersey—close enough to New York so that the top executives presumably can arrive in time, but far enough away to escape being vaporized with the rest of the hoi polloi. Inside, AT&T telephones, desks, and computer terminals are all empty and waiting for the busy signal. Delicate switching equipment is mounted from the stone ceiling by huge rubber bands—to withstand the expected shock waves—and an AT&T official was quoted in the June 17, 1981, *Wall Street Journal* extolling Ma Bell's ingenious plans to keep the telephones ringing: "If New York were knocked out, somebody in Boston could still call Washington, perhaps by way of San Francisco."

If the charade wasn't so potentially dangerous, it would be downright comic, although we might wonder whether Ivan and Yuri would appreciate the joke. Thus, MGM is defending itself against nuclear war by storing hundreds of old movie negatives in deep crypts maintained by Underground Vaults and Storage, Inc. Citicorp and Mobil Oil are also partaking of the new underground movement, and it is indeed reassuring to know that even if its customers are all blown away, Pizza Hut has had the foresight to store its franchise records!

In the now-classical 1964 movie *Dr. Strangelove, or How I learned to Stop Worrying and Love the Bomb,* one of the climactic comic scenes shows agitated high-level politicians worrying about a "mineshaft Gap." In an equally classic case of reality imitating fiction, the U.S. Congress was actually briefed on a possible mineshaft Gap, eight years later.

Official U.S. manuals advise us not to forget our "credit cards, social security cards, sanitary napkins, wills and savings account books" as we respond to a "national emergency." And publication H-20 from the Defense Civil Preparedness Agency, titled *Protec-*

*tion in the Nuclear Age,* advises: "If you get caught in a traffic jam, turn off your engine, remain in your car, listen for official instructions, and be patient. Do not get out of the line to find an alternate route. All routes will be crowded." Going now to the truly ridiculous, Richard T. Barnet recalls a civil defense manual from the early 1960s titled "How to find a Job in the Post-Attack Environment." On the cover was a cheerful government official behind a desk; in front of him an applicant was filling out a form. Behind him, a mushroom cloud was just beginning to disperse. The U.S. Postal Service has even printed Emergency Change of Address Cards, Form 809, to be sent in (postage free, mind you!) in the event of a nuclear war.

Responsible government officials on both sides recognize that "civil defense" makes no sense. But even if they have the good judgement to see through their own posturings and propaganda, they may nonetheless take each other's seriously. What seems ludicrous when done by one's own country suddenly seems ominous when done by the other side." Civil defense" itself merits no credibility; the "civil defense" Gap deserves, if anything, even less.

## The War-Winning Doctrine Gap

Richard Pipes, the hawk from Harvard now an influential national security adviser to the White House, announced recently that "the Soviet Union thinks it can fight and win a nuclear war." This claim, reiterated by President Reagan, ushers in a new and particularly pernicious Gap—a supposed doctrinal Gap about whether nuclear war can be won. Deterrence has long been the cornerstone of our fragile nuclear peace, based on the notion that neither side would start a nuclear war because if it did, both sides would be destroyed. Obviously, if either side believed that it could fight and win such a war, then that side might no longer be deterred.

Even more troublesome, perhaps: if we believe that the U.S.S.R. seriously expects to win a nuclear war, then this can spur the U.S. into 1) increased, useless, investment in "civil defense"; 2) increased, dangerous, investment in even more destructive nuclear weaponry—to convince the U.S.S.R. that they could not, in fact, win—which in turn would only spur the Soviets to a reaction of building yet more weaponry themselves; or, most dangerous yet, 3) initiating a nuclear war against them before they can do the same against us. Thus, if our leaders become convinced that the Russians are no longer inhibited against attacking us, then we may automatically become less inhibited about attacking them, since by attacking we are just "getting it over with" sooner and maybe by surprising them, we will come out of it less badly than otherwise.

And finally, for an even more bizarre twist: if the Soviets become convinced of *our* belief that they (the Soviets) can win a war, then they might be more likely to strike us first, since to their thinking, we might be moving toward a first strike, as just described. (Believe it or not, tortured reasoning like this really does occupy strategic planners, on both sides!) A crucial question therefore becomes: do the Soviets really believe that they can win a nuclear war?

This claimed Gap is based on two things, both of them misunderstandings. For one, Russian military thinkers outspokenly admire Karl von Clausewitz, the Prussian strategist of war who maintained that "war is the continuation of policy by other means." But a central part, perhaps *the* central part of Clausewitzian doctrine is that "since war is not an act of senseless passion but is controlled by its political object, the value of that object must determine the sacrifices to be made for it in magnitude and also in duration. Once the expenditure of effort exceeds the value of the political object, the object must be renounced and peace must follow." This message should actually be rather reassuring to the West, since love of their homeland makes it clear that no political gain would warrant the sacrifice of Mother Russia.

The other basis for the supposed Russian belief in war-winning is the manual *Military Strategy* by Marshall V. D. Sokolovskiy. In short this book claims that whereas the U.S.S.R. does not seek war, it would fight if necessary and if so, it fully expects to win. We must realize that the Soviets had been under unceasing pressure since the late 1950s, accused by Maoist China of "revisionism." When Sokolovskiy wrote, in 1961, the U.S.S.R. was outnumbered in warheads, bombers and missiles by about ten to one. It was a stage of U.S.-Soviet relations characterized by Khrushchev's bluff and bluster, designed to compensate for a very real strategic inferiority.

There is no reason to accept such writings as accurately reflecting Soviet policy at that time. And it is simply inexcusable to read Sokolovskiy for a statement of *current* Soviet doctrine on war-winning.

In fact, the influential current texts, such as *Marxism-Leninism on War and Army,* and the journal *Military Thought* show neither warmongering nor an optimistic view of winning any future nuclear war. Rather, they reveal an obsessive fear of being attacked, not itself greatly reduced since Sokolovskiy's day. On balance, there is at least as much horror and revulsion at the prospect of nuclear holocaust in their writings as in ours. Military thinkers dealing with nuclear weaponry on both sides have a difficult job: maintaining morale and support for a system that must never be used. One way of succeeding—on both sides—is to suggest that, just possibly, exercising their profession might not be suicidal. Ironically, giving that impression too well might itself be a contributing step toward that suicide.

Most Soviet public officials have actually been quite explicit about the consequences of nuclear war. At the first SALT negotiating session in Helsinki, November 18, 1969, the Soviet chief delegate said in his opening statement: "Even in the event that one of the sides were the first to be subjected to attack, it would undoubtedly retain the ability to inflict a retaliatory strike of crushing power. Thus, evidently, we all agree that war between our two countries would be disastrous for both sides. And it would be tantamount to suicide for the ones who decided to start such a war." Since the Soviet rulers keep a very tight reign on the actions and pronouncements of their negotiators, we must assume that these sentiments were written, or at least, cleared by the very top leadership.

A group of American doctors, known as Physicians for Social Responsibility, has been conducting an increasingly successful program of public education regarding the ghastly medical consequences of nuclear war. Those attending the various PSR symposia, and even sometimes members of the press, have often asked whether comparable efforts were being made to inform the average Soviet citizen that nuclear war could not be survived. The implication was that the controlled Soviet press would never permit dissemination of such information, presumably, once again, because

Soviet leadership claims that nuclear war could be won. An international organization has recently been formed, the International Physicians for the Prevention of Nuclear War. The U.S.S.R. sent a high-ranking delegation to the first meetings, headed by Dr. E. Chazov, Deputy Minister of Health and Brezhnev's personal cardiologist. These meetings described and documented the gruesome effects of all-out nuclear war, in mind-withering detail. Far from being suppressed in the Soviet Union, accounts of these findings were reported more widely even than by the U.S. press.

Upon his return to the U.S.S.R., interviews with Dr. Chazov appeared on the front pages of *Pravda* (circulation 10 million), *Komsomolskaya Pravda* (10 million), and *Izvestia* (8 million), and major articles were published in the *Literary Gazette* (2.5 million), and *Medical News* (1 million). The *Soviet Medical Gazette* wrote: "In the case of a nuclear war, a complete breakdown of the social structure would occur. Society would be reduced to ruins, to primordial chaos." In his interview with *Komsomolskaya Pravda* on April 10, 1981, Chazov was quoted as saying that the international physicians' community "understands that one cannot wait idly as the threat to the very life of mankind hangs over every day of existence. But the broad masses, of course, have not fully realized all the horrors which such a war can bring. And the importance of our movement is especially to bring the truth of the catastrophic consequences of nuclear conflict to the public."

Dr. Chazov provided the Russian public with detailed accounts of those consequences, describing the results if a one megaton bomb exploded on a city of one million persons: about one-third would be killed instantly, another third seriously injured. He explained that there would be virtually no medical care available for the others, adding "even those who survive will die slowly." This somber message, quite different from a belief in the winnability of nuclear war, was vigorously *promoted* by the Soviet government. Thus, Chazov even appeared on the television show "Vremya," which has over 100 million Soviet viewers. His message: "In our age of thermonuclear power, man has at his disposal nuclear weapons capable not only of annihilating enormous numbers of people, but also, for all practical purposes, capable of destroying the very foundations of life in general."

If the Soviet government wanted to condition its people for

fighting and somehow winning a nuclear war, the controlled media certainly wouldn't expose the public to such material.

In an interview with *Pravda,* published in October 1981, Brezhnev said "Among ourselves we are saying . . . that it is a dangerous madness to try to defeat each other in the arms race and to count on victory in a nuclear war. Only he who has decided to commit suicide can start a nuclear war in the hope of emerging a victor from it." What clearer message can be sent? And yet, on the very same page reporting this interview a major Seattle newspaper headlined another article: "Russians Feel They Can Win Nuclear War, Claims Reagan." The Soviet Union has made its position abundantly clear, again and again, and yet U.S. hawks simply keep trumpeting the same scary line, imputing an attitude to the Soviets which they explicitly reject.

If there is a "war-winning doctrine Gap," then regrettably, U.S. hawks have contributed greatly to it, not only by misrepresenting the Russians, but by staking out their own dangerous and untenable position on this issue. To be sure, high-ranking American officials have, in the past, understood that nuclear war is not winnable. Thus, Douglas MacArthur wrote that "war has become a Frankenstein to destroy both sides. . . . No longer does it possess the chance of the winner of the duel—it contains, rather, the germs of double suicide." And JFK was equally clear in 1961: "Mankind must put an end to war—or war will put an end to mankind." But there have always been those who felt that the risk was somehow tolerable, and that in any event, we should strive for victory. Consider this gem from Richard Russell, when he was chairman of the Senate Armed Services Committee: "If we have to start all over again with Adam and Eve, then I want them to be Americans and not Russians."

Senator Russell is no longer alive to propound his peculiar vision of nuclear war-winning, but his intellectual descendants are still with us, and with the election of Ronald Reagan in 1980, "thinkers" of this sort now occupy the upper echelons of U.S. policy-making. Thus, Colin S. Gray, former Director for National Security Studies at the prestigious and oft-consulted Hudson Institute, wrote the following in an article titled "Nuclear Strategy: The case for a theory of victory," appearing in the journal *International Security:* "Any American president should know that the only kind of war his country can fight, and fight very well, is one where there is a clear concept of victory—analogically, the Marines raising the flag on Mount Suribachi is the way in which a president should think of American wars being terminated." And Paul Nitze, in the respected magazine *Foreign Affairs:* "The question of military or political victory if deterrence fails would depend upon the net surviving destructive capacity of the two sides. . . ." Mr. Nitze, former leader of The Committee on the Present Danger (more accurately, "The Committee on *Increasing* the Present Danger") was a leading opponent of SALT II and is now President Reagan's chief negotiator on European missile reductions.

During the 1980 presidential campaign, candidate George Bush echoed Nitze's line, claiming that victory in a nuclear war could be achieved by "survivability of command and control . . . of industrial potential, protection of a percentage of your citizens," and ". . . a capability that inflicts more damage on the opposition than it can inflict on you." During his confirmation hearings, when General Haig was asked whether the avoidance of nuclear war should be the prime goal of U.S. foreign policy, he replied that there are "some things that Americans should be willing to fight for." On the subject of nuclear war, there are indeed some things that Americans should be willing to fight for: one of them is that their officials leave no doubt about the unwinnability of nuclear war. At least, they should be as clear on this as their Soviet counterparts, whom they regularly ignore and misrepresent.

### The International Success Gap

Just as the grass is always greener on the other side of the fence, it seems that geopolitical success always looks greater on the other side of the Iron Curtain. Americans who look to a major military build-up in the 1980s are often captured by two assumptions: assumption #1 is that the U.S.S.R. has been riding a great wave of international successes in recent years. Assumption #2 is that this international success Gap has developed because we have allowed the Russians to close the military Gap between us. A third assumption follows: by massive new increases in our military strength, we can presumably reverse this Gap and recapture the geopolitical successes that are rightfully ours. All three of these assumptions are false; as we have already seen, the U.S.-Soviet military Gap has definitely not been closed, although it is closer than it once was. In any event, the U.S.S.R. has *not* been particularly successful in recent years (although, to be sure, neither have we). Finally, there is no evidence that international successes in recent years have correlated with the military strength of the two superpowers—certainly not their nuclear weaponry.

Americans have been shocked by the Soviet invasion of Afghanistan, humiliated by the American embassy held hostage in Iran, frustrated by repression in Poland. All this has contributed to a feeling of frustrated impotence, of being pushed around once too often, a worry about becoming what Richard Nixon called a "helpless, pitiful giant," while the U.S.S.R. goes about chalking up one international success after another. Let's stop for a moment, however, and try to see the world as it must look to the old men in the Kremlin: away to the east sits Japan, strongly allied to the U.S., the economic and technologic giant of Asia, and under increasing U.S. pressure to expand its military as well. To the southeast lies China, the world's most populous nation, formerly your close ally, and now your bitterest enemy, a nuclear power with whom you have a 4,500-mile border and an ongoing territorial dispute. Moving west, Pakistan is a right-wing military dictatorship, closely allied to the U.S. and China, and about to obtain nuclear weapons. The southern border merges into Islamic nations in which violently conservative Moslem fundamentalism is gaining ever greater power. The overthrow of the Shah, for example, is hardly comforting to the Soviets, who have more than 50 million potentially restless Moslems within their own borders. Iraq alternately embraces, then villifies the Kremlin, and Turkey is another right-wing military dictatorship, firmly in NATO. Even in Eastern Europe, maintained ever since World War II as a buffer against allied attack, the Albanians are overtly hostile, Czechoslovakia and Hungary are occupied nations, sullen and resentful, Yugoslavia is a leader of the nonaligned states, and Poland, the largest and strongest of non-Russian Warsaw Pact countries, is under control, but certainly not a friend. If the Kremlin was vaporized tomorrow, hardly a Lithuanian, Estonian, or Latvian would shed a tear. In short, the Soviet geopolitical situation is hardly a picture of comfortable security. In fact, there is only one nation on earth wholly surrounded by hostile Communist states—and that is the U.S.S.R.!

In the U.S. (as probably in the U.S.S.R. as well) there is a tendency to forget successes and dwell on failures. Thus, most Americans have forgotten that the Soviets sent about $1.5 billion in military aid to Indonesia in the early 1960s, only to be cast out utterly in 1965 along with a massacre of hundreds of thousands of communists. Similarly, they spent billions more wooing Egypt and once had 20,000 military advisers in that country; all were expelled in 1972 and Egypt (even without Sadat) is firmly in the U.S. camp. The Soviets spent about another billion dollars backing Somalia, after which they supported Ethiopia in a dispute with Somalia over the Ogaden region; as a result, the Somalis kicked the Russians out and offered us the enormous Russian-built naval base at Berbera. Angola and Mozambique have received extensive Soviet military aid, but in return, have refused Soviet requests for military bases. Vietnam and Cuba may appear to be ongoing triumphs, but they are also ongoing economic drains, costing several million dollars per day just to keep afloat; several more "successes" like these and the Kremlin will be bankrupt.

The spectacular tragedy of Vietnam has left many Americans with the impression of deteriorating power vis-a-vis the U.S.S.R. Nonetheless, a recent study by the respected Center for Defense Information, titled "Soviet Geopolitical Influence Around the World from 1945 to 1980," concluded that Soviet influence has *decreased* worldwide during that time. Out of 155 countries in the world, the U.S.S.R. has the allegiance of only 19. Moreover, the U.S. commands about 70 percent of the world's military and economic power.

The Russian occupation of eastern Europe after World War II left most Americans with the impression of an aggressive U.S.S.R., bent on world domination. In fact, Soviet actions strongly suggest that their motivation is overwhelmingly defensive, based partly on a paranoid view that the rest of the world—led by the U.S.—is out to get them. Russia was, after all, defeated by Japan at the beginning of the twentieth century, invaded by Germany in World War I, then invaded again by twenty Western nations (including U.S. forces) in 1920, intent on "strangling Bolshevism in its cradle," as Winston Churchill put it. They were then disastrously invaded once again by Hitler—not to mention the earlier depredations of Napoleon a century ago. If there is any theme to Soviet military defensiveness, it is "Never Again." Unfortunately, preparations that are intended as defensive by one side often appear offensive to the other.

On the question of Soviet military and political motivation, former CIA Director William Colby testified as follows before the Senate Foreign Relations Committee:

> You will find concern, even a paranoia, over their own security. You will find the determination that they shall never again be invaded and put through the kinds of turmoil that they have been under many different invasions. . . . I think that they . . . want to overprotect themselves to make certain that that does not happen, and they are less concerned about the image that presents to their neighbors, thinking that their motives are really defensive and pure and therefore other people should not be suspicious of them.

Certainly, the brutal suppression of revolts in Hungary (1956) and liberalizaton in Czechoslovakia (1968) seem far from pure; but it is important to remember that the Soviet leadership has been very cautious about commiting Russian troops abroad—both Hungary and Czechoslovakia involved efforts to maintain the *status quo*, since the U.S.S.R. perceives its European satellites as defensive buffers against the West. In both cases, military power was used *not* to achieve new, aggressive ends, but rather, to prevent a potential weakening of what they see as their defensive position. By contrast, the U.S. has been much less circumspect, in Korea, Iran, Guatemala, Lebanon, the Congo, Vietnam, Laos, the Dominican Republic, Cambodia, and El Salvador.

But what about Afghanistan? This Moslem nation has had a quietly pro-Soviet government since 1937. Then, a vigorously ideological Marxist takeover in 1977 generated stiff opposition from the conservative Islamic majority. These rebels began receiving aid from China, Egypt, Iran, Kuwait and Saudi Arabia in 1978; even the CIA sent supplies and guns. Moscow grew nervous that an avowedly *anti*-Soviet government might come to power, right on their vulnerable southern border. Their invasion of Afghanistan in December 1979 was brutal and in fact, stupid, but it was almost certainly *not* a move against either the U.S. or the Persian Gulf, any more than our tragic involvement in Vietnam was a move against the U.S.S.R.

The invasion of Afghanistan did not so much indicate Soviet aggressiveness, emboldened by their military strength, as it showed their *weakness* and their continuing paranoia about the security of their borders. Sitting as we are with an ocean between us and our opponents, bordered only by friendly Canada and Mexico, and not invaded by hostile armies since 1814, it is difficult for Americans to appreciate the sense of exposed, embattled vulnerability that pervades Soviet geopolitical thinking. The U.S.S.R. has extensive land borders with many different nations, most of them potentially or actively hostile. Their policy has been singlemindedly directed toward securing those borders, as in eastern Europe. Hence, although we are free to view their invasion of Afghanistan as a dastardly example of unending Soviet expansionism, this would be a tragic mistake—even more tragic, perhaps, than the invasion itself. This is not to excuse that invasion; however, we do ourselves and the cause of mutual survival a grave disservice if we mistake Soviet anxiety about their own security as a direct threat to ours. Moreover, it would be particularly tragic if we allow such actions to stampede us into further military posturing which will only increase Soviet anxiety and lead to more militarism and *reduced* security on both sides.

In many ways, the world is neither a peaceful nor a pleasant place. Certainly, it is a lot less tidy and less manageable than we might like. Gratuitous insults at the U.S., the infuriating ingratitude of our client states, the stubborn nationalism of two-bit groups we have never heard of, living in places we cannot even pronounce, make us want to reach for our gun. And in fact, to get an even bigger gun. But the old concepts of ideology and power don't explain very much anymore: some of the bitterest wars, for example, have recently been fought among Communists—China and Vietnam, Cambodia and Vietnam, and as the Falklands crisis has shown, not all enemies of the U.S.S.R. are friends of each other. Local nationalistic and religious issues are forcing major change, often violent and revolutionary: $20 billion in U.S. arms did nothing to save the Shah of Iran, and military power was equally useless to the feudalistic government of Ethiopia's Haile Selassie. Our defeat in Vietnam was admittedly military but not because we lacked military power; rather, because of the limits to what military power could achieve. This is especially true of nuclear military power—which leads us to the third fallacy of the "international success Gap," that by building up our nuclear arsenal we will somehow enhance our situation in the world.

Safely ensconced behind our nuclear Gap in the 1940s, we had hoped to brandish the Bomb and scare Russia out of eastern Europe. No such luck. Indeed, the history of U.S.-Soviet relations since Hiroshima makes it clear that our nuclear superiority does not make the Russians one bit more tractable. No matter how much we add to our nuclear arsenal, we can never again achieve anything even approaching the Gap we had in the late 1940s, throughout the 1950s, and even the 1960s. And yet during that time we had to deal with a coup in Czechoslovakia, the Berlin blockade, the defeat of Chiang in China, the Korean War, and Vietnam. Overwhelming nuclear superiority did us no good whatsoever, simply because nuclear weapons are so extreme and so dangerous as to be useless in directing the conduct of international affairs. As international lawyer Roger Fisher points out, making the world work by nuclear explosions is like making a marriage work by dynamite. Can we solve the crisis in northern Ireland by blowing up Belfast, or Dublin? Would we have kept the Shah in power by threatening to incinerate Teheran? For their part, would the Soviets gain anything by annihilating Kabul—or Warsaw for that matter? Imagine a policeman armed with an atomic bomb—could he stop a robbery? Nuclear weapons are simply too blunt to accomplish anything but mass destruction or at best, deterrence; expecting to use them to influence world affairs is like trying to fix a pocket watch with a sledge hammer.

"The nuclear bomb is the most useless weapon ever invented. It can be employed to no rational purpose," wrote George F. Kennan, former ambassador to the Soviet Union, and the dean of American diplomatic historians. "It is only something with which, in a moment of petulance or panic, you commit such fearful acts of destruction as no sane person would ever wish to have upon his conscience."

A true weapon is at best something with which you endeavor to affect the behavior of another society by influencing the minds, the calculations, the intentions, of the men that control it; it is not something with which you destroy indiscriminately the lives, the substance, the hopes, the culture, the civilization of another people.

We live in an era of preposterous overkill; although in fact we have more and better warheads, better available missiles, and more and better bombers than the Soviet Union, it would not matter if *they* did. If the U.S.S.R. could blow up the world one million times over, and we could only do it 900,000 times, this would not make us less secure than they. You can only die once. Moreover, it would not even give them greater leverage for achieving international successes. In a speech to the National Press Club, two weeks before Jimmy Carter took office, Henry Kissinger commented that since each side can annihilate the other, "What in the name of God, is strategic superiority? What is the signifince of it politically, militarily, operationally at these levels of numbers? What do you *do* with it?"

A recent study by the prestigious Brookings Institution, titled "Force Without War," examined 205 occasions between 1946 and 1975 when the United States used armed force to achieve political aims. It concluded that we did nothing at all with our strategic superiority. American international successes were not influenced at any time by the relative strengths of the U.S. and the U.S.S.R.

A frequent Reagan refrain during the 1980 campaign was that the U.S. has never gotten into a war because it was too strong. This is wrong: in the nineteenth century we got into both the Mexican-American and the Spanish-American wars because we were too strong; the temptation for empire-building at the expense of second-rate nations was just too great. In the twentieth century, a good case can be made that we also got into the Vietnam War because we were too strong. We assumed that with our strength we could regulate the affairs of southeast Asia, regardless of what the southeast Asians had in mind. And even at the outset of World War II, the Allies were much "stronger" than Germany and Japan. If the question is deterrence, being strong enough to deter another country from attacking us, then consider this: Robert McNamara calculated that about 400 deliverable one megaton warheads would be sufficient to deter an attack on the U.S. We now have about 12,000—more than 30 times McNamara's recommendation. It is simply not possible that we are too weak. But it is entirely possible, indeed likely, that we are too strong. Thus, if we are so strong as to threaten the deterrence of our opponents, then we make them jumpy and make war *more* likely. Moreover, we gain nothing from this "strength."

As we have seen, there has been no international success Gap. It may be that neither the U.S. nor the U.S.S.R. has been especially successful these days in getting its way with the rest of the world. But if so, this is because the world is made up of many different, feisty people who increasingly refuse to take direction from either of the superpowers (witness OPEC, for example, or the Islamic movement, or tribal rivalries in Africa, disaffected peasants in Central America, or Catholics and Protestants in Ireland). We simply cannot close this gap by nuclear weapons, but we can make nuclear war more likely if we keep on trying.

The conclusion is painful, but inevitable: time and again, we have been fools, duped by the professional cold warriors, stampeded by hair-raising, exaggerated tales of Soviet strength and made to feel insecure despite our own strength. Then—as we augment our strength yet further in response—we actually make ourselves *less* secure. There is a new and lucrative profession in the U.S., practiced by recently retired admirals and generals who proclaim American military weakness and some newfound Gap—often just prior to joining one of the major defense industries. Such pronouncements do more harm to American security than would a new Soviet arms system, not only by reducing the credibility of the enormous power that we actually do have, but by forcing us into a steady, relentless and mindless increase in our nuclear arsenal. As George Kennan puts it:

> We have gone on piling weapon upon weapon, missile upon missile, new levels of destructiveness upon old ones. We have done this helplessly, almost involuntarily; like men in a dream, like lemmings heading for the sea, like the children of Hamlin marching blindly behind their Pied Piper. And the result is that today we have achieved, we and the Russians together, in the creation of these devices and their means of delivery, levels of redundancy of such grotesque dimensions as to defy rational understanding.

Our need—our desperate need—is for a halt to the increases, followed by *reductions,* and yet incredibly, the Gappers are demanding yet more, piling new weapons on our sprawling, grotesque pile. Even more incredibly, some Americans still believe them. We are all too quick to think the worst of our capabilities, all too ready to succumb to Gap-pap that we are behind. Moreover, we remain all too convinced that security comes from more and better weapons. In the days of conventional war, this may have been true, but not in today's nuclear age. "Once we are sure that, in retaliation, we can destroy the Soviet Union and other potential attackers as modern societies," concluded McNamara's analysts, "we cannot increase our security or power against them by threatening to do more." Several decades before, Winston Churchill had marveled at the obsession of his bomb builders, trying to "make the rubble bounce."

Today, national security is not for sale; we cannot solve that problem by throwing money at it—or warheads. But we can make things worse, as the Reagan Administration now seems determined to do. We (and the Russians) are caught in a Chinese finger puzzle: the more we try to muscle our way out, the more tightly are we held. The Gappers plan as though when it comes to a military innovation or build-up, ours will always be the last move. But every escalation by us has always led to a comparable escalation by them, until our fingers—our lives—are held tighter than ever before.

Now, in the 1980s, there is a particular irony in our Gap-happiness and the reaction it invariably produced in the Soviet Union. Thus, following their gradual military build-up of the 1970s, it may well be that the Russians have finally achieved their goals—not true equality in military strength, but at least, sufficient strength relative to the U.S. that a freeze and then perhaps mutual and balanced arms *reductions* could take place. But if instead, we embark on a new effort to widen the Gap, then they surely will respond similarly—and here we go again.

"Both sides have to convince their military establishments of the benefits of restraint," said Henry Kissinger in June 1974. "And that does not come easily to either side." The benefits of restraint are especially clear when we recall one of the unique aspects of nuclear weaponry: because a single bomb can do almost unimaginable damage, the offense has an overwhelming edge over the defense. If 2,000 warheads are launched at the U.S. and by a superhuman effort, fully 90 percent are deflected or somehow shot down, the 200 warheads that got through would destroy us. Every new weapon on our side impels them to introduce a comparable innovation; as a result, whenever we stimulate the arms race, whether because of misinformed fear of Gaps or the hope of a temporary advantage, we only make ourselves more vulnerable and less safe in the long run.

Moreover, "talking tough" to the Russians is not likely to do us any good; aggressive bombast by our leaders has the same effect on the Soviets as tough statements by them have on us. As Averell Harriman pointed out, "they pull the rug out from under the more moderate and strengthen the arguments of the militants and other hard-liners." The result: heating up the arms race, closing no meaningful Gaps at all, and making the world yet more dangerous.

"The real question," as Adlai Stevenson once wrote, "is not who can stand up to, or talk back to the Russians. That's too easy. The real question is who can sit down with them at the bargaining table and negotiate with them. . . . The real question is not who is tough and who is soft. The real question is who is wise and who is foolish, who likes to play with words and who likes to get things done."

As we have seen, despite all the claims, there is no U.S.-Soviet military Gap; certainly, none that favors them. There is a very important Gap, however—not between the U.S. and the U.S.S.R., but rather between the builders of nuclear weapons and their would-be controllers. There is no question who is winning the arms race: neither the U.S. nor the U.S.S.R., but rather, the weapons builders. In fact, the Gap is increasing and plans for the 1980s call for it to grow even more rapidly. Every day it yawns wider—and someday soon, if we don't move quickly, it just might swallow us all. As George Kennan has pointed out, we all therefore have an obligation

> to assure that we of this generation, here and elsewhere, do not, in deference to our military fears, commit the supreme sacrilege of putting an end to the civilization out of which we have grown, the civilization without which our children and grandchildren can have no chance for self-realization, possibly no chance for life itself.

This book is not anti-U.S. We take no joy in pointing out our folly—even, we might say, our guilt. But the fact is, although the

Soviet Union clearly has not been an innocent bystander, we have led every step of the way; we have initiated virtually every new and dangerous escalation in this madness. But in a sense this is a reason for hope rather than despair, since if the Russians were the prime culprits in the nuclear arms race, the task of reversing things would be harder still. Fortunately, it is easier to change our own behavior than theirs. And ours needs changing. It is we who pioneered the atomic bomb, the hydrogen bomb, the submarine-launched missile, the intercontinental bomber, the MIRVed missile, the neutron bomb, we who have refused countless requests to negotiate a "no first use policy," and we alone who used nuclear weapons to incinerate tens of thousands of helpless civilians. It is we who see Gaps under every bed and who are now poised on the brink of the biggest, most expensive, least justified, and overwhelmingly perilous escalation in the sorry history of the nuclear arms race. And it is we who live in a democratic society which can—and must—listen to our fear, our outrage, and our determination.

# 6. Deterrence to War-Fighting:

## Going from MAD to Worse

In Xanadu did Herman Kahn
A fearful atom bomb decree
Where Alpha radiation ran
Through fallouts measureless to man
Down to a poisoned sea . . .
—NORMAN CORWIN

I will not burn houses or destroy them unless there is a knight inside. I will not root up vines. I will not attack noble ladies traveling without husbands, nor their maids, nor widows or nuns, unless it is their fault.

—oath of ROBERT THE PIOUS (tenth century, England)

In his book *Common Sense and Nuclear Warfare*,° Bertrand Russell posed the following hypothetical situation: imagine that a particularly vicious form of rabies has broken out in Berlin. Thousands of striken dogs, lethal to people, are running about the city. Can anyone doubt that government authorities, East and West, would cooperate to eliminate the mad dogs? Would we leave the West's dogs uncontrolled, in the hope that they would bite more communists than capitalists? Or alternatively, would we parade ours around with detachable muzzles, as "deterrents," ready to unleash them in case the other side sics theirs on us? Would we refuse to destroy ours, for fear that the other side might not destroy theirs? Life in a city full of mad dogs would not meet anyone's conception of "security." And yet, this is precisely how we live today. Nuclear weapons are today's mad dogs, and rather than destroy them, we have been content to live with them, and have even gone further, devising schemes whereby they can be used.

° The title, admittedly, is something of a contradiction, like "Happiness and Hemorrhoids."

Prior to Hiroshima and Nagasaki, military strategy involved such nitty-gritty questions as how best to attack fixed machine-gun implacements, avoid encirclement, or deploy a brigade of tanks. Today's nuclear strategists use computer printouts in governmental think tanks, playing esoteric war games with theoretical moves and countermoves in which hundreds of millions of lives hang in the balance. "They have become the alchemists of our times," wrote Lord Zuckerman, Britain's chief scientific adviser, "working in secret ways which cannot be divulged, casting spells which embrace us all."

Since they embrace us, we should understand them: know thy embracer. And it is not really all that difficult. Although the details are often secret, the general theory is straightforward enough. And yet, most people only vaguely understand these issues upon which their lives depend. We like to leave sorcery to the sorcerers. As a result, most people are not aware of how close they live to nuclear annihilation. Worse yet, they are generally unaware of recent developments in strategic sorcery, beginning about two decades ago and peaking during the 1980s, which are making things even more dangerous than ever before. In this chapter, we shall describe the strategists' work: how and why the United States has lived with its nuclear mad dogs, and how and why we plan to use them.

Just after the Hiroshima bombing, Einstein commented that when he was young he had been taught that ancient history ended with the fall of Rome. Now, he said, that had changed: ancient history ended in 1945. The political theoreticians were not slow in recognizing this. Truman's Secretary of War, Henry Stimson, pointed out that nuclear weapons represented a fundamental change in our relationship with the universe, and Bernard Brodie, one of our first nuclear strategists, emphasized in 1946 that "everything about the bomb is overshadowed by the twin facts that it exists and that its destructive power is fantastically great." Brodie also pointed out that whereas the previous function of armed forces (during the days of "ancient history") had been to fight wars, its primary function must henceforth be to *prevent* them. As we shall see, it was a change to which the military agreed, but only grudgingly.

## The Theory of Deterrence

The theory is simple enough: we have our mad dogs and they have theirs. If they unleash theirs at us, we will do the same to them. Both of us would die. So, neither of us would ever be the first to set loose these new dogs of war.

In the early years of American diplomacy, especially while John Foster Dulles was Secretary of State under President Eisenhower, the official policy was that "massive retaliation" would follow if we or our allies were attacked. Then, as the Soviets developed their own nuclear weapons and with them, the ability to destroy American society no less than we could destroy theirs, massive retaliation and "brinksmanship" were replaced by a more subtle concern: second-strike capability. Once more, however, the idea is not difficult: if our nuclear weapons are to deter attack upon us, then we must be able to absorb a surprise strike and still retain enough power to strike back with devastating force. The goal here is not revenge, but rather, deterrence. As long as we can cause "unacceptable damage" to a would-be aggressor, that aggressor would be forever deterred. Or so goes the logic. "Safety will be the steady child of terror," as Winston Churchill put it, "and survival, the twin brother of annihilation." The strategic goal of deterrence thus became to insure that an enemy would not have an advantage if it struck first. This should eliminate any incentive to do so—and of course, if no one strikes first, then no one strikes at all.

Thus was born the policy of Mutually Assured Destruction— appropriately known as MAD. The two antagonists were mutually assured that if one attacked the other, both would be destroyed. By the ghoulish logic of MADness, deterrence is best served when offensive weapons are as invulnerable as possible, and each other's population as vulnerable as possible. Thus, by mutual agreement and solemn vow, the great cities of each nation are exposed to the nuclear weapons of the other.

We and the Soviets therefore live with our breasts bared to one another. The stark fact is that if the Kremlin leadership ever decided to wipe out the United States, it could do so, and in about half an hour. There is nothing we could do to stop them. Similarly for the U.S. leadership. Both sides stake their survival on the assumption that the other will be deterred by the threat of retribution. Moreover, they go further: both sides seek to make themselves more secure by threatening ever more awful retribution. A very effective cartoon shows two men, armed with bow and arrow, standing in front of each other with the arrows aimed at one another's chest, each straining to pull his own bow as tightly as possible. The caption shows the thoughts of both: "The tighter I pull it, the safer I feel."

Not unexpectedly, there are some problems with this posture. For one, it relies on rationality; we can be confident that *rational* leaders on either side will not attack the other. But not all world leaders have been rational, and moreover, it takes extraordinary optimism to imagine that no irrational leader will ever arise in the future. As Richard J. Barnet, founder of the Institute for Policy Studies, once put it, the leaders of the U.S. and the U.S.S.R. are like "chess players in the dark, absorbed in a game they can barely see. Each player depends upon the other not to upset the table." If for whatever reason a player on either side suddenly decided to quit playing by the rules and to knock over the board, then the game is over.

There is also the moral problem. As Dr. Jack Geiger has pointed out, there is something dreadfully wrong with a society that guards its bombs as its most exquisite treasures, while exposing its children to incineration. Even when the whole arrangement is ostensibly to protect those children. In fact, a basic tenet of the whole MAD doctrine is that strategic weapons must be well-protected indeed. In his State of the Union address, January 30, 1961, President Kennedy said, "If we are to keep the peace, we need an invulnerable missile force powerful enough to deter any aggressor from even threatening an attack that he would know could not destroy enough of our force to prevent his own destruction." Robert McNamara underlined this shortly afterward: "In this age of nuclear-armed intercontinental ballistic missiles," he explained in Congressional testimony, "the ability to deter rests heavily on the existence of a force which can weather or survive a massive nuclear attack, even with little or no warning, in sufficient strength to strike a decisive counterblow." Shortly afterwards, he explained "We are emphasizing survivability," by which he meant survivability of the nuclear weapons.

Out of this concern for "survivability" came the American decision to rely on a "triad" of strategic nuclear forces—land-based ICBMs, strategic bombers (the B-52s), and submarine-based missiles. The theory, again, was simple: if each leg of the strategic triad is capable of destroying the U.S.S.R. independently, then attack against the U.S. should be deterred. Indeed, it should be triply deterred. The strategic wisdom in such a decision was considerable, aside from the moral questions. (By contrast, Soviet strategic planning seems to have been less farsighted, since they invested three-fourths of their deterrence in land-based ICBMs, which are less survivable than either submarines or bombers—whatever the survivability of their children.)

Another moral dilemma of deterrence is that it relies on the threat, and hence the training, expectation, and readiness, to murder tens of millions (perhaps hundreds of millions) of totally innocent men, women, children, the elderly, animals, even perhaps, the planet itself—in case deterrence fails. "Our method for preventing nuclear war," as described by former ACDA director Fred Kile, "rests on a form of warfare universally condemned since the Dark Ages—the mass killing of hostages."

This posture seems unlikely to appeal to anything high-minded in the military, either. It demands that our strategic warriors must be prepared to be attacked, and then to retaliate by killing millions of helpless civilians on the other side. If there is any honor in the military profession—and we are willing to concede the possibility— then it must rebel at deterrence theory.

The heart of the Strategic Air Command, ten miles south of Omaha, is Offutt Air Force Base. Under the official SAC motto, "Peace is our profession," some wag once added, "Mass murder is our specialty." In a nutshell, that graffito is the morality of deterrence. We cannot know the moral cost of making this pact, of living by grace of such a declaration. We also cannot know the cost in emotional insecurity, instability, loss of faith in the future, and distrust of authority at the same time that authority necessarily becomes ever more centralized, secret, and demanding of obedience. We cannot know these things with accuracy, but we cannot ignore them either.

Not surprisingly, the moral problems of nuclear deterrence also pose a real difficulty for religion, especially the Catholic Church's doctrine of a "just war." San Francisco's Archbishop John Quinn has commented that the devastation of nuclear weapons has made a just nuclear war a contradiction in terms. Historically, a "just war" has been one that is in response to an aggressor, and that respects noncombatants. Hitler clearly violated both these guidelines, beginning in 1937 at the Spanish city of Guernica, later immortalized by Picasso's painting. Japan behaved similarly at Nanking. It is little appreciated that in the early stages of World War II, Britain vowed to refrain from saturation bombing of civilian targets, but rather, to engage in precision bombing of strategic targets only. This was given up in 1942. The U.S. also joined the policy of mass, obliteration bombing of civilians, with notable results in Berlin, Dresden, Hamburg, Tokyo, and of course, Hiroshima and Nagasaki. The history of modern war has been a history of more and more death to civilian "noncombatants." There is little doubt that World War III will continue this trend, perhaps to its ultimate resolution: the deaths and casualties will be almost entirely civilian. Another "just" war or not, it certainly will not be just another war.

Aside from these moral issues, however, deterrence theory also has a triad of skeletons in its conceptual closet, just as our strategic deterrence in practice rests on a triad of forces. These three skeletons are: 1) how much is enough? 2) keeping the deterrent secure; and 3) credibility. These three, in turn, lead into difficult and dangerous new problems; notably, the problem of deterrent security is closely related to the ominous development of counterforce weaponry, and the problem of credibility has led, in part, to scenarios for the fighting of "limited" nuclear wars. Although these three skeletons are closely intertwined with each other, it is easier if we first consider each one separately.

*Skeleton #1: How much is enough?*

As usual in strategic doctrine, the question is simple; the answer, difficult. The question: how much destruction must be available for an opponent to be deterred? Unfortunately there is no guaranteed yardstick for measuring the adequacy of deterrence. We can never say that an enemy would willingly suffer so many hundred thousand, million or tens of millions of deaths, but if we can threaten them with a hundred thousand and one, or a million and one deaths, then they will be deterred from attacking. Similarly, no nation could confidently say anything comparable about us. In a sense, this uncertainty is one of the strengths of deterrence. In any event, nuclear weapons are immensely destructive, more so than anything the world has ever known before. As such, it seems likely that their deterrent value, the deterrent value of even a very small number, would be very great. McGeorge Bundy, Special Assistant for National Security Affairs under Presidents Kennedy and Johnson, wrote:

> Think tank analysts can set levels of 'acceptable' damage well up in the tens of millions of lives. . . . They are in an unreal world. In the real world of real political leaders—whether here or in the Soviet Union—a decision that would bring even one hydrogen bomb on one city of one's own country would be recognized in advance as a catastrophic blunder; ten bombs on ten cities would be a disaster beyond history; and a hundred bombs on a hundred cities are unthinkable.

Nonetheless, given that a country possesses nuclear weapons, and that the purpose of those weapons is to be deterrence, that country needs to decide how many it needs for that purpose. Robert McNamara, JFK's defense secretary, liked precision and detailed analysis—it was he who moved our policy from massive retaliation to MAD. He also pushed for an analysis of "bang for the buck," or more precisely, how many Russians would be killed and what percentage of their economy would be destroyed, by different numbers of American nuclear warheads. The results were fairly clear: the Soviets have about one-third of their population and two-thirds of their industrial capacity concentrated in their 200 largest cities. It would require the equivalent of about 400 one megaton bombs to destroy them. Up to this point, every U.S. bomb provides a large return in Russian deaths and destruction (i.e., in "deterrence") but from here on, the curve flattens out; economists would say we reach the point of diminishing returns. Not that we couldn't employ more bombs—it is just that the difference between hitting them with 1,000 bombs as opposed to 999 is not nearly as great as the difference between 10 bombs and 9. The "break point" is at about 400. Since it would be most efficient to aim for this level of destruction, this was decreed as appropriate for deterrence. Being conservative, however, McNamara decided to provide *each leg* of the strategic triad with the ability to deliver this level of destruction.

In 1968, he wrote that assured destruction is the "ability, even after absorbing a well-coordinated surprise first strike, to inflict unacceptable damage on the attacker." His estimates were actually somewhat less than those upon which government policy were then based: "In the case of the Soviet Union, I would judge that a capability on our part to destroy, say, 1/4 of her population and 1/2 of her industrial capacity would serve as an effective deterrent." We long ago surpassed that capability. We have more than 4,000 megatons in nuclear weapons, the equivalent of more than 300,000 Hiroshimas divided among 30,000 warheads. Even in the bloodless, analytic world of strategic analysts and cold-blooded computers, things clearly have gotten out of hand.

The extraordinary accumulation of ever more accurate nuclear warheads, grossly more than are needed even for MAD, is part of a new crazy pursuit of instability. Since there is no clear answer to the question: "How much is enough?" we (and the Russians) have gone on piling bomb upon bomb. In a sense, MAD doctrine is frustrating for military planners. After all, it is a nonaggression pact. In its pure form, it is entirely defensive, giving no options for getting one's way in the world. So both sides press on, hoping to gain security by excess, and also to devise the ultimate gadget that might somehow provide the decisive edge. For such people, the arms race must never stop, or we shall have given up on "winning." As George Kennan points out, however, in our pursuit of deterrence we have reached the point at which our bombs make us *less* safe:

I have never been an advocate of unilateral disarmament, and I see no necessity for anything of that sort today. But I must say that if we Americans had no nuclear weapons whatsoever on our soil instead of the tens of thousands of nuclear warheads we are now said to have deployed, I would feel the future of my children and grandchildren to be far safer than I do at this moment; for if there is any incentive for the Russians to use such weapons against us, it surely comes in overwhelming degree—probably, in fact, entirely—from our own enormous deployment of them.

## Skeleton #2: Security of the deterrence

If both sides would be content to sit glaring at each other across their mutual, MAD stockpiles, things would be bad enough. But instead, ongoing efforts, on both sides, continually threaten to upset the balance by reducing the security of the other side's deterrence. "Only when our arms are certain beyond doubt," said JFK in his 1961 Inaugural Address, "can we be certain beyond doubt that they will never be used." The same applies to the other side's arms: only when the U.S.S.R.'s arms are certain beyond doubt can we be certain that they will not be used against us. And yet, both U.S. and Soviet policy regularly attempt to reduce this certainty.

For example, take the problem of Anti-Ballistic Missiles (ABMs). At first glance, defensive weapons of this sort seem to be a good idea, stabilizing the nuclear balance. But in fact, they are highly provocative and destabilizing. Here is why: if an ABM system was used exclusively for defense against a first strike by the opponent, then it would in fact be acceptable. But neither side can ever be sure that the other's ABMs will not also be used to enable it to strike first and then be safe from retaliation.

So if our side begins deploying an ABM system, it becomes necessary for the other to deploy more and more warheads, so as to insure the continuing security of its deterrence; presumably, no matter how effective the ABM shield, some retaliating warheads will get through, if enough are launched against it. ABMs, therefore, lead to a greatly accelerated arms race with no winners, only losers. Both the U.S. and the U.S.S.R. finally recognized this, and agreed to a treaty limiting ABM deployment, as part of the original SALT I agreement. Regrettably, however, any triumph of sanity seems generally short-lived in the nuclear arms race, and there is danger in the 1980s that the very useful and security-inducing ABM treaty may be scrapped in our anxiety to use ABMs to defend our new missiles, notably the MX. In fact, some form of BMD

(Ballistic Missile Defense) system is being actively considered by the Reagan Administration at this moment.

The MX is a highly accurate new missile. It is also controversial. Most of the debate has concerned its "basing mode"—whether the MX should be placed in circular loops or a multiple racetrack shell game, in super-hardened silos, on constant airborne patrol, in a "dense pack" or underground (Deep Underground Missile Basing, or DUMB). But the really crucial point concerns the missile itself and its supposed justification. The MX is avowedly a counterforce missile, designed to destroy other missiles in their silos; otherwise, there would be no need for its extreme accuracy. The strategists' justification is this: imagine a Soviet first strike that removes most of our land-based ICBMs—in that case, they say, we need the ability to destroy their remaining missiles in a second-strike response, or else those Soviet missiles will hold us hostage, threatening a counter-city attack to which we could not respond. We would have to surrender.

Let us briefly examine this argument. First, our cities are *now* hostage to Soviet missiles, just as theirs are to ours—this is deterrence. We would not be any more hostage following a counterforce attack against our ICBMs. Second, as we have seen, an attack against our ICBMs would also cause enormous civilian damage and would be an unmistakable act of war. The U.S.S.R. could never assume that we would not retaliate, just as they must assume that we would retaliate against an attack directly on our cities. Third, even with complete elimination of our ICBMs (which, as we have seen, would be impossible), the remaining invulnerable submarines alone—not to mention the surviving bombers and forward-based, tactical weapons—provide more than enough overkill to destroy the U.S.S.R. in retaliation. So, however we choose to base it, the MX missile simply is not necessary.

More important, however, it is dangerous. It will make things worse, not better. This is because, like an ABM system, the MX missile makes the balance of terror less stable by threatening the security of the other side's deterrence. Whereas ABMs threaten to make deterrence ineffective, the MX threatens to eliminate it altogether. As we have just seen, an opponent can never be confident that ABMs will be used only to deflect an aggressor; rather, there is always the chance that they will be used as a shield for one's own aggression. Similarly, the Soviets could never be sure that the MX, once deployed, would only be used by us in the event that they attacked us first; rather, from their viewpoint, there is always the chance that we will use the MX missile as a first-strike weapon ourselves. Moreover, for just this reason, rather than repelling attack, the MX missile will be a magnet, inviting attack in times of crisis. Again, this is because the MX threatens the security of their deterrence, and hence, its mere presence could drive them toward a preemptive attack, in tragic pursuit of the illusion of their own security. And finally, deployment of the MX could well drive the Soviets to a "launch on warning" posture. When one side threatens the security of the other side's deterrence, especially with a weapon such as the MX, which is both fast and accurate, it pushes that side into a hair-trigger anxiety, in which a small computer or radar error could bring the whole fragile structure of deterrence crashing down about our heads.

There is profound and tragic irony here: the U.S. and the U.S.S.R are spending billions annually, seeking technologic breakthroughs that might reduce the other's security by threatening its deterrence, totally unmindful that by doing so they threaten their own security as well. The MX is not an isolated case. For example, the Defense Advanced Research Projects Agency annual report for 1977 eagerly advised the reader to "ponder the consequences of an ability to not only detect but to localize and track quiet submarines at long range." We have an enormous and growing lead over the U.S.S.R. in antisubmarine warfare. Submarines have long been the most invulnerable of deterrents. If we persist in threatening their deterrence, we only threaten ourselves. And yet, the work goes on.

If some day our scientists, filled with patriotic fervor perhaps, invented a weapon enabling us to guarantee the destruction of Soviet strategic forces, the very best thing they could do is to destroy it instantly and probably commit suicide as well. Because a "rational" Soviet response to such a weapon could well be to strike us immediately, out of fear that otherwise we might someday attack them with impunity.

*Skeleton #3: Credibility (bluffs, counter-bluffs and blind-man's bluffs)*

Picture the scene: deterrence has failed, for whatever reason.

Thousands of nuclear warheads are about to explode all over the nation. What do we gain by annihilating millions of Russian children as well? Or alternatively, imagine a more limited, but nonetheless devastating attack: let us say that all U.S. oil refineries, airports, or military bases are attacked. Or what if the Grand Canyon is bombed? Or the Mormon Temple? Is it worth risking the obliteration of the surviving country by devastating the U.S.S.R. in return? Thus we come to one of the most troublesome skeletons in the closet of horrors named deterrence: credibility.

Credibility is such a problem that it makes nuclear strategists nervous even to raise the issue. This is because the whole structure of deterrence rests on credibility, the other side's belief that we would retaliate. And in fact, that belief verges on the incredible. The problem is that the whole business simply does not make sense—we are damned if we do (retaliate after an attack) and damned if we don't. But more damned if we do. The *threat* of nuclear retaliation may be useful in preventing an attack against us, but in the event of such an attack, retaliating is totally illogical since this would gain nothing but revenge, and moreover, it would only insure that any Americans still alive would be clobbered by a counter-response from any remaining Soviet warheads. But we could never admit that.

Walt Rostow, national security adviser to President Johnson and one of the principal architects of our Vietnam fiasco (also brother of Eugene Rostow), wrote in 1964: "Credible deterrence in the nuclear age lies in being prepared to face the consequences if deterrence fails—up to and including all-out war." Can any sane person honestly say that he or she is prepared for those consequences?

Any American who is *really* willing to plunge the nation and the world into all-out nuclear war, for any reason whatsoever, should probably be certified insane and automatically disqualified for any high office. On the other hand, an essential part of deterrence is to proclaim one's willingness to do just this! As a result, the American citizenry is in a real quandary: when we hear our leaders proclaim their determination to use nuclear weapons under certain cases, we cannot tell if such statements are intended only for Soviet consumption (in which case they have at least some justification), or if they are real (in which case they do not). Perhaps this uncertainty is itself appropriate, since deterrence—as a massive bluff—relies on Soviet uncertainty as to how we will respond.

One way out of this dilemma is to take the decision process out of human hands, to adopt a "launch on warning" system which automatically fires our missiles upon warning of a Soviet attack. Since the machine would simply be following its programmed instructions, and since it has no conscience, it would have higher credibility of retaliating, and hence, it should add to deterrence. The overwhelming and insoluble difficulty with such a scheme, however, is that accidents do happen. We might enhance the credibility of deterrence for a time, but at the unacceptable risk of virtually assuring that some day, some time, we will have a nuclear war by accident. In the movie *Dr. Strangelove* the Russians had solved the problem of credible deterrence by installing a "doomsday bomb," which would destroy the planet if a nuclear explosion was detonated on Russian soil—only, they forgot to tell the Americans about it! Maybe both sides could use the opposite, something we told each other about, and which was believed, but which really doesn't exist!

On the other hand, perhaps there is some limited hope for continued effective deterrence, at least until the whole business can be improved. (That is, abolished.) McGeorge Bundy, former security advisor to JFK, has pointed out that deterrence does not work in theory, only in practice. Thus, if the Soviet Union were to invade western Europe, or even attack parts of the U.S. with nuclear weapons, the only rational U.S. response would be to do nothing at all, because our use of nuclear weapons could only make things worse. So in theory, deterrence should not work; it is rational up to a point, but if push ever comes to shove, it becomes the greatest irrationality of all time. And yet, so far at least, deterrence *has* worked. The Soviets have refrained from provocations against critical U.S. interests, just as we have refrained from similar provocations against theirs. Why? Because despite the seeming illogic of deterrence in a crisis, despite the fact that reason demands the bluff be empty, there is always the possibility that it is for real, that in the final decision process unreason will prevail and holocaust will ensue. "The Emperor Deterrence has no clothes," writes strategic analyst Lawrence Freedman. "But he is still the emperor." If deterrence works at all, then, it is because of that bottom-line uncertainty, and because the costs of miscalculation are so great.

According to Charles Yost, career diplomat and former U.S. ambassador to the U.N.,

> It is almost impossible for any sober observer to imagine any Soviet leadership, particularly the present array of septuagenarians and sexagenarians, risking such hazards. Soviet doctrine requires them to nudge history along in their direction but not to give it so brutal a shove as to send it sprawling—very possibly with themselves underneath.

Let us turn now to the two ghastly, ill-begotten offspring of deterrence: counterforce and "limited" nuclear war.

### Counterforce

As we have seen, counterforce is an attack upon the other side's deterrence. It sounds relatively humane—let the military attack the military, not the innocent civilians. It is the Western hero, shooting the gun out of his opponent's hand. But as we have also seen, counterforce is perilous because it is potentially destabilizing. In its origin and justification, counterforce is closely related to the triple problems of how much is enough, security of the deterrence and credibility of retaliation, with a dose of technological sweet tooth thrown in.

If MAD was the only goal of nuclear weaponry, the arms race would have ended long ago. Thus, for example, the U.S.S.R. has 5 major population centers and 145 other cities with more than 100,000 people. Five hundred "deliverable" bombs would be excessive deterrent; 1,000 is grotesque. We have about 10,000—counting strategic bombs only. The U.S. nuclear stockpile grew, it is said, because the Soviets' grew, forgetting that if deterrence is the goal, the real question is not how much *they have,* but rather, how much *we need* to achieve deterrence. The U.S.S.R. had 30 ICBMs in the early 1960s, over 500 by 1967 and 1,000 by 1969. The original justification for American MIRVing (which multiplied severalfold the number of warheads) was that it was necessary to counter their supposed ABM system. But the bulk of the U.S. MIRV program has been carried out *after* the ABM treaty, which the U.S.S.R. has studiously obeyed. There can be only one "rational" explanation for MIRVing and the rapid growth in U.S. warhead number: a response to Soviet rocket expansion, a continuing effort to keep the U.S.S.R.'s deterrence within our gunsights.

According to the official Pentagon line, this counterforce capability is not intended for a first strike, but rather, to provide an ability to respond to a *Soviet* first strike by eliminating any Soviet missiles that are still unlaunched. Aside from the problems already raised with regard to the MX, one effect of possessing such a counterforce capacity is to insure that in the event of a Soviet first strike, no missiles will be held back! Moreover, any ability on our part to destroy their remaining missiles after they have first attacked us—and when they are presumably alert and expecting possibly retaliation—would mean that we also had the ability to strike first ourselves.

For sixteen productive years, Robert Aldridge was deeply involved in the American missile program, as chief engineer for Lockheed, the nation's number one military contractor. His job was secure and he made a good living doing what he liked and did well. Nonetheless, he suddenly quit his job in the 1970s when it became apparent to him that his future was not really secure, just as ours is not, because of emerging military policy. In particular, Bob Aldridge became alarmed at the extreme accuracy being demanded of the ICBMs he was designing. Not only were our missiles exceeding any reasonable number for MAD deterrence, they were also achieving the accuracy that spoke all too clearly of first-strike designs. Aldridge's book *The Counterforce Syndrome* was first published in 1977, then revised in 1979. It details the technical characteristics of U.S. first-strike weaponry, making the strong case that whereas we do not quite yet have this capacity, we are rapidly moving toward it.

Why? Why threaten their deterrence, thereby making ourselves less secure? In part, simply because it could be done; MIRVing in particular was "technically sweet," and so the pressures to do it became irresistible. In addition, as we ran out of targets, saturating the civilian and industrial centers, Soviet missile silos presented themselves. There may also be some influence wielded by the mentally myopic purveyors of the need for a "second strike counterforce" capability, as described above. But finally—and perhaps most importantly—there is that old bugaboo of deterrence: credibility.

Here's how it works. Deterrence theorists have worried that because of the mind-boggling consequences of nuclear war, the credibility of the nuclear deterrent would be doubted—and hence, it might no longer serve as a deterrent after all. Richard Nixon was quite clear on this in 1970:

> Should a president, in the event of a nuclear attack, be left with the single option of ordering the mass destruction of enemy civilians, in the face of the certainty that it would be followed by the mass slaughter of Americans? Should the concept of assured destruction be narrowly defined and should it be the only measure of our ability to deter the variety of threats we may face?

In fact, the U.S. (and, presumably, the U.S.S.R.) have had a strategy of targeting each other's military strength for quite some time. In an important policy speech delivered at the University of Michigan in 1962, Secretary of Defense Robert McNamara stated:

> The United States has come to the conclusion that, to the extent feasible, basic military strategy in a possible general nuclear war should be approached in much the same way that more conventional military operations have been regarded in the past. This is to say, principal military objectives, in the event of a nuclear war stemming from a major attack on the alliance, should be the destruction of the enemy's military forces, not of her civilian population.

As technology improved, and both the numbers and accuracy of missiles increased, it became increasingly "feasible" to target the opponent's military forces, and this policy was reaffirmed regularly. Thus, in 1964, McNamara spoke of the desirability of "building into our forces a flexible capability." In 1967, his successor, Clark Clifford, emphasized the importance of "providing our (nuclear) forces with characteristics that will permit them to be used effectively in a limited and controlled retaliation as well as for assured destruction." Clifford's successor, Melvin Laird, reported in 1973:

In order to maintain needed flexibility, we design our (nuclear) forces so that we have strategic alternatives available for use depending on the nature and level of provocation. This means capabilities that enable us to carry out an appropriate response without necessarily resorting to mass urban and industrial destruction.

This argument was clarified for Congress by James Schlesinger (who followed Rumsfeld, who followed Laird) in his testimony to the Senate Foreign Relations Committee's Subcommittee on Arms Control, in March 1974. This was the occasion at which Schlesinger also developed the (now admittedly fallacious) argument that a Soviet counterforce attack on the U.S. could be both effective and "surgical," leaving us with relatively few civilian casualties, and therefore requiring us to maintain a "second strike counterforce" capability so as to avoid being at the mercy of their blackmail.

The next major public statement regarding counterforce came on July 15, 1980, just before the hotly contested Democratic National Convention, when President Carter signed Presidential Directive 59. PD 59, as it was known, spelled out the U.S. policy of targeting Soviet military installations, including missile silos. Although it was considered by some journalists to be a new step in U.S. counterforce doctrine, it was not. As we have seen, it was only the continuation of a longstanding and developing tradition.

Let us reiterate: the linchpin of MAD is that both sides must keep a secure second-strike capability, thereby assuring that each side has a strong incentive not to strike first. If the U.S. ever achieves a first strike capacity, then two things follow, both of them bad. For one, it gives the U.S. incentive to strike first. And for another, it gives the U.S.S.R. incentive to beat us to the punch and/ or to interpret a false alarm as the real thing. Where nuclear war is concerned, fear is a much more likely cause than is cold-blooded, rational decision-making—fear that if we don't strike first, they will. By threatening the other side's deterrence, this fear is increased. In short, going from deterrence to counterforce is going from MAD to worse.

The only reasonable argument consistently advanced for counterforce is the need for "flexibility" in our strategic nuclear forces. Flexibility may well be desirable, counterforce is not. In fact, flexibility exists without counterforce, and has existed for a very long time: it is easy to target oil refineries, munitions centers, power plants—all of these are "softer" than missile silos and therefore they are easier to destroy and do not require great accuracy. Even now, every missile or bomber has multiple targeting options. For example, the Minuteman III is equipped with a new Command Data Buffer system, with which computers on board the missiles can be reset, from launch control centers, in about thirty minutes. In short, there is no reason to go from MAD to worse. MAD is bad enough.

## *"Limited" nuclear war*

There is something inherently unlimited about nuclear war. And yet, strategists—especially in the U.S.—have busily been developing the concept of "limited" nuclear war. Mutually Assured Destruction appears even more mad when people in authority begin to consider that maybe our destruction isn't assured, and hence, it may be acceptable. Once again, our old friend credibility rears its head.

"It is absurd to base the strategy of the West on the credibility of the threat of mutual suicide," explained Henry Kissinger in 1979. (Note: according to the good doctor, the absurdity lies not in the potential for mutual suicide, but in the credibility of the threat. Presumably, credible suicide would be acceptable.) In his 1957 book, *Nuclear Weapons and Foreign Policy,* Kissinger had sounded a similar theme: "The more powerful the weapons, the greater becomes the reluctance to use them." Dr. K's solution? "A strategy which makes room for the possibility of fighting limited (nuclear) wars . . ."

So, MAD is under attack, and not only from the antiwar camp. A new doctrine has been taking shape, one that espouses the possibility of fighting limited nuclear wars. In an article appearing in the influential *Technology Review,* in 1979, Jack Ruina and Howard Margolis suggested an appropriate acronym: the exponents of limited nuclear war are Nuclear Utilization Theorists—in short, NUTs. According to the NUTs, we can make nuclear war less likely by making it more credible, and hence, more effective as deterrent. And we do this by increasing the possibility of limited nuclear wars. NUTs indeed.

The early patron saint of NUTs is Herman Kahn, celebrated thinker about the unthinkable. St. Herman has identified no fewer than forty-four distinct "rungs" of potential nuclear escalation, starting with such lowly half-hearted efforts as "slow motion counterproperty," through the delicacies of "augmented disarming attacks," and culminating in all-out "spasm or insensate war." Despite the intellectual charm of Kahn's carefully worked-out manual of strategic foreplay, the likelihood is that we would all reach wargasm very quickly indeed. President Kennedy wrote that "inevitably the use of small nuclear armaments will lead to larger nuclear armaments on both sides until the world-wide holocaust has begun." Lord Mountbatten, formerly Chief of the British Defense Staff, made it equally clear: "I repeat in all sincerity as a military man I can see no use for any nuclear weapons which would not end in escalation, with consequences that no one can conceive."

The chaos, disorganization, and panic during the brief, early stages of a "limited" nuclear war would make it virtually impossible for it to stay limited. Communications would be cut or at least, seriously disrupted. Without effective radar each side would be blinded, not knowing whether additional strikes are occurring at any given time. The pressure to escalate, and quickly, would be overwhelming. In a crisis, the hardest thing to do is nothing at all. Moreover, since war plans on both sides target the opponent's leadership and communication facilities, how will the precise niceties of limited, pinpoint nuclear attacks be controlled? Finally, if hostilities are ever to be ended, short of all-out "spasm," who will order the cease-fire or surrender, since leadership, communications, and command and control centers are prime targets for early destruction on both sides? With these out, all restraint vanishes. With no one clearly in command, and no one with a calm overview of the whole situation, can we expect launch control officers to do anything other than what they have rehearsed thousands of times?

"Limited" nuclear war is a monstrous fallacy; in fact, the whole concept is worse—much worse—than deterrence, since it aims to make nuclear war "thinkable," and hence, more likely—although it cannot be kept limited. The phrase "limited" nuclear war is a contradiction, like being "partially" pregnant or—more to the point—"somewhat" dead.

Incredibly, however, "limited" nuclear war is not just a plotter's pipe-dream, the demon lunacy of some psychotic Strangelove—it is a serious policy option, considered daily by respected military and political planners. In fact, nuclear war-fighting (instead of just deterring) is so completely integrated into U.S. military doctrine that it would probably take an extraordinary effort of will for the U.S. to fight a war without using nuclear weapons. For example, even as far back as 1965, when President Johnson ordered an aerial bombardment of North Vietnam, neither the Air Force nor the Navy had any contingency plans that did not involve nuclear-armed missiles or bombers. (Perhaps one positive result of the Vietnam experience is that conventional war has been reestablished as qualitatively distinct from nuclear war.)

But "limited" nuclear war lingers on, with more adherents than ever before. During James Schlesinger's Senate testimony in 1974, he was pressed by Senators Fulbright and Humphrey about how a nuclear war could ever be kept limited. The Secretary of Defense replied:

> If we were to maintain continued communications with the Soviet leadership during the war and if we were to describe precisely and meticulously the limited nature of our actions, including the desire to avoid attacking their urban industrial base . . . political leaders on both sides will be under powerful pressure to continue to be sensible.

If the subject was not so dreadfully serious, it would be high comedy. Imagine this conversation:

*U.S. President:* "We regret your destruction of our submarine bases at Charleston, South Carolina and Bremerton, Washington, and your devastation of our Minuteman silos in North Dakota and Nebraska, In retaliation, we are about to destroy your submarine base at Murmansk, one-third of your ICBMs and the vodka distillery at Kiev. Please don't be unduly upset."

*Soviet President:* "Good shot, America! We are now undertaking a limited attack upon your Strategic Air Command B-52s, but only those in states beginning with the letters G through T. Please don't take this gesture amiss."

On March 30, 1980, President Carter's national security advisor, Zbigniew Brzesinski, was asked by a reporter from *The New York Times:* "Are you saying that you want the United States to be able to fight a "limited" nuclear war?" The answer: "I am saying that the U.S., in order to maintain effective deterrence, has to have choices which give us a wider range of options than either a spasmodic nuclear exchange or a limited conventional war." In other words, yes.

Beyond its fascination for the strategists, "limited" nuclear war has a special, almost hypnotic appeal to the military as well. Thus, by making nuclear weapons usable at last, it holds out to them the opportunity of doing what they do best, what they have been trained to do, and what they must periodically do in order to validate their profession and themselves: fight. And so, we are all walking backward toward a precipice, insisting all the while that we mean to go the other way. Why? Because "the world in its madness is guided by military men who," as Thomas Merton put it, "are the blindest of the blind." (At least in the early 1980s, this may be unfair to the American military. Thus, the real crazies in the Reagan Administration are, in fact, the civilian appointees, not the Joint Chiefs of Staff, who appear like pillars of pacifism by contrast.

A special aspect of this blindness is in the difference between capabilities and intentions. We may be capable of all sorts of terrible acts; our intentions (or so we hope) are quite different, however. But when viewing the Soviets, our leaders assume that the capability to do something is also accompanied by the intention of doing it. "Worst-case" planning, once again. When it comes to "limited" nuclear war, this yields results that are bad indeed. Thus, in order to conduct a "limited" nuclear war, one must have precise, pinpoint accuracy. This capability must exist. The problem, however, is that such a capability is absolutely indistinguishable from the capability of initiating a counterforce, first strike. Even if this is not our intent, we can scarcely blame Kremlin strategists from playing the same "worst-case" games that we do. So the more we prepare for "limited" nuclear war, the more likely we make it that such a war will occur, and then rapidly expand.

There is another important reason why "limited" nuclear war would be unlikely to stay limited. Just as it takes two to tango, it takes two nations to dance the intricate nuclear minuet choreographed by the strategists of thinkable war. And the U.S.S.R., for its part, has made it very clear that it will not follow the correct steps as spelled out in our manuals. Thus, while the intellectual descendants of Herman Kahn write scholarly treatises about how many different kinds of nuclear war can dance on the head of a pin, those boorish Russian bears refuse to join the debate, insisting steadfastly that they will not respect the niceties of "limited" nuclear war if the firebreak between conventional and nuclear weaponry is ever crossed.

Why, then, do we keep planning for "limited" nuclear war? Maybe that too is a bluff. Or maybe the Soviet denial is itself a bluff. Thus perhaps we would not *really* respond to a Soviet provocation, even a serious one, with carefully orchestrated nuclear strikes. Perhaps we just claim that we will, so as to deter their provocation in the first place. And for their part, if a war starts and we do escalate to a restricted use of nuclear weapons, maybe the Soviets would not really go into the threatened all-out spasm, and burn down the dance floor. Maybe their rejection of "limited" nuclear war is a bluff to prevent U.S. planners from ever employing nuclear weapons, in any conflict. If so, let us hope that they succeed.

Because, make no mistake about it, if nuclear weapons are ever exchanged between the U.S. and U.S.S.R., whatever the plans of the strategists, there is an overwhelming probability that the well-laid plans will go to hell and very, very quickly. Perhaps some day a truly limited nuclear war will break out between two countries of limited nuclear capabilities—say, between India and Pakistan, or Israel and Libya. But the only thing limited about U.S.-Soviet nuclear war is the judgement of those who are now planning for it. You should be very clear on this: when government analysts design plans for "limited" nuclear war, they are planning your death.

### Europe: A Special Case

As British science writer Nigel Calder described it, East and West meet head-on in Europe—and especially in Germany—like two huge tectonic plates. The two superpowers, with their client states, grind together in this small, crowded and historic continent, with all the tension, strain, and buckling that goes with such geologic forces. And most experts agree that if World War III ever starts, it may well start here, in this European collision zone. Not surprisingly, then, much ink has been spilled over the defense of

Europe, and the Pentagon and Kremlin computers have been working overtime, developing strategy and tactics which, although not made in Europe, are designed to be used there.

First, we must make a distinction: between strategic weapons and tactical weapons. Strategic weapons are intended for use against the homeland of one's opponent; ICBMs, submarine-launched ballistic missiles and intercontinental bombers are the strategic delivery systems for both the U.S. and U.S.S.R. By contrast, tactical weapons are intended for battlefield use. Tactical weapons are delivered over a much shorter range and they are typically smaller than their strategic cousins—although this distinction is not clear-cut, since many tactical warheads (especially those deployed by the U.S.S.R.) tend to be relatively large, and the new generation of accurate, strategic U.S. weaponry may be smaller than their older, tactical versions. Tactical weapons are intended for use in a particular "theater," whereas strategic weapons are aimed by us at the Soviets and by the Soviets at us. Of course, one person's theater is another's reality, and thereby hangs a tale.

To many American planners, a tactical bomb is one that explodes in Germany. Since the beginning of the Cold War, both sides have been fearing and also preparing for a confrontation in Europe. Neither side can benefit from attacking the other, and both sides know that, but each side keeps insisting that the other does not. For Americans and Russians, the situation is bad. But for the Europeans, it is even worse. After all, we fought World Wars I and II on their soil, and they are something less than enthusiastic about another go-round. Their reluctance is understandable, given that the extreme destructiveness of nuclear weapons would utterly devastate the continent, making the depredations of World War II look like a Sunday school picnic. And yet, a keystone of NATO planning has been the "nuclear umbrella" held over western Europe by the United States. Once again, we are faced with the peculiar irony of deterrence; war is to be averted by threatening an even greater war which would be so intolerable as to make the threat difficult for the Soviets to believe and increasingly impossible even for our allies to tolerate.

Even the word "theater" implies something unreal, a make-believe of posturing and play-acting. But our theater is where the

Europeans *live*, and for them it is theater of the absurd and of unacceptable horror.

First, a bit of history, to set the stage for our European theater: the Bolshevik revolution of 1917 produced a double distrust of Soviet communism among the western democracies. Not only did the communists pull Russia out of World War I, leaving the allies to deal with Germany unaided, but communism also seemed likely to spread, especially via labor unions, to the democracies themselves. This fear was not lessened by the avowed commitment by Lenin, Trotsky, and Stalin to "worldwide revolution," and it was only with the onset of World War II and the German invasion in June 1941 that the U.S.S.R. became clearly if temporarily allied with the West. Indeed, the Cold War did not really begin at the end of World War II; rather, the period of 1941-1945 was merely the temporary interruption of a longstanding mistrust and antagonism. Even during the war, moreover, East-West relations were never very warm. In particular, Western leaders kept postponing the long-promised "second front" against Hitler in France, prefering to let Stalin absorb the brunt of German aggression. The U.S.S.R. lost twenty million people, more than all other combatants combined.

Following the war, Europe (including the U.S.S.R.) was in ruins and the Soviets quickly established client states in eastern Europe—in their mind, as a buffer against any future attack, but in the view of many Western leaders, as an initial effort at world conquest. The Red Army remained large and (in Western eyes) threatening, while (in Soviet eyes) it was justified by the even more threatening nuclear weapons of which the U.S. had a monopoly. In 1949, President Truman ordered the Strategic Air Command to include "retarding" nuclear strikes in its war planning; prior to that, all U.S. nuclear warheads had been relegated to strategic, intercontinental bombers. The first tactical nuclear weapons were installed in Europe in 1954, by order of President Eisenhower as part of his military "New Look," and in an effort to achieve maximum deterrence at minimum cost.

From the end of World War II, the U.S. had committed itself to the recovery of western Europe, partly out of humanitarian impulses, and partly in response to the Soviet threat, which had been magnified by their occupation of eastern Europe. Paul Nitze, later

200 • STOP NUCLEAR WAR! A HANDBOOK

a prominent nuclear strategist, was architect of the Marshall Plan for the economic recovery of western Europe. We proclaimed that American security was irretrievably tied to the security of western Europe, and the leaders of western Europe were pleased and reassured by that proclamation.

But as Soviet nuclear strength grew, our defense commitment to Europe began to seem less dependable. The culprit? That old skeleton in the closet of deterrence: credibility. When the U.S.S.R. developed its own arsenal of ICBMs, directly threatening U.S. cities, western Europe grew even more nervous. Could we be relied on, if our own lives might be at stake? Would the U.S. risk Boston to save Hamburg? Christian Herter, Eisenhower's Secretary of State during 1959-1960, commented, "I cannot conceive of any President engaging in all-out nuclear war unless we are in danger of all-out nuclear destruction ourselves." And in his book *Nuclear Weapons and Foreign Policy* (1957), Henry Kissinger had pointed out: "however firm allied unity may be, a nation cannot be counted on to commit suicide in defense of a foreign territory."

In 1962, responding in part to the diminishing credibility of the American commitment to Europe, Robert McNamara emphasized the doctrine of "flexible responses" to any Soviet invasion, developing scenarios of "limited" nuclear war as well as the use of conventional forces to repel conventional attack. Although Europe remained skeptical, worried that we were seeking to decouple our security from theirs, they acquiesced, and by 1967 flexible response became official NATO policy. In the meantime, some European powers remained unconvinced. In particular, France's DeGaulle maintained that he could not count on an American president being willing to sacrifice New York to defend Paris. France accordingly developed its own *"force de frappe,"* withdrawing from NATO's military command. (At the time, other factors were also involved, including DeGaulle's yearning for French military grandeur as well as anxiety over U.S. adventurism. This had been heightened in 1966 when Dean Rusk declared that the "western flank" of NATO was in the Pacific—thereby horrifying Europeans with the prospect that they might be drawn into a U.S.-China war over Vietnam.)

Like a recurring nightmare, however, the stubborn question of credibility would not go away. In truth, the nuclear defense of

Europe was (and still is) based on what Herbert York called an "awesome bluff," which must never be called. Some European leaders (notably Helmut Schmidt of West Germany) have worried that the U.S.S.R. could engage in a "sanctuary" nuclear war, using the Soviet homeland as a sanctuary from which to launch missile attacks on western Europe, since the U.S. would not retaliate, fearing retaliation upon U.S. cities in return. In response to this worry, they supported deployment of intermediate-range missiles—ground-launched cruise missiles and Pershing IIs—which have the range to strike cities and military targets in European Russia. Hence, these missiles would be a strategic threat to the U.S.S.R. and would insure that in the event of war in Europe, the U.S. would be involved.

One of the deepest European fears is that the U.S. and U.S.S.R. might be preparing to fight a "limited" nuclear war, using Europe as their battleground. This explains the furor in Europe caused by President Reagan's casual comment on October 16, 1981, that he "could see where you could have the exchange of tactical weapons in the field without it bringing either one of the major powers to pushing the button." In fact, just as we have seen that strategic nuclear war would almost certainly be "unlimited," there is no doubt that nuclear war in Europe would rapidly escalate. It is hard to imagine that Soviet leaders would bother distinguishing whether the nuclear-armed missiles destroying their country were launched from Europe (cruise and Pershings) or from North Dakota (Minutemen). Moreover, SS-20 bases are often located very close to Soviet ICBM silos, so that an attack on the SS-20s—presumably, part of the NATO plan for "limited" nuclear war in Europe—would look very much like an attack on the Soviet strategic deterrent.

Indeed, from the Soviet viewpoint, there is no real difference between tactical nuclear weapons blowing up SS-20 bases within the U.S.S.R., and strategic nuclear weapons blowing up ICBM silos, also located within the U.S.S.R. In short, there simply is no valid military reason for these intermediate-range NATO missiles. In addition, because of the extreme accuracy of cruise missiles, and the speed of Pershing IIs (six minutes from Bonn to Moscow), installing these missiles is likely to make the Russians more nervous than ever, leading to a dangerous, hair-trigger expectancy on their part.

Actually, the credibility of NATO's nuclear deterrent in Europe is doubly undermined—first, as we have just seen, by the uncertainty over whether the U.S. would use nuclear weapons and thereby risk strategic nuclear war, and second, by the realities of potential war in Europe. Herbert York, Director of Defense Research for President Eisenhower and Kennedy, put it best:

> On the one hand, NATO says that if the Soviets launch a massive attack on Europe, even without using nuclear weapons, then NATO will reply with nuclear weapons and thus set in motion a series of events which could easily result in the destruction of most of Europe's cities and the death of most of its people.

> On the other hand, most European political leaders, and probably most of its military leaders, would not in fact be willing to deliberately set in motion events leading to such a result. However, the public admission of such an unwillingness would, as the experts say, "undermine the credibility of the deterrent," and thus increase the probability of an attack.

The nuclear bluff is probably more transparent in Europe than anywhere else. There is no other place on earth that is so ill-suited to be "defended" by a nuclear war. Europe has no vast expanses of desert or uninhabited mountains; rather, the continent is densely populated. As one official put it, the villages in Germany are only about two kilotons apart! Under such conditions, to defend Europe with nuclear weapons is to blow it up. As Helmut Schmidt, chancellor of West Germany, has written, "a war which, though regarded as a limited war by the super-powers, would be no less than a war of annihilation for the countries of the battlefield." Even aside from the immediate effects of blast and heat, about 400-500 medium-sized bombs, exploded on the ground, would produce enough fallout to make all of Great Britain, Belgium, the Netherlands and West Germany radioactively lethal. The tactical arsenals of both sides consist of more than ten times that number.

Out of this concern comes another effort to shore up the deterrent by making nuclear war more credible: the neutron bomb. This modified hydrogen bomb produces about six times more prompt radiation—mostly neutrons—than an atomic bomb of equivalent yield. Since these high-energy neutrons can penetrate steel, they are attractive to NATO military planners as potential antitank weapons. And tanks, of course, are a major part of the Warsaw Pact military arsenal. Thus, for example, a one kiloton neutron bomb would kill twice as many tankmen as would a 10 kiloton atomic weapon, but with only one-fifth the blast damage. This has led some to describe the neutron bomb as the "ultimate capitalist weapon," since it kills people while leaving property intact.

The idea, once again, is to maintain credibility by presenting a weapon which is *usable*. Given the crowded conditions of Europe, as well as the probability that if war breaks out, tanks will be among the major combatants, the neutron bomb has been attractive to NATO strategists. It has two major drawbacks, however.

For one, neutron bombs are not at all free of "collateral damage," as the war-planners call the death and destruction of innocent civilians. A typical atomic bomb, for instance, releases about 50 percent of its energy as blast and 35 percent of its energy as heat; by contrast, a typical neutron bomb will release about 40 percent of its energy as blast and 25 percent as heat—so, neutron bombs will give out a total of 65 percent blast and heat, as compared to 85 percent blast and heat produced by atomic bombs. Even allowing for their smaller expected yields (around one kiloton), neutron bombs will therefore still pack a tremendous wallop, and their "collateral damage" will also be enormous—somewhat less than other nuclear weapons, but enormous nevertheless.

The other, and even greater, danger of neutron bombs is the same as the danger of planning for "limited" nuclear war: by making nuclear weapons more usable, we make it more likely that they will be used. That is the avowed purpose of neutron bombs, acknowledged by their advocates as well as their opponents; the hawks claim they will make deterrence more credible while the doves claim they will make nuclear war more likely.

Faced with all these moves toward war-fighting instead of war-deterring, as well as an increased belligerence between Washington and Moscow, Europe in the early 1980s has been convulsed by an epidemic of sanity. As of late 1981, 72 percent of the Dutch people favor unilateral nuclear disarmament, as do more than 60 percent of the British. It seems increasingly unlikely that cruise missiles or Pershing IIs will be implanted on European soil, and if they are, they will immediately become major items of contention within their "host" countries, and may well fracture NATO. The European peace movement is one of the most stupendous events in modern history, with hundreds of thousands of demonstrators in the streets of just about every major city. The more NATO insists on making nuclear war thinkable, the more Europeans have been doing just that—thinking about it, and rejecting it.

Yet there seems little doubt that both NATO and the Warsaw Pact are busily planning for nuclear war in Europe. Thus, when NATO officers speak enthusiastically about the new "integrated battlefield," they are not concerned with civil rights! Troops are being taught such useful things as how to calculate their distance from a nuclear blast by estimating the "flash-to-bang time"—just as we can estimate distance from a lightning strike by counting the number of seconds before hearing thunder. If war comes to Europe, NATO is ready, willing and able to make it nuclear.

Given this avowed policy, it may be that the Red Army will be more cautious than otherwise. But the same stance that may help keep the peace also runs a greater risk of losing everything if hostilities ever break out. "The first level of escalation for use would, of course, be to nuclear weapons," said General Bernard W. Rogers, Alexander Haig's successor as NATO Supreme Commander. As to the Russians, "their doctrine calls for preempting our first use. If they could figure out when we might escalate, then they would hit us first, with nuclear weapons if they thought we were going to strike with them." Whether or not this is a true statement of Soviet policy, the expectation provides a reason for NATO to preempt them. At the same time, of course, Soviet expectation of our preempting them may make them likely to preempt our preempting—and so it goes.

And what about the Russians? In the same interview quoted above, General Rogers concluded by noting "I cannot believe that any Soviet leader, current or future, is going to expose his people to that kind of nuclear exchange." Soviet military planners have also shown an attitude which must be terribly frustrating to NATO planners: just as in their attitude toward strategic nuclear war, leaders of the U.S.S.R. have consistently denied the possibility of "limited" tactical nuclear war. Part of their motivation is clear enough: the Russians consider themselves Europeans, and war in Europe is war on their own soil. Hence, they have little patience for the niceties of precise, computer-plotted tactical nuclear exchanges. They believe in Clausewitz, who wrote "To introduce into the philosophy of war a principle of moderation would be absurd. War is an act of violence pursued to the uttermost." This is not necessarily as bellicose as it sounds. It says: if war breaks out, do not delude yourself into thinking you will be spared. The only sane course, then, is to avoid war altogether.

In fact, Soviet warheads are generally larger than their NATO counterparts—most are over 20 kilotons and 600 missiles are in the 500 kiloton to 3 megaton range. Hardly the stuff to limit "collateral damage." Moreover, Soviet missiles are less accurate, making it even more difficult to spare the noncombatants. Any way you look at it, the whole business is difficult indeed.

### Some Realities of Deterrence

In a way, most Americans know about their country's preparation for nuclear war in about the same way that an adolescent knows about sex: a rather hazy sense of the whole mysterious process combined with almost total ignorance as to the sweaty details. For most of us, the details of nuclear deterrence may seem to be unimportant. But without details, it is all too easy to pretend that nuclear weapons, and our plans for using them, don't really exist. Most adolescents grow up and experience sex. We hope that most Americans will not ever experience nuclear war. But just as sex education is supposed to prevent mistakes, perhaps a bit of nuclear war education will make our lives safer as well.

Meet the Minuteman III missile: 60 feet long, 6 feet wide, powered by 3 solid fuel rockets and carrying 3 warheads. It weighs 7,800 lbs and can travel 6,500 miles, from the U.S. over the North Pole to the Soviet Union, at 15,000 miles per hour—almost 20 times the speed of sound. Each one lives in its own Little House on the Prairie, marked with a little sign that says "US Government Property—No Trespassing—Use of Deadly Force Authorized." That's for sure: the Minuteman missile is the embodiment of deadly force. The Air Force has authorized 2,600 young men to use this deadly force. They are young, typically in their twenties, lieutenants and captains paired off in missile combat teams. They sit 50 feet underground, during 24-hour shifts at their launch consoles, each armed with a .38 revolver. They neither see nor touch the missiles they have been trained to launch and they do not know precisely what part of Russia their missile is targeted to destroy. (Presumably, they have no "need to know," in the Pentagon jargon. Moreover, if it became known that a particular missile, for example, was aimed at Minsk, and if one of its launch officers happened to look up Minsk in the encyclopedia, and perhaps see a picture of some smiling, bright-faced children playing in a park, and if he noted that there are tens of thousands of such children, and that they don't seem very different from his own children at home—well, that officer just might hesitate to launch his missile if the call ever came. And of course, the possibility of such a hesitation would undermine the "credibility of the deterrent.")

Each young man has a key, undistinguished looking, like a brass house key. To launch a missile, two men must insert their keys and turn them within a second or so of each other, and two pairs of two men each must "vote" identically. For the keys to work, they must be twisted, like an automobile ignition key, and then held against slight resistance for two seconds. It requires just a bit of determination, a wee bit of continuing pressure, signifying that the turner of the key really means it.

Above, each missile is shielded by a massive concrete slab resting on a short stretch of railroad track; the track carries the slab smoothly to the side and out of the way when blown open by a small explosive charge, just before the big birds are sent on their one-way migration. They are not evil men, these wielders of the keys in their concrete crypts. Most are married and many have children. They don't have dueling scars or look like Gestapo officers. If you saw one at a supermarket, you wouldn't even notice. Often they attend night school in their spare time, studying to be accountants, computer programmers, college professors. They practice turning their keys, changing the target patterns on their missiles, responding to various levels of alerts—thousands of times, so that when the call comes, they will do what they have practiced so well. Not for vengeance, mind you, but for the deterrence.

There are also submarines. Unlike the missile officers, who receive regular commands and controls from their Air Force superiors, submariners lead a more isolated life. It is difficult to talk to a submerged submarine, because the water gets in the way, and to avoid detection, submarines are not only nuclear-armed but also nuclear-powered, designed to remain underwater for weeks at a time. To talk to the men in the submarines, we have the "Tacamos," "take charge and move out" airplanes, which fly low over the water, dragging literally miles of antenna line behind them in the ocean.

We have 12 Poseidon submarines, each fitted with 16 of the newest Trident missiles, and each missile is MIRVed to carry up to 17 warheads. That's 204 warheads in a single submarine, nearly 2,500 warheads in all, each several times the power of the Hiroshima bomb. There are also 19 Poseidon submarines with their original Poseidon missiles, 16 missiles to a submarine, and each missile with from 10 to 14 warheads apiece. The latest generation of submarines, the Trident, is now being delivered. A single Trident submarine weighs 18,000 tons, more than twice that of Poseidon, and carries 24 Trident missiles; each MIRV to carry up to 17 warheads. With 24 missiles and 17 warheads per missile, a single Trident submarine will carry 408 warheads. The first 10 will be docked at Bangor, Washington, and the rest at King's Bay, Georgia.

There are also B-52 bombers, 8-engined behemoths known as Stratofortresses, dispersed around the 46 Strategic Air Command bases. Each airplane can carry several nuclear gravity bombs, as well as SRAMs (short-range attack missiles) with a range of 25 to 100 miles, and long-range Hound Dog missiles, with a range up to 600 miles. Air-launched cruise missiles, with a range of 1,200 miles, have also been ordered for the B-52s, and the first ones have already been built by Boeing. Each B-52 can carry up to 12 of these. Each B-52 is also equipped with elaborate electronic countermeasures, and lead shielding for the windows. The crews are trained to take off blindfolded, if their airfield is under attack and they cannot look outside.

Military planners used to talk about "command and control." This has now expanded to become $C^3I$ (pronounced "see cubed eye"), or "command, control, communications, and intelligence." If nuclear weapons are the muscle and sinews of American nuclear war-fighting, then $C^3I$ is the brain and nerves.

The eyes of $C^3I$ are the satellites, in many shapes and sizes. The

Defense Satellite Communication System (DSCS) consists of 6 transmitter satellites in 22,000-mile geosynchronous orbit. There are also 3 early warning satellites, each with 2,000 infrared sensors; one each surveys the Indian, Atlantic, and Pacific Oceans, for the hot exhaust "signatures" by which missiles are known.

The nerves are communications, with a combination of radio, telephone and teletype lines, and satellite transmitters. There are several brains, including the Strategic Air Command base at Offutt Field, near SAC Headquarters in Omaha, Nebraska, and the NORAD headquarters located under a quarter mile of solid granite in Cheyenne Mountain, near Colorado Springs. Cheyenne Mountain is an underground, windowless city, humming softly behind 25-ton steel doors. There, 15 steel-walled buildings (11 of them more than 3 stories high) stand on 1,319 steel springs, each weighing 1,000 lbs. There is a gym, a snack bar, barbershop, a 2-bed infirmary and 6 million gallons of water.

Since there is no real "defense" in a nuclear war, only the threat of retaliation, the danger of having one's own $C^3I$ destroyed is a potentially powerful threat, since it could eliminate one's ability to retaliate, and hence, to deter attack. So, the SAC also maintains a fleet of specially modified Boeing 707s, with one of them constantly airborne, 24 hours a day. While aloft, each plane makes an erratic flight over North America for 8 hours at a time. This is the "Looking Glass" airplane, with its command officer authorized to order nuclear war and hence, to take us all through the looking glass into a wonderland never before experienced by this planet.

Sitting ever ready at Andrews Air Force Base, just 10 miles from the White House, is a specially equipped Boeing 747, the "Doomsday Plane," officially known as NEACP (pronounced "kneecap"), the National Emergency Airborne Command Post, from which the president and his advisers will survey the desolation that was America while they conduct a nuclear war. It is not clear where such an airplane would eventually land, and accordingly, a "ground mobile command post," disguised as a commercial vehicle, has been ordered for the President, and delivery is expected in 1982 or 1983. It may be some consolation to know that following a nuclear war, our leader may be tooling around whatever is left of the interstate highway system in his own special souped-up Winnebago.

In case the President chooses to go underground instead, there is always Mt. Weather, a hollowed-out mountain 80 miles west of Washington, D.C. More than 300 employees are permanently assigned here.

It is also rumored—but not confirmed—that one or two Minutemen do not carry warheads at all; rather, they are equipped with "Doomsday Tapes," computer-keyed messages whose job is to insure that any unfired missiles, any laggard bombers that have not gotten the message, discharge their final duty. In the last agonies of all-out nuclear spasm, these guardians of our security will rise to the occasion, hang gloriously in the stratosphere, and wail out the final call to arms. Nigel Calder described what would follow: "Out of battered silos and the ocean depths and neglected airstrips come forgotten warheads, badly aimed, to pick like vultures over the corpse of our civilization. . . ." The mindless vengeance of dead men? Of course not, the planners will say—credibility of the deterrent.

Actually, there is a detailed, carefully worked-out plan for conducting nuclear war. It is the SIOP ("Single Integrated Operational Plan") and is one of the best-guarded secrets of government. In fact, the Joint Chiefs of Staff don't even divulge the secrets of the SIOP to their civilian superiors. The priorities of the SIOP seem clear: nuclear facilities, including military bases, missile sites, submarine ports; radar, military headquarters and communication centers; airports; fuel stores and munitions depots. Although big cities are presumably targeted as well, it seems likely that they have lower priority. Thus, Vladivostock is probably not really a "choice" target, compared, say with Petropavlovsk (a port for nuclear-armed submarines). Similarly, we can assume that Grand Forks, North Dakota and Malmstrom, Montana, with their nearby Minuteman missiles, are more directly in the Soviet gunsights than Bismarck or even, perhaps, Chicago.

In the bowels of the greatest Pentagon computers, the SIOP resides. It whirs and blinks about nuclear war, 24 hours a day, playing theoretical games against the supposed Russian plan, known as RISOP. Among all the myriad moves and countermoves that SIOP makes on our behalf, there's one thing it never does—it never thinks about surrender. It seems that in 1958, a Rand Corporation analyst by name of Paul Kecskemiti wrote a study on *Strate-*

*gic Surrender,* in which he thought about that something which is
even more unthinkable than nuclear war. The furor was such that a
bill was rushed through Congress, prohibiting the use of any federal
funds even to study the possibility of American surrender. In the
index of Henry Kissinger's book *Nuclear Weapons and Foreign Policy,* the index listing under "unconditional surrender" reads *See*
Victory, total."

Somewhere between total victory and unconditional surrender,
then, the SIOP keeps spinning, updating its recommendations,
ready to whisper its carefully considered, statistically verified advice. But to whom does the SIOP speak? Ultimately, not to another
machine but to a person—the Commander-in-Chief, or if need be,
his surviving descendants in command. This person, then, must
make a decision. Based on what? The data inputs to the Pentagon's
War Room are staggering in complexity. No one person can be
expected to interpret them all. In 1976, a former Deputy Director
of Defense Research and Engineering testified before Congress as
follows:

> It is no use to give (the President) a room full of status boards and say
> 'Here it is, boss, make a decision.' It has to be boiled down to a scale—
> for example green, yellow or red—and he can decide by how far the
> needle moves, what he should do.

Whoever controls "the needle" would control our destiny. Who
chooses the appropriate color for a given situation? How does the
nation finally decide what provocation deserves what response?
Will there be any Monday-morning quarterbacks left alive to sec-
ond-guess a bad decision?

Finally, since uncertainty seems to be at the very hub of nuclear strategic doctrine, let us end this section on the realities of
deterrence with a little understood wild card, a real live joker in
the nuclear deck: something called electromagnetic pulse (EMP).
In some ways, EMP embodies many of the uncertainties of this
whole crazy business.

On July 8, 1962, a Thor rocket carried an H-Bomb 248 miles
above Johnston Atoll in the Pacific. When it exploded, street lights
failed, burglar alarms sounded, and electrical systems generally

went haywire in Honolulu, Hawaii, 800 miles away. Everyone was puzzled. Since then, physicists have gotten a pretty good idea of what happened. It seems that gamma rays, produced by nuclear explosions high above the atmosphere, bang into electrons, forcing them to emit a sudden and very intense electromagnetic pulse, EMP. When it reaches an electrical conductor, this EMP causes a split-second surge of electric current, tens of thousands of volts per meter. In the early 1960s, when EMP was just being noticed for the first time, vacuum tubes were the heart of electronic circuits; now, with the semiconductor revolution (which has brought us low-cost home computers and miniaturized circuits), vacuum tubes have been largely replaced by transistors and microprocessors. These new, state-of-the-art components are also much more fragile than their predecessors—in fact, integrated solid-state circuits are about ten million times more sensitive to EMP than their "primitive" ancestors had been.

The implications are staggering. A single nuclear explosion, in the stratosphere above Nebraska, for example, would perform an electronic lobotomy on computer memories throughout North America. The accompanying surge in voltage would also have an unknown but clearly unhelpful effect on all other electronic equipment. What effect would EMP have on bombers attempting to complete their doomsday missions? What about incoming—or outgoing—ICBMs, with their complex and delicate circuitry? What about deterrence? At Kirtland Air Force Base in New Mexico there stands an extraordinary structure, twelve stories high and built entirely of wood: it is even joined together with 200,000 wooden bolts. It is an EMP-simulator, intended to help discover the best ways of "hardening" B-52s against these electronic jolts. The Defense Nuclear Agency currently spends $11 million per year to maintain 165 people on Johnston Atoll, so as to test the EMP effects of a high-altitude nuclear blast, at a moment's notice if the limited test-ban treaty is ever abrogated.

In the event of a nuclear war, and after hurried consultation with the great god SIOP, the President will presumably want to send the Emergency Action Message, the final call to arms. There are now 43 different ways of sending the EAM, including a wide array of cables, microwave relays, satellites and special radio transmitters: high, ultra-high, and low frequency. "It may take hours, and we might have to send runners with handwritten messages," said a Pentagon official commenting on the EMP problem, "but somehow the message will get out." Actually, however, no one knows the effect of even a single high-altitude explosion on today's delicate electronics, not to mention a possible dozen or even hundreds.

For years, though, the Bell System has been hardening its underground cables, wrapping steel around switching centers, repeater stations and command posts. It has cost hundreds of millions and possibly even billions in design and construction during the 1970s, and yet the Defense Department did not pay a penny. Rather, the extra costs were simply—and covertly—passed along to the consumer in higher telephone bills (An interesting example both of the hidden societal costs of our military efforts, and of the incompleteness of official Defense Department military budgets.) In any event, this practice has stopped in the 1980s, since the government has begun allowing competition in long-distance communication. Because Bell no longer has a comfortable monopoly, it has become more price-sensitive, and so the Department of Defense—and not the telephone customer—will now have to pay directly for EMP protection. For example, fiber-optic tubes (immune to EMP) are due to be installed between Washington, D.C. and Boston by 1984.

What about the rest of the $C^3I$ network? Will hardening work? We don't know. In his 1981 official posture statement, former Secretary of Defense Harold Brown stated:

> We need to maintain forces able to survive a Soviet attack and deal a victory-denying counterblow while maintaining significant forces in reserve, *assuming that we have command and control to operate these forces.* (our italics)

In truth, there is tremendous uncertainty regarding EMP and its effects on our ability to command, control, and operate nuclear forces during a war. This has major implications for any ability to fight a "limited" nuclear war. John Steinbrunner, a senior Brookings Institution think tanker, wrote of EMP that "the precariousness of command channels probably means that nuclear war would be uncontrollable, as a practical matter, shortly after the first tens of weapons are launched." The uncertainty itself increases the pressures for launching our entire strategic arsenal in the event of a nuclear war, since the *expectation* of failed communication links can make it seem necessary to do so now or never: Use 'em or lose 'em. Just like with counterforce.

So, if hardening and other anti-EMP measures will help shore up C³I and also appease that never-satisfied demon, the "credibility of the deterrence," then it might be a good thing. On the other hand, insofar as it makes "limited" nuclear war seem more feasible once again, then it certainly is a bad thing, since if nothing else, *we will never really know if such a war can be limited.* To some strategists, our ignorance of EMP cries out to be corrected. But in this case, ignorance is strength—neither U.S. leaders nor their Soviet counterparts know what would happen if deterrence fails. And someday, somehow, it will fail. As analyst Lawrence Freedman has pointed out:

> An international order that rests upon a stability created by nuclear weapons will be the most terrible legacy with which each succeeding generation will endow the next. To believe that this can go on indefinitely without major disaster requires an optimism unjustified by any historical or political perspective.

Carefully, then, but firmly, we must extricate ourselves from the terrible clutches of deterrence. Certainly, we must not let things get any worse.

# 7. Psychology: Thinking and

## Not Thinking About the Unthinkable

When it comes to nuclear war, human psychology has been against us. Thus, our ways of thinking (and not thinking) have made our predicament in the first place, and human psychology has generally made things worse rather than better. For reasons we shall now explore, most of us avoid thinking about nuclear war, and when we do, we often think about it wrongly. If we are ever to turn things around, however, we need to deal not only with the "hardware"— the weapons and delivery systems—but also with the human "software," the psychology that makes us rely on these weapons, that enables some of us to contemplate their use, and that keeps most of us from thinking about it at all, and hence, from acting on our own behalf.

Let us therefore confront the murky processes of human thought, seeking to identify how and why we think and do not think about nuclear war. If we can get a clear look at ourselves, maybe then we can break free of our mental shackles and begin acting, under our own orders, and for our own salvation.

### The Neanderthal Mentality

"The splitting of the atom has changed everything but our way of thinking," wrote Einstein, adding "and hence, we drift toward unparalleled catastrophe." A world of splittable atoms is clearly dangerous, and yet as Einstein foresaw, much of the problem seems to lie elsewhere, in "our way of thinking." For example, Britain and France each have enough nuclear firepower to obliterate the other, and yet European strategic planners do not lie awake nights worrying about preemptive strikes between London and Paris. Between these nations at least, there is a different way of thinking than between us and the U.S.S.R. Even within the United States, the Navy and Air Force are each immensely powerful (and competitive); yet they restrict their fighting to the football field and Congressional appropriations committees. Clearly, the possession of nuclear weapons, although bad enough, does not in itself assure unparalleled catastrophe. Combined with an outmoded way of thinking, however, the splitting of the atom threatens us all.

That outmoded way of thinking has been described by Charles Osgood as the "Neanderthal mentality." In a sense, it is a misleading phrase, not even anthropologically accurate (we probably did not evolve from Neanderthalers). It is useful, however, as a caricature—an exaggerated shorthand for primitive and universal mental habits of human beings. It is also appropriately unpleasant-sounding.

The Neanderthal mentality persists because it has long been adaptive, contributing to the success of its possessors. In ages gone by, during 99.999 percent of our evolutionary and cultural history, our Neanderthal mentality served us well. But ever since August 6, 1945, the situation has changed dramatically while, as Einstein emphasized, our way of thinking has not.

Fortunately, however, all is not lost. We can change our behavior, overcoming our Neanderthal mentality. The anti-nuclear war movement in Europe and the U.S. may well represent the beginning of a major breakthrough: the triumph of the human intellect over our Neanderthal tendencies. If so, it is welcome, and none too soon. If we are to change our way of thinking—and change it we must—it might help to recognize it. Here, then, are some examples of the Neanderthal mentality:

1. *"Fighting pays."* Most living things will fight if it is worth their while. So will people. Numerous studies of primitive human beings have shown that under certain circumstances—when food or mates are scarce, or when the young warriors have little to lose and much prestige to gain—people go to "war." Typically, however, such battles are more like skirmishing than the nuclear war of civilized nation-states, and fatalities are rare. Now, we have Joint Chiefs of Staff and nuclear arsenals, but our inclination to fight may well have been established, at least in part, during our long history when warfare was much less dangerous. With nuclear weapons, war can only be a losing proposition. But the Neanderthal within us may have a hard time understanding this.

2. *"We win: you lose."* For the Neanderthal, like the modern-day sports fan, winning is everything. Certainly it never occurs to either that winning is literally *impossible*. Football coaches are fond of noting that a tie is about as satisfying as kissing your sister: the implication is clear; one winner, one loser—nothing in between. So each team strives to win. It was ever so, presumably, in battles between rival groups of humans and before that, pre-humans, and in the competition between *Homo sapiens* the predator, and his prey. Moreover, our early social experiences incline us in the same competitive direction: the payoffs of Western schooling and the marketplace go to the successful (winning) competitors. But times have changed, and the Neanderthal must learn to accept a tie—not as a regrettable and unsatisfying outcome, but as a permanent situation; indeed, as a triumph—the only acceptable ending. In conflict between nuclear-armed states, if either side loses, then both lose. We must therefore restrain the Neanderthal within us, forget about winning, and try to figure our how to arrange a permanent tie. For these days, that is the only way to win.

3. *"In-group, out-group: either you're with us or you're against us."* Sociobiologists have recently emphasized the importance of shared genes in promoting altruism among living things. Social psychologists and sociologists, for their part, have emphasized the notion of "in-group amity, out-group enmity." Whatever its interwoven causes, the phenomenon seems real enough: even in our daily lives, the boundaries of our concern are strangely limited to family and friends, and nepotism appears to be a crosscultural universal. It has even been expedient to designate the out-group as not quite human. But suddenly, there is no out-group. Somehow, the highly discriminating Neanderthal must understand the new demands of enlightened self-interest: the narrow boundaries of our earlier concern must be widened. John Donne is finally correct—no one is an island these days, although some of us are still dangerously and stubbornly insular.

We typically dehumanize our enemies, making it easier to kill them: gooks, commies, kikes, krauts, niggers and japs are easier to hate and kill than if they were people like us. On the other hand, there is some hope in the speed with which we can change our perceptions. For example, during World War II, surveys showed that Germans and Japanese were described by Americans as "war-like," "treacherous" and "cruel." By 1966, none of these adjectives applied to the Germans and Japenese any more, for we had become allies. Instead, the Russians (previously our allies and hence, well-regarded) had become "warlike" and "treacherous." Similarly, in 1966, the mainland Chinese were "warlike," "treacherous" and "sly." Following President Nixon's visit, however, they became "hard-working," "intelligent," "artistic," "progressive" and "prac-tical."

The atomic bomb is a masterpiece of human cooperation by a devoted in-group. Ironically, it may be used in the ultimate state-ment of blinkered noncooperation. We must somehow learn to re-establish the boundaries of our group, encompassing all who inhabit this planet. "We must either learn to live together as broth-ers," said Martin Luther King, "or we are going to perish together as fools."

4. *"If we do it, it's good; if they do it, it's bad."* When we introduce troops in support of a locally unpopular foreign govern-ment that we support (as in Vietnam), it is portrayed as a noble cause. But when the Soviets do something similar (as in Afghanistan), it is a dastardly act of international aggression. Sim-ilarly, we can introduce missiles into another country (Turkey) ca-pable of striking deep into the U.S.S.R., and it is acceptable defensive strategy. But when the Soviets follow suit (Cuba), it is unacceptable and in fact, worth precipitating a crisis bringing the world to the brink of disaster. We readily justify a "margin of safety" in our military forces; but we accuse them of maintaining more than is clearly needed for defensive purposes. Our bombs are clean, theirs are dirty. God is with us, not with them.

5. *"Flight or Fight."* Physicians have long recognized this syn-drome, in which the body responds to emergency conditions by activating the sympathetic nervous system: the heart beats faster, blood is shunted from the gut to the muscles, the pupils dilate and the adrenals begin pumping. Is there a mental effect as well? Ac-cording to Charles Osgood, the Neanderthal mentality includes "cognitive stereotypy," in which increased stress results in stronger (habitual) tendencies gaining the upper hand over weaker (less fa-

miliar) behaviors. As a result, there is a shift away from creative flexibility. This occurs, paradoxically, just when we most need our intellect. The "flight or fight" syndrome, with its likely mental effects, was probably appropriate for Neanderthals, however: when confronted by a sabre-tooth, an unfriendly Neanderthal, or a thunderstorm, success may well have gone to the one who responded quickly and automatically, and who spent little time lost in thought. But the world has changed, and lightning reflexes for a right uppercut or a missile launch will not serve us well these days.

6. *"Ostrichism."* We seek gratification, positive reinforcement, experiences that have always been consistent with success. When possible, we try to spare ourselves discomfort, not only physical but also mental. And few things are as mentally uncomfortable as "thinking about the unthinkable." So, paradoxically once again, our psychological "defense mechanisms" make us *more* at risk. We blissfully substitute the illusion of security for real security, preferring to contemplate the manageable and the mundane over the dangerous and distant. Nuclear war is painful to imagine; thinking about it will probably not help you to "have a nice day." But unless we begin facing our danger and enduring the mental pain, the Neanderthal will be caught with his head in the sand—and the rest, regrettably exposed.

Similarly, we may well be programmed to pay attention to immediate, pressing needs; anything else seems unreal by contrast. Although thousands of megatons are at this moment poised for your incineration, on a day-to-day basis you probably worry more about paying the milkman or the nocturnal barking of a neighbor's dog. In an invited lecture to a U.N. colloquium in 1978, Osgood wrote:

> The more people can avoid thinking about negatives (like there being no more fuel for cars or a nuclear holocaust)—particularly when they seem remote in time and are highly symbolic in nature—the less likely they are to try to do anything about them until it's too late. Seated in the backyard on a nice spring day, watching the kids at play, and sipping a beer, the Neanderthal within us simply cannot conceive of the trees suddenly blackened and the voices of the children stilled—or there being no more beer.

The Russell-Einstein Manifesto, issued on the tenth anniversary of the bombing of Hiroshima, described the problem faced—or rather, not faced—by human ostriches:

> They can scarcely bring themselves to grasp that they, individually . . . are in imminent danger of perishing agonizingly. . . .

In part, the planning and theorizing all seems so bloodless and cerebral, that a single soldier with a rifle can feel more threatening. As psychiatrist Jerome Frank pointed out: "Since nuclear weapons in distant countries poised for annihilation cannot be seen, heard, smelled, tasted or touched, a constant effort of imagination is required to keep in mind how threatening they are." The SIOP machine in its smoothly humming Pentagon computer, the tidy missile silos and well-groomed young men sitting at their precise consoles, the strategies and counter-strategies . . . all these produce a world of unreality in which ostriches can thrive. At least for a time.

7. *"It can't happen here—certainly not to me."* The psychiatrists call it "denial": when faced with something very unpleasant, some people just say it isn't so. But denying it does not make it go away. T. S. Eliot once remarked that "Humankind cannot bear very much reality." In the case of nuclear war, however, humankind cannot survive much more denial. Yet, we shrink from such thoughts, often dwelling in a fantasyland of personal survival. The book and movie *On the Beach* depicted the end of the human species following a nuclear war. Toward the end, only a handful of people were still alive; hundreds of millions had already died. And yet, most of the audience secretly imagined themselves to be included among those survivors!

On the island of Martinique, most of the residents prepared for the eruption of Mount Pelee, but inadequately—they couldn't believe it would be that bad. Similarly with the eruption of Mount St. Helens: on Saturday, May 17, 1980, cabin owners pressured sheriff's deputies into letting them visit their property. The mountain exploded the next day, surprising everyone with its force, and causing scores of deaths. In general, we adapt quickly to immediate situations, but have a hard time believing in overwhelming catastrophe; actually, we can believe in them—intellectually—but the realization is so staggering that we repress any gut-level understanding. In his book *Age of Uncertainty,* John Kenneth Galbraith wrote that

> Man has learned to live with the thought of his own mortality. And he now has accomodated to the thought that all may die, that his children and grandchildren will not exist. It's a capacity for accomodation at which we can only marvel. I suspect that our minds accept the thought but do not embrace the reality. The act of imagination is too great or too awful. Our minds can extend to a war in some distant jungle and set in motion the actions that reject it. But not yet to the nuclear holocaust.

> A commitment to this reality is now the supreme test of our politics. None should accept the easy evasion that the decision is not ours. . . . For after the first exchange of missiles . . . the ashes of Communism and the ashes of Capitalism will be indistinguishable. Not even the most passionate ideologue will be able to speak of the difference, for he, too, will be dead. In an age when so much is uncertain, there is one certainty: this truth we must confront."

But confronting such truths will not be easy for the present-day Neanderthal. We are tuned in to the wavelengths of our workaday world—birth, death, fighting, and sex—not to the first-and-only volcanic eruption of impending worldwide doom, for which nothing has prepared us. The Hiroshima bomb killed about 100,000 people immediately, then probably another 75,000 within a few months. Let us take a total of 100,000—a very conservative estimate, especially since today's bombs dwarf the primitive Hiroshima effort. At 100,000 apiece, 10 bombs equals one million deaths; 10,000 bombs equals one billion. (What *is* one billion?) Between the Soviets and ourselves, there are about 50,000 bombs. The mind wavers, our antennae numb to the signals, as from outer space—messages on some totally novel wavelength, for which we have no receivers. The catastrophe would be unearthly, so we cannot comprehend it. We draw a blank, and turn away: denial.

Goethe proposed a motto for the eighteenth-century Age of

Enlightenment: *Sapere Aude* ("Dare to Know"). It would be a good one for today.

8. *"It hasn't happened, so it won't happen."* There really is very little new under the sun. In general, therefore, it is a good rule to assume that the future will be like the past. In fact, most living things learn rather quickly when something is not going to happen—psychologists call it "habituation," the most primitive form of learning. Simply put, we cease responding to things that don't quickly lead on to something else. This is why, for example, we stop hearing the hum of a refrigerator or become oblivious to a pungent smell after being exposed to it for a while. We *habituate.*

Living things can even habituate to *changes*, if they are gradual enough. If you place a frog in a bucket of cold water, and then heat the water very gradually, the frog will never notice the change, and won't jump out. It will simply get hotter and hotter (or so it is said) until eventually it cooks. Since 1945, we have been surrounded by nuclear weapons which have gradually, almost imperceptibly, increased in numbers, in accuracy, and in danger. If we don't notice soon, we may suffer the same fate as the habituating frog. As President Carter commented in his farewell address, we have grown accustomed to nuclear weapons, like our eyes to the dark.

And besides, they haven't been used in anger since 1945. Of course, many things have not yet happened; nonetheless, we would be fools to deny their eventuality—our own deaths, for example, even if by natural causes. Nuclear war, for another, unless we take it seriously.

9. *"Whistling in the Wind."* There is, generally, a certain wisdom by which people gauge how to spend their energies. We adjust our efforts to the size of the task at hand, avoiding those that seem unmanageable. We may occasionally whistle in the wind, but always fully aware that we cannot cause it to change direction by doing so. The Neanderthal shies away from wrestling with earthquakes, arguing with hurricanes or defying a volcano, and for perfectly good reasons. Indeed, we are rarely rewarded for taking on an oversized opponent. And as opponents go, nuclear war is grossly oversized, in two important respects. First, the weight of political,

social, bureaucratic, and military inertia, combined with the enormous numbers of people involved, and compounded by the above-mentioned Neanderthal traits, make the task seem larger than any mountain, more intractable than any earthquake, more indifferent to personal efforts than a solar eclipse. Why bother whistling in the wind when your breath can be more profitably employed in your own personal exertions? Second, we shy away from the enormous destructive power of nuclear explosions themselves, feeling dwarfed, inadequate, or sometimes unable even to care. In the short run, it may be personally beneficial to avoid whistling in such a nuclear wind. But the short run is running out, and we must begin making contact with another part of ourselves, a part that goes beyond immediate success or failures, and that sometimes even enjoys tilting at windmills.

10. *"More is better."* Dr. Nicholas Humphrey, professor of animal behavior at Cambridge University, once told the following story, which we might call "The Parable of the Happy Tortoise": It seems that when he was a child, Professor Humphrey had a pet tortoise named Ajax. One autumn day, Ajax was looking for a place to spend the winter, and in his wanderings he happened upon a pile of brush and wood. As it turned out, that pile was being prepared for Guy Fawkes Day, celebrated in England every November 5 with bonfires. We can imagine the growing contentment of Ajax, as tinder was heaped up around him, offering more and more protection from rain and cold. On the appointed day, Ajax may well have felt differently about the arrangement, but not for long.

Dr. Humphrey asks: "Are there some of *us* who still believe that the piling up of weapon upon weapon *adds* to our security—that the dangers are nothing, compared to the assurance they provide?" The answer is yes. Moreover, those people are in control.

It is almost certainly a very primitive concept, this Neanderthal insistence that more is better: more money, more goods, more leisure, more weapons. The traditional route to military superiority was to have more and better weapons than your opponent. And when faced with a new problem, the Neanderthal tries to solve it by the same old methods that worked in the past. But nuclear weapons really are a *new* problem, and they don't fit into the old categories and the old ways of thought. The Neanderthal, in particular, suffers from a dangerous illness: hardening of the categories. It may well take a reworking of our thought patterns to establish new categories and realize that sometimes, more is worse.

According to Greek mythology, human beings obtained fire as a gift from Prometheus; the gods, however, were angry with him for sharing their power with us. Now, in the twentieth century, we Neanderthals have obtained atomic power as well. The gods punished Prometheus by chaining him to a mountain in the Caucasus, where a vulture came to feed every day upon his liver. Will we punish ourselves instead? In *Prometheus Bound*, Aeschylus asks:

> Prometheus,
> Prometheus, hanging upon Caucasus,
> Look upon the visage
> Of yonder vulture:
> Is it not thy face,
> Prometheus?

Two thousand years later, Pogo said it more simply: "We have met the enemy and he is us."

The Neanderthal mentality is a formidable obstacle to survival in the nuclear age, but it is not insurmountable. As the Russell-Einstein Manifesto suggested, "we have to learn to think in a new way." To do so, we must first recognize our old ways of thinking, identifying our fetters, if we are ever to cast them aside. Accordingly, one step in learning to think in a new way is to recognize the Neanderthal within us, and within others. When you see it, name it. Tell modern-day Neanderthals to wake up to the realities of the nuclear age. In public office, we find them on both sides of the political aisle, among socialists such as France's Mitterand and conservatives such as Britain's Thatcher. Among Democrats such as Senators Henry Jackson, Sam Nunn and John Stennis, and among Republicans such as John Tower, Jesse Helms and Strom Thurmond. And just about anyone in the upper echelons of the Reagan Administration. Neanderthals all. The sooner we recognize the Neanderthal in others and in ourselves, the safer we are against extinction.

The Neanderthal mentality is not the only psychological problem we face in the struggle against nuclear war. Here are some others:

## Cognitive Dissonance

We try to keep our thoughts—our cognition—from clashing, from becoming dissonant. It is unpleasant, so we find ways to avoid cognitive dissonance. For example, since we are taught that killing people is bad, we tell ourselves that our enemies aren't quite human, thereby allowing us to kill them without being bad. Similarly, we think of ourselves as kind, decent, caring people. If we also allow ourselves to see nuclear war—its horror as well as its imminence—and do nothing to help avert it, then we can no longer keep our self-image as kind, decent and caring. To avoid the dissonance, then, we avoid the issue altogether.

If, because of cognitive dissonance, we cannot accept the problem of nuclear war and still lead our lives as usual, then there is only one answer: we must stop leading our lives as usual.

## Seeking the Technologic Fix

Pierre Curie received a Nobel Prize for his discovery of radium in 1898. Upon receiving the prize, he wrote:

> The question arises whether it be to the advantage of humanity to know the secrets of nature, whether we be sufficiently mature to profit by them or whether the knowledge may not prove harmful. Take, for instance, the discoveries of Nobel—powerful explosives have made it possible for man to achieve admirable things, but they are also a terrible means of destruction in the hands of those great criminals who draw nations into war.

But Curie remained an optimist: "I am among those who believe that humanity will obtain more good than evil from future discoveries." Fifty years later, after Hiroshima, would he still agree?

Whatever the final verdict on scientific discoveries in general, it seems clear that solutions to the problem of nuclear weapons will not come from science and technology alone. Technology put us into this fix; that is the only technologic fix on the horizon today.

### *"Nuclearism" or the "Strangelove Syndrome"*

A small but important minority of people actually develop a seeming fondness, almost a passion, for nuclear weapons. Psychiatrist Robert Jay Lifton calls it "nuclearism," and describes it as

> the passionate embrace of nuclear weapons as a solution to death anxiety and a way of restoring a lost sense of immortality. Nuclearism is a secular religion, a total ideology in which grace and even salvation—the mastery of death and evil—are achieved through the power of a new technological deity. The deity is seen as capable not only of apocalyptic destruction but also of unlimited creation. And the nuclear believer as nuclearist allies himself with that power and feels compelled to expound on the virtues of his deity. He may come to depend on the weapons to keep the world going.

Journalist William Lawrence gave us this description of the first atomic test, at Alamagordo, New Mexico, in 1945:

> On that moment hung eternity. Time stood still. Space contracted to a pinpoint. It was as though the earth had opened and the skies had split. One felt as though he had been privileged to witness the Birth of the World . . . the big boom came about a hundred seconds after the great flash—the first cry of a newborn infant.

Because of Lawrence's almost religious enthusiasm, he was chosen by the U.S. military to be the official chronicler of nuclear weaponry during the late 1940s.

While he was meeting with Stalin and Churchill at Potsdam, Truman received the following report of the first successful atomic test:

> It lighted every peak, crevasse and ridge of the nearby mountain range with a clarity and beauty that cannot be described but must be seen to

be imagined. It was the beauty the great poets dream about but describe most poorly and inadequately.

Can such beauty, such transforming energy, be all bad? It can lead to a kind of love, a strange love indeed, but stranger things have happened. In fact, physicist Edward Teller, identified by Lifton as a classic nuclearist, was the inspiration for Dr. Strangelove of the movie subtitled *How I Learned to Stop Worrying and Love the Bomb*.

Beware the Strangeloves among us.

### Social Pressures, Fashionable Fatalism and Feeling Silly About Doing Good

To talk about nuclear war is to break a powerful social taboo, like talking about sex in Victorian England. Nuclear war is about as socially gauche as announcing that you have terminal cancer at a cocktail party. There are several reasons for this social pressure. (Interestingly, none of these have anything to do with the validity of the concerns.)

For one, nuclear war is a real "downer." Thinking about it will make people sad, and people don't like to be sad.

For another, there is a chic blend of cynicism and bravado, a kind of fashionable fatalism. Like the bullfighter who gets applause by exposing his back to the raging horns, some people flaunt a machismo that admits yes, the world is in substantial danger of nuclear holocaust and in fact, it will almost certainly happen, but *c'est la vie*, or rather, *c'est la morte*. Such fatalism is a good deal less fashionable if you begin picturing your children, your mate, your parents, and your friends suffering from third degree burns or radiation sickness. It may be socially acceptable to disregard one's own peril; there is nothing cute or admirable, however, about casually accepting the fate of others.

Finally, the problem is so big, and each person is so small, that it seems absurd even to start on such a quest. People don't like to seem ridiculous, and let's face it, there is something ridiculous about a personal campaign to save the world. For example, Alistair Cooke once wrote the following description of Bertrand Russell in the *Manchester Guardian*:

A midget suspended against a huge Cinemascope screen . . . a charming puppet straining for a miracle and in the act wobbling the tiny wire frame of his body . . . 'It is,' he said in his high nasal voice, 'the most important question men have ever had to decide in the whole history of the human race!'

In fact, it *is* the most important question men have ever had to decide in the whole history of the human race. And they have not yet decided it. At the time Cooke wrote, Bertrand Russell was one of the greatest mathematicians in England, and certainly its greatest philosopher. He could shoulder abuse. But what about the rest of us? It is downright embarrassing to pronounce oneself a modern-day Messiah, especially without the credentials. Moreover, it feels particularly silly to announce to a friend, "The world is in grave and increasing danger of nuclear holocaust. Please pass the mustard."

But that's the way it is.

### Nukespeak*

Language can be a great cover-up. It can hide what we are doing, not only from others, but from ourselves as well. Nowhere is this more apparent—and more dangerous—than in the case of "nukespeak," that strange and bloodless language by which the planners of nuclear war drain the reality from their actions. Nukespeak is the sanitization of the world's dirtiest words. It is at least partly because of nukespeak that hundreds of otherwise decent Eichmanns can go about their work with sanity and a feeling of personal decorum, removed from what they are actually doing. It is because of nukespeak that the targeting centers and institutes of strategic planning seem more like banking offices or accountancy

*Throughout this book, we shall carefully avoid the word "nuke," which we consider the grossest of obscenities. Whether used as a verb ("nuke'em") or a noun ("thousands of nukes") we find it wholly objectionable. It is too flip and glib, too easy to say, too chummy and familiar: nuke, fluke, kook; cucumber cuke, newcomer nuke. I nuke, you nuke, he she or it nukes. It is a friendly diminutive, like Chuck or Bill. We don't make diminutives, however, out of obscenities. To say something, and to say it easily, is the first step toward making it ordinary, banal and acceptable. We must not casually invoke nuclear weapons, either in practice or in speech.

firms than designers of death. Hitler spoke of "the final solution" to the Jewish problem—not mass murder. And our own strategists speak of "demographic targeting"—not the incineration of people. But genocide by any other name still stinks.

Here are just a few examples: "delivery vehicle" = bomber or missile; "reentry vehicle" = missile warhead that enters the atmosphere; "overkill" = the ability to kill more people than actually exist; "collateral damage" = the murder of innocent civilians (especially women, children, the elderly) as well as the destruction of homes, businesses, farms, etc.; "device" = bomb; "counterforce" = blowing up the opponent's missiles or bombers; "countervalue" = blowing up the opponent's cities.

The third edition of an encyclopedic tome, *The Effects of Nuclear Weapons*, was prepared and published in 1977 by the Department of Defense and the Energy Research and Development Administration, and is available from the U.S. Government Printing Office. It includes analyses of explosions of all types (air, surface, underwater, and underground), as well as detailed information on the various effects of pressure, heat, wind, and radiation on buildings, vehicles, and people. The sections on people are notable for their bloodless nukespeak: accounts are provided, for example, of the various "translational velocities" of a human body (the speeds at which you will be hurled through the air) by explosions of different intensities. There have been studies of "human tolerance to decelerative tumbling during translation in open terrain." For this purpose, various objects were dropped "onto a flat, hard surface from vehicles traveling between 10 and 60 miles per hour," and it was concluded that "a person tumbling over a smooth surface, free from rocks and other hard irregularities, might survive, even if the initial velocity is quite high, if he could avoid head injury and did not flail his limbs." When it comes to "deceleration against rigid surfaces" (i.e., smashing into a wall), it's not the takeoff that will do you in, so much as the hard, fast landing: "Although there may be some hazard associated with the accelerative phase of body displacement (translation) by a blast wave, the deceleration, particularly if impact with a solid object is involved, is by far the more significant." There are charts showing, among other things, the injuries caused by 10-pound objects striking a human body at different velocities, the explosion intensity required to cause first, second, and third degree burns among light, medium and dark-skinned individuals. And lots more—all very dry and technical, rigidly accurate and understated; a marvel of nukespeak.

The purpose of nukespeak is to cause us to think about something without really thinking about it—or rather, without feeling it. "Translational velocity" is a problem in physics, not crushed lungs or fractured skulls. Even the phrase "nuclear war" is misleading, suggesting some continuity with earlier wars. Perhaps our thinking would be clarified if we stopped talking about *a* nuclear war and substituted *the* nuclear war. Or better yet, maybe we should call it what it really would be, namely *The End.*

In the late 1950s, the Air Force began writing about "baby H-bombs." How innocent; almost adorable. "Delivering baby H-bombs" to Leningrad begins to sound like the act of a good Samaritan. (Maybe we could even devise a new "delivery vehicle," and call it a Stork.) Similarly, a 1968 Air Force *Fact Sheet* described the Minuteman III as the "newest member of our ICBM family." We can almost see the proud father, the smiling mother, the rambunctious little brother and sister missiles. Maybe this is what anthropologists really mean when they refer to the "nuclear family." Maybe, instead, it's time for us to get rid of nukespeak altogether, and start calling a spade a shovel.

### Thinkables, Unthinkables, Pessimists, and Optimists

It may be that national leaders and military strategists, even more than average citizens, deny the seriousness of nuclear war. Because their lives are necessarily closer to the awful reality and because their own actions could make it happen, they may well shy away even more vigorously than the rest of us, to protect their own psyches. Responsibility for nuclear war is the heaviest burden that anyone could bear. So it is not surprising that psychological defense mechanisms may be used to ease that burden. There is only one problem: while making things easier for themselves, these mechanisms make things more dangerous for the rest of us.

Harvard psychiatrist John Mack has identified two kinds of people who deal with the prospect of nuclear war. He calls them the "thinkables" and the "unthinkables." In reality, of course, people of both persuasions *can*—and *do*—think about nuclear war; they differ, however, in *how* they do so. The thinkables believe that nuclear war is a realistic prospect under certain circumstances, and that we should therefore plan for it, developing scenarios and various possible contingencies: "civil defense," "limited" nuclear war, etc. The unthinkables, by contrast, believe that it is not meaningful to plan for nuclear war and that therefore the only way to think about it realistically is to think about preventing it. According to Dr. Mack, the thinkables are especially prominent among government officials who, oppressed by the enormity of their responsibility, seek to make it tolerable by making it manageable—that is, thinkable. For their part, the unthinkables tend to have a deeper anxiety about nuclear war, and their concern has led them to reject it as a thinkable option. According to this analysis, those who find nuclear war thinkable are attempting to make the unacceptable, acceptable; as a personal strategy for reducing one's inner conflicts, "thinkability" is reasonable, consistent and even, perhaps, healthy. But as the primary mind-set of those responsible for whether we will have peace or war, it is unhealthy in the extreme—for us all.

If the unthinkables withdraw altogether—as they generally have been doing, at least in the United States—then the danger is magnified severalfold. Because the field is then left to the thinkables, who aren't planning so much for preventing nuclear war, as for its eventuality. The solution? Unthinkables of the U.S. unite; you may lose some peace of mind and some free time that you now spend doing other things, but you have a world to save.

There are costs to being an unthinkable. Dr. Mack has surveyed hundreds of adolescents and has found a deep-seated pessimism and anxiety behind a superficial, seemingly indifferent exterior. Thus, many of today's youngsters are fundamentally disheartened about their future—their prospects for living happily, for raising a family, for achieving their life's ambitions. And as a result, there is a tendency to have fewer ambitions, and to focus on immediate gratification rather than long-term goals in a world which may not hold out the prospects of continuing into the "long-term." Living under the shadow of The Bomb has caused us all to wilt a little. The future is not what it used to be.

Psychiatrist Robert Jay Lifton has written similarly about "the new ephemeralism," the sense that not only are our own lives temporary—after all, we won't live forever, and every healthy person knows this and accepts it—but that for the first time the previously unbroken line of life's continuity may finally come to an end. Death is one thing, a normal ending to every life. Annihilation, on the other hand—the destruction of civilization and of all our descendants—is quite different and unique to the nuclear age. As individuals, we are ephemeral, and have always been. What is new, however, is the perception that our descendants, our species, our projects and hopes, even all life itself, may at long last be ephemeral as well. The sun is destined to go out some day, but that is about ten billion years from now, and few of us feel immediately threatened by the prospect. Nuclear war is very different. It threatens the immediate continuity of ourselves and those we love. It is something wholly new in human experience.

But we are an optimistic people and we shy away from gloomy thoughts. If we are ultimately to have cause for optimism, then, we must find ways to think optimistically about getting out of the fix we are now in. We must learn to think positively, not about surviving nuclear war, and not about denying it altogether, but rather, about *preventing* it.

### Shall We Overcome?

*Religion*

Others may find it incredible, but there actually are many people, especially among the more fundamentalist Christian faiths, who believe that nuclear war will be the final judgment of God upon man, and hence, that it is to be accepted—even welcomed. Conceivably, a religious zealot might see a tornado or an erupting volcano as the hand of God. But we doubt that even the most ardent would refuse to stand aside from the lava flow or to seek shelter from the wind, believing that his destruction is necessarily God's will. We all duck when a rock flies by and we keep our hand away from the hot stove. It is our obligation to strive for what is right and perhaps only in the *extremis* of certain death to submit helplessly to the "will of God." Certainly, when the event is caused directly by human action (or inaction), then it is all the more absurd to deny our human responsibility. Even deeply religious people do not drive blindfolded at high speed in heavy traffic, trusting to God. Yet, when it comes to nuclear war, we are in fact driving at high speed and on very dangerous roads. It is nothing less than idiotic to do it blindfolded, trusting to anyone, whether President or God. Indeed, just as it is the ultimate cop-out to say that the prevention of nuclear war is someone else's job, it may be the ultimate blasphemy to deny human responsibility and blame it on God.

According to a traditional religious view, "final judgement" is rendered by God, for spiritual reasons, eventually establishing His kingdom. This seems very different from our own *self*-destruction, and for such banal reasons as error, misunderstanding, empire-building or personal pride, prejudice and pigheadedness. Regarding the Second Coming and Armageddon, Jesus said "But of that day and that hour knoweth no man, no not the angels in heaven" (Mark 13:32). Thus, blaming God for nuclear war is not only personally immoral, but also grossly sacreligious.

More and more, in fact, religious leaders are urging us face the man-made problem with man-made solutions. Not only the traditional peace churches, such as the Quakers, Mennonites and Brethren, but even the mainline Protestant denominations and especially the Roman Catholic Church are rapidly assuming their Christian obligation toward peace. In Europe, the churches are the backbone of the burgeoning antiwar movement. In the U.S., Leroy Mattiesen, bishop of Amarillo, said "Let's stop this madness. . . . We beg our administration to stop accelerating the arms race; we beg our military to use common sense." All twelve Roman Catholic bishops in Texas concurred with this statement. Archbishop John Roach of Minneapolis-St. Paul, president of the National Conference of Catholic Bishops, has publicly questioned the neutron bomb and strategies of "limited" nuclear war, adding that "The church needs to say 'no' clearly and decisively to the use of nuclear arms." The U.S. Leadership Conference of Women Religious (America's nuns) have condemned the neutron bomb and the MX missile, and the President of the National Federation of Priests' Council, Father Neil McCaulley, says that the neutron bomb "brings the human family to the brink of destruction."

"The teaching of the Church is clear," said Archbishop John R. Quinn of San Francisco. "Nuclear weapons and the arms race must be condemned as immoral." Furthermore, Archbishop Quinn emphasizes, "not only the peace of the world but the very survival of the human experiment is at stake."

Nor are the Protestant churches remaining silent. "We are not known as a 'peace church' year in and year out like the Mennonites," said William Winslow, communications officer for the 1.8 million-member United Church of Christ. "But our synod felt it's the most pressing issue now, as our forebears felt the abolition of slavery was the most pressing moral issue in the last century." Bishops of the Episcopal Church are advocating a "weekly act of fasting and prayer for the peace of the world," and a pastoral letter sent to about 7,000 Episcopal churches pointed out that "massive nuclear overkill poised for instant use represents deadly insecurity," and expressed the hope that "our actions may reflect a new resolve of leadership in peacemaking." Signs of a similar new resolve are apparent even among the usually conservative Southern Baptists, despite their strong military tradition. Thus, seven Southern Baptist state conventions have recently adopted statements on peace.

In short, whereas religion may give support in time of suffering, meaning in time of doubt and hope in time of despair, it certainly does not counsel self-immolation, or even our acquiescence in the destruction of ourselves or others at the hands of those in power who should know better but apparently do not. Moreover, organized religion may soon be taking the lead in generating a much needed form of nuclear sanity.

## Morality and Sanity

At its root, nuclear war is a moral problem, and morality is out of fashion these days. In his book *The Undiscovered Self*, the great psychoanalyst C. J. Jung wrote:

> It is not that present-day man is capable of greater evil than the man of antiquity or the primitive. He merely has incomparably more effective means with which to realize his proclivity to evil. As his consciousness has broadened and differentiated, so his moral nature has lagged behind. That is the great problem before us today.

For their part, generals are not usually a source of great moral

234 • STOP NUCLEAR WAR! A HANDBOOK

wisdom. And yet, Omar Bradley, Chairman of the Joint Chiefs of Staff from 1949 to 1953 and widely known as the "GI's general," was acutely sensitive to Jung's great moral problem:

> We have grasped the mystery of the atom and rejected the Sermon on the Mount. The world has achieved brilliance without wisdom, power without conscience. Ours is a world of nuclear giants and ethical infants. We know more about war than we know about peace, more about killing than we know about living. . . .

Bradley went on to state that he was not so much distressed by the magnitude of the problem, but by the average citizen's colossal indifference to it.

There is something elemental about nuclear weapons, like Faust's dilemma of achieving overwhelming power, but at unacceptable cost. By what right do we wield the power to destroy everything? We have neither the strength to master such forces, the wisdom to use them wisely, nor the forbearance to refrain from using them at all. We have overstepped our limits—not the limits of what we *can* do, but of what we *ought* to.

Before he went on trial for his life, Adolf Eichmann was examined by Israeli psychiatrists. The Nazi who masterminded the extermination of six million Jews was declared sane. Thomas Merton, the brilliant Jesuit theologian, wrote an essay about this, a "devout meditation" on sanity and morality. Eichmann apparently slept well, ate well, loved his family and was loved in return. He was a loyal subject, a capable if unimaginative bureaucrat who hated disorder and inefficiency, and who was uncomfortable with the sight of blood. He did his job well, and in a rational manner. He was sane, although he certainly was not moral.

Merton comments that despite our legitimate worry about terrorists, psychotic world leaders, or plain old-fashioned errors (both human and electronic), our greatest danger probably lies in those totally sane, rational, amoral planners of strategic doctrine who bloodlessly, fastidiously, with abundance of care and absence of conscience, design scenarios for mass suicide, blueprints for megadeath. Modern-day Eichmanns, they coolly estimate "acceptable" losses in the tens of millions of victims. By contrast, the ban-the-bomb types are just a bit crazy, worried as they are about death and destruction, making moral judgments where well-adjusted, order-following sanity is supposed to reign supreme. "It is the sane ones, the well-adapted ones," writes Merton

> who can without qualms and without nausea aim the missiles and press the buttons that will initiate the great festival of destruction that they, *the sane ones,* have prepared. . . . No one suspects the sane, and the sane ones will have *perfectly good reasons,* logical, well-adjusted reasons, for firing the shot. They will be obeying sane orders that have come sanely down the chain of command. And because of their sanity they will have no qualms at all. When the missiles take off, *it will be no mistake.*

Perhaps some people, as Merton suggests, can be well-adjusted in hell itself. In any event, we can ask whether they have a right to make a hell of our earth. We can also ask whether sanity has any meaning at all in a world devoid of moral values. "We have two tasks," reported a young launch control officer at an ICBM base near Omaha. "The first is not to let people go off their rockers. That's the negative side. The positive side is to ensure that people act without moral compunction."

*Beyond Psychic Numbing*

In his landmark study *Death in Life: Survivors of Hiroshima,* Robert Jay Lifton reported that survivors experienced "a sudden and absolute shift from normal existence to an overwhelming encounter with death." For the A-bomb survivors, or *hibakusha,* this shattering experience produced a peculiar but widespread deadening of the emotions, which Lifton called "psychic numbing." Looking at photographs of the victims from Hiroshima and Nagasaki, one is struck by the near-total devastation, the seemingly unbearable wounds, combined incongruously with faces that are virtually blank and expressionless. This is not legendary Japanese stoicism. Rather, the *hibakusha* describe themselves as *muga-muchu*—"without self, without center," because their experience has broken down the usual boundaries between life and death, by a death-immersion that has left them almost literally numb.

The Japanese government has officially defined A-bomb victims as those who 1) were within 4 kilometers of the epicenter, 2) entered within 2 kilometers within 14 days, 3) aided or helped dispose of such victims, and 4) were *in utero* or whose mothers fall into categories 1 through 4. But *hibakusha* literally means "explosion affected person," and accordingly, we are all *hibakusha*. We have all been affected by the explosions at Hiroshima and Nagasaki, whether we become thinkables or unthinkables; whether we hide among our armaments like Ajax the tortoise, or choose to protest against them; whether we seek respite in the Strangelove Syndrome; however we deal with social pressures, morality and nuke-speak; whatever our particular brand of Neanderthal mentality; and however we let religion enter into our private, nuclear consciousness. Most Americans are "explosion affected persons" through their own personal psychic numbing, in which they emotionally reject the experiences of Hiroshima and Nagasaki, not only as historical realities, but also as warnings for our own future. Moreover, today's American *hibakusha* are numb to the nuclear arms race and to their own peril.

On a personal level, for those who have experienced great traumas, psychic numbing may be helpful. But in our current predicament, it is counterproductive, since psychic numbing, like any other form of numbing, leaves us unknowingly vulnerable to injury. We have nerves—for pain as well as pleasure—that warn us of danger and help us keep alive. It is dangerous to be numb. And fortunately, we don't have to be.

After all, throughout history human beings have shown themselves to have unquenchable spirit: willing, able, and even eager to conquer staggering odds, once they can get their psychology working for them instead of against them. There is no better time than now. The U.S. is full of caring, intelligent, and resolute people. We have the warmth of love, a genius for innovative and effective action, a political system that responds to the will of its people, and the determination and self-confidence born of past successes. Look within yourself, and see what there is. You should be pleased and encouraged by what you find. John F. Kennedy made the following suggestion, in a speech at American University on June 10, 1963:

> Every thoughtful citizen who despairs of war and wishes to bring peace should begin by looking inward, by examining his own attitude toward the possibilities of peace, toward the Soviet Union, toward the

course of the cold war, and toward freedom and peace here at home.

First: let us examine our attitude toward peace itself. Too many of us think it is impossible. Too many think it unreal. But that is a dangerous, defeatist belief. It leads to the conclusion that war is inevitable, that mankind is doomed, that we are gripped by forces we cannot control.

We need not accept that view. Our problems are man made. Therefore they can be solved by man. And man can be as big as he wants. No problem of human destiny is beyond human beings. Man's reason and spirit have often solved the seemingly unsolvable, and we believe they can do it again.

## Hollanditis: The European Epidemic
## (or, How to Stop Worrying and Start Fighting the Bomb)

There is an old German melody, given words by an unnamed prisoner in a Nazi concentration camp in 1933. It is called *"Die Moorsoldaten"* (The Peat Bog Soldiers). Even in the concentration camps, the prisoners sang this song, and with such enthusiasm that the SS finally banned it altogether. "The Peat Bog Soldiers" became a symbol of resistance to oppression, of faith and hope amid despair. Prisoners in the concentration camps would gather secretly, to lift their spirits by singing of an end to winter, and a new springtime of freedom.

Even in Dachau, they sang. As Americans in the 1980s, do we really have less hope than they did? Have we so much accepted the inevitability of nuclear war, and the destruction of everything that we have ever loved, that we have less will to resist than the prisoners of Dachau?

But in the streets of Europe, the children are singing *"Die Moorsoldaten"* once again, accompanied by guitars, some with flowers in their hair. They are joined by hundreds of thousands of others—middle-aged, elderly, even babies. Why are the Europeans singing together now?

There are several reasons. For one, they seem less inclined to a Neanderthal mentality than we. They have known wars on their soil, and what seems distant and impossible to us is just yesterday and very possible for them. They know that more weapons is not better; they know that neither side can win; etc. Tragedies have been too real and too frequent for fatalism to be fashionable, and they are not numb.

For another, the European peace movement is not narrow, not ideological, not the creation of Moscow propagandists. Rather, it is a broadbased movement for human survival, with wide support from people of all ages, religions, political parties, and occupations. There is no question of changing society, no thought of revolution; rather, the *preservation* of society is the unifying principle.

Here is the dominant symbol of the Dutch peace movement, seen on thousands of posters throughout Amsterdam, Rotterdam, and The Hague:

This lady is not a hippie! She is a middle-aged, middle-class Dutch hausfrau, cleaning up her world as she would her own house. She is angry, determined, but also very human and somehow accessible. She could be us, or you. Indeed, in this local, grassroots movement, each person has a niche. People talk to their neighbors, and whole communities thereby become involved.

Thus, the form of the European peace movement seems to follow its function. The life of the community is enhanced, because people begin to confront their neighbors and talk to them about the one surpassing issue: survival. A local "working group" in Holland becomes a group of friends, licking envelopes and designing posters while the very fabric of their social life is enriched. Each demonstration is more a celebration of life than a confrontation with death. People make new friends, buy hot dogs, flaunt their new clothes or the creativity of their posters, banners, and makeup. The singing and clapping is fun. There is a party atmosphere, in which human relationships are enhanced rather than distanced.

At one "small" torchlight demonstration in The Hague in November 1981 (unnoticed by the U.S. press), 10,000 women of all ages, some with babies on their backs, were all singing together. Older women had chartered buses, decorated them with posters and banners, and those who could not walk, rode. Their faces were flushed, their voices firm as they chanted

> Hey friends, come and resist.
> No more missiles and no more bombs.
> We want peace, and we insist
> Hey friends, come and resist . . .°

Millions of Europeans are singing for survival, together. We have been silent too long. We, the American people, must start to sing.

°To the old folk tune "Hey-ho, Nobody Home."

# 8. How a Nuclear War Might Start:

## Many Roads Lead to Ruin

> Some say the world will end in fire
> Some say in ice.
> From items on the AP wire
> I hold with those that figure fire.
> —Norman Corwin

> This is the way the world ends
> This is the way the world ends
> This is the way the world ends
> Not with a whimper but a bang.
> —Norman Corwin

According to Greek legend, one of the courtiers of Dionysius the Elder, tyrant of Syracuse, was a man named Damocles. He was a jealous flatterer, always exaggerating his king's wealth, happiness, and good fortune. One day, Dionysius invited Damocles to a great feast, where, surrounded by opulence, he happened to look up and see a sword, dangling directly above him, suspended by a single hair. This sword symbolized the daily danger under which the ruler lived. Thus did Damocles learn that power and wealth are often bought at great risk. The predicament should be familiar. President Kennedy once pointed out that "every man, woman and child lives under a nuclear sword of Damocles, hanging by the slenderest of threads, capable of being cut at any moment by accident, miscalculation, or madness." In this chapter, we shall face our precarious situation, evaluating just how the slender thread could break.

Since Nagasaki, on August 9, 1945, the thread has held. But this does not mean that it always will. We have no guaranteed inhibition against using nuclear weapons; certainly, we cannot assume that just because they have not been used recently in anger they never will be, or that the seriousness of the act would necessarily stay our hand, or the hand of anyone else holding a nuclear trigger.

In the twelfth century, crossbows were considered so dangerous that anyone who used one against another person risked immediate excommunication. That taboo did not last long. Similar hesitancy surrounded the first use of gunpowder, poison gas, flamethrowers, napalm. And yet, one million soldiers were gassed in World War I, flamethrowers and saturation bombing of cities were common in World War II, and napalm and herbicides were used in Vietnam. Indeed, atomic weapons have already been used, as the Japanese well know. To the military strategist, nothing is unthinkable. "It is the business of military strategists to prepare for all eventualities," wrote Reinhold Niebuhr, "and it is the fatal error of such strategists to create the eventualities for which they must prepare."

It would be nice to think that nuclear weapons are so destructive that they have made war obsolete. But unfortunately, this is more like wishful thinking than an accurate reading of history or of what may yet take place. It is also not new. Thus, in 1910, Norman Angell, an Englishman, wrote a book called *The Grand Illusion*, which was widely read and discussed. Its thesis: war could never happen again, because nations had become so interdependent, and furthermore, the consequences of "modern" war were so devastating that no one could win. "Commercial disaster, financial ruin and individual suffering" would be so great that nations would simply shy away from it. Four years later, the "guns of August" were sounding and Europe suffered the most intense and devastating war in its history up to that time. Angell was correct about the consequences of war; he was wrong, however, in thinking that nations would always act rationally, in their own best interests.

During our closest brush with nuclear war, the Cuban missile crisis of 1962, President Kennedy expressed fear that sometime in the future a historian might write about "the missiles of October," telling the tale of yet another tragic misunderstanding—that is, if anyone would be alive to write it, or to read it. In fact, World War I was a big misunderstanding, a war no one wanted. Austria mobilized to show that it was really upset about the killing of one of its nobles, the Archduke Ferdinand, and intending by this show of resolve to keep Russia out of any conflict; Russia then mobilized, concerned that Austria had designs that went beyond little Serbia; Germany mobilized to show its support for Austria; France mobilized to show its support for Russia and in case Germany went west instead of east; England mobilized to show its support for France. Now, communications are better, and we might hope that misunderstandings are less likely. But the response speed is also much greater, measured in minutes rather than the weeks required for mobilization. We are already "mobilized," and in that sense, much worse off than Europe in 1914. In addition, of course, our ability to destroy each other has multiplied literally millions of times.

The costs of a mistake are greater now than ever before, but sadly, this does not mean that the chances of making such a mistake are any less. As we shall now see, there are many ways that a nuclear war might start; many roads lead to ruin.

### Boob Attack

The most obvious is also probably the least likely—a Bolt out of the Blue ("Boob"). No one really believes that some fine morning the President of the U.S.S.R. (or the U.S.) will wake up, rub his hands fiendishly together, and announce that it is time to destroy the U.S. (or the U.S.S.R.). Nonetheless, it is precisely against such a Boob attack that the radar and satellite systems of both nations are constantly watchful. It is also unlikely (although less unlikely) that a Boob attack will one fine day be launched against the opponent's missiles—that is, a counterforce attack. Either type of attack, especially without the provocation of some sort of international crisis, could only occur if the attacking president was either crazy (and hence oblivious to the consequences of his action) or woefully misinformed (and hence overestimating the likely efficiency of his own counterforce strike, and underestimating the retaliation available to the victim). Neither is likely, but either is possible.

### "Chicken"

Bertrand Russell first pointed out that the behavior of nations, especially those armed with nuclear weapons, resembles the behavior of irresponsible teenagers playing "chicken" with automobiles. Two drivers head toward each other; the one who turns away first, to avoid a collision, is branded a "chicken." He loses. To win you must continue straight ahead, counting on the other to turn aside. The complication, of course, is that if both drivers are determined not to swerve—that is, to win—then they collide head-on, and both lose. When teenagers play chicken, it is delinquency at least. When nations do it, it is the pinnacle of diplomacy.

During the Cuban missile crisis, Kennedy and Khruschev played chicken and Khrushchev swerved. He "lost," and that is why we are alive to write this book, and you are alive to read it. During the Vietnam War, President Johnson vowed that he would not be the first U.S. president to lose a war. When a nation swerves aside during international chicken, that nation's leadership loses face, at the very least. It may also lose influence, territory, trading partners, etc. (and maybe even the next election). The more costly it is to lose, the less likely a nation is to turn aside, even if the cost of not turning aside may be the greatest of all.° Given the current cold war climate, Americans seem impressed by would-be leaders who are willing to "stand up to the Russians," with little appreciation of what this could really mean. Perhaps the most dangerous situation of all is when the two nations bear down on each other—cheered on by the hawks and disdaining to be a chicken—with both leaderships determined not to turn aside and convinced that the opponent will. The result? Both sides, whether chicken or not, end up fried.

### Accidents

Accidents happen. No thing, no person is infallible. And yet, nuclear things and nuclear people must be, since the consequences of failure are so catastrophic. In a sense, nuclear war via a boob attack or fried chicken would be "rational"—at least in that it would have been planned, even if miscalculated. There is also, however, plenty of room for nuclear war by accident. We shall now consider three categories of accidents: nuclear weapons accidents ("broken arrows"), accidents of command, control and com-

---

°As if nuclear chicken wasn't crazy enough, some strategists have actually suggested that leaders should intentionally appear irrational, to enhance the credibility of the bluff. Since a rational person can be expected to swerve, something might be gained by persuading your opponent that you are crazy!

munications ("false alarms"), and accidents in which the wrong person pushes the button ("unauthorized use").

A. *Broken arrows*. The immediate result of a broken arrow can be a localized disaster, as when a nuclear weapon goes off unintentionally somewhere. In itself, this might not lead to nuclear war, although for the people locally involved, there would be little difference. However, the explosion of a nuclear weapon might well be seen as a sneak attack rather than an accident. Even a small spark, struck by error, could thus initiate war.

Here is a list of *announced* U.S. broken arrows:

1. April 11, 1950: A B-52 crashed at Manzano Air Force Base, New Mexico. At least one nuclear bomb case was "demolished."

2. August 5, 1950: a B-29 crashed on takeoff from Fairchild Air Force Base, California, killing 19 persons. The high explosive charge in its nuclear weapon was detonated.

3. March 10, 1956: A B-47 was lost over the Mediterranean. No trace of the plane, its crew, or the two nuclear bombs aboard was ever found.

4. July 27, 1956: An unarmed B-47 crashed into a stockpile of nuclear weapons at the Royal Air Force Lakenheath Base in East Anglia, Britain. The crew was killed. The local population was not informed until 1979.

5. March 22, 1957: A B-36 dropped a nuclear weapon shortly after taking off from Kirtland Air Force Base, New Mexico. The bomb's high explosive made a 12-foot crater.

6. July 28, 1957: A C-124 cargoplane dropped two nuclear weapons off the Atlantic coast. Neither were ever found.

7. February 5, 1958: a B-47 collided with a smaller plane in flight. A nuclear bomb was dropped into the ocean from 7,500 feet, off the Georgia coast: it was never recovered.

8. March 11, 1957: a B-47 accidentally dropped a nuclear bomb over one megaton in power, near Mars Bluff, South Carolina. The conventional explosive trigger obliterated a farmhouse, killing several people.

9. November 4, 1958: a B-47 carrying nuclear weapons crashed near Dyess Air Force Base, Texas.

10. July 6, 1959: a C-124 transport plane, carrying a nuclear weapon, crashed on takeoff at Barksdale Air Force Base, Louisiana.

11. September 25, 1959: a Navy P-5M anti-submarine warfare plane ditched in Puget Sound, off the coast of Washington. The nuclear weapon aboard has not been recovered.

12. October 15, 1959: a B-52 collided with another plane in midair near Hardingsburg, Kentucky. Four persons were killed and the two nuclear weapons aboard were found near the crash site.

13. June 7, 1960: a fire at McGuire Air Force Base, New Jersey, destroyed a nuclear-tipped BOMARC ground-to-air missile.

14. January 24, 1961: a wing fell off a B-52 in flight. Two nuclear bombs were jettisoned over Goldsboro, North Carolina. At least one of these was 24 megatons (almost 2,000 times more powerful than the Hiroshima bomb). Both were recovered, unexploded: one was leaking uranium onto surrounding farmland, and the other was found hanging in a tree—of its six "fail-safe" safety switches, five had been tripped when its parachute cords became entangled in the branches. The sixth held.

15. January 13, 1964: a B-52 carrying two nuclear bombs crashed in the Cumberland Mountains of Maryland. The crew was killed but the bombs were found "relatively intact."

16. December 5, 1964: a Minuteman missile fell apart while on test alert at Ellsworth Air Force Base, South Dakota.

17. December 8, 1964: a B-58 carrying five nuclear bombs crashed and burned.

18. December 5, 1965: a Navy A-4 attack plane rolled off its elevator from an aircraft carrier about 500 miles offshore in the Pacific Ocean. Neither the pilot, the plane, nor the nuclear weapon aboard was ever recovered.

19. January 17, 1966: a B-52 collided with its refueling tanker above Palomares, Spain. Five crewmen died and four H-bombs were accidentally dropped. One was recovered on land and another at sea after an extensive search. The conventional explosive in the other two exploded when they hit the ground, contaminating an extensive area.

20. January 21, 1968: a B-52 crashed and burned on the North Star Bay ice floe when attempting a crash landing at Thule Air Force Base in Greenland. Four H-bombs were aboard; the high explosive triggers of all four were detonated, scattering plutonium across a wide area.

21. January 21, 1968: the attack submarine *Scorpion* sank in the Atlantic, 400 miles north of the Azores. An unknown number of nuclear antisubmarine torpedoes went down with her.

22. September 2, 1980: fuel vapors exploded at a Titan II ICBM base near Damascus, Arkansas, after a mechanic had dropped a wrench and ruptured the liquid fuel tanks. The resulting explosion tossed the warhead 200 yards in the air. The damaged warhead was then shipped to Texas for repairs, on a flat-bed truck marked with the appropriate warning sign, "Do Not Drop."

This list includes only *nuclear weapons* accidents. If we include military accidents in general, even considering only cases that could have involved nuclear weapons, but did not simply because of chance, the list would grow much longer. For example, on September 17, 1978, an unarmed cruise missile crashed near Lampoc, California. On July 15, 1981, the guided missile destroyer USS Coontz, undergoing routine maintenance prior to a scheduled test firing, accidentally launched a Harpoon missile toward the island of St. Croix. Although this particular missile was not nuclear-armed, Senator John Bell, leader of the majority coalition in the Virgin Islands Senate, had this to say: "I am damned disturbed to hear about this!"

We have very little information about Soviet broken arrows, at least partly because of their penchant for secrecy. In addition, since they rely relatively more on land-based missiles and less on airplanes, the Soviet accident rate may actually be lower than ours. There have, however, been reports of Soviet broken arrows, especially involving submarines:

1. January 10, 1970: a "Foxtrot"-class submarine collided with the Angelina Lauro, an Italian cruise liner, in the Bay of Naples. The Soviet submarine, generally believed to carry nuclear-armed torpedoes, suffered a 25-foot hole in her bow.

2. January/February, 1970: a very large explosion was detected, by infrared monitoring satellites, at the Gorki submarine yards. Immediately afterward, the Volga river and Black Sea estuary were radioactively contaminated.

3. April 12/13, 1970: a nuclear-powered "November"- class submarine sank with all hands 150 miles off the British coast when its nuclear reactor exploded. Its nuclear weapons were never recovered.

4. September, 1973: an "Echo-II"-class submarine was sighted in the Caribbean with "an enormous gash" in her hull; this class submarine normally carries eight SS-3 nuclear missiles.

5. October 27, 1981: a "Whiskey"-class submarine, apparently on a spying mission, and armed with nuclear-tipped torpedoes, became grounded near the top-secret Swedish Naval facility of Karlskrona.

B. *False Alarms.* Accidents are bad, but false alarms are worse. Since there is no defense against a nuclear attack, only a retaliation, if either side thinks it is being attacked, it might well respond with an attack of its own. This danger is magnified by the quick reactions that must be involved: it takes only thirty minutes or less for opposing missiles to devastate each other's homeland. Therefore, as Senator Mark Hatfield (R-Oregon) put it, "leaders on both sides will inevitably be forced to make decisions over the continuance of modern civilization in brief moments of awesome tension." Hatfield concludes, "This volatile mixture of fear and weaponry may set the stage for perhaps the most tense period in the history of civilized life."

The North American Radar Air Defense system (NORAD) had 151 nuclear false alarms labeled "serious" and 3,703 lesser alarms in just the 18 months preceding June 30, 1980—according to a report of the Senate Armed Services Committee. There were also 33 Strategic Air Command alerts during the period 1945–1975. For example, during the early 1970s, an early-warning satellite detected a Soviet missile and predicted that it would hit California. It didn't; it was a test, splashing down in the Pacific. Before that was recognized, however, the SAC went into high alert, and silo launch officers prepared to turn their keys upon a command—which fortunately did not come.

On October 18, 1975, infrared sensors on a U.S. spy satellite reported a sudden burst of heat in northern Siberia, near the Soviet land-based ICBMs. It looked at first like a missile launch; it was, in fact, a fire in the nearby gas pipeline. On other occasions, notably during the tense Berlin crisis, radar had picked up flocks of migrating geese, and seen them as missiles. Even the man in the moon has looked sinister: on October 5, 1960, the Ballistics Missile Early Warning System, located at Thule, Greenland, reported a Soviet missile attack, which was, in fact, the lunar reflection of radar signals. False alarms have not been limited to radar and satellite sensing errors: twice during 1971 alone, U.S. Polaris submarines accidentally released Submarine Emergency Communications transmitter buoys, signaling that the submarine releasing it had been attacked and destroyed—presumably by the U.S.S.R. Since submarines are an important part of the nation's strategic deterrent, a real attack upon them would be an unmistakable act of war. . . .

The sophisticated computers of C³I have also had their share of false alarms. On November 9, 1979, someone fed a practice wargames tape into one of the North American Air Defense Command computers. The computer took it seriously, and so did the Air Force: fighters were scrambled. After six minutes, the false alarm was discovered. Had our bombers taken off (the likely next step in our response plan), the Soviet satellites would doubtless have recorded this and possibly thought that we were attacking them, whereas in fact, we thought they were attacking us! Twice in June

1980, microchips failed in the ·Data General NOVA computer at
NORAD; as a result, our missile-firing submarines went into a yellow alert, and the ICBM crews, a red alert. (In cases of red alert,
the launch keys are inserted into their slots—the next step is to turn
them.) Faced with this astonishing situation, General David C.
Jones, Chairman of the Joint Chiefs of Staff, was not at all abashed.
Instead, he took it as an occasion to lecture the Soviets. Their
leaders "had better know that we are ready," warned the General,
"and that we can respond in a very few minutes." He might have
added that we are so ready that we might even "respond" in the
absence of a provocation!

We have been playing Russian roulette with ourselves. So far,
the barrel has been empty, and so, we keep on playing. As for the
Russians, we know nothing about their record of false alarms, but
their computers are generally agreed to be inferior to ours. It therefore seems likely that they have also been spinning the revolver
chamber. After reviewing the dismal history of computer errors,
Senator Hatfield asked: "Knowing of our own momentary failures
in these critical areas, is it rational to pursue a nuclear policy that
places the fate of the Western world in the hands of an edgy Soviet
leadership operating under enormous stress and depending on inferior Soviet systems of identification, command, and control?"

During the strategic military environment of the 1970s and
early 1980s, both sides have been able to scrutinize reports of Soviet attacks with some calm and deliberation—that is, with a leeway of fifteen to twenty minutes. This is bad enough. But in the
brave new world of counterforce planned for the mid to late 1980s,
that margin for verification and decision will be cut sharply—to five
minutes or perhaps ten at most. This is much worse. It is caused by
the new, emerging threats to each side's deterrence. Since fast,
highly accurate missiles will threaten each other's missiles, during
warning of attack the pressures will be immense to fire the home
side's missiles quickly, before they can be destroyed in their silos.
For example, consider this scenario:

> Late in the 1980s, the Soviet Union has just changed leadership, and
> their new, younger men expect to be challenged by the West. Jockey-
> ing for position in the Middle East has raised tensions, and the invec-
> tive has been hot, each side accusing the other of threatening its

strategic interests and of seeking an excuse for war. Then, at three o'clock one morning, following a Soviet tank incursion into Iran, Soviet radar picks up a massive missile attack coming over the North Pole and due to reach the U.S.S.R. within 25 minutes. Soviet submarines report close surveillence by U.S. anti-submarine warfare airplanes; frantic efforts for confirmation of the attack give conflicting results: satellites show no heat images (but perhaps the U.S. missiles have been outfitted by some new, heat-diffusing afterburner?) whereas radar stations continue to report the attack (which actually exists only in the overloaded circuits of their own computers). The edgy, sleep-deprived Soviet leaders are urged by their military advisors to fire their missiles immediately or risk having them destroyed. There is no more time to think, to hesitate or to regret.

This could happen, and it could happen either way—just substitute American for Soviet or Europe for the Middle East, etc. Moreover, don't count on the "hotline." Let's assume that on our hypothetical morning, the agitated Soviet leaders call up the White House to report what their computers have just told them, asking for confirmation or denial. The U.S. president denies any attack, of course. So what are the Soviet leaders to conclude? If the U.S. were attacking they certainly wouldn't admit it in advance, especially since surprise and temporary paralysis of the opponent count for so much. So, the attacker would be expected to allay any aroused Soviet fears. And rest assured, Soviet hawks would point this out. If the situation were reversed, would we believe them?

C. *Unauthorized use.* Nuclear war would be equally bad whether started by the "correct" authorities or by underlings who are not authorized to do so. However, it seems reasonable that the more centralized the war-starting authority, the less likely an accidental war, if only because fewer people will have their fingers on the button. Moreover, it also seems reasonable that the small number of "authorized" war-starters will have been carefully scrutinized, both by the electorate and by others in power, so that irrational orders for nuclear war-starting will be less likely. (This assumes, of course, that orders for the use of nuclear weapons can ever be given for rational reasons—a questionable assumption.)

So it would seem that the more centralized the war-starting power, the better. On the other hand, since deterrence relies on credibility, and credibility depends not only on the willingness to retaliate but also on the *ability* to do so, pressure mounts for *de*-centralizing the necessary authority. Thus, if only the president can order a nuclear retaliation, then an enemy attack need only kill the president, or destroy the communication channels from him to his subordinates, to incapacitate the whole system. So, whereas safety from unauthorized war-starting requires that authority be central-ized, on the other hand, credibility of the deterrence requires that authority be decentralized, so that in the extreme case, each missile can be launched independently, even if all the other missiles and their control centers were destroyed.

We know next to nothing about Soviet arrangements to prevent unauthorized war-starting. However, we do know that the old men in the Kremlin like to keep power to themselves, sharing it only with great reluctance. Thus, during the SALT negotiations, Soviet diplomats were constantly obliged to contact Moscow for instruc-tions, having been given very little leeway by their bosses. Sim-ilarly, as we shall see, guided missile submarines must necessarily be given freer reign than either ICBM or bomber crews; this may partly explain why the Russians have very few submarines on open ocean patrol at any one time. In any event, it seems likely that the Soviet government has delegated very little responsibility to their field commanders, almost certainly less than we have.

How likely is it that a subordinate officer will someday start World War III? Not very. But nothing is really "fail-safe." And given the consequences of failure, just one failure, it is hard to be very optimistic about the long haul. Preventing a nuclear war is like trying to save a grove of redwood trees: you may succeed a thousand times, but if you fail just once, you have failed for good. The Department of Defense seems to have done an outstanding job of forestalling such a failure; indeed, perhaps everything that is humanly possible. But given the risks, is that enough?

ICBMs have the most reliable communication, and hence they are also the most reliably protected against unauthorized firings. Missile launch officers are kept from launching their missiles by Permissive Action Links. These aptly named PALs do us all a great favor, by preventing unauthorized use until the correct numerical code is inserted into the electronic system: this code can only be obtained after the PAL unlock has been authorized from above, and the missiles can then be "armed." For B-52s, the "go code" provides capability; until this is received, nuclear weapons cannot be armed. Once the code is transmitted, the pilot, radar navigator, and electronics warfare officer must all cooperate. For submarines, the situation is less clear: to be invulnerable against attack, nuclear missile submarines must remain submerged, but while submerged, they have great difficulty receiving or sending messages. Accordingly, it is almost certain (although never officially confirmed) that unlike ICBMs and B-52s, submarines can fire their nuclear weapons without transmission from the outside—that is, capability for nuclear war exists within each submarine.

Inside each sub, several "reliable" men, including the captain, first officer, and electronics warfare officer, must act together to fire their weapons. Errors seem unlikely, but they are not impossible. Thus, for example, on at least one occasion, a communications officer misread a message calling for a surprise drill as "the real thing," the dreaded Emergency Action Message. Fortunately, the captain caught the error, but then he did an interesting thing: to test the performance of his officers, he kept the error secret, allowing them to proceed as though it really *was* the real thing. They did very well, whereupon the captain, satisfied, ended the suspense by revealing the truth. An interesting exercise. But what if the captain had died of a sudden heart attack or stroke during the "drill," leaving his crew about to start a nuclear war? (This is not so far-fetched: pilots and train motormen have died at their controls, and the results, although tragic, have been mild by contrast.) Note also that there have been nine *reported* collisions between U.S. nuclear submarines and "hostile vessels" in Soviet waters during the 1970s alone—and five of these involved Soviet nuclear-armed submarines.

Clearly, men at the nuclear trigger should be "reliable." The Air Force operates a model Human Reliability Program, specifically concerned with screening personnel for nuclear duty. At the Strategic Air Command offices, about 2,000 servicemen are rejected every year for such assignments. After two years of service, however, disqualifications are almost unheard of. Perhaps this is because the Human Reliability Program does such a good screening job the first time around. On the other hand, it is also possible that after having lasted two years, most servicemen become socially incorporated within the personal network at their installation, making them immune from real scrutiny.

In 1969, a Cuban defector flew his MIG safely to Florida, right through the coastal radar defenses, without arousing any alarm. The resulting investigation of Nike-Hercules missile crews resulted in the arrest of thirty-five men assigned to these crews; they were charged with using drugs, including LSD (which can cause delusions and hallucinations). We leave it to the reader whether to be reassured by the portestations of Admiral W. P. Mock, chief of the Defense Department's drug abuse program: "only 10 had responsible positions—and there was only one per battery. In other words, no battery had more than one case in it." In addition, although the Air Force claims that the men in the ICBM silos are the sanest people on earth, rumors abound of heavy use of both marijuana and LSD. During a recent five-year period, 3,300 military personnel have been removed from nuclear weapons duty because of drug or alcohol abuse.

Finally, what about an insane or temporarily deranged president? The President of the United States, by definition, could not order *un*authorized nuclear war, because he *is* the final authority; his is the ultimate authorization. Should a president decide to order a nuclear attack, either in rataliation or even as a totally unprovoked Boob attack, the Secretary of Defense and the Chairman of the Joint Chiefs of Staff would be constitutionally and thus legally obliged to go along, whatever their moral objection might be. There is no PAL, no multiperson corroboration, no armed forces reliability test for a president. Indeed, there is not even a clear-cut procedure for relieving a president if he becomes mentally incompetent. Both Reagan and Brezhnev are over seventy; one frequent consequence of age is arteriosclerosis, resulting in impaired blood flow to the brain and often impaired judgment as well. President Eisenhower had two strokes while in office. As a result, his speech was noticeably slurred and by his own admission he sometimes had difficulty remembering what he was doing while seated at his desk in the Oval Office. Senator Thomas Eagleton, for a time vice-presidential candidate in 1972, had previously been treated for psychotic depression. It is widely recognized that during his "final days," Richard Nixon was on the brink of emotional collapse: crying, praying, pounding on the floor of the Lincoln Room. During that time, Defense Secretary Schlesinger is said to have taken extraordinary precautions that he be informed of any unusual orders involving nuclear weapons by the distraught president. Had such

254 • STOP NUCLEAR WAR! A HANDBOOK

orders been given, however, it is not clear what Schlesinger could have done.

History is filled with psychotic or deranged leaders: Caligula, Mad Ludwig of Bavaria, King George III. And can anyone have great confidence in the likes of Idi Amin or Muammar Qaddafi? It seems likely that when power is obtained by a coup, it is easier for a mentally incompetent leader to get control of a nation than when a lengthy political process insures some degree of scrutiny. Are we willing to bet our lives on the results? And further, are we willing to bet our lives on another country's choice of leaders?

If a psychotic, power-mad, nuclear-armed national leader ever emerged, the world would be faced with a crazy, intolerable choice: either capitulate to his/her demands, whatever they might be, or face nuclear oblivion. Deterrence, insane as it is, relies nonetheless on rationality. But irrationality exists, and for this reason alone, MAD cannot protect us indefinitely.


## Terrorism

Before the Arab oil boycott, virtually no one thought about an "energy crisis." Then, suddenly, it was one of our widely recognized problems. Right now, only a few experts worry about nuclear terrorism, but sometime within the next decade or two, terrorists using nuclear weapons may well burst on the human consciousness, making gasoline waiting lines seem the most trivial of inconveniences. Just as before 1973 only a small band of conservationists worried very much about energy supplies, most people probably will not think about nuclear terrorism until after it happens. It is just a matter of time.

Would-be nuclear terrorists would not have to recreate the Manhattan Project in order to get a bomb or two; there is no more secret. The word is out. The mountain has been climbed and the route well-marked. In their 1974 book *Nuclear Theft: Risks and Safeguards,* Mason Willrich and Theodore Taylor note that

A few persons, possibly even one person working alone, who possessed about 10 kilograms of plutonium oxide and a substantial amount of high explosive could, within several weeks, design and build a crude fission bomb. . . . This could be done using materials and equipment that could be purchased at a hardware store and from commercial suppliers of scientific equipment for student laboratories.

Shortly afterward, John A. Phillips, an average twenty-one-year-old undergraduate physics major at Princeton, used public documents to design a perfectly feasible working bomb in about four months. But, you might say, to actually build a bomb terrorists would need the fissionable material, either uranium 235 or plutonium 239. In fact, this is so easy that it may well have already happened, or be happening right now.

Thus, an average reactor makes from 5 to 400 pounds of plutonium per year. Plutonium is very difficult to measure accurately. Not only is it the most toxic substance known, it is also complex and fickle in its chemistry, adhering to surfaces and migrating out of containers. The Nuclear Regulatory Commission (successor to the AEC) keeps bookkeeping accounts of plutonium stores within the U.S. NRC bureaucrats have a large and growing category: Missing Unaccounted For, or MUF. And when it comes to plutonium, we have really MUFfed it. For example, in 1978 the NRC announced, begrudgingly, that over one ton of plutonium was Missing Unaccounted For! Although the likelihood is that most—perhaps nearly all—of the MUFfed plutonium is in fact missing and not in the hands of would-be terrorists, the prospect is not reassuring, especially when we consider that only about 5 to 20 pounds would be enough to make a bomb. During 1965/1966, 164 kilograms of highly enriched (bomb grade) uranium disappeared from the NUMEC plant in Apollo, Pennsylvania; the loss was not even reported publicly until a decade later. During a single two-month period in the fall of 1980, 22 kilograms of highly enriched (bomb grade) uranium couldn't be accounted for at the naval reactor fuel facility at Erwin, Tennessee.

One option for a would-be nuclear terrorist, then, is to accumulate plutonium or highly enriched uranium over a period of time, so that the losses are hidden in the statistic "noise" of accidental MUF. On October 22, 1970, the city of Orlando, Florida received a "ransom" note demanding $1 million—or, claimed the writer, the city would be blown up by a nuclear bomb. The note included a sketch of a bomb, one that was realistic enough that the threat had to be taken seriously. Moreover, AEC officials could not assure the mayor's office that fissionable materials, in the amount needed for the bomb, had not been stolen! The money was paid and the culprit apprehended shortly afterward; it was a fourteen-year old boy.

If they weren't concerned about keeping their operation secret, terrorists could assault one of the many plants and storage depots where fissionable materials are kept in large quantity. Security is incredibly lax, and for a group willing to risk the murder of hundreds of thousands, killing a guard or two would not be prohibitive. Bomb-usable materials could also be intercepted in transit. Uranium and plutonium are trucked all over the country; for example, fuel may be produced in Oak Ridge, Tenn., fissioned in a reactor in Oregon, then sent back to West Valley, N.Y. to be reprocessed. The fact is that a determined group, willing to resort to violence, could obtain the necessary fuel for a nuclear bomb. Moreover, such a group could even steal some ready-made bombs directly from the military. Our 30,000 or so nuclear bombs are not all carefully and securely guarded; often they simply wait in storerooms behind barbed wire and a sentry or two, lie about on airfield runways, or are trundled here and there in trucks.

Even a crudely made "fizzle yield" bomb of less than one kiloton, exploded in, say, the area of Wall Street in downtown Manhattan, could kill several hundred thousand persons. The gamma rays from even a one-fiftieth kiloton bomb could kill everyone in the Rose Bowl. One kilogram of plutonium is about the size of a golf ball. One kilogram of marijuana takes up about twenty times the space; yet, tons of marijuana are successfully smuggled across patrolled borders every week. Enough plutonium to blow up a large city could easily be smuggled anywhere by one person in the pockets of his coat. A one kiloton, do-it-yourselfer's delight, exploded just outside the restricted access area during the State of the Union address, could kill everyone in the Capitol building at the time: President, Vice-president, the Cabinet, the Senate, House of Representatives, Supreme Court justices, and the Joint Chiefs of Staff. And bombs can easily be made small enough to fit inside a large suitcase, or placed in the trunk of a car parked innocently at a curb.

Aside from the immediate death and destruction from such an attack, and the susceptibility of great nations to blackmail, there is the possibility that small-scale nuclear terrorism of this sort could precipitate the ultimate in nuclear terrorism: nuclear war. After the chaos and utter destruction of a sudden nuclear explosion in a big city or a military base, how would we know who did it? Sift the wreckage for clues? Would a victim state lash out blindly after being struck by an unknown assailant? What would the SAC officer in the Looking Glass plane do if Washington, D.C. disappeared in a flash, tomorrow. Or SAC headquarters?

During conventional wars, surprise attacks could always occur, but they could not be disavowed once they had taken place. Thus, Hitler surprised the world by the sudden blitzkrieg that overran Poland, but he could hardly deny having done it. Similarly with the Japanese attack on Pearl Harbor. With nuclear weapons, however, especially in the guise of terrorism, it is now possible for one nation to devastate another and to do so anonymously! "Surrogate terrorism" could well erupt within the next few decades. For example, Libya is angry with Egypt—a few bombs could be exploded in Cairo, Alexandria, the Aswan Dam, and blamed on Palestinians, Israelis, etc. Iraq could provide bombs to one of the radical Palestinian liberation groups, for use in Tel Aviv, Jerusalem, and Haifa; North Korea could give some bombs to the Japanese Red Army for use in South Korea; the possibilities are endless. A nation could even pretend to have some of its bombs stolen, so as to absolve it from responsibility.

At this point, it seems unlikely that any of the superpowers will resort to such tactics; however, for unstable, highly ideological and downright fanatic leaders of militant, smaller countries, the possibility cannot be excluded. Political scientist Louis Rene Beres points out several reasons why nuclear terrorism is more likely now than ever before: 1. Many nations tolerate and even support terrorist groups. 2. These groups cooperate with each other, crossing national boundaries and readily exchanging bomb materials. 3. Terrorist groups, by definition, are insensitive to public morality which would shrink from the murder of large numbers of innocent persons; they are ideologically committed to the end justifying the means. 4. They have already shown a penchant for indiscriminate, often suicidal violence. 5. Information, technology and the necessary materials for building bombs are available today as never before.

The conclusion is unavoidable: the risk of nuclear terrorism and of nuclear war ignited by terrorism is high during the 1980s. Much too high.

## Escalated War

Although there has not yet been a nuclear war, the world since 1945 has hardly been at peace. There were 97 civil and cross-national wars during the period 1945–1969, and more people have died from warfare after World War II than during it. According to a report from the Brookings Institution, the U.S. has deployed a military "show of force" 215 times between the close of World War II and 1977. To our knowledge, American and Soviet troops have not fired a shot at each other in more than 30 years, and perhaps we can take some comfort from this fact. If conventional war should ever break out between the superpowers, however, pressures to use nuclear weapons would be intense, and perhaps irresistible. Whichever side is losing, its military leaders will be hard-pressed to accept defeat when they still possess powerful and perhaps decisive weapons, still unused. Similarly, the winning side might conclude that the loser is about to cross the "fire-break" separating conventional from nuclear war. Indeed, as we have seen, recent developments, especially in U.S. war-planning strategy, have been emphasizing "limited" and tactical nuclear war. This blurs the distinction between conventional and nuclear war, making escalation more likely once fighting has broken out. Finally, either side might use nuclear weapons if conventional war results in a prolonged stalemate. In summary, conventional war between the superpowers could readily become nuclear war if one side is losing, winning, or tied. That pretty much covers the possibilities.

Nuclear confrontation could also begin indirectly. There have been several near-uses of nuclear weapons by the U.S., any of which could have expanded into a U.S.–U.S.S.R. confrontation. For example:

1. When U.S. troops were being pushed back by Chinese forces in Korea during 1951, Truman threatened to bomb Moscow. Not surprisingly, tensions were high. Early warning radar picked up a "bomber attack" coming over the Canadian arctic; it turned out to be a flock of geese.

2. In 1954, John Foster Dulles offered two bombs to France, one for use in the defense of Dienbienphu and the other for use against China, near the Vietnamese border.

3. In 1958, the National Security Council tentatively approved the use of nuclear weapons to help Chiang Kai-shek hold the islands of Quemoy and Matsu.

4. During the Laos crisis of 1961, the Joint Chiefs of Staff recommended use of nuclear weapons against the Pathet Lao.

5. During the Berlin crisis of 1961, Lauris Norstad, NATO supreme commander, favored the possible use of nuclear weapons.

6. During the Cuban missile crisis of 1962 the threat was open on both sides.

7. When the U.S. Marine base at Khe Sanh was surrounded and under siege in 1968, during the Vietnam War, President Johnson asked General Earle Wheeler, Chairman of the Joint Chiefs of Staff, about the possible use of nuclear weapons. General Westmoreland, commander of U.S. military forces in Vietnam, established a working group to evaluate the "nuclear defense of Khe Sanh," and the General remains convinced that "the use of a few small tactical nuclear weapons in Vietnam—or even the threat of them—might have brought the war to an end." It seems likely that use of nuclear weapons in Vietnam was forestalled largely by threat of adverse public opinion.

Following the Soviet invasion of Afghanistan and the end of détente in December 1979, President Carter made it clear that any perceived threat to the Persian Gulf region could bring about nuclear war. From southeast Asia, southwest Asia, the Middle East, to the restless satellites of eastern Europe, and even the Caribbean, there is clearly no shortage of sites for possible U.S.–Soviet military confrontation. Nonetheless, superpower wariness of each other will probably continue. Washington and Moscow will undoubtedly strive to avoid any conventional war, which could so easily escalate. Even if they succeed, however, the world is rife with lesser countries, lacking the inhibitions of the superpowers, filled with local hatreds, and also allied in one way or the other with either the U.S. or the U.S.S.R. The stage is therefore set for "catalytic" war in which fighting between other countries catalyzes nuclear war between the superpowers.

The conflict between the U.S. and the U.S.S.R. is primarily ideological. Among smaller quarreling countries of the world, by contrast, the disputes are more immediate, clear-cut, and impassioned, as contrasted with such theoretical issues as who has more influence in the world at large. For example, Israelis or Palestinians argue about particular chunks of real estate. Pakistan worries about being carved up any further (thereby becoming the Poland of the late twentieth century). Leaders of such countries feel that the stakes are high. In addition disputed borders are often directly touching, as between Pakistan and India, North and South Korea, Chile and Argentina, or Israel and her neighbors. In the latter case, for example, Israeli conventional forces can only be pushed back a few miles before Jerusalem, Haifa, or Tel Aviv is directly threatened. With their backs to the wall, countries could readily jump across the nuclear firebreak.

The Middle East may well be the most dangerous and potentially catalytic place of all. For example, on the second day of the 1973 Yom Kippur War, Israel is widely acknowledged to have assembled its small but potent nuclear arsenal (about two dozen atomic bombs), in case their conventional forces were unable to stem the Egyptian advance. On October 13, 1973, the Soviet Union responded by shipping nuclear warheads from its naval base at Odessa to Alexandria. Russian Scud missiles, capable of carrying these warheads to Israeli territory, were already in Egypt. The U.S. responded with a worldwide red alert. At about the same time, with Israel clearly on the ropes and down to only a few days' worth of tank ammunition, President Nixon began a massive airlift of needed military supplies. This aid was clearly instrumental in Israel's eventually turning the tide (and also, in generating the subsequent Arab oil boycott). What is less widely appreciated is that at the time, Israel had almost certainly equipped her French-made MD-660 surface-to-surface missiles, capable of reaching Cairo or Damascus, with nuclear warheads. Since there was also little doubt that if pushed far enough, the Israeli government would have used these weapons, the U.S. airlift was at least in part a response to nuclear blackmail.

However, a new danger soon surfaced. Israeli forces had essentially encircled the Egyptian Third Army and could have destroyed it, leaving Egypt defenseless. The Soviet Union then threatened to intervene on Egypt's behalf, placing seven divisions on alert. The next day, the U.S. again responded with a worldwide alert. This time, however, decentralizing procedures, needed for actual combat, were not begun. On that same day, the U.N. passed resolution 340, calling for a cease-fire and a peace-keeping force. The U.S. alert was then canceled. But once again, the catalytic potential of local wars was made terrifyingly clear.

There are many other possible trouble spots, in which either the U.S. or the U.S.S.R. or both, have allies: Taiwan and China, North and South Korea, Cuba and its Central American neighbors, India and Pakistan, South Africa and its black neighbors. Even if neither superpower is immediately drawn in, nuclear war between two lesser powers would generate powerful pressures for other countries to obtain similar weapons for their own "defense." Moreover, it would also break down the crucial psychological firebreak, however fragile, that now separates conventional and nuclear warfare. Just as it often requires a fatal accident before a community gets a needed traffic light for a dangerous corner, it may well take a little nuclear war (if this is possible) before the world wakes up to the peril.

We don't necessarily even have to wait for other countries to use their own nuclear weapons—maybe someone will go ahead and use ours. Thus, during the July 1974 crisis between Greece and Turkey over Cyprus, the U.S. Sixth Fleet was ordered to stand by with a detachment of Marines aboard helicopters to recover the dozens of nuclear warheads which were (and perhaps still are) stored there by our NATO forces.

Fledgling nuclear powers are especially liable to use their weapons. Thus, an important factor, rarely noted by most observers, is that whereas the U.S. and U.S.S.R. have stable second-strike deterrence, a newly arrived nuclear nation does not. For each superpower, second-strike deterrence means that each side is deterred from striking first because the would-be victim's nuclear arsenal is so enormous that even after a surprise attack, enough warheads would be available to destroy the attacker. By contrast, consider a fledgling nuclear nation that has, say, five atomic bombs. These bombs may be a substantial threat to an opponent, but they could also be destroyed with relative ease by that opponent in a preemptive attack. Therefore, during a war—or even a crisis—either side may be tempted to attack the other, not only because the devastated opponent would be unable to retaliate, but also because that same opponent would presumably be under the same temptation to strike first as well!

But it doesn't even end here: because of these risks, it seems likely that second-rate nuclear powers would be much jumpier than either the U.S. or the U.S.S.R. Moreover, permissive action links, human reliability programs, and the like may appear to be costly extravagances. So, fledgling nuclear nations would almost certainly have fewer controls against accidental or unauthorized use, and also a greater likelihood of delegating launch responsibility to forward-based field commanders who are liable to be somewhat trigger-happy. Furthermore, as demonstrated by the Israeli attack on the Iraqi reactor at Osirak, even the *threat* of nuclear weapons production may generate anxiety, leading to a preemptive attack.

## Proliferation: I. Politics

> If all this capacity for destruction is spread around the world in the hands of all kinds of different characters—dictators, reactionaries, revolutionaries, madmen—then sooner or later, and certainly by the end of this century, either by error or insanity, the great crime will be committed.
>
> —letter from British Prime Minister Harold MacMillan to President John F. Kennedy

Why? Why are so many countries busily acquiring nuclear weapons? There are several reasons. One is pride and prestige—

which clearly influenced DeGaulle's decision to develop a French *force de frappe*, and doubtless motivates many third world leaders today. Thus, Pakistan's Zufikar Ali Bhutto said that his people would "eat leaves and grass, even go hungry" to pay for their own bomb. There may even be some religious pride as well. Thus, Bhutto added, "There is a Hindu bomb, a Jewish bomb and a Christian bomb. There must be an Islamic bomb." (Libyan money, using stolen Dutch plans, is now sponsoring development of such a bomb in Pakistan, which will almost certainly be complete in the 1980s).

There is also fear of a nuclear-armed opponent. Thus, Pakistan points to India's nuclear explosion; India, in turn, points to China; China points to the Soviet Union; and the Soviet Union, of course, points to the United States. Chain reactions, it seems, are not limited to nuclear physics; they apply to nuclear politics as well. Not surprisingly, once a nation joins the nuclear club, then it usually seeks to close the door to any further entrants. But it can't be done. Acquiring nuclear weapons is like killing the top-ranked gunfighter in the Old West: it may confer prestige, but it is unlikely to bring any security, since all the other hotshots are likely to come gunning for you. For example, once Argentina gets its own bomb (as it seems to be doing), in order to be "safe," then Brazil will doubtless feel unsafe. So it will get one, too. When both are nuclear-armed, both will be less safe than either is now.

Some theorists actually maintain, however, that a proliferated world may be safer than today's. They espouse the "porcupine theory": just as porcupines walk safely through the forest, too spiny for any predator to swallow, if every nation has nuclear weapons, peace will follow, or so it has been claimed. Unfortunately, the porcupine theory is almost certainly incorrect. It recalls the old joke: "How do porcupines make love?" "Carefully." By obtaining nuclear weapons, any country raises the risks enormously. As we have seen, it may provoke a first strike against it, just by the threat of possessing these weapons. As more countries get their own bombs, the threat to all increases exponentially, not only from calculated attack, but also from accident, false alarm, unauthorized use, or terrorism. In fact, even porcupines have predators: the fisher (a relative of the weasel) flips them over and rips at their soft, unprotected bellies. And more to the point, other predators, less adroit, often kill porcupines as well, although in the process, they suffer grieviously from their prickly prey.

By 1985, nearly forty countries will have enough plutonium from the spent fuel in their power reactors alone to make atomic bombs. That's forty countries. Thomas Schelling, professor of political economy at Harvard University, wrote in 1979:

> Although, by temperament, I may be an optimist, a reasoned evaluation of where we may be in 25 years suggests that we will not be able to regulate nuclear weapons around the world by 1999 any better than we can control the Saturday-night special, heroin or pornography today.

Here are some brief examples of how it has been going: in November 1968, the freighter Scheersberg sailed from Antwerp with 200 tons of uranium ore. It never arrived at Geneva, its destination. The Scheersberg was later found empty in Turkey, and its owner revealed as an Israeli secret agent. The boat had apparently been hijacked off the coast of Italy, and sailed to Haifa—the apparent work of Mossad, the Israeli CIA. About the same time, several hundred pounds of highly enriched uranium (hidden as MUF) was almost certainly diverted from the Nuclear Materials and Equipment Corporation (NUMEC) plant at Apollo, Pennsylvania. It is now clear that Israel has been accumulating the materials for nuclear bombs at its top-secret Dimona Atomic Research Community in the Negev Desert—not open for international inspection and so heavily guarded that during the 1967 war the Israelis shot down one of their own airplanes which strayed over it. Although Israel has not openly tested any bombs, the Israelis have cooperated actively with scientists from the Union of South Africa, and in September 1979, satellites detected a bright flash off the southern Indian Ocean, suggesting an explosion of 2–3 kilotons.

In 1976, Egyptian foreign minister Ismail Fahmi announced, "If Israel explodes an atomic device, Egypt will obtain a similar weapon or manufacture it." Thus far, Israel has not publicly acknowledged exploding an atomic "device," and Egypt does not seem hell-bent upon getting its own. On the other hand, Iraq purchased a nuclear reactor from France in 1975. Iraq is rich in oil and has very little need for electricity; accordingly, the Iraqi goal is quite clear—not electric power, but bombs. The reactor core had been awaiting shipment from the French town of Seyne-sur-Mere when it was blown up, presumably by Israeli agents. A prominent Iraqi physicist was also murdered while in Europe. Then, in June 1981, after a new core had been installed, Israel used American F-15 jets in a novel role, as temporary nonproliferation devices.

Libya has also been seeking nuclear weapons, and once more, it seems to be only a matter of time. Following the 1967 Arab-Israeli war, Muammar Qaddafi announced: "The nuclear monopoly is about to be broken. Soon the atom will have no secrets for anybody. Some years ago, we could hardly procure a fighter squadron. Tomorrow we will be able to buy an atomic bomb and all its parts." He sent his top aide, Abdul Salem Jalloud, to China in 1969, seeking to buy an atomic bomb. The Chinese refused. But by 1975 he had signed an agreement to purchase an atomic reactor, which of course, makes plutonium. In addition, Libya and probably Saudi Arabia are financing the aggressive Pakistani bomb-building program.

Meanwhile, India shocked the world in 1974 by exploding an atomic bomb of 15–20 kilotons, underground in the Rajasthan desert, east of New Delhi. The Indian government claimed that the explosion was for "peaceful uses," although no one believes that. The Indian bomb had been constructed with material from Canadian-built reactors; Canada responded angrily and ceased all nuclear-related assistance to India. The guilty reactors had been fueled with uranium supplied by the United States. Nonetheless, President Carter subsequently pressured Congress to approve an additional 38 tons of uranium fuel for the Tarapur reactor, near Bombay.

Over in the Far East, Taiwan is operating a 40-megawatt research reactor, also Canadian-built, like the ones used by India to construct its bomb. Moreover, Premier Chiang Ching-kuo commented in 1977 that Taiwan "has the capability of developing nuclear arms." The Chung Shan Institute is widely acknowledged to be working on missiles, guidance systems, rocket fuels, and warhead design. The government in Peking, of course, is noting this well.

Even in our own hemisphere, there is little cause for complacency. In July 1975, U.S. intelligence reported that Argentina secretly removed 50 kilograms of plutonium waste from its Atucha power plant, enough for 5 atomic bombs. Despite this, in October

1981, the Reagan Administration agreed to waive regulations and sell additional supplies of enriched uranium to Argentina. Ominously, Brazil has signed a huge, multibillion dollar deal with West Germany, obtaining power stations, enrichment plants and plutonium reprocessing plants.

Finally, there is a novel way for a country to obtain nuclear weapons: revolting or seceding from the parent state. If North Dakota ever left the union, it would outrank France, Britain, China, and India as a nuclear-armed power. No one seriously considers this likely, but can we say the same about other countries? For example, it is widely believed that during the Cultural Revolution in China during 1967, the military commander of Sinkiang Province threatened to seize the nuclear base if the provincial government had been overturned. And what if, following a military coup in, say, Turkey or Spain, our nuclear weapons stored in those countries were suddenly overrun?

With so many countries slavering to indulge in a nuclear orgy, we might ask: why have others refrained? Those countries that seem about to develop nuclear weapons fall into two categories: on the one hand, third world states that perceive themselves directly threatened by a neighbor or that are ideologically committed to certain local antagonisms. On the other, developed, technological nations that are outside the major power blocs. In the first case we find the Arab states, as well as South Korea, Pakistan, and India. In the second, Israel, South Africa, and Taiwan—lonely, isolated and endangered. It is striking that some of the world's most technologically sophisticated nations, with both the wealth and knowledge to develop nuclear weapons, have *not* done so: Holland, Sweden, Canada, Australia, Norway, Switzerland, Italy. At the slightest whim or provocation, these nations could readily develop nuclear weapons. They are not currently doing so because they feel relatively safe, either by virtue of their neutrality, their membership in NATO, or their recognition that such a move would make them less safe, not more. And let's not forget those two great economic and industrial giants, Japan and West Germany. Because of their own experiences during World War II, as well as the terms of their surrender, neither country has attempted to develop nuclear weapons of its own, although it is certain that either one could do so within weeks—perhaps days—if it ever made the fateful decision.

And significantly, the U.S. is pressuring both of these countries, especially Japan, to take a more vigorous military posture.

Nor can we take much comfort in the lack of "delivery systems." After all, nuclear weapons do not have to be delivered by bomber or missile. Since a little bit goes such a long way, bombs can arrive by van, motorboat, or even parcel post. There is also the cruise missile, which so enchants American military leaders at present. Cruise missiles are not only easy to hide, they are also cheap. Armed with atom bombs and cruise missiles, countries like Libya, Pakistan, or even Upper Volta can threaten any nation on earth.

This review is necessarily brief, but the point should nonetheless be clear: nuclear weapons and the ability to make nuclear weapons have been proliferating like weeds. In the words of economist-turned-strategist Albert Wohlstetter, we are "moving toward life in a nuclear-armed crowd." And for modern-day cave men armed with atomic weapons, the phrase "nuclear club" takes on a new and ominous meaning.


### Proliferation: II. Power

> Human society is too diverse, national passion too strong, human aggressiveness too deep-seated for the peaceful and the warlike atom to stay divorced for long. We cannot embrace one while abhoring the other; we must learn, if we want to live at all, to live without both.
>
> —JACQUES IVES COUSTEAU

Proliferation is politics: the decision "to proliferate or not to proliferate" is a political one. Thus it is subject to all the emotion, history and economics of other political decisions. But certain things make that decision more likely or less so, and among these, one of the most important is the ease with which a country can go ahead and make bombs if it wishes. And nothing makes bomb-building easier than nuclear power. Indeed, just as biologists view a chicken as an egg's way of making more eggs, Amory Lovins has suggested that a reactor is a bomb's way of making more bombs. Nuclear reactors are, in fact, virtually useless for their avowed purpose: making energy, but they are fiendishly efficient for their forbidden purpose: making bombs. Nuclear power technology can be directly applied to nuclear bomb technology. And even more important, the stuff of reactors is the stuff of bombs.

As it happens, atomic bombs can be made either from material that goes into reactors (fuel), or from material that comes out of them after they have been operating for a time (spent fuel, or waste). The latter is the easiest, so we shall concentrate on it here. The most popular reactors operate by fissioning $U_{235}$. In the process, some of the $U_{235}$ absorbs neutrons and gets transformed eventually into plutonium. Two things can be done with plutonium: it can be used as a fuel itself, in so-called "breeder" reactors, which make additional plutonium, and it can be used to make bombs. Indeed, it is more efficient than uranium at making bombs. For reasons best known only to itself, the Atomic Energy Commission chose a particular technique, the "Purex" method, for reprocessing spent reactor fuel. This technique has accordingly been spread worldwide, largely through our largesse. It is also the preferred method for getting especially pure plutonium for bomb production.

The U.S. commercial reprocessing plant, at West Valley, N.Y., has been closed down, hopelessly contaminated with radiation. But at this moment, plutonium is being separated at commercial reprocessing plants in Atucha, Argentina; Barseback, Sweden; Latina, Italy; Vandellos, Spain; Biblis, West Germany; and Muhleberg, Switzerland. India constructed her own reprocessing plant to make the 1974 bomb out of the effluent of several power and research reactors. In 1974, about 4 tons of plutonium was made commercially in the world; by 1978, 14 tons. According to the Stockholm International Peace Research Institute, by 1990 there will be about 450 tons, enough for 80,000 to 90,000 bombs. (This is NOT counting military production!)

Research reactors alone are very efficient at making plutonium. Here is the output for a few countries: India–12 kilograms per year; Taiwan–12; Switzerland–9; Israel–8; Canada–72. And so it goes. Inspections by the International Atomic Energy Administration in 1976 revealed that of 41 countries checked, 7 had at least 5 kilograms of plutonium, and another 13 had at least that much, unseparated. The U.S. essentially gave away 26 reactors, fueled by highly enriched uranium, to South Korea, Pakistan, Iran, Israel,

Brazil, Spain, and Taiwan. (Highly enriched uranium can be used directly to build bombs, and it also makes plutonium quickly and well.) India had to "buy" its Tarapur reactor, financed at .75 percent annual interest, a 40-year repayment schedule, and a 10-year initial deferment!

You should know a little more about plutonium, since the world seems to be moving rapidly toward a "plutonium economy," in which the stuff will be shipped around all over the place, like coal or take-home pizza. Even aside from its bomb-building potential, plutonium has other charms. Thus, it is probably the deadliest thing on earth, 20,000 times as toxic as cyanide. One pound of reactor plutonium contains 338 million cancer doses, more than enough for all of North America. Distribute 10 pounds equally, and every man, woman, and child on earth will have a high probability of dying from cancer. It was named, aptly enough, for Pluto, the Greek god of the dead. It has a half-life of 24,000 years, and is dangerous to people for 500,000 years. Thus, to deal with it successfully, we must be assured of keeping it safely stored for more than 50 times longer than civilized life has existed on our planet. It is a silvery-white metal, naturally present in only minute quantities; thus, it is essentially man-made, unknown to this planet until its creation, in a reactor, in 1940. In small pieces, it burns spontaneously in the air, making a smoke that is virtually invisible and of which one millionth of a gram, inhaled, will cause cancer. We might expect such a substance to be abhorred. And yet, the AEC estimated in 1972 that U.S. reactors alone will have made 50,000 tons of plutonium. This is the legacy we are leaving our children.

Uranium is not nearly the same immediate public health risk as plutonium. Uranium is stolid, almost immobile and inert compared to plutonium. It is not so carcinogenic. But the isotope $U_{235}$, if sufficiently concentrated, can make dandy bombs. Gas diffusion has long been the favored technique for getting high-grade $U_{235}$, but it is incredibly expensive and only 7 such plants exist in the world: one each in the U.S.S.R., Britain, France, and China, and 3 in the U.S. Other processes have recently been developed, enabling the user to "enrich" uranium ore to the concentration desired—about 3 percent for reactor fuel, about 90 percent for bombs. There are now gas centrifuge and laser separation techniques, and an aerodynamic process developed by West Germany. South Africa has apparently discovered yet another, cheaper, and more efficient way. (In hot pursuit of its own bombs, Pakistan stole plans for an advanced uranium centrifuge design from Holland.) But there can be no doubt, the U.S. is responsible for most of the nuclear technology that is so widely diffused about the world today.

Since we are so threatened by plutonium and its allies, why in heaven's name are we pushing reactor technology to anyone who will accept it? There is no rational answer (except for the fact that some companies make money on it). But some history might help.

We exploded the first H-bomb in October 1952. The world was shocked and scared. Then Russia exploded its H-bomb, in August 1953. Things looked even worse. So several months later, in December 1953, President Eisenhower made a momentous speech at the U.N., unveiling his "Atoms for Peace" plan. Its goal was to make the H-bomb and nuclear technology politically acceptable. Now, there is almost a religious commitment to the "peaceful" atom, and an incredible refusal to consider the risks. In fact, Atoms for Peace must go down in history as one of the stupidest blunders of all time.

But isn't nuclear energy safe, you ask? Of course it's safe. That is, providing there is no sabotage, no mechanical breakdowns, no wearing out of containment vessels, no wars, no riots, and no human error. Acts of God are strictly forbidden. But the greatest danger is not in the area of reactor *safety*, which concerns breakdowns, meltdowns, and other sorts of screw-ups, but rather in the area of *safeguards*—that is, the problem of protecting against the use of reactor products to manufacture bombs.

Safeguards are the job of the IAEA, the International Atomic Energy Agency. Sad to tell, these safeguards are at best inadequate. They give reassurance to the world community, whereas in fact, real anxiety is warranted. For example: (1) Each host country can veto a would-be inspector. Thus, Iraqi nuclear facilities have been inspected only by Soviet and Hungarian nationals. (2) The IAEA must give several weeks' notice prior to an inspection, since visas must be obtained. Thus, a "pop quiz" is impossible, and would-be violators have plenty of time to cover up their activities. (3) As long as any country claims that a particular facility is not processing plutonium or making uranium fuel, the IAEA cannot insist that it be inspected. (4) As part of their operating rules, the IAEA cannot and does not look for clandestine violations. Like the three monkeys, the IAEA sees no evil, hears no evil, and speaks no evil. (5) Uranium ore, known as yellowcake ($U_3O_8$), is not subject to any safeguards whatever. (6) Although plutonium is relatively difficult to divert from light water reactors, it is quite easy to do so in research reactors, since part of reactor research typically involves inserting different substances into the reactor for varying periods of time. If uranium is used instead of some test material, out comes plutonium. Thus almost any power, super or not so super, can get plutonium. And thus, proliferation flourishes.

In summary, here is how a nuclear war could start: boob attack, chicken, accidents (broken arrows, false alarms, and unauthorized use), terrorism, escalated conventional war, catalytic war, and via proliferation. Some, like the renowned British historian and anti-nuclear activist E. P. Thompson, state that nuclear war is a "virtual certainty." Our job is to prove him wrong.

There has not yet been a nuclear war. Perhaps this is because we have been wise. More likely, we have been lucky. In any event, disaster is not inevitable, but unless we recognize the problem and resolve to do something about it, our luck seems bound to run out someday. To say the least, it is unwise to bank on nuclear war not happening, simply because it has not happened yet. Recall the fellow who jumped off the roof of the Empire State Building, and who calmly announced as he sped past the thirty-first floor, "Well, so far, so good."

# 9. Stars on Earth: The Immediate Effects of
## Nuclear Explosions

> And the fifth angel blew his trumpet, and I saw a star fallen from
> heaven to earth . . .
>
> REVELATIONS, 9:1

Nuclear explosions are different. Their sheer power makes them different from conventional explosions, not only quantitatively but qualitatively as well. In less than one millionth of a second, they can release the force equivalent to millions of tons of TNT, with temperatures measured in the millions of degrees. When we multiply anything by a million or so, we effectively change it altogether. You may have a few dollars in your pocket. Multiply by a million and you are a multimillionaire. Your life will have changed, not only quantitatively, but qualitatively. Walking down the street, you move at about three miles per hour. Multiply by a million, and you are going fast enough to leave the planet altogether. The point should be clear: multiply anything by a million, and it becomes something new. Nuclear weapons, then, are different, and yet, we must somehow include them within our thinking. Otherwise, we fail to grasp our peril.

The mind flinches, writhes, then often gives up entirely, and we wander adrift in a sea of numbers. Numbers can be numbing—the reality, by contrast, would be abrupt and all too real. So we must stretch our imagination, to feel the heat, light and power of the sun and the stars raining down upon this fragile, green planet. It will not be easy or pleasant, but it is important, because only by knowing the effects of nuclear war—emotionally as well as intellectually—will you know (in your guts as well as your brain) that it must never be allowed to happen. Poet Archibald MacLeish has pointed out the danger of separating fact from feeling: ". . . knowledge without feeling is not knowledge, and can only lead to public irresponsibility and indifference, conceivably to ruin . . . (When) the fact is dissociated from the feel of the fact . . . that people, that civilization, is in danger." In the next two chapters, we will try to provide you with the facts and also the feel of those facts, so that we can all act, together, to reduce our danger.

The advocates of peace are often accused of being unrealistic, but it is the hawks and the nuclear war planners who are out of touch with reality: the reality of what a nuclear war would be. As former SALT negotiator Paul Warnke pointed out, "People teetering at the edge of the abyss cannot afford to ignore the law of gravity." They also should have no illusions as to their fate when they reach the bottom.

Beyond this, you must also be able to counter those who argue that we can somehow walk on air, or land daintily on our feet, after we fall. Thus, two separate and influential groups of people have been proclaiming that "it wouldn't really be so bad." (It is hard to imagine a more glaring case of civic irresponsibility on the part of government officials—like the policeman on the suicide-prevention squad who tells would-be jumpers that the pavement is actually quite soft.) The first, largest, and most dangerous of these groups are government agencies throughout the world, in Russia, Sweden, England, Switzerland, and the U.S. among others, entrusted with "civil defense" preparations. In the U.S., the bomb-shelter schemes and air raid drills of the 1950s have now given way to expensive plans for evacuating American cities when a Soviet nuclear attack on the U.S. mainland is expected. FEMA, the Federal Emergency Management Agency, is to receive $4 billion over the next five years to develop such plans, and for industrial "civil defense." The second, smaller group are the "survivalists," who claim that nuclear war is probably inevitable, but, they say, with sufficient personal preparations, you and perhaps your family can sit it out in safety, and then return to a more rugged but nonetheless passable lifestyle when the dust settles. A typical spokesman for this "survivalist" movement is Bruce Clayton, author of *Life after Doomsday*, who states:

> Nuclear war will be the greatest social and biological catastrophe our world has ever known. It will be unprecedented, but it will not be difficult to survive it.

All you have to do is buy his book. . . .

These claims of survivability are dangerous, appealing to part of our Neanderthal mentality: "When the going gets tough, the tough get going." In the past, neither wars nor natural disasters have been *total*—otherwise we wouldn't be here. Our natural, Neanderthal inclination is to treat nuclear war as we have treated past experiences. First, we rely on strength or a big stick to deter conflict. If conflict seems imminent (or desirable), governments prepare young men to fight, and women and children, if possible, are kept in the background. If a battlefront moves toward a town, the town evacuates, the noncombatants hide in rural areas, then return to towns that are somewhat damaged but basically functional. The society may change governments, sustain casualties, it may win or lose, but it does not cease to exist.

Similarly for natural disasters: the Neanderthal inside knows that if he lives near a volcano, and the ground starts to shake, he'd better run. It may be a matter of luck whether he escapes—which way the lava flows, where the landslides occur, and so forth. In any event, however, running as far and as fast as possible from a natural disaster would seem to make good sense.

But nuclear war is fundamentally different from anything in human experience, and therefore the compelling calls of our biological and cultural heritage no longer make sense. A nuclear bomb exploding is like a small, intense star falling to earth, an event unprecedented in history. To grasp it, we must shake off our preconceptions of temperature, sound, distance, and the reliability of our senses. In our workaday world, the temperature of boiling water (100°C.) is very hot, and even dangerous. Only by forcing our imaginations can we conceive 100,000,000°C.—the temperature inside a fusion bomb. We are used to poisons that taste or smell bad, not radiation that has no taste or smell. Our planet has been scarred by war before, but never sterilized.

Therefore, let's begin by describing a few smaller, past holocausts as a tool to engage the imagination. The Black Plague reduced the population of Europe by about 50 percent. From 1347 until 1351, about 20 million Europeans died. In the twentieth century, we may have grown accustomed to 20 million as the number of deaths associated with a run-of-the-mill holocaust. Twenty million Russians died in World War II. The United States Office of Technology Assessment report on *The Effects of Nuclear War* estimates 20 million immediate deaths as the upper limit for a counter-force nuclear war, and 20 million immediate deaths as the lower limit for a "countervalue" or all-out nuclear war with Russia. As the number is repeated, we become numb to its personal, ethical, social, and biological impact. Twenty million is a nice round number that Pentagon planners seem to have accepted as expendable in nuclear war. (As we shall see, even this number is wildly optimistic and a likely underestimate.)

It is only when we begin to look at the plight of individuals, or small groups, that the catastrophe becomes real, and we start to feel the tears. A few examples may suffice. A few years ago, an earthquake rattled Italy, killing thousands. As the Italian government and world health relief organizations mobilized to aid the survivors, the world's attention was riveted instead on the plight of one small boy who fell down a mineshaft. The personal drama was gripping; the collective catastrophe, by contrast, seemed less real.

*The Diary of Anne Frank* has made the Nazi holocaust real for millions who would have ignored the photographs of Auschwitz corpses. Does the image of a boxcar full of baby shoes, found at Auschwitz, say more than the figure of six million dead? The individual Vietnamese monks who cremated themselves may have had more impact than the mass graves at My Lai.

And thus we must turn again and again to Hiroshima and Nagasaki, and the experiences and pictures of the victims, to sense even a small fraction of what nuclear war would be like. Even then, these two bombs are tiny by today's standards. Hence, they can only offer a metaphor for nuclear war today, in which thousands of nuclear bombs, exploding almost simultaneously, could be the last holocaust.

The immediate effect of a nuclear explosion is first heat, and then blast. Of course, the most notorious effect is radiation, both immediate and then fallout. Many people seem to believe that a nuclear explosion is just like a conventional one, only with radiation. Therefore, they fear the radiation (which they are surely correct in doing), but they almost ignore the blast and thermal effects, which is surely incorrect. We shall now review all three effects, our nuclear trinity: heat, blast, and radiation—first separately, then together in an imagined attack.

## Heat

The hills which looked on Christ will heave and crackle,
and quarries vaporize as meekly as the dust of Pharoahs:
The earth, the tamed and tonsured earth with all its gardens
and substances, its places, breeds and patterns,
its letters and its airs, will plummet out of grace, will fail its orbit:
And soon enough will be a blistered ash, its moon trailing
ungoverned like a dog after his master's corpse.

—N. Corwin *(Now About That Next War, Son)*

Our only example of a useful or friendly thermonuclear explosion is the sun. Only because it is so far away however, (93 million miles), is it friendly. The sun glows yellow because its surface temperature is about 5,500°C. (10,000°F.). Its interior is probably about 10 to 30 million degrees C. A thermonuclear bomb is precisely like a small sun, exploding much closer to home.

At the moment of detonation, the heat of the fusion reaction is between 20 to 100 million degrees C., hotter than the interior of the sun. The bomb vaporizes and the hot gases plus intense electromagnetic radiation are quickly absorbed by air, producing a fireball. About 35 percent of the energy released is in the form of heat, pure infrared radiation. This burst of heat is called the "thermal pulse," and it travels at the speed of light.

A small nuclear explosion, say 20 kilotons like the one that devastated Nagasaki, reaches a burst temperature of millions of degrees within a millionth of a second after detonation. Less than a millisecond later, a sphere with a uniform temperature of about 300,000°C. and a radius of 15 meters is formed. Thereafter, pressure builds up and the fireball splits into two concentric regions, a hotter inner region and a cooler, rapidly expanding shock wave, or outer region. The outer region reaches a temperature of about 8,000°C. in about 0.2 seconds, and then begins to fall. However, it takes a full 10 seconds before the brightness of the fireball disappears. Within this interval, 0.2 to 10 seconds, vast amounts of pure infrared rays are emitted. Just in its heat alone, therefore, a nuclear explosion is totally outside of human experience. Not only is the heat unimaginably intense, it is also *persistent*, continuing for many long seconds, and not just a quick flash.

The bomb that destroyed Hiroshima at 8:15 AM on August 6, 1945, had the explosive force of about 12,500 tons of TNT; Nagasaki was decimated by a slightly larger bomb equivalent to 20,000 tons of TNT. By the end of 1945, an estimated 140,000 people died of bomb-related injuries in Hiroshima, and an estimated 70,000 in Nagasaki. Severe burns, caused by the heat, were the primary cause of thousands of deaths.

Persons closest to the blast were simply vaporized by the heat, some leaving their shadows engraved on concrete walls. Those farther away became instant masses of crispy charcoal; and farther yet, like sudden baked potatoes, with charred skin and burned innards. Those far enough to survive, at least for a time, often had their faces literally melted away. At greater distances, women wearing flowered kimonos had the patterns burned into their flesh, as the darker figures absorbed the heat which was reflected by the white background.

The horrible image of burned victims particularly characterizes the individual stories of the *hibakusha*. For example, in his book, *Hiroshima*, John Hersey reported on the nightmarish experience of Father Kleinsorge, the day after the bombing. He heard a voice ask, "Have you anything to drink?" and went toward the bushes.

> When he had penetrated the bushes, he saw that there were about twenty men, and they were all in exactly the same nightmarish state; their faces were wholly burned, their eyesockets were hollow, the fluid from their melted eyes had run down their cheeks. (They must have had their faces upturned when the bomb went off; perhaps they were antiaircraft personnel.) Their faces were mere swollen, pus-covered wounds which they could not bear to stretch enough to admit the spout of a teapot.

R. Katsutani reports a similar tale:

> The sight of the soldiers was more dreadful than the dead people floating down the river. I came upon I don't know how many, burned from the hips up; and where the skin had peeled, their flesh was wet and mushy.

They must have been wearing their military caps because the black hair on the top of their heads was not burned. It made them look like they were wearing black lacquer bowls.

And they had no faces. Their eyes, noses, and mouths had been burned away, and it looked like their ears had melted off. It was hard to tell front from back. . . ."

Painful as it is, we must burn the images of *their* burns into *our* minds.

The severity of burns is characterized by the depth of skin that is injured. For example, most sunburns are first degree burns, with pain and reddening of the skin; but since underlying skin cells are uninjured, no special treatment is necessary. Second degree burns involve blistering of the skin, and will result in severe pain, swelling, and dehydration; but again, since the deepest layers of rapidly dividing skin cells are not killed, second degree burns rarely require skin grafting—although they can be life threatening if more than 20 percent of the body is involved. Third degree burns involve the death or carbonization of the entire skin layer. Even a small third degree burn requires intensive medical treatment. Indeed, third degree burns are the most painful human injury, and also among the most difficult to treat.

Even a small second or third degree burn in a critical place can cause severe disability or death. For example, any facial burn that causes swelling of the nose and throat poses immediate medical emergency. Many of the Hiroshima and Nagasaki victims had severe burns, so that a common sight was people whose skin was loosened, burned, and dropped down in grotesque flaps. Many victims received direct burns to internal organs, following blast injuries, and most of these died within hours.

Often, third degree burns, even over a large part of the body, are not immediately fatal. After all, our skin is not normally considered a vital organ, like the brain, heart, or lungs. However, without immediate and intensive medical efforts, severe burn victims eventually die, and in great agony.

Mortality rises several hours after a severe burn, when the sufferers begin to lose enormous quantities of fluid, and the adjacent tissue begins to swell. During the initial period of burn management, huge quantities of intravenous fluids, including both plasma and blood products, are essential. Shock or vascular collapse may occur. The dead, burned skin can no longer protect the victim from infection or fluid loss, so the fluid replacement program must be supplemented with antibiotics, and possibly strict reverse isolation—that is, putting the victim in a "life island" with its own sterile air supply and an infection barrier between the patient and his or her caretakers. Using these techniques, plus extensive surgical procedures for skin grafting, and provided that the patient has 24-hour intensive nursing care, some individuals with even 80–90 percent total body third degree burns will survive. Total cost? In 1982 dollars, around $500,000. There are only about 2,000 beds for severely burned patients in the entire United States—and virtually none would exist following a nuclear war.

The Shriners currently maintain three specialized burn hospitals; with only about 30 beds each, these burn hospitals use about the same budget as the Shriner's 19 orthopedic hospitals. And even so, the intensive care required by burn patients means that each hospital can handle only 2 or 3 fresh, severe cases at one time. Dr. John Constable, burn specialist and plastic surgeon at Harvard, stated that from a single nuclear explosion, "the medical facilities of the nation would choke totally on even a fraction of the burn casualties alone"—assuming that the facilities themselves were intact. Dr. Howard Hiatt, dean of Harvard's School of Public Health, recounts the example of a twenty-year-old man, brought to a Boston area hospital with third degree burns over 85 percent of his body. He required: 281 units of blood, 147 units of additional packed red blood cells, 37 units of platelets, 36 units of serum albumin, 6 surgeries (including allo-grafts, homografts, and artificial skin), and the full-time services of numerous highly skilled specialists and technical machinery. Yet, after straining the resources of one of the nation's great medical centers, he died on the 33rd day. All of New York City has beds for only about 50 such patients; an attack on New York City would undoubtedly produce hundreds of thousands of similar victims, and (if it mattered any) all of the burn beds would have been destroyed.

With 10-mile visibility, a one megaton nuclear airburst will cause first degree burns in all unprotected persons at 7 miles from the epicenter; second degree burns at 6 miles, and third degree burns at 5 miles. A one megaton bomb is 70 times bigger than the

Hiroshima bomb. A 20 megaton bomb is 1,400 times bigger (again, the mind boggles). It would cause first degree burns at 30 miles from the epicenter, plus spontaneous ignition of many materials, like rayon; people 21 miles away would suffer second degree burns, and at that distance, newspaper would ignite; at 18.2 miles, (an area of 1,040 square miles), people would suffer third degree burns, and cotton fabrics and leaves would ignite. For a 20 megaton bomb, the sheet metal on auto bodies will melt at 5.2 miles, and metals will vaporize and glass will melt at 3.4 miles.

The spontaneous ignition of flammable materials, such as listed above, can cause additional burns, called "secondary" because they are flame burns, resulting from the combustion of these materials, not the direct effect of the bombs. But the burns can be equally severe, and cover a wider area. Depending on the number of "ignition points" per acre, the fires may coalesce into either of two kinds of huge blaze: a "conflagration" results when the fire front moves outward from the center, as in serious forest fires; a "firestorm" results when the fire front moves inwards, causing enormous heat and the total destruction of the area. Such firestorms occurred in Hamburg, Dresden, and Tokyo, in addition to Hiroshima; it is interesting to note that the only survivors were those who fled their bomb shelters. Even days after the fire-bombing of Dresden, the temperatures within the shelters remained so hot that new fires broke out spontaneously when the shelters were opened, and oxygen was let in. It is estimated that temperatures within the shelters rose as high as 800°C., thereby becoming ovens, cremating their inhabitants. Occurrence of a firestorm extends the lethal radius 5 times beyond the effects of the bomb alone. Firestorms also result in winds up to 150 miles per hour, strong enough to uproot trees, rushing inward, *toward* the flames.

Finally, eye injuries are guaranteed among the victims, varying in severity. As noted previously, the eyeballs of some Hiroshima residents were literally melted. Focal retinal burns may occur in anyone who glances by reflex at the fireball, and permanent blinding may result. Animals were blinded by retinal burns more than 300 miles from a thermonuclear atmospheric test in the 1950s. A conservative estimate is that a person glancing at the fireball 35 miles from a one megaton airburst, or 50 miles from a 20 megaton explosion would probably receive retinal burns. In addition, temporary but disabling "flashblindness" may occur 13 miles from a one megaton explosion—53 miles at night.

To sum up: thermal effects and secondary fires are an early consequence of nuclear explosions, and even alone, they will cause tremendous, unprecedented and intolerable damage. In the event of an isolated or small attack, the treatment of the burned patients alone would be impossible and would overwhelm the entire country.

## *Blast*

> Earth rocks and shudders,
> The roar of thunder, echoing from the
>   depths
> Bellows beside me.
> Fiery wreaths of lightning flash, and
> whirlwinds toss the
>   swirling dust;
> Blasts of all winds leap forth
> In dreadful striving.
> The sky is confounded in the sea.
>
> —AESCHYLUS *(Prometheus Bound)*

About 50 percent of the energy from a nuclear explosion is released as blast and shock. By contrast, a conventional chemical explosion releases almost 100 percent of its energy in this way, with little or no thermal energy given off. In any explosion, a sudden release of energy causes increased temperature and pressure. In a nuclear explosion, the temperatures are so high that all nearby materials are vaporized, or converted into extremely hot, compressed gases. By conventional laws of physics, such gases expand rapidly, pushing and heating air molecules and atoms in front of them. The wall of air and gases that expands from the center of a nuclear explosion is called the "shock front"; it travels faster than the speed of sound, but far slower than the infrared "thermal pulse" which precedes it at the speed of light. Therefore, slow motion movies of nuclear explosion tests show that the thermal pulse causes structures to start melting or catch fire several seconds before the blast wave flattens them.

The blast is really composed of two parts. The steady, sustained pressure of the wall of hot gases and air is called "static overpressure" and is measured in pounds per square inch (psi). The powerful accompanying winds are called "dynamic overpressure." Wind velocity is measured in conventional units, say, miles per hour. The shockwave itself expands evenly, depending on the contours of the ground, several times faster than the speed of sound. The larger the explosion, the greater the overpressure, and the longer it lasts. For example, a 20 kiloton airburst produces overpressure at a distance from 1 to 2 miles that lasts 1 to 1.4 seconds; a 1 megaton airburst would produce overpressures lasting as long as 2.5 seconds at a similar range. This means that unlike a clap of the hands, or a clap of thunder, overpressure goes on and on, for seconds at a time, as though a great hand hits—and then keeps pushing. The unit of measurement, psi, gives a deceptively low perspective on the actual forces involved. For example, 1 pound per square inch may not sound like much, but it equals 144 pounds per square foot, or 1,296 pounds per square yard. An average window measures about 2 square yards, so at "only" 1 psi it would receive 2,592 pounds of pressure.

Nuclear weapons can be exploded anywhere, on the land, underground, at sea, under the sea, within the atmosphere or in outer space. Technically, a bomb that explodes so that its fireball touches the ground is called a "surface burst"; a bomb exploding in the air is an "airburst." Strategic targets, those with military or industrial value, will generally be attacked with groundbursts. For example, groundbursts are preferred when trying to "take out" missile silos that may be hundreds of feet underground, and surrounded by concrete (so-called "hard targets"). If delivered accurately, a groundburst would produce a crater where the missile silo—used to be.

Much of the energy of a groundburst goes into the ground. Therefore, the destruction of cities and people can be better accomplished with airbursts, because the static overpressure extending from such an explosion has a much larger radius. While it may take 50 to 100 psi to destroy a heavily protected, hardened target, even .5 to 1.0 psi will cause glass windows to shatter into millions of pieces that become deadly little missiles traveling at high velocities. A mere 2 psi will destroy most frame or even brick houses. Clearly, it is much easier to kill people and damage cities than it is to destroy military structures that are built to withstand anything but a direct hit. For this reason, people and cities are referred to as "soft targets."

The human body itself is actually quite resistant to over-pressure, and it is not uncommon for scuba divers to endure static overpressures of more than 30 psi. However, there are two areas of the body that are particularly vulnerable to pressure. Lung damage may occur at from 8 to 15 psi, and severe damage from 20 to 30 psi. The tiny airsacs (alveoli) at the end of the bronchial tree have very thin membranes. With severe overpressure, the alveolar mem-branes rupture, producing hemorrhage, and possibly permitting ac-tual air bubbles (emboli) into the blood. Air emboli are particularly dangerous for the brain, because they may block the passage of blood through the tiny vessels. Therefore, considerable suffering and death can result from pulmonary effects alone.

In addition, the eardrums are very sensitive to pressure changes. This is why young children with even minor ear infections often cry piteously when they are in descending aircraft. As the pressure decreases, an imbalance between the pressure within their ears and the outside air pressure causes the eardrum to hurt. The satisfying feeling of one's ears "popping," after yawning or chew-ing gum, occurs when air finally gets through the eustachian tubes to the middle ear, restoring equilibrium of pressure. As little as 5 psi may cause eardrums to rupture, and 15 to 20 psi virtually guar-antees it. A ruptured eardrum produces a functionally useless ear, in addition to pain and likely dizzyness. Therefore, many bomb victims will be deaf (as well as burned, blind, crushed, pierced, flattened, etc.).

When it comes to actual killing, however, blast effects gener-ally do their work indirectly, rather than by overpressure alone. Similarly, high winds that accompany the shock wave are dan-gerous not because of direct effects, but rather because high winds pick up people and objects, and transform them into missiles, hit-ting other objects or structures at high speeds. For example, some-one in a reinforced concrete building at the 3 psi overpressure zone is most likely to be injured by glass from the disintegrating win-dows, or to be swept out of the windows along with the contents of the building, into what was formerly a street. High velocities and high pressures do not in themselves usually hurt the human body; sky and scuba divers attest to this fact. Rather, rapid deceleration against solid objects causes the injury; as witness the sky diver whose parachute fails to open. Winds of 300 to 600 mph are to be expected within the 10 psi zone for a 1 megaton airburst. This greatly exceeds the strongest hurricanes or tornadoes ever known.

Winds initially sweep away from the epicenter, trailing the shock wave but not far behind. A low pressure zone is therefore created at the center. After the fireball begins to fade, the center begins to cool, and the winds that have been blowing outward suddenly reverse, flying back toward the center—carrying dust, debris, and people.

Deaths due to blast would mostly result from structures collapsing, and from objects being blown onto or against people and people being blown out of, or against structures. A collapsing, obliterated city would suddenly be transformed into a huge fragmentation grenade, with small dartlike pieces of wood, metal, concrete and glass, and also enormous chunks including whole buildings—all traveling at lethal speeds and perhaps on fire as well. Objects striking human bodies will produce innumerable open injuries, such as lacerations, as well as closed injuries, such as skull fractures or concussions. Bleeding may occur externally or internally. For example, automobile accident victims who appear uninjured frequently go into sudden shock and die from internal bleeding, particularly from ruptured organs such as the spleen.

In fact, blast injuries are very much like auto accident injuries, because the forces are similar. When a car, traveling 60 miles per hour, strikes a cement wall, the front of the car decelerates abruptly from 60 mph to 0 mph. The passenger not wearing a seat belt will continue to move forward, at 60 mph, until his head strikes the windshield, causing skull fracture, brain contusion or internal bleeding, rupture of the arteries or veins of the brain, lacerations, stress to the neck, and so on. Or, he may be tossed from the car, hitting the ground and suffering fractures of the long bones, lacerations, broken spine and ribs, ruptured internal organs, ruptured arteries and veins. If he has a seat belt on, the victim may be held in place, but smashed against the steering wheel, cut by glass and/or crushed and pinned by the vehicle itself. A one megaton airburst 8,000 feet above the surface produces winds over 160 miles per hour at 4.4 miles from ground zero. Therefore, the speeds of the objects (or the people) flying through the air would be greater than the velocities of most car crashes. The injuries would be similar, but more severe. Moreover, we must imagine not just one accident victim, but many hundreds of thousands—or, if the city is large enough, millions—all having their "accident" simultaneously.

There is substantial disagreement among experts about the exact consequences of nuclear explosions, and the directions of disagreement seem to be predictable, once we understand the aims and goals of the experts. For example, "civil defense" booklets, prepared by governments primarily to reassure civilians before war breaks out, give the impression that it is easy to survive a nuclear blast simply by lying down and covering your eyes with your hands or arms. Soldiers, who are being prepared to fight a "theater" nuclear war are similarly reassured. (If told the truth, they might refuse to cooperate at all!) For example, Dutch soldiers receiving training from NATO in the use of tactical nuclear weapons, are apparently told "If you see a white flash, lie down on the ground and count to 90. Then get up, see which way the wind is blowing, and run as fast as you can in the other direction."

U.S. Government documents, such as Glasstone's *Effects of Nuclear Weapons,* and the Office of Technology Assessment's report on *The Effects of Nuclear War,* are less obviously biased, but both works nonetheless minimize the potential catastrophe by chosing very simplified scenarios, or emphasizing nuclear effects singly rather than combined. However, the OTA report is probably the most conservative estimate that is officially available. (It may not be purely coincidence that military planners always assume worst-case scenarios, while "civil defense" planners always assume the most optimistic cases!) Even these OTA calculations assume 98 percent fatality, 2 percent injured in the 12 psi zone; 50 percent dead, 40 percent injured, and 10 percent "safe" at 5 psi; and 25 percent injured, 75 percent safe at 1 to 2 psi. These estimates apparently take only direct and indirect blast effects into account, not fires or firestorm. Furthermore, they consider only *immediate* consequences, totally ignoring intermediate and long-term effects, which (as we shall see in the next chapter) will be devastating.

When both thermal *and* blast effects are taken into account, the size of the concentric circles of destruction increase: at 12 psi, 100 percent fatality and all structures destroyed; at 5 psi, 100 percent fatalities due to burns plus trauma, plus all light structures destroyed and heavily reinforced structures severely damaged; even at 2 psi, there would probably be at least 50 percent casualties, primarily injuries due to secondary fires and blast effects, and all frame and brick houses severely damaged. (Note that we still haven't mentioned radiation.)

Still looking only at blast and thermal effects, the medical consequences of nuclear explosions are beyond comprehension. The OTA report states that if even one bomb went off—say, a one megaton surface burst in Detroit—there would be 250,000 fatalities, and 500,000 injuries. Most of the injured would receive essentially no medical care, because all of the hospitals in Detroit would be gone, along with most of the physicians, nurses, medical supplies, drugs, and equipment. From just one such bomb, the rest of the country would be faced with a massive, unprecedented relief job that might last for years. It was four years before attempts were made to rebuild downtown Hiroshima. And that was a single, tiny bomb. And then, there was an "outside."

### Radiation

The word itself is frightening. And appropriately so: it can't be seen, smelled, heard, or touched. Almost unknowable, it defies our senses, and likewise our sense of rightness. The sun emits radiation other than light, and physicists can detect these emissions with cloud chambers, photographic emulsions, and other techniques. Human senses, however, respond only to visible light, because for the four billion years of our evolution, background radiation from radioactive materials in the earth itself and from stars played only a very small role. However, a full 15 percent of the power of a nuclear bomb is released as radiation, and perhaps because we are unequipped by evolution to cope with this phenomenon, we respond with horror and fear. Nuclear radiation poses a direct threat to the machinery of our cells, particularly to our own cell nuclei that contain our personal genetic instructions: how to reproduce, and also how to function enzymatically from day to day.

By convention, when a bomb yield is measured, only the energy released within the first two minutes is counted. This includes all of the primary blast and thermal effects, but only about one-third of the radiation that is unleashed. This initial radiation represents only about 5 percent of the total explosion. An additional 10 percent of the energy is released slowly, as fission fragments decay, and this factor is not usually counted in the force calculations. Thus, a "100 kiloton" bomb actually releases about 110 kilotons of energy; the additional 10 kilotons (almost the size of the Hiroshima weapon) are released slowly, in a matter of days to millions of years, as radioactive decay. The next chapter will deal with the delayed radiation effects, or fallout. For now, let us concentrate on the immediate emission—the prompt, deadly 5 percent.

Nuclear reactions produce many different kinds of radiation, with a wide range of energies. There are four main types: the first is gamma radiation. This is basically electromagnetic waves or photon particles, like visible light, only with a shorter wave length, much like x-rays. The initial gamma rays may be of very high energy, and these particles rapidly penetrate skin. However, they may easily be absorbed by dirt, concrete, or even paper. "Civil defense" calculations for various types of fallout shelters generally refer to gamma radiation protection, when they speak of the "protection factor" offered by various structures or materials.

The second type of released radiation is in the form of electrons, or beta particles: small, negatively charged particles that may be accelerated close to the speed of light, thus carrying high energy. Although beta particles may burn the leaves of exposed deciduous trees, they are generally more important in the consideration of fallout effects and other long-term contamination.

Alpha particles, the third type of radiation, consist of naked helium nuclei, which are very heavy (two protons and two neutrons). The effects of external radiation with alpha particles are minimal, since alphas don't even penetrate skin, but they are very important when considering long-term effects, since once eaten, they attack us from within.

Finally, there are neutrons, particles that are as heavy as protons, more than 2,000 times the mass of an electron, but uncharged. All nuclear explosions release neutrons, but in varying amounts, depending on the amount of the fusion reaction, and the composition of the outer shell of the bomb. Because neutrons have no charge, they pass readily through most materials, including tanks, until they are finally absorbed.

Neutrons and gamma rays do very different things to human tissue. Gamma rays interact with the electrons that orbit the nuclei of atoms, causing increased energy that may disrupt the chemical bonds of the tissue. Neutrons, on the other hand, interact with the atomic nuclei directly, coliding with them and setting in motion a shower of sub-atomic particles.

The interactions of the neutrons are particularly important because 1) higher amounts of neutron irradiation are associated with more death and destruction than the same amounts of other kinds of radiation and 2) the neutron bomb or "enhanced radiation warhead" emits large quantities of high-energy neutrons, designed as a battlefield weapon to kill soldiers.

Radiation produced by nuclear reactions is called ionizing radiation, because it disrupts chemical bonds, producing chemically unstable molecules called ions. Gamma rays are referred to as "sparsely ionizing," because the tracks of the energetic electrons they produce are well separated in space. By contrast, heavy particles like neutrons, protons, and alpha particles produce a denser track of ionization. Such particles don't travel very far, but they are very damaging. An x-ray is like a small bullet passing through tissue; the chance of injury to any one cell is small. By contrast, an alpha particle marches like Sherman through Georgia, leaving a swath of destruction in its wake.

Of course, the most significant damage that can occur to an individual cell is death. However, for the rest of the body, a dead cell may be less troublesome than a cell gone wild. One common theory of cancer holds that certain genes regulate when a cell reproduces. Distortion of these instructions may therefore cause the cell to go out of control, reproducing rapidly, with no regard for its neighbors or the needs of the organism. Radiation, then, may produce cell death, by damaging the enzymatic machinery necessary for the daily life of the cell, or it may produce rampaging, insensitive cells whose reproduction is out of control: cancer.

The measurement units of radiation may be confusing, because several different terms are used almost interchangeably. A "Roentgen" (named for the discoverer of x-rays) is a unit of exposure to gamma rays, measured by its ionizing power; a "rem" is derived from the first letters of the term "roentgen equivalent in man," and it refers to radiation that is actually absorbed by human tissues. Finally, a "rad" is also a unit of absorbed dose of radiation. Heavier particles, however, such as neutrons and alpha particles, cause more intense cellular damage than lighter ones, so for these characters, a rem equals a rad multiplied by a "quality factor" (that's destructive quality!). When measuring immediate radiation effects, we are primarily concerned with gamma rays and beta particles, and thus rads equal rems. When measuring internal contamination, over the long run, we are primarily concerned with alpha emitters, and the units must be clearly specified. Also, note that normal, background radiation is about one-tenth of one rem.

As we have seen, when an average nuclear bomb explodes, 5 percent of its energy is released as "initial radiation," primarily gamma rays and neutrons. For large bombs, the energy released as blast and thermal effects is so huge that the diameter within which everyone dies from blast and heat is far greater than the diameter within which there is significant initial radiation. In other words, if a large bomb is targeted for your neighborhood, you are more likely to die from blast and fire than from radiation. (Or, for another way of looking at it: most of those people guaranteed to be killed by radiation will first be killed by heat and blast. There is, perhaps, some comfort in knowing that we can only die once!) However, for "small" bombs—less than 100 kilotons—the radiation effects are important.

For example, in Hiroshima 31 percent of the survivors and 16 percent of those who eventually died of bomb related injuries exhibited initial symptoms of radiation sickness on the day of the explosion. For a normal human population, 400 rems is generally considered the dose at which half of those exposed will die. Doses over 1,000 rems are universally fatal. It is impossible to tell from the initial symptoms whether an exposed victim has received a lethal dose of radiation or whether he or she might eventually recover. Thus, medical "triage" is impossible; doctors cannot separate those who are certain to die from those who might benefit from treatment with antibiotics, blood transfusions, or other procedures (assuming, of course, that such treatment is even available).

The symptoms of radiation sickness consist of gastrointestinal problems such as nausea, vomiting, diarrhea, loss of appetite, cramps, salivation, fluid loss, dehydration, and thirst, along with neuromuscular symptoms of fatigue, apathy, listlessness, sweating, fever, headache, and hypertension. Any or all of these symptoms may be seen at doses of 200 to over 10,000 rems.

At doses of 5,000 to 10,000 rems, central nervous system effects predominate, and the victim will die of the "central nervous system syndrome," probably caused by an increased fluid content in the brain, and pressure built up within the skull. Severe nausea and vomiting develop within minutes, followed by disorientation, loss of muscle coordination, respiratory distress, diarrhea, siezures, coma, and death. There is no treatment.

Doses of 1,000 to 5,000 rems produce death inevitably within three to ten days, primarily from a "gastrointestinal syndrome" consisting of severe nausea, vomiting, and diarrhea. The symptoms resemble those of cholera or bacterial dysentery: severe, bloody diarrhea leads to dehydration, emaciation, exhaustion, and death. There is, again, no effective medical treatment, because the diarrhea is caused by the death of the epithelial cells that line the intestine. Normally, these intestinal cells reproduce very quickly, and thus, they are especially sensitive to radiation. The cells at the surface of the gut slough off, and the surface is denuded. Normally, the small intestine absorbs water, but following radiation, when the intestinal cells are killed, water and plasma leak through the gut wall, causing severe dehydration. The intestinal epithelium is normally a barrier to infection, so when it is gone, overwhelming infection may also be a cause of death.

At doses of 200 to 600 rems, humans suffer from a "hematopoetic syndrome" thar results from the death of the blood-making cells in the bone marrow. At about three weeks to a month after radiation exposure, the hair begins to fall out, and the victim suffers chills, fever, fatigue, anemia and hemorrhages in the skin. Depletion of white blood cells demolishes resistance to infections, both bacterial and viral. In addition, blood clotting is impaired, resulting in the rupture of small capillaries in the skin, and a tendency to hemorrhage internally as well as externally that complicates the anemia.

After experiencing a dose of 300 to 500 rems, half of all middle-aged victims will die of this hematopoetic syndrome. In addition, the very young and the very old are more sensitive, and will die in greater numbers. For individuals who are exposed to high doses of radiation where medical care is available (say, after industrial accidents), there are several techniques that may prolong survival: first, good nursing care and adequate rest, food, and fluids; second, it may help to put the patient in a germ-free environment, bathing in antiseptic baths, and treating with high doses of antibiotics, to prevent infection. A third technique is to transplant normal bone marrow into the radiation victim. Bone marrow transplants are technically difficult, expensive, and have a high incidence of complications. After a nuclear war, when medical treatment would be essentially unavailable, less than 300 rems would probably kill one-half those exposed.

In addition, even among those estimated in government documents to be "injured," a very high percentage will in fact die. This is because of the combined effects of different injuries, each of which might be sub-lethal alone, but deadly in combination. Although 100 rems is unlikely to be fatal to a healthy adult, for example, such exposure would seriously impair the victim's ability to recover from burns, and would also render him or her more likely to die of infection at the same time. Recovery from massive puncture wounds, for another example, would be greatly complicated by simultaneous burns (plus radiation, plus infection, plus lack of food, water, sanitation, etc.).

If the victim survives, convalescence from radiation sickness alone may be prolonged, up to a year. Thus, particularly in those areas that are attacked by small nuclear weapons, initial radiation effects will weaken those who survive the blast and heat, and who will also face the overwhelming difficulties of survival in a socially and ecologically shattered world.

## What it Would Be Like—the Barrage Period

In imitation of military and civil defense planners, let us examine a "scenario" of the prompt or acute phase of nuclear war in the 1980s. This will consist of two parts, a "barrage" period, when nuclear warheads will actually be going off, and in the next chapter, the so-called "shelter period," including the prospects for post-attack survival.

Whether war began as a total surprise, perhaps because of a false alarm in either nation's computer warning system, or as the culmination of increasing tension, the results would be very much the same. In the desperate climate before a first strike, the leaders of both nations would, if possible, doubtless attempt to save "key" people, usually men (and including of course, themselves). These few individuals could probably be evacuated without attracting attention. In the United States, certain individuals have been given special identification cards, guaranteeing them entrance to federally operated blast shelters. No doubt, their Soviet counterparts also exist. Either side could evacuate a few hundred of these powerful, usually wealthy men, leaving the rest of us to bake or to fry, without generating the enormous traffic jams that would be the sure signal of mass evacuation.

Suppose that the Soviets launched a boob attack on the United States, at around 3AM on a summer weekend. It would take 30 minutes for Soviet ICBMs to leave their silos, cross the North Pole, and begin to dismantle the cities of the New World. It only takes 12 minutes for Soviet submarine-launched ballistic missiles to leave their tubes and begin to rain down on coastal cities like New York, Boston, San Francisco, or Seattle. It takes about 14 minutes for the attack to be detected and a second strike launched against the Soviet Union. By 1985, with "launch on warning," it may take as little as 3 minutes for the attack to be detected, and the missile silos emptied. Fifteen minutes after the start of the attack, the Early Warning Defense system air raid sirens would begin to scream, and the familiar tone that Americans have grown to ignore (announcing a test of the Emergency Broadcasting System) would begin to wail, only this time without the comforting addition "This is a test. . . ." Therefore, coastal cities would have minus 3 minutes of warning, and the inhabitants would die suddenly, without a moment of anticipatory panic. However, residents of inland cities such as Chicago or St. Louis would be awakened by the sirens, and then have about 5 or 10 minutes to panic before the bombs started to explode.

The Federal Emergency Management Agency has analyzed in detail a 6,559 megaton attack on the United States, 4,000 megatons to be detonated on urban and population centers and 2,559 megatons detonated on military and economic targets. This attack is the equivalent of 524,720 Hiroshima bombs. High priority attack targets include ICBM silos; Trident and Poseidon submarine stations; Strategic Air Command bases; military installations; transport and logistic facilities; basic industries and energy plants, such as dams, electrical generators, natural gas pipelines, oil refineries, and nuclear power plants; airports and railyards; and population centers of 50,000 or more. The Arms Control and Disarmament Agency estimates that in addition, 80 percent of towns with populations of 25,000 or more are targeted. There are, in fact, enough Soviet warheads to target populations centers of 1,500 or more, and Jonathan Schell suggests that even individual people of particular importance may be targeted with nuclear bombs.

Bombs would begin to explode on coastal cities 12 minutes after the attack started, and the inland cities would be destroyed within 20 to 30 minutes. In 18 minutes or so, about 86 million Americans (about 40 percent of the population) would die, and an additional 34 million people would be injured severely, with no prospect of medical attention. The total population of the United States is 225 million. Therefore, in less than 20 minutes, one-half of the population of the United States would be killed or severely injured and doomed, by the combination of thermal effects and fires, blast, and immediate radiation. One half hour later, United States warheads would begin to rain down on Soviet cities, and the scene would repeat itself.

But what would it be *like?* Again, because the imagination is strained by large numbers, let us simplify, and describe the effects of a single one megaton bomb detonated in one large city. A one megaton bomb equals 70 Hiroshima bombs, exploding within a millionth of a second. (Bear in mind, if you can, that the FEMA attack hypothesizes 6,559 megatons, or the equivalent of 6,559 one megaton bombs.) Let us assume that the attack occurs on a clear night in the summer, with 15 minutes or less warning. . . .

The bomb explodes with the heat of the sun and the stars, and within the first 2 seconds, the center of the city, including steel and concrete buildings, asphalt, roads, bridges, brick, glass, people, plants, and animals are vaporized. If a groundburst, the center of the city is turned into a crater, 1,000 feet in diameter and 200 feet deep, surrounded by a rim of highly radioactive debris of about twice this diameter.

Within the first 2 seconds after the detonation, the fireball grows rapidly, emitting gamma rays and neutrons, as well as infra-red radiation, pulsing outward at the speed of light. The blinding flash melts the eyeballs of anyone looking on from close to the explosion, and causes retinal burns to anyone who reflexly glances at it from within 50 miles. Within a radius of 1.75 miles, steel surfaces evaporate, concrete surfaces explode, glass melts, and people are melted and then charred. At 2.75 miles, aluminum siding evaporates, auto sheet metal and lucite windows melt. (People fare no better.) At 4.35 miles, wood, plastics, and heavy fabrics burst into flames, and asphalt surfaces melt. At 5.5 miles from the deto-nation, upholstery, canvas, and clothing burst into flames, and painted surfaces explode. Watching the destruction of a city with a nuclear bomb, one would first see it melt, char, then collapse. Whatever is left would then likely roar into flames. An individual human being, say 2 miles from ground zero, within the first 2 sec-onds would receive fatal total body irradiation, plus third degree burns. Her clothing would catch fire, along with her skin, and she would quickly be reduced to a charred corpse.

Within the next 10 seconds, the blast wave would squeeze the city like a giant fist, and the buildings would start to disintegrate. As Jonathan Schell has observed, a city is like a series of valleys (the streets) surrounded by mountains (the buildings). When the blast wave strikes, the mountains fall down and the valleys fill up, bury-ing and crushing the corpses.

One thing that you can do, right now, to sear these points into your consciousness, is to take a map of your hometown, and graph the effects of a one megaton airburst exploding over you. Even if you live in a very small town, there are probably strategic targets in your neighborhood, and no one can guarantee the accuracy of the incoming missiles once the explosions start to occur. Some bombs destined for Denver may well land in Wyoming. Assume that you are targeted, and find out what will be left of your city or town. Use a compass and draw six concentric circles, like the ones in the figure opposite. Then mark each circle with the appropriate effects. You can use this map as the basis of future meetings and discussions in your community. The data given here are from the U.S. Arms Control and Disarmament Agency; if you like, you can even write to them directly, and ask for the map that they have probably prepared of your area. For another perspective, call your

# ONE MEGATON NUCLEAR WEAPONS AIR BURST
## Approximate Immediate Effects

**5 MILES**
- Spontaneous ignition of clothing, other combustibles
- Likely complete burnout of area encircled

**4 MILES**
- Overpressure 5 psi
- Winds 160 mph
- Brick and wood frame houses destroyed
- Exposed people seriously burned

**1½ MILES**
- Overpressure 20 psi (pounds per square inch)
- Winds 500 mph
- Reinforced concrete buildings destroyed (office-type, multi-story steel framed/reinforced buildings)
- Most people killed

**3 MILES**
- Overpressure 10 psi
- Winds 300 mph
- Stone and concrete buildings destroyed ("monument-type" wall-bearing buildings)
- Exposed people critically burned if not killed

**8½ MILES**
- Overpressure 2 psi
- Brick and frame houses moderately damaged (structure cracked, glass broken, inside walls knocked down, roofs partly torn off)
- Second-degree flash burns (blisters) to exposed skin

**6 MILES**
- Third-degree flash burns (charring) to all exposed skin

Each circle indicates an average range for the effects listed. Actual effects at a given range could vary considerably according to the weather, specific design of buildings, degree of exposure of individual people, and irregularities in weapon yield.

Additional longer-lasting effects could result at various ranges from radioactive debris and dust, fallout, uncontrollable fires, and perhaps ozone depletion in the atmosphere that would let in damaging ultra-violet radiation from the sun.

Wilkins & Peterson, 1982. adapted from the Arms Control and Disarmament Agency, 1979.

local "civil defense" office, or the Federal Emergency Management Agency, and ask for maps of the high risk areas in your state. Remember, there are the equivalent of 10,000 one megaton bombs targeted at the U.S., and a similar number targeted at the Soviet Union. Try to visualize what's in store for you, when deterrence fails.

It is not at all fanciful to assume that within the first 10 minutes of a nuclear barrage on the United States, more than half of its population will be fried, baked, crushed, irradiated, minced, sliced, diced, battered, blinded, and broiled. In short, "We have arrived at that point, my friends, where war does not present the possibility of victory or defeat. War could present us only the alternative of degrees of destruction. There can be no truly successful outcome." (President Eisenhower).

# 10. Anarchy is Loosed Upon the World:

## "Civil Defense" Myths

> . . . Things fall apart, the centre cannot hold;
> Mere anarchy is loosed upon the world,
> The blood-dimmed tide is loosed, and every-
>    where
> The ceremony of innocence is drowned . . .
>    —W. B. YEATS *(The Second Coming)*

So much for worldwide wargasm. But what about the morning after? In the last chapter, we estimated that about half the population of the U.S. and a similar proportion of U.S.S.R. citizens would be killed immediately by blast, burns, and immediate radiation within the first day of our next nuclear war. What about the other half? Could they simply reconstruct society as it was, only with new cities in different locations, shorter shopping lines, less traffic on the freeways? The Federal Emergency Management Agency (FEMA) instructs American evacuees to pack "as though going on a vacation" when the President announces that our hour has come round at last. What kind of vacation will this be, and what will people find, if they survive the shelter period and try to return to their homes? ("The only thing wrong with shelters," quips Robert Jay Lifton, "is going into them, staying in them, and coming out of them.")

During the Second World War, hundreds of thousands of East European Jews trudged into cattlecars, denying fearful rumors they had heard, and choosing instead to believe their Nazi overlords who said they were to be "resettled for work in the East." Instead, of course, they went to the death camps or to hastily dug roadside graves. Many Americans are similarly gullible today, quieted by reassurances that they will be "evacuated to safety" in the event of a nuclear war. Don't you believe it.

More than $4 billion is being allocated to FEMA over the next five years, to develop a strategy of "civil defense" for the United States. Of course, "civil defense" is not new; for years it has been the post-Hiroshima opiate of the masses, a sedative to quiet our nuclear nightmares. Now the symptom hasn't changed, but the treatment has become even more misleading. Indeed, FEMA officials (and presumably, other high government functionaries as well), these days actually seem to believe in their own prescription: FEMA claims that with three to eight days of warning, through mass evacuation and sheltering, up to 80 percent° of the American people and substantial parts of our economy and industry could be "saved" in an all-out nuclear war between the U.S and the U.S.S.R. Don't worry, they say—just remain calm, stay orderly, and follow our instructions: we shall take very good care of you. (Can you see the cattlecar, gaping before you?)

In this chapter we shall examine evacuation, survival in fallout shelters, the social, economic, medical, and psychological challenges of the post-attack period, and finally, extinction. The point of this chapter is: Never again should human beings queue up in orderly lines, innocently conniving in their own annihilation.

## Before the Sirens Scream

Just for the sake of argument, let us imagine that international tension increases so that nuclear war seems imminent. What will happen?

First, when the threat is still vague, look for reduced participation in society, as people become anxious, preoccupied with individual and family survival. One immediate result will be economic slowdown. Anxious people work more slowly and less accurately, and are more easily distracted. Citizens will be less likely to buy furniture, homes or cars, invest in retirement plans, save money, or even reproduce. Altruistic behavior will almost certainly decrease, as people feel less secure themselves, and as they perceive less opportunity for reciprocation.

° The derivation of this number is interesting, and characteristic of what passes for planning and analysis in the "civil defense" community. Thus, the estimate of 80 percent was not really derived from anything; rather, it was an "entering assumption," introduced into a 1977 computer model, and thereafter taken as a *result* of the study, which it assuredly was not.

Within families, heightened fear and insecurity will affect parents and children alike. Younger children would probably become more dependent, clingy, and less self-confident. Nightmares would plague both young and old. Among adolescents, hedonistic behavior such as drug use, and other forms of antisocial behavior and "acting out" would probably increase. Some parents may become neglectful or abusive under stress. One thing is clear: families will be hard-pressed to perform their basic function of preparing children to assume the tasks of adulthood.

The conditions of the pre-attack period may sound familiar—economic slowdown, hedonism, disrupted family life—because in a sense, we are in that phase right now! Harvard psychiatrist John Mack has studied the correlation between adolescent drug use and fear of nuclear war, and he concludes that a pervasive loss of confidence in the future is a major reason why adolescents give up and "space out." Fear of the future may well be an important cause of the current recession (in addition to the wasteful, inflationary influence of the arms race, to be examined in the next chapter). In fact, a record number of Americans have already begun taking the logical next step: voluntary evacuation.

Australia and New Zealand are deluged by requests for immigration. Among the stay-at-homes, the survivalist movement is particularly strong in Southern Oregon, northern California, and the mountains of Colorado: literally thousands of people have already abandoned the cities and fled for the hills.

For those of you who are beginning to think about Tasmania for your next home, let us reassure you: you probably won't be able to go. Australia and New Zealand have strict immigration policies, requiring that you already have a guaranteed job before immigration is even considered. The question of safety is also unclear; for example, a nuclear submarine base, sure to be targeted, is being built near Perth, Australia.

Oregon is no refuge either. Maximum stratospheric fallout deposition, over the long run, is predicted at 45 degrees North latitude, on a line running through Portland, Minneapolis, Ottawa, Bordeaux, Turin, Venice, Belgrade, Tashkent, and Vladivostock. The distribution would be especially intense from 30 to 60 degrees, blanketing most of the United States. In other words, we are all stuck. Unlike some Jews in Eastern Europe—those who recognized their danger and had some options for flight to America—you and your family have nowhere to go.

## The Last Traffic Jam

As tension mounts, there will doubtless be increasing numbers of voluntary, unplanned evacuations. Following the nuclear reactor accident in 1979, evacuation of the area around Three Mile Island showed that even without instructions from the government, many people will evacuate their homes from fear of catastrophe. In Pennsylvania, 145,000 people were evacuated from an area of 706 square miles surrounding the damaged reactor.

Voluntary evacuation will further hamstring the country. Businesses, factories, hospitals, and schools will falter, and possibly close. The reliability of the monetary system will be questioned, and credit cards and checks will seem increasingly unreal. Massive withdrawals of cash may force banks to close. But even money may quickly lose its value.

As people watch their neighbors, friends, and colleagues skipping town, insecurity and fear would spread rapidly, and chaos and panic might ensue. The president might then be forced to proclaim a national evacuation, trying to forestall the chaos of spontaneous flight from the cities. Of course, the start of a national evacuation program might trigger the start of war, because spy satellites would quickly demonstrate the movements of populations, and each side would worry that the other side was planning a first strike. (In this regard, we must note a crucial distinction between planning for natural disasters and planning for nuclear war: if people living near a volcano flee when the earth begins trembling they may well save themselves, and they do not make the eruption itself any more likely. By contrast, however, if people flee when the earth begins trembling on the brink of nuclear war they almost certainly will *not* save themselves, and even more important, they almost certainly will make the eruption *more* likely. This last point seems utterly lost on FEMA officialdom.)

When it comes to nuclear war, we all live near the volcano.

What if it really starts rumbling? What would happen if suddenly the air raid sirens started to wail, and the harsh tone of the emergency communication system interrupted radio and television shows throughout the land? Today's young adults grew up in the 1950s when civil defense drills were commonplace, and most of us have a hidden, inner fear of nuclear war. We might well be reduced to the mental state of terrified children waiting for our nightmares to become real. Panic is a small word to describe the engulfing fear of the flames, the blast, and the radiation.

Amid the panic, concern for family members and fear of separation would predominate. In urban centers, parents often work at considerable distances from their children's schools and day care centers. The sirens would send both children and parents into further panic, and any official government planning for organized traffic patterns would almost certainly be disrupted by desperate parents, wives, and husbands trying to locate one another. During the accident at Three Mile Island, children were frightened by seeing other children and teachers removed from school in tears. Some children were abandoned at locked houses, left to fend for themselves; some schools were evacuated *en masse* without informing parents. Fear of separation would be heightened by uncertainty of the time of the attack, and fear that the separations would be final.

The TMI evacuation revealed (and produced) enormous distrust of government information and plans. With the threat of imminent nuclear war, who would patiently wait his or her turn for evacuation? FEMA has designed schedules for evacuation, neighborhood by neighborhood, but who could resist the impulse to cheat, to try to sneak in line on the freeways and leave the high risk areas quickly? In some regions, FEMA is proposing that even-numbered license plates will evacuate on day one, odd-numbered on day two (perhaps vanity plates will wait patiently for day three!). Traffic jams will be unprecedented as some individuals rush for the evacuation routes while others try to return to the cities to rescue relatives. Even in peacetime, large traffic jams try the patience of many normal people, and turn others into beasts behind the wheel. In this last traffic jam, angry and aggressive behavior would be rampant, particularly in response to delays. For example, an unfortunate family that runs out of gas on a narrow road might be the victim of vicious attempts to throw the car off the road rather than altruistic attempts to share gasoline.

Civil servants have no monopoly on courage, devotion to duty, or altruism. But neither do they have notable excesses of the same. Would the call to protect one's family and self be less strong on a bus driver or policeman than on a businessman or florist? Probably not. Then, as the evacuation progressed, vital community services such as police, ambulance, transportation, and health care services would collapse. The evacuation of hospitals poses an interesting dilemma. Which of the sick and injured would be evacuated, and would health care personnel abandon their own families and self-interest to care for those who could not be evacuated? In Seattle, a specific person is apparently designated to go to the zoo when evacuation is announced, to shoot the poisonous snakes, so that they would not pose a risk to the survivors. Is there someone in each hospital who has similarly been designated to euthanize the ill, rendered terminal by their immovability, when it is time to go?

It is possible that many people would defy the evacuation orders, and choose to die in their own homes with their families, rather than face the risks and insecurities of evacuation. Take the case of Harry Truman, the elderly innkeeper at Spirit Lake, Washington, who ignored the scientists' warning of the forthcoming eruption of Mt. St. Helens in 1980, and died at home in the mudslide. A common sentiment is, "When the bomb goes off, I hope I'm at ground zero." Fear of radiation sickness, starvation, and riots may be greater than the fear of being vaporized, and many people may choose to stay home, anticipating such an end. Mass family suicides are also likely, miniature Jonestown massacres; perhaps Kool-Aid and cyanide will take their place alongside aspirin and vitamin pills in the family medicine chest.

The Crisis Relocation Plan from the Massachusetts Civil Defense Agency claims that

> while no one can guarantee perfect behavior in such an unprecedented situation as crisis relocation, the judgment of those who have studied peacetime and wartime evacuations is that constructive and law-abiding behavior would be predomionantly, and indeed overwhelmingly, the case. In an emergency, people tend to be jolted out of

their normal routines and patterns, and many people go out of their way to help others.

This optimistic, cheerful expectation of human behavior contrasts remarkably with the behavior of the Hiroshima survivors, who were generally too demoralized and dazed to respond to the needs of any but immediate family members. The "Boat People" of Cambodia suffered stresses analogous to shelter inmates: isolation, hopelessness, and despair complicated by danger, demoralization, thirst, dehydration, and starvation. There are reports that some refugees killed and ate young children so that the adults might survive.

FEMA documents compare the behavior of individuals evacuated from the scene of natural disasters such as hurricanes with projections of human behavior during evacuations preceding nuclear war. People can, in fact, be evacuated from hurricanes with minimal social or psychic disruption. However, nuclear war is fundamentally different from natural phenomena. First, it is beyond human experience, and has only two precedents, Hiroshima and Nagasaki, both limited ones at that. Human beings habituate very quickly to stress, but only when it is predictable. For instance, the initial evacuation of the Mt. St. Helens area in 1980 was frightening and stressful. By contrast, evacuation of the same region in March 1982 was relaxed, accompanied by much joking. Because nuclear war is unfamiliar and portended to be catastrophic, people would be unlikely to respond with aplomb. Moreover, government officials are totally unjustified in using the American response to natural disasters as a measure of how we would respond to the disaster of nuclear war. In all the twentieth century, the greatest single disaster to befall our country was the Galveston hurricane in 1900, which killed about 6,000 people. Nothing since then has even come close. As we saw in the last chapter, nuclear war would be qualitatively different; the human response might very well be equally unique. Certainly, it cannot be predicted.

Second, in the case of a hurricane, volcanic eruption, or hotel fire, the event is time-limited, affecting a specific region, and victims know that the outside world exists, providing not only refuge but also relief. In a nuclear war there will be no outside, and no rational person could expect to return to everyday life. The duration of the crisis will probably be as long as the survivors survive.

And finally, government planners really have no more information than the rest of us. The "security" of evacuation is almost entirely a dream, and as we have seen, a very bad one at that. Soviet missiles could easily retarget evacuation centers, or simply guarantee overwhelming amounts of lethal fallout by detonating groundbursts upwind of the "host" areas. Moreover, no one can say confidently which areas are targeted and which are not; even the government can't get its signals straight. For example, the federal government considers Missoula, Montana a likely target for Soviet missiles, while at the same time that state's Crisis Relocation Plan has targeted Missoula in a different way, as a "host" city for Montanans fleeing the state capital, Great Falls. According to Rick Leavell, Civil Defense Coordinator for Missoula County, "The state and feds can't get together on whether good ol' Missoula, Montana is going to be a hole in the ground or a reception center."

## The Shelter Period—Life Underground

> Physical survival of some people is quite probable. . . .
> —Office of Technology Assessment, U.S. Government

The Office of Technology Assessment estimates between 20 million and 160 million immediate deaths, out of a total population of 225 million U.S. citizens. The remaining population would presumably cower in makeshift shelters in rural areas, except for high-ranking government officials who are designated to go to well-equipped blast shelters buried deep in the mountains.

"Civil defense" is based on the notion that certain areas would be spared immediate thermal, blast, and radiation effects, and that these areas could be identified in advance. If that were the case, fallout would be the next danger. Any American can contact his or her local Civil Defense agency or FEMA and obtain information on how to build and equip a fallout shelter, designed to protect his or her family for a period of up to two weeks, the duration of intense gamma and beta radiation from fallout. Plans can be obtained for the construction of fallout shelters that can double in the event of peace as utility rooms, as one cheerful booklet suggests "a place where Mrs. Housewife does so many important jobs, and where she stores soaps, cleansers, polishes, brooms, etc. It can be a happy place, too, where she can iron and watch TV." FEMA further recommends that a home shelter can be used as a snack bar, wine cellar, or sauna, and another booklet advises that equipping your home with a fallout shelter increases its marketability "by offering home buyers a better way of life, as well as security without creating consumer resistance." This elaborate program of evacuation and sheltering assumes that external radiation from rapidly decaying fallout particles is the major threat in the post-attack period. Accordingly, some protection would seem achievable by burying people for about two weeks, in shelters that are impermeable to fallout particles, gamma and beta rays. Then, "civil defense" authorities would have us believe that we could emerge, dust ourselves off, and continue where we left off.

We think the reality would be very different. FEMA's pamphlet on how to build a home fallout shelter which doubles as basement storage, shows a man, woman, and teenage child in a closet-sized area, calmly reading, perhaps to one another. In truth, only a few powerful government officials, mostly men, will sit out two weeks in a shelter that is fit for human habitation. Rural residents, and those city dwellers who successfully evacuate, will go to makeshift shelters that will only prolong their deaths.

The initial shelter problem would be to determine who gets in, because even primitive shelter space is extremely limited. Take, for example, the small town of Shelton, Washington. Many designated shelters are similar to Shelton's—a long, narrow concrete tunnel under the local prison that could accommodate some 6,000 people under intolerably crowded conditions. Approximately 65,000 people, from neighboring Thurston County, are scheduled to seek shelter in Shelton. There are approximately 10,000 residents of the town itself. Who gets into the shelter? Those left outside have not been forgotten, however. Thomas K. Jones, a former missile planner at Boeing, and now Deputy Under Secretary of Defense in the Reagan government, suggested to the Los Angeles *Times* that Americans simply "Dig a hole, cover it with a couple of doors, and then throw three feet of dirt on top. Everyone's going to make it if there are enough shovels to go around. It's the dirt that does it." How clever, Mr. Jones. If we each dig our own graves, then climb obediently inside . . . indeed, the dirt will do it: less clean-up afterward.

Then there is fallout.

> The bomb comes on little cat feet.
> It obliterates harbor and city
> and raises a cloud
> which then moves on.

—N. CORWIN (*Fireside Album of Familiar Verse*)

Any nuclear explosion creates a wide range of radioactive products, resulting both from the fission products themselves and from radioactivity induced by neutron bombardment of earth, rock, and debris. Such radioactivity is very intense if the explosion occurs at or beneath the ground, or if the fireball even touches the ground. The most intense radioactive fallout would occur if a nuclear weapon vaporizes the core of an existing nuclear reactor, in which case the long-lived isotopes of the reactor core are added to the fallout plume, and the lethal zone of fallout is increased by thirty times. It should be noted that most nuclear reactors are probably targeted, particularly in Europe where power reactors are often located near military facilities. Wherever they are, however, reactors are ideal targets for an enemy wishing to produce devastating fallout with only a small expenditure of bombs.

Within the first 24 hours after the explosion, heavier particles will descend to earth, emitting large quantities of short-lived but intense gamma and beta rays. This early fallout spreads in a cigar shaped pattern, narrow near the burst point, then widening out depending upon the wind and atmospheric conditions. Fallout particles may adhere to raindrops, causing an oily "black rain" as in Hiroshima, with "hot spots" of intense radioactivity at unpredictable times and distances from ground zero. Near the explosion, fallout particles may be visible as a fine sand.

A one megaton surface burst will produce a fallout finger that would expose an unprotected individual to a dose of 300 rems within a week of the explosion over an area of about 150 miles long and 20 miles wide, given prevailing winds of about 15 miles per hour. A 15 megaton groundburst on Bikini Atoll in 1954 covered about 7,000 square miles with lethal fallout. The initial explosion of Mt. St. Helens was equivalent to about 6 megatons, and it blanketed eastern Washington, Idaho, and Montana with *non*radioactive fallout that was so heavy it stopped cars and clogged machinery. Particles of volcanic dust were detected throughout the eastern United States, Europe, and Asia; finally, the dust circumnavigated the globe and returned to Washington. A 10,000 megaton attack would equal 1,667 Mt. St. Helenses. Of course, Mt. St. Helens erupted after several months of prior warning rumbles, in a rural area with low population density. Nuclear war would occur in densely populated regions with probably very little warning, and it would spew fallout that is intensely radioactive and toxic to plants, animals, and people.

Radiation from fallout decays over time, declining roughly by a factor of 10 for every sevenfold increase in time from the explosion. So, if at one hour the radiation intensity from fallout is 1,000 rads per hour, at seven hours it will be 100 and at 49 hours (7x7) it will be 10. Recall that 100 rads causes significant radiation sickness in men and women, and 600 rads is almost certainly fatal.

Larger, heavier particles will fall quickly to the ground as local fallout. Smaller particles drift down more slowly, and are therefore carried farther downwind. The amount of fallout in any given area will depend on the wind speed and direction, and the distance from ground zero. The radiation dose increases as more fallout arrives, and then decreases as the fission products decay. For example, according to the *British Medical Journal,*

> At a point in the open 20 miles downwind of a two megaton attack, with 15 mile per hour winds, the dose rate at one hour is three rads an hour, rising rapidly to over 500 rads an hour between one and two hours. Then it will decrease to 200 rads an hour at 6 hours, and 50 rads an hour at 18 hours.

Anyone exposed to this radiation will have an accumulated dose of over 2,000 rads, which is rapidly lethal.

Radiation sickness from fallout is identical to radiation sickness from immediate radiation, although people are slightly more tolerant to radiation that builds up over time as opposed to a single blast. In addition, fallout may emit large amounts of beta particles (electrons) that literally cause local burns to skin, and additionally burn the leaves of plants. Deciduous trees are particularly susceptible, and may die as a consequence of losing their leaves.

Many rural shelters are not underground. For example, traffic tunnels are often designated shelters, mere concrete tubes lacking any sort of food, water, or sanitary facilities, lighting, heat, or air filtration systems. Although underground shelters are more protected from blast, fire, and fallout, most have no provisions for lighting, and minimal ventilation. Underground evacuees will therefore find themselves huddled in the dark lacking food, water, and communication devices. Those in aboveground shelters will scarcely be better off. Only a few shelters will have radios, and because one effect of nuclear explosions is to disrupt communication systems, most shelters will be isolated from the world outside. Fear of an incipient attack and speculation about the fate of the world may produce further feelings of demoralization, helplessness, and apathy.

Most shelters will lack means to measure radiation levels, so there will be chronic anxiety about the "invisible contamination" of radiation sickness. Both at Three Mile Island and Hiroshima, hypochondriacal complaints mimicked the actual symptoms of early radiation sickness: weakness, headache, nausea, loss of appetite, vomiting, and lethargy. It will be impossible to tell who is going to die of radiation sickness in hours, days, or weeks, and who will recover from the low doses of radiation or hysterical symptoms. The care of the sick will be complicated by the problem of disposal of the corpses. A physician describes the scene in Hiroshima:

> Patients who could not walk urinated and defecated where they lay. Those who could walk would feel their way to the exits, and relieve themselves there. Persons entering or leaving the hospital could not avoid stepping in the filth, so closely was it spread. The front entrance became covered with feces overnight, and nothing could be done, for there were no bed pans, and even if there had been, no one to carry them to the patients. Disposing of the dead was a minor problem, but to clean the rooms and corridors of urine, feces, and vomitus was impossible.

## The Emergence Period: Coming Out . . . to What?

And when it is all over what will the world be like? Our fine great buildings, our homes will exist no more. The thousands of years it took to develop our civilization will have been in vain. Our works of art will be lost. Radio, television, newspapers will disappear. There will be no means of transport. There will be no hospitals. No help can be expected for the few mutilated survivors in any town to be sent from a neighboring town—there will be no neighboring towns left, no neighbors, there will be no help, there will be no hope.

—Lord Louis Mountbatten

What will the veterans of World War III face when they emerge from their caves and bunkers?

The social fabric of modern life will be gone, leaving the cave men in an appropriately primitive environment. Massive food and water shortages will probably be their first concern, complicated by the ubiquitous radiation and contamination. Agricultural effects will depend partly on the season. If nuclear war comes in the fall, when crops have been harvested and plants are dormant, food shortages will be less severe than if the attack comes in the spring or summer. Fruits and grains that have been harvested and sheltered will only be contaminated with external fallout. Furthermore, some seeds are fairly radiation resistant, and may still germinate in the spring. Young plants, however, are particularly vulnerable to radiation, so if war comes in the spring, most will die.

Livestock will generally be dead. (No shelter plans exist for cows and pigs.) Most will perish immediately from fallout. Cattle and sheep are more sensitive than humans to radiation; swine, horses, and poultry are about the same or somewhat less sensitive. In animals, as in humans, the very young and the elderly are most radiation-sensitive, and will die sooner and at higher rates than young adults. Interestingly, irradiated cows that do not die may produce as much milk as normal cows, but this will be irrelevant to the survivors: after a cow has not been milked for several days, her milk dries up. Furthermore, contamination of the milk with iodine-131 and strontium-90 would generally make the milk unfit for consumption; similarly with cesium-137 in the muscles of surviving animals. During the certain famine of the post-attack period, however, survivors would probably worry very little about long-term contamination, in their desperate race for calories.

Some food crops are radiation resistant, particularly rice, which may survive as much as 15,000 rads. Lima beans, sugar beets, and broccoli are also said to be resistant. Onions are particularly sensitive, along with small grain cereal crops such as wheat, barley, and oats. Although a world without Wheatena and oatmeal is not unimaginable, it will be difficult to provide sufficient calories, protein, and balanced vitamin and mineral regimes for a population subsisting on small quantities of rice and broccoli. (Assuming, of course, that available stockpiles can somehow be distributed to the survivors.) Again, children will be the most vulnerable to malnutrition, and any infants and children who survive the shelter period may become mentally and physically retarded, or simply die of starvation.

There is an inverse correlation between grain stores and population in the United States, but a positive correlation between grain stores and land-based missile silos. The most fertile and productive land in our country is in the midwest, home of the Titans and Minutemen. Most of the dairy and beef cattle are raised in Nebraska, Iowa, and Kansas. An attack on the Strategic Air Command Headquarters in Omaha is also an attack on over a million cows in Nebraska. In the post-attack period, obtaining grain that has been stored in the midwest would be a crucial survival task. But, who would volunteer to enter the devastated region in order to bring food to the survivors?

In addition, efficient production of crops and livestock depends on the availability of irrigation, farm machinery, seeds, and fertilizers. A severe energy shortage will not only impair food distribution, but also food production. It would be very easy to destroy or bottleneck the energy production facilities of both the United States and the Soviet Union. It doesn't take an accurate warhead to immobilize an oil refinery or electrical generating plant; even an inaccurate airburst will do. Modern agriculture will then cease, and postwar farmers will have to scratch in the dirt, lacking even the facilities to mine iron ore or to smelt steel to make shovels. Horses will be dead. Can you imagine the plight of a modern executive, "rescued" in a plush shelter for a month while 90 percent of Americans die, who emerges almost literally into a Stone Age?

Water will be a chronic problem. Strontium-90, with a half-life of 28 years, and cesium-137, with a half-life of 30 years, are both water soluble. There is no way to strain or filter these chemicals out of the water. There will be no sewage systems, since they require fuel for their operation. Billions of rotting human and animal corpses will contaminate water supplies, but there will be no laboratories which can evaluate the bacterial contamination of the water. The midwest relies on massive amounts of water being pumped from underground aquifers for irrigation, industry, and drinking. Southern and Central California would quickly revert to desert, without their massive system of man-made aquaducts, dams, and water supply systems. Without fuel and energy, these water projects would cease. There would be no technology to drill wells, or fuel for the drills.

Exposure will probably kill a significant number of survivors, because housing will be destroyed, and heating fuels will be unavailable. Wood for heating and construction will be in short supply, because evergreen trees are extremely susceptible to radiation, and once dead, will easily catch fire. Massive forest fires are likely, with no fire fighters.

Dr. Herbert Abrams, Chairman of the Radiology department at Harvard University Medical School, has analyzed the medical problems of the postwar period. His conclusion? A significant likelihood of massive epidemics of infectious diseases, in a scope that equals or surpasses the long-term problems of radiation, and that will probably exceed anything our species has ever endured. Survivors will be particularly vulnerable to infections for two reasons: 1) radiation injures the bone marrow and lymph nodes, thus directly lowering white blood cell count and resistance to infection, and 2) hardships of the post-attack period will further weaken the victims. Trauma, burns, and radiation sickness directly increase human susceptibility to infection. Malnutrition, dehydration, and poor sanitation will compound the problems. The millions of rotting human corpses, along with countless dead animals, will be breeding grounds for the relatively resistant insects, bacteria, and viruses. One report predicts, "The fly population would explode. . . . Trillions of flies would breed in the dead bodies." Most supplies of insecticides will be gone, so there would be no way to control either human or agricultural pests:

> Dogs will die but not the flea
> Tubers die but not TB
> Trees will die but not the blight
> Day will end but not the night.
> —N. CORWIN *(View From the Ark)*

U.S. government sources estimate that casualties in health personnel will be higher than the population as a whole, with easily 80 percent of physicians dead in the first month. The government estimates that the remaining physicians will have 32 million severely injured patients. There will be few diagnostic laboratories left. Most stores of antibiotics will be vaporized in the attack, and existing antibiotics have a brief shelf-life. Many viral diseases cannot be treated, but can be prevented with immunization. However, even immunized persons will still be susceptible to infections for which they had already received shots, because radiation will directly impair their immune responses. Furthermore, most Americans have no resistance to cholera, typhoid, typhus, malaria, rabies, or encephalitis, and the appearance of mutant strains would render previous immunity useless in any event. Respiratory infections, such as flu and pneumonia, and gastrointestinal infections, such as cholera, would almost certainly become epidemic among the survivors.

Dr. Abrams also argues that tuberculosis and plague may become major threats. TB was common in Dachau, and is likely to increase under conditions of stress and crowding. Rodents, particularly rats, are relatively resistant to radiation, as are their ubiquitous fleas. Both bubonic and the dread pneumonic plague might well be carried by the rats into the scraggly clusters of surviving humanity. Both plague and TB are extremely difficult to treat; they lurk just beneath the surface of our civilization, waiting for its veneer to wear thin. Nuclear war would probably do the trick.

Even routine medical problems that can readily be treated in complex modern hospitals might prove lethal in the post-attack period. FEMA's lovely little book, *Protection in the Nuclear Age,* thoughtfully includes a section on first aid. In simple language designed to reassure any Boy Scout, it explains the treatment of burns, bleeding, respiratory arrest, and broken bones. Strangely lacking, however, is a do-it-yourself guide to Caesarean sections, bone marrow transplants, coronary bypass surgery, or intravenous alimentation. There is nothing on how to deliver a baby (perhaps because most fetuses that are exposed while *in utero* will die). The Office of Technology Assessment points out that "a lack of medicines would accentuate the smallness and hardiness of the surviving population."

Society as we know it will cease existing, period. Our hypothetical survivors will confront not only Stone Age survival conditions and Stone Age agriculture, but Stone Age economics, Stone Age politics and a universal Stone Age psychology as well. In this sense, our analysis of medical and agricultural problems is really only a metaphor for all the problems of social collapse. Moreover, the Office of Technology Assessment is quite clear that following a nuclear war, things will get progressively *worse,* not better, for quite some time—that is, if they ever get better. There will be a race between consumption of remaining supplies and production of new ones. From what we now know, it takes a supreme article of faith to bet on the latter.

Arthur M. Katz attempted to evaluate *Life After Nuclear War.* Interestingly, the largest attack scenario that he analyzes consists of "only" 500 one megaton bombs on the 71 largest U.S. population centers, and 200 to 300 100 kiloton bombs targeted at 8 key industries—in other words, only a maximum of 800 bombs, comprising 530 megatons. As already indicated, the U.S. and U.S.S.R. together have about *20 times* this in their strategic arsenals, so Dr. Katz's estimate is conservative in the extreme. Nonetheless, he demonstrates that such an attack would kill 110 million people, 55 percent of the nation's population, and destroy 70 percent of our manufacturing capacity. Deputy Undersecretary of Defense T. K. Jones, our foremost proponent of industrial "civil defense," claims that industrial recovery would be possible, and in only a few years. "After all," he points out, "the streetcars were running in Hiroshima within 3 days of the attack." He neglects to mention that it took four years to start to rebuild the center of the city, and that with the aid of a mobilized and repentant "outside world."

In the post-attack world, money will have no meaning. Similarly for credit cards, checks, stocks, and the like—all are symbols of worth, not really of any value in themselves. Our financial and monetary system, no less than theirs, is based on a concept of underlying national stability. In the great equalizer of the postwar world, money will no longer be an incentive. Instead, primitive barter or simply rule by force will replace communism and capitalism, both of which are actually very complex and sophisticated ways of life. As John Kenneth Galbraith aptly points out, the world's two great systems will be indistinguishable among the ashes.

## Will the Center Hold? Long-term Effects of Nuclear War, and the Question of Extinction

Human beings have tangled with the forces of the sun and the stars for only about forty years, and there has only been one very small nuclear war. Therefore, predictions about the long-term effects of a large nuclear war must be uncertain. The scope of the potential destruction is as large as the imagination of the predictor. Science fiction novels such as *On the Beach* and *A Canticle for Leibowitz* may have as much to tell us as the Office of Technology Assessment, precisely because our imaginations may be constrained by our own self-interest. FEMA and Department of Defense scenarios tend to be optimistic about the long-term consequences, probably because of an underlying assumption that nuclear war may be inevitable, and it is best not to scare people. Moreover, FEMA bureaucrats, just like all other functionaries, have a vested interest in keeping their jobs, and if possible even expanding their empires. No government is likely to spend money on a project deemed hopeless, not to mention the consequences of admitting that even to plan for nuclear war is to make it more likely. So, FEMA and the likes of T.K. Jones make nuclear war sound uncomfortable, but somehow tolerable.

*On the Beach* was deliberately frightening, intended as it was to fuel the early ban-the-bomb movement. The Office of Technology Assessment commissioned a writer to produce a scenario called "Charlottesville," portraying the first year after a nuclear war as difficult but not impossible; long-term medical and ecologic damages are simply not addressed. In this section, we shall ask more questions than we answer, because the truth is not known. The possibilities, however, are staggering. In fact, we may well be facing the extinction of the human species, the extinction of all mammals and the extinction of most, if not all, life on earth.

Much ink has been spilled on. the medical and genetic consequences of the low level radiation from persistent fallout. Although intense local fallout may dissipate within a month, leaving only low levels of radiation that can remain for years, certain long-lived fission products may be deposited in the stratosphere, from which they will drift slowly to earth over many years. For example, plutonium from atmospheric bomb tests of the 1950s still persists in the stratosphere. Plutonium-239 has a half-life of about 24,000 years, and it is considered to be biologically toxic for 240,000 years. It can be inhaled, in which case even exceedingly small doses will cause cancer. It can also be ingested, in which case it concentrates particularly in the reproductive system—the ovaries in women and the testes in men. Plutonium is an alpha emitter, which means that its radiation doesn't travel very far, but packs a lot of punch. Most of us probably already have small amounts of plutonium in our reproductive organs, courtesy of the Atomic Energy Commission and the Department of Defense, not to mention the governments of Russia, France, Britain and China. However, this does not necessarily mean that our own children will have obvious mutations: dominant mutations, and most major chromosomal defects, will usually be spontaneously aborted, probably experienced as nothing more than an irregular menstrual period. It takes many generations for recessive mutations to become manifest, so our children may be born "normal," but carrying damaged genes that will be revealed in future generations.

Unfortunately, the victims of Hiroshima and Nagasaki can give us no more than a clue to the genetic effects of atomic bomb radiation. Genetic studies to date of children born to exposed parents have yielded no abnormalities.° However, no studies are being done on the grandchildren of the Hiroshima and Nagasaki victims;

° This must be distinguished from the very high level of abnormalities found among children who were *in utero* during the bombings, and hence, were exposed to radiation while they were developing. Many of these victims were born with essentially no heads, and other serious and incurable defects.

316 • STOP NUCLEAR WAR! A HANDBOOK

it is "too expensive." Hence, there is no current effect to determine possible genetic effects in these first victims.

Nonetheless, based on animal studies of radiation, the Office of Technology Assessment estimates that there would be 400,000 to 9 million genetic effects within the U.S. after a "comprehensive attack," and 1.5 to 15 million genetic effects outside the United States. In addition, OTA estimates 150,000 to 6 million spontaneous abortions within the U.S. caused by chromosomal damage, and 500,000 to 5 million abortions outside the U.S.

There is no doubt that the Hiroshima and Nagasaki victims, and others who have been exposed to radiation, such as the inhabitants of Rongelap (in the South Pacific), those exposed to Nevada atmospheric testing, and uranium miners have an increased incidence of cancer. Leukemia and lymphatic cancers appeared within three to five years in the Japanese victims, afflicting not only those who received immediate radiation from the blast itself, but also those who entered the cities shortly afterward, in search of relatives or to aid the rescue operations. Cancer of the thyroid was also significantly increased, probably because iodine-131 concentrates in the thyroid gland. Cancers of the lung, breast, ovaries, salivary glands, and other tumors were also significantly elevated. The Office of Technology Assessment estimates, rather conservatively we believe, that a nuclear war would produce 1 to 5 million cancer deaths and 1 to 2 million thyroid cancers in the United States, and 900,000 to 9 million cancer deaths and about 3.2 million thyroid cancers outside the United States. Because no medical treatment will be available, we can assume that most thyroid cancer victims will die, thereby yielding a conservative prediction that between 3 and 19 million people will die of cancer in the post-attack period.

Dr. Edward Radford, former chairman of the National Academy of Sciences Committee on the Biological Effects of Radiation, has concluded that with a worldwide exposure of 300 rems per person, just about everyone would develop cancer and perhaps half of the remaining population would die from it. (That, of course, assumes that enough people lasted the five or more years necessary for cancer to develop!) Similarly, accelerated aging is another possible result of radiation, but it can only be experienced if enough people survive the ensuing famines, plagues, riots, and cancers, and then live to begin growing old.

It is possible that *no one* would survive, not so much because of radiation, but because of the major ecological disruption caused by the explosions themselves. One hypothesis for the extinction of the dinosaurs, after they had dominated life on earth for over 200 million years, is that a large meteor may have collided with the earth, kicking up an enormous cloud of dust that could have obscured the sunlight for a few years. If the earth were darkened, even for a short time, geologically speaking, green plants would die and the ecosystem could collapse. The dinosaurs may thus have starved to death, in the dark. Even a year or a summer without normal sunlight would have major, unpredictable consequences. No one knows how many explosions it would take, or what megatonnage, to cause sufficient dust to be deposited in the stratosphere to darken the globe, and extinguish most life on our green planet. But it is a real possibility, especially with a large number of groundbursts. For example, when volcanic Mt. Krakatoa exploded in 1883, the world was darker and colder for more than a year thereafter. We can only wonder about the possible effects of several thousand Krakatoas, blowing up simultaneously.

As if we haven't already given you enough to worry about, there is more. In fact, if the world doesn't become dangerously dark, it could become lethally light, although we wouldn't actually see the new light—in fact, we might very well not see at all. A layer of ozone currently surrounds the earth, protecting it (and us) from the sun's dangerous ultraviolet light. In 1975, the National Academy of Sciences reported that a nuclear war could destroy this ozone layer, which would subject the earth to toxic ultraviolet radiation never experienced on this planet since life first appeared, several billion years ago.

Life probably evolved on earth when high-intensity UV light stimulated the chemical interaction of carbon, hydrogen, and nitrogen, forming complex molecules and ultimately DNA. However, many millions of years later, life on land was only possible because of the ozone shield which now surrounds the earth, protecting living things from the burning intensity of UV light. Ozone is composed of three molecules of oxygen ($O_3$) formed when sunlight hits molecular oxygen ($O_2$). The ozone layer developed when a sufficient quantity of oxygen had been formed by photosynthesis.

Ultraviolet light is biologically toxic; in fact, surgical instruments are often sterilized by UV lamps. UV light kills lower micro-organisms; it rarely kills higher organisms, at least not right away. Rather, it burns them and blinds them.

The National Academy of Sciences report pointed out that nuclear explosions create enormous quantities of nitrogen oxides, which react chemically with ozone and destroy it. No one knows how many explosions it would take to destroy the earth's ozone layer, but Kosta Tsipis, professor of physics at MIT, estimates that depletion of the ozone layer by even ten percent would blind all unprotected eyes. In theory, at least, all humans could wear glasses, but what about the birds, insects, reptiles, and mammals? They would be blinded, and hence the entire ecosystem could collapse. For example, blind bees couldn't find and pollinate flowers; unpollinated flowers would not make fruit; and so on. How would blind birds find insects? Dr. Tsipis estimates that the detonation of only twenty percent of the world's nuclear arsenal could bring about total ecological collapse. (Maybe the moles, not the meek, would then inherit the earth.)

We know virtually nothing about the effects of low level radiation and ultraviolet light on the microorganisms of the oceans, the tiny algae whose steady and thankless task has been to provide most of the oxygen renewal that takes place on the globe. These minute plants, absolutely crucial to life on earth, float in the oceans close to the surface. They comprise a significant portion of our planet's living stuff, and they could well be lethally burned by the UV light, causing the oceans to be sterilized like an operating room. The result? No more oxygen in the atmosphere.

Furthermore, note that cesium, strontium-90, tritium, deuterium, and even carbon-14 are highly radioactive, with long half-lives. As those substances leach from the contaminated land masses, adding their pollution to the existing fallout, the seas would also become radioactively contaminated. Algae, once again, are particularly vulnerable, because they reproduce quickly.

The reduction of the world's ozone layer would have unpredictable climatic consequences as well. The National Academy of Science 1975 report noted that the surface of the earth could be warmed by several degrees, by permitting more solar radiation to reach it, or cooled, for example by an increased cloud or dust cover. An average temperature change of less than five degrees either way could cause either a new ice age, or alternatively, melting of the polar ice caps and significant flooding of all coastal areas, where a large part of the world's population now lives.

Thus, the new cave men, when they emerge from their holes, will find a world very different from the one they left behind. It may be a darker world, with the sun obscured by gray-brown dust, and all green plants wilted in the shade. It may be a cloudier world, rent by hurricanes and storms, as the atmosphere convulses to find a new equilibrium. Perhaps the world will be sickeningly bright, as rampaging sunlight pours through the damaged atmosphere. If so, white-skinned people will be subjected to third degree sunburn if they stray out of their caves unprotected for more than three minutes. After the first month, very few of the blinded, sickened animals will be crawling through the wreckage, and corpses of butterflies will mingle with those of the children.

For any people that survive, the psychological consequences of this overwhelming immersion in death may be extreme. The problems of life during the post-attack period will be like surviving on the moon. There will be unending tasks: finding food, water, and even air to breathe. Most survivors will have lost their families or will watch them die, perhaps slowly. Friends and foes alike will be dead. Will revenge be consoling? As the survivors lament their dead children, will it give them joy to know that "the enemy" is also destroyed?

Any who survive will not dare return to their cities, transformed into smoldering radioactive ash-heaps. The veterans of World War III will have lost their property, their livelihoods, their family homes, and their cultural ties. Even if the various ecological disasters somehow do not come to pass, rebuilding society may be impossible. Evacuation "host" areas are far from populations precisely because they lack water, habitable terrain, necessary resources or viable climates. It will be exceedingly difficult to reconstruct a social network that resembles the United States, because the map will be pockmarked by vast radioactive craters and the landscape transformed into huge banks of charred rubble. Communication between isolated islands of survivors will be minimal, and transportation virtually nonexistent. There will be no meaningful trade. There could be no effective centralized government. Who will lead these groups, and how will they make decisions? Instead of democracy, we might expect a series of brutish, tribal bands, lacking ethics or morality except survival. The depravity of *Lord of the Flies* may be a good model for the behavior of isolated and desperate human beings.

Alternatively, the poor, weak, frightened survivors (if indeed there are any) may well drag through their remaining days as did the prisoners of Auschwitz: demoralized, dehumanized, oblivious. Will these walking corpses be able to form relationships with one another? Will they dare to make friends or alliances? Will anyone in the post-attack period dare to fall in love, or to have children? Commenting on the aftermath of a nuclear war, Khrushchev noted that "the living would envy the dead." But even this may be optimistic: will the living harbor any recognizable human emotions? More likely, as sociologist Kai Erickson and psychiatrist Robert Jay Lifton have suggested, the living will *resemble* the dead.

Perhaps the most basic meaning in life is continuity, through successive generations—usually by parenthood, but also through teaching and creating new forms that will endure beyond the scope of individual survival. With the end of love will come the end of meaning.

As we have seen, in addition to psychological and social extinction, the human race may face physical extinction as well. This is something entirely new. We all must face individual death, both the thought of it, and ultimately, the reality as well. But until the specter of nuclear war, we could at least be confident that something, someone will go on. Before now, human actions were always accountable in the here-and-now, with occasionally some lingering consequences for future generations. Never have we had to contemplate the wholesale canceling of all generations yet unborn. Now we must.

We have not enjoyed leading this tour of hell. But it is for your own good, and ours. Scare stories? Absolutely—because scared is just the way you ought to be. We must all have no illusions as to what nuclear war would be like, for we shall never have the chance to apologize, to take it all back, explaining that we didn't know it would be quite so bad. It is all too easy to dismiss the likes of T. K. Jones and his soul-brothers at FEMA as bungling bureaucrats, and to laugh at their absurd flights of fancy. But don't discount them so quickly—their quaint misperceptions are the stuff upon which governments base *their* actions and *your* death. So when presidential counselor Edwin Meese, in an address to the U.S. Civil Defense Council on March 1, 1982, called nuclear war "something that may not be desirable," he is dousing you and those you love with gasoline. The next step is to strike a match.

> I have set before you life and death . . . choose life.
> —Deuteronomy 30:19

# 11. The Arms Race at Home:

## A Cross We All Bear

> Every gun that is made, every warship launched, every rocket fired, signifies in the final sense a theft from those who hunger and are not fed, those who are cold and are not clothed. The world in arms is not spending money alone. It is spending the sweat of its laborers, the genius of its scientists, the hopes of its children.
>
> —PRESIDENT DWIGHT EISENHOWER

Death and taxes: the only two certainties in life, or so it is said. In the latter part of the twentieth century, however, we go the cynics one better, buying death *with* taxes. And moreover, our purchases along the way have made our lives not richer but poorer, not happier but more miserable. The road to hell may be paved with good intentions; the road to our nuclear hell is paved with economic ruin. Like Christ carrying his cross up Golgotha, we stagger under an incredible military burden—on the way to our own peculiar crucifixion.

Ironically, however, perhaps we should rejoice at the cost of our military "preparedness," since it is a cost that is immediate, real, and undeniable. It may therefore help save us. Thus, short-sighted men, like those running our country, see only the issues immediately in front of them. In general, this works to the detriment of us all. But our salvation, in this case, may lie in this same mental myopia: to the self-styled "pragmatists" who govern the U.S., nuclear annihilation may seem distant and unreal. But inflation, unbalanced budgets, loss of productivity, unmet social needs, unemployment—these are real, even to the more near-sighted. And much of the blame for these problems lies squarely with our military spending. In this chapter, we shall look first at the actual amount of that spending, but this is only one way of measuring cost. The really painful immediate costs will be examined next: inflation, loss of productivity, unmet social needs, and fewer jobs. The cost of our military effort is a cross that we all bear, often unknowingly. Yet we shall continue to bear it until we recognize our folly, until we realize that it is a cross of our own making, and which we can and must lay aside before our journey reaches its horrid end.

## The Amount of Military Spending

To describe military spending is to risk the same numbness that comes from describing the effects of nuclear weapons, only substituting billions of dollars for millions of degrees. Like a nuclear explosion, military spending occurs on a scale so vast that it is almost beyond our comprehending—as with nuclear war itself, military spending is not difficult to *understand*, however; it is difficult to *believe*.

The world spends about $500 billion per year on arms. That is about $1.4 billion per day, or better than $1 million per minute. During the period 1960 to 1978, NATO countries spent about $3,137 billion on arms; the Warsaw Pact countries spent about $1,401 billion during this same time. This represented 5.6 percent of NATO gross national products, and 8.5 percent of the Warsaw Pact's. During the years 1977 to 1980, U.S. military expenditures were $97.5, $105.2, $117.7, and $135.85—all billions, of course. Reagan Administration requests for 1981 through 1984 are: $162.1, $188.85, $226.05, and $255.60. Reagan Administration budget projections for 1986 reach *$374 billion,* with no end in sight. Even the proposed $226 billion budget for 1983 is the largest peacetime increase in U.S. history. During the 35 years from 1946 to 1980, we spent a total of $2,000 billion on the military; the Reagan Administration is now seeking to spend about $1,500 billion in just the next 5 years. (By way of contrast, the value of all corporations listed on the N.Y. Stock Exchange is about $900 billion. This suggests that the business of America is no longer business, but rather, military spending!) During the period of the Korean War, from 1950 to 1954, the Truman and Eisenhower Administrations shifted 18.5 percent of general funds from the domestic sector to the military; Reagan is proposing a shift of 23.6 percent and supposedly, we are now at peace.

Much of the annual U.S. budget is relatively "uncontrollable," tied up in programs such as veteran's benefits, social security, railroad retirement, and highway trust funds. Of the "flexible" programs that are budgeted at the discretion of each government, military expenditures account for no less than two-thirds. Thus, for example, the Carter budget for fiscal year 1982 budgeted $197.7 billion in flexible funds, of which $116.3 billion was for the military.

Even though nuclear weapons generally make up a relatively small part of the total military budget, they are not cheap. Here is a breakdown of the Reagan Administration's strategic nuclear weapons requests, for 1982–1987 (in $ billions): bombers–63, SLBMs–51, ICBMs–42, nuclear warheads and bombs–30 to 35, air defense and "civil defense"–29, $C^3I$–22, and cruise missiles–15. Total: $252 to 257 billion. Given the Pentagon's legendary cost-overruns, this estimate is almost certainly conservative. Indeed, Richard DeLauer, head of weapons research and procurement at the Pentagon, told a closed meeting of the Joint Chiefs of Staff in January 1982 that the total estimate of $1.5 trillion might well be 50 percent too low! When this news was leaked to the nation's press, the Reagan Administration responded, not by reevaluating their budget demands, but with an unprecedented muzzling of top officials, including lie detector tests and a requirement that all news contacts be cleared in advance.

Before World War I, British Foreign Secretary Sir Edward Grey described the world's obsession with weaponry as a "satire on civilization." What would he say if he saw us now?

## The Costs of Military Spending

### 1. Inflation

There is a widespread myth: "military spending is good for the economy." In fact, military spending is sometimes good for a *depressed* economy, and for one simple reason—it is wildly inflationary. It is generally accepted that World War II got the U.S. out of its Great Depression, and this is almost certainly correct. But to equate military spending with economic health is almost certainly *in*correct. Going back as far as the Revolutionary War, prices went up sharply along with military spending. The same trend has continued during the War of 1912, the Mexican-American War, the

Civil War, the Spanish-American War, and so on. In the 1980s, with inflation widely identified as a prime economic evil, our government is nonetheless insisting upon record military expenditures, hoping in part to exploit the myth that it will be good for the economy. It just won't work. As William Winpisinger, president of the International Association of Machinists and Aerospace Workers put it, the Pentagon is a "perpetual inflation machine." And the *Wall Street Journal* (hardly a tool of radical peaceniks) pointed out editorially that "Defense spending is the worst kind of government outlay," precisely because it is so inflationary.

How does military spending fuel inflation? Several different ways; for one, look at the basic law of supply and demand. If demand goes down, or alternatively, if supply goes up while demand stays the same, then prices go down; on the other hand, if demand goes up, or if supply goes down while demand stays the same, then prices rise. When prices go up, of course, we have inflation. Military spending fuels inflation both ways. Thus, it increases demand by pumping money into the economy through military contracts, while at the same time *reducing* supplies, especially such important and basic items as aluminum and other metals. If money and materials are spent producing something in the "civilian sector" that people can buy, such as automobiles, TV sets, or toasters, then inflationary pressures are balanced by the increased supply—that is, with more automobiles, TV sets, or toasters to choose from, prices are kept down. But no one can go to the local hardware store and purchase a missile, or a bomb. In short, military spending produces objects which are of no domestic economic value, and which drive up the prices for other things.

Military spending therefore drives up domestic prices because it puts money into the economy without increasing the supply of buyable goods. It also fuels inflation by *reducing* the supply of raw materials. Thus military procurement competes with domestic uses, and the military wins. For example, when Northrop or Boeing buys up large quantities of aluminum for building military aircraft, this raises the cost of aluminum for the rest of us as well. Moreover, military contracts are typically on a "cost plus" basis, in which the contracting firm is guaranteed to make a certain profit, on top of whatever the production costs might be. As a result, industry—bolstered by the largesse of the American taxpayer—freely bids up the price of raw materials, thereby generating prices which are even more inflated, and which further plague the taxpayer when (s)he goes out to buy something at the store.

We do not have the heaviest military burden, per capita, in the world. That dubious distinction goes to Israel, for obvious reasons. For equally obvious reasons, Israel is also staggering under a nearly incredible inflation rate: about 100 percent per year. That's right, 100 percent.

In 1965, the U.S. inflation rate was only 1.7 percent. Then came the Vietnam War, and a 6 percent build-up in military spending during the period 1965 to 1968. Most observers agree that our current inflationary spiral was initiated when President Johnson insisted on having both "guns and butter," without a tax increase. Now, in the 1980s, the Reagan Administration has orchestrated a massive tax *reduction*, combined with plans to increase military spending by 52.8 percent during the period 1981 to 1986 (in 1972 dollars). The effect is unavoidably inflationary. Moreover, as the economy fails to respond vigorously to Reagonomics, and the government nonetheless insists on its massive military program, it will be necessary for the government to borrow additional money, driving interest rates yet higher.

The conclusion is unavoidable: military spending and inflation go hand in hand.

## 2. Loss of productivity

In addition to inflation, military spending leads to reduced productivity. There is only so much available in the American social, scientific, economic and financial pie. The larger the military's slice, the less is available for the rest. As the ecologists like to point out, there is no free lunch. President Eisenhower was quite clear on this:

> There is no way in which a country can satisfy the craving for absolute security—but it can easily bankrupt itself, morally and economically, in attempting to reach that illusory goal through arms alone. The Military Establishment, not productive of itself, necessarily must feed on the energy, productivity, and brainpower of the country, and if it takes too much, our total strength declines.

How much is "too much"? In terms of national security, no amount is too much, no economic cost too great, if real security is being purchased. However, given that we are buying insecurity not security, and instability not stability, then our military purchases are clearly too much, even if they enhanced productivity. Which, in fact, they do not.

The prestigious Council on Economic Priorities recently studied the economies of thirteen major industrialized nations during the 1960s and 1970s. The findings were clear: lower military expenditures correlated with more investment in the domestic economy, more productivity, and faster economic growth. Higher military expenditures correlated with reduced domestic investment, less productivity, and less growth. For example, Japan, Austria, and Canada had the lowest military expenditures and the healthiest economies; West Germany, Belgium, and Sweden were intermediate in military spending and also intermediate in their economies: the United States and Great Britain had the greatest military drain and the most stagnant economies. This lack of productivity could not, incidentally, be traced to higher U.S. wages—our wage scale was intermediate among the countries studied. Similarly, it could not be attributed to "wasteful" social spending—of the thirteen countries, only two spent less on social needs, per gross national product, than the U.S.

Data compiled by economist Ruth Leger Sivard tell an identical story: Looking at nine industrial giants (Japan, Denmark, Canada, Italy, Sweden, West Germany, France, Great Britain, and the U.S.), the higher the military expenditure—in percentage of GNP—the lower the annual rate of growth in manufacturing productivity. Similar results have also been found by economist R.P. Smith, of the University of London, who studied the economies of fifteen industrial nations over a period of eleven years: high military spending leads to low civilian investment.

This is a new and very painful experience for our country. As Columbia University professor of industrial engineering Seymour Melman points out, for decades the American economy was characterized by a 3 percent increase in industrial productivity output per employee per year. Year after year, this was America: 3 percent increase, as much a part of our country as the purple mountains' majesty or the fruited plains. Since 1965 (not coincidentally, the year the Vietnam War went into high gear), this productivity rate has been dropping. In the late 1960s, it declined to 2.1 percent and by 1975 it was down to 1.8 percent, the lowest of any industrialized country! As a result, production costs could no longer be offset by increased availability of goods as they had always been before, so cost increases were passed along increasingly to the consumer. The result? More inflation.

Why does military spending lead to diminished productivity? We have already considered the major reason—money spent in the military sector is simply not available for the domestic sector. The American steel industry, for example, is using outmoded, inefficient equipment—the worst and least productive of any major western power. It should come as no surprise that Japanese and West German steelmaking, unhampered by the drain of large military budgets, have become preeminent in the world. Money desperately needed to revitalize our domestic economy is sucked down the drain of military spending. And current plans call for this to increase.

In addition to money that might otherwise go toward modernization and machinery repair, the military sector also diverts scientific and technological expertise. Thus, the U.S. is behind every other industrial nation in the percentage of its Gross National Product spent on civilian research and development. A whopping 50 percent of federal research and development funds goes to the military, as compared to 12 percent in West Germany and 2 percent in Japan. That is why we import Volkswagens, Toyotas, and Sonys. The U.S. military-industrial complex employs from 35 to 50 percent of all our scientists and engineers, about 500,000 people. That is why we can design sophisticated MIRVs and neutron bombs but can't seem to figure out how to build a car that gets 50 miles to the gallon. (The Germans and the Japanese, incidentally, are well on their way to accomplishing just this, while the U.S. auto industry is in shambles and Chrysler is a basket case.)

In a sense, the Germans and Japanese have it made. Given their roles in World War II, both nations are inhibited from developing nuclear arsenals—the Germans by world opinion, the Japanese by domestic opinion. (If these prohibitions against nuclear weapons were suddenly lifted, we can imagine Japan turning out hydrogen bombs like Hondas—at least for a while.) At present, however, our defeated former enemies have enjoyed the luxury of turning their economic power inward and they have waxed strong. When economist John Kenneth Galbraith testified before the Senate Foreign Relations Committee, detailing the connection between the reduced military spending of Germany and Japan, and their postwar economic "miracles," Senator Fulbright asked him—tongue only partly in cheek—whether we could ask the victorious Vietnamese government to prohibit our continued arms build-up, in order to bring about an *American* economic miracle!

Admittedly, there have been some advantages in productivity from beneficial "spin-offs" of military research and development. But these have been few, far between, and certainly trivial compared to what could have been achieved if the research and development were aimed specifically at achieving this end—that is, at helping people instead of killing them. Even in the areas of undoubted spin-offs, our military obsession keeps us from pressing any advantage. Thus, solid-state circuits are now built better and for less money by the Japanese, who put them into inexpensive, reliable TVs, stereos, and recorders. Similarly, Lockheed and McDonnel-Douglas—both huge defense contractors—are halting their airliner production, leaving Boeing as the only American producer in this major market. Because of the style of defense contracts, U.S. military firms compete to add "improvements" which dazzle the Pentagon planners, rather than to produce reliable products at the lowest possible cost. As a result, in the computer chip industry, our military emphasis has led to obsession with ever higher speeds, regardless of the ever higher costs, while the Japanese develop cheaper, reliable components that may well dominate the civilian sector during the mid-1980s.

It will be truly ironic if sometime soon, the U.S. economy becomes unable to compete in civilian products, leaving us the world's best builders of armaments, and nothing else!

### 3. Unmet social needs

In June 1980, the U.S. Presidential Commission on Hunger estimated that 50,000 people die of starvation or hunger-related diseases *every day*. Five hundred seventy million people in the world are undernourished. Waterborne diseases kill about 25,000 per day; yet in 1974 alone the world spent about $400 billion on weapons, while 10 million people starved. The eradication of malaria, which now strikes millions annually, would cost about a weekend.

In 1980, the United States spent more than 4 times as much on military research and development as on health ($15.1 billion versus $3.7 billion.) Just 2 Trident submarines cost about $3.42 billion—approximately equal to all federal funds appropriated for elementary and secondary education. Just 8 Lance surface-to-surface missiles cost more than $1 billion, exceeding the total federal funds appropriated for alcohol, drug abuse, and mental health. Just 22 F-15 fighters cost $382.58 million, $60 million more than was spent on the entire operation of the National Park System—before the Reagan cuts. The $9 billion budgeted for a "rapid deployment force" could rapidly deploy commuters on new subway systems for 5 major U.S. cities, creating about half a million new jobs in the process and also reducing our dependence on foreign oil.

There is, moreover, a direct connection between the already bloated yet nonetheless expanding military budget and a wide range of pressing domestic needs. Thus, as money goes to the Pentagon, it is withdrawn from other spheres. The Reagan Administration is cutting over $1 billion in federal Medicaid funds and another $1 billion in U.S. Public Health Service programs in 1982—while spending $2.4 billion for additional development of the MX missile. To take a smaller example, the Public Health Service Hospital in Seattle was scheduled for closure in 1982 because federal funding was being withdrawn; the total annual budget for this hospital was $20 million, less than two-thirds the cost of a single AH-64 military helicopter!

The list could go on and on. Let's conclude, however, with this statement by the Public Health Association of New York City, presented at the Statewide Conference on the Public Health Crisis, in May 1980:

> The health of the people of New York City is actively endangered by the already imposed cuts and by the threatened cuts in funding for health care services and for medical care services. To express ourselves in clear language, so there is no misunderstanding: we are talking about dead babies whose deaths can be prevented; we are talking

about sick children and adults whose illnesses can be prevented; we are talking about misery for older people whose misery can be prevented. We are speaking of these unspeakable things in a wealthy country and in a wealthy state, whose people deserve better. The malignant neglect of federal, state and local governments is literally killing people now and will kill, and destroy the lives of, many more in the future. . . .

## 4. Fewer jobs

Military expenditures employ some people; there can be no doubt about that. But this does *not* mean that military expenditures make more jobs than equivalent money spent in a domestic economy. In fact, when we compare military spending with domestic spending, we find that military expenditures cost the nation hundreds of thousands of jobs; there also can be no doubt about this.

According to the U.S. Bureau of Labor Statistics, every $1 billion spent on the military creates on average 75,000 jobs. The same $1 billion spent on mass transit creates on average 92,000 jobs; construction, 100,000; health care, 139,000; education, 187,000. In fact, military spending creates the fewest jobs of any major sector of the economy. It does this for one simple reason: weapons manufacturing is what economists call "capital intensive." That is, it requires expensive, sophisticated gadgetry and expensive, sophisticated materials—but relatively few people. Hence, $1 billion buys fancy alloys, high-technology electronics and state-of-the-art metallurgy, but relatively few jobs. In the aerospace industry, "headhunters" get $1,000 for each highly skilled employee they can recruit for military contractors eager for electronics experts, chemical engineers, and solid-state physicists—a very small percentage of the work force, and a group that already has a low unemployment rate. It hires relatively few trade, service, and industrial workers—those most in need of jobs. On average, for example, 9 out of 10 jobs in U.S. industry are in production, whereas in aircraft manufacturing, this shrinks to only 5 out of 10, and in electronics, communications, and guided missiles, a mere 3 out of 10. Accordingly, Marion Anderson, economist for Employment Research Associates, has concluded that for every $10 billion switched from domestic to military purposes, the nation *loses* about 34,000 jobs.

For one example, take the state of Washington, home of Boeing, a major defense contractor. When healthy, Boeing makes a major contribution to Washington's economy, employing about 55,000 persons. During the "Boeing depression" of 1969–1970, the state's entire economy was disrupted, real estate values plummeted, and people left. It got so bad that a sign was erected along the major highway leading east over the Cascade mountains: "Will the last person to leave Seattle please turn out the lights!" But Boeing is not the state's only employer. The lumber and wood products industry hires 48,000, and construction, another 62,000. As of early 1982, there was great excitement in the Seattle area, since record military budgets were expected to increase employment at Boeing, perhaps by as much as 3,000 new jobs.

However, more than 5,000 Boeing employees were being laid off at the same time, because of the drastic slump among domestic airlines. Moreover, the construction industry is in desperate straits, largely because of the continuing high interest rates, which stifle new construction. And these high interest rates, in turn, are necessitated by government deficit spending, to meet the costs of our vast military budget. In addition, these high interest rates are also putting Seattle-area lumber workers out of work, as mills close. For example, unemployment among loggers and sawmill workers now hovers around 40 to 50 percent, and the Seattle Master Builders Association estimated in 1981 that 16,000 homebuilders were out of a job.

These facts have led Seattle economist and businessman Robert Lamson to estimate that "if policies at the national level continue as planned, each defense-related job gained at Boeing will be paid for by the loss of two to five jobs elsewhere in Washington." A similar pattern almost certainly holds for other industries in other states. Military contracts are not gift horses; we *should* look them in the mouth. In fact, they are more like Trojan horses, with unemployment and unpredictable boom/bust cycles hidden inside the shiny, exterior promise of a few new jobs.

So, military spending creates fewer jobs, not more. But the fact remains, those jobs that it does create are real, as against a *potential* number of jobs that exist, for now, only in the never-never-land of a future civilian-oriented system as opposed to our present military economy. One problem in achieving a civilian economy, therefore, is to confront the prospective loss of military contract-related jobs.

Beating swords into plowshares is child's play compared with making missiles into subway cars. But even this task pales by comparison with the more fundamental one: changing people—people whose livelihood and prestige now depend on a war-oriented economy—into people whose skills are used for life instead. As everything else in the new peace movement, it will not be easy, but it is not impossible.

Economic "conversion" therefore deserves attention, more than it is now getting from the federal government (about zero!). For assembly-line workers, conversion to a civilian economy would be easy, requiring only the actual retooling. Just as during World War II auto factories switched smoothly to making tanks, jeeps, and armored personnel carriers, there are no fundamental barriers to a switch in the opposite direction. According to G. Dargity, secretary-treasurer of District 751 of the Machinists Union (28,000 members at Boeing alone), "a tool and die maker, a journeyman machinist or a machine operator could move to anything: railroad cars, plastics, airplanes—it would make no difference."

Conversion of most military-industrial plants would take from six months to two years. Unskilled and semiskilled laborers would switch most easily, although as we have just seen, even highly skilled workers would probably have little difficulty. The greatest problem would be posed by senior, high-level personnel: the engineers and project managers. Military contracts call for high performance, with generally no penalty for high costs. By contrast, civilian markets are much more sensitive to costs; successful conversion would therefore call for new ways of thinking, designing and subcontracting. Presumably, however, these intelligent, highly educated people have some flexibility. (Moreover, a number of nuclear engineers are guaranteed a living in any case. Because of the tons of high-level nuclear waste already created, more than 99 percent of it from bomb-building programs, thousands of generations of radiochemists, materials physicists, etc., are assured of steady employment even if we stop our nuclear weapons build-up tomorrow!)

We have virtually no information about the possible course of economic conversion in the Soviet Union. We do know, however, that the U.S.S.R. has its equivalent of our military-industrial complex, with particular emphasis on the role of military bureaucrats.

Thus, insufficient supply is the ongoing bottleneck in the Soviet economy, and military procurers always get top priority. (This, incidentally, is part of the reason why military competition with the U.S.S.R. is the least favorable avenue for us to choose; the one thing the Soviets do efficiently and well is build weapons.) In the Soviet Union, military production, and therefore military managers, have high prestige, high pay, incentive bonuses, etc. Hence, when Professor Seymour Melman raised the issue of economic conversion with a leading Soviet military manager, he got the laughing reply "Do you expect us to convert to making sausages?".

In fact, more sausages is exactly what the Russians need. Complaints about meat shortages led to the rapid rise of *Solidarity* in Poland, and yet, Russians eat *less* meat, per capita, than do Poles. By contrast with his Russian counterpart, there is no evidence that, in the U.S., high-level managers for General Foods or Texaco are treated any less well than comparable executives at Lockheed or General Dynamics. So we may find economic conversion less painful than the Soviets.

U.S. politicians—especially regional representatives—currently tend to be captives of their military contractors. Thus it is difficult for a California legislator to vote against Lockheed or for a Washington legislator to disagree with the immediate interests of Boeing. And yet, Senator Alan Cranston of California and Congressman Mike Lowry of Seattle have managed to combine nuclear/military sanity with getting elected. When the electorate realizes the connection between military contracts and inflation, loss of productivity, unmet social needs, and fewer jobs, it will become difficult indeed for politicians to continue with the kind of insanity that has been all too popular thus far.

Finally, it might be sobering for constituents to rethink one of the old standbys of the present military/political connection: the pride with which politicians point to the military contracts they bring to their districts. For example, when he was chairman of the House Armed Services Committee, Mendel Rivers brought to his district in South Carolina an Army depot, Marine Corps Air Station, and Polaris (now Poseidon) submarine facilities. There were, admittedly, some new jobs. But Charleston also became a prime, #1 target! Maybe Congressional hawkishness could be made self-limiting, once the American people realize that their favorite pork-barreling Pentagon-booster is slitting their throats—not only economically, but literally as well.

## Who Makes What?

In a sense, the arms race is not really out of control; it is just out of *our* control. The arms race is being controlled rather well by those who profit from it.

This includes most of the nation's largest companies. A listing of major military contractors reads like a Who's Who on Wall Street. Even when it comes to the manufacture of top-secret, ultra-classified nuclear weapons, the work—and the profit—gets spread around. Since most firms are rather tight-lipped about their role in making weapons of mass destruction, we shall take a special look at them.

The hydrogen bomb is a composite of American corporate know-how, with contributions from some of our best-known companies. The neutron generator, crucial for the initial atomic explosion, is produced near Tampa, Fla. at the Pinellas Plant of Ronald Reagan's former employer, General Electric ("Progress for People"). The explosives used to compress the fissionable fuel to critical mass are made by Monsanto ("Without chemicals, life itself would be impossible") at their Mound Laboratory in Miamisburg, Ohio, ten miles southeast of Dayton. Plutonium and beryllium components, for the atomic trigger, are fashioned by Rockwell International ("Where science gets down to business") at its Rocky Flats plant near Denver, Colo. Tritium gas—part of the fusion fuel—comes from Du Pont's ("Better living through chemistry") plant at Savannah River, S.C. Deuterium, uranium, and lithium—for the fusion and second fission explosion—come from Oak Ridge, Tenn., courtesy of Union Carbide ("Today, something we do will touch your life"). Polystyrene foam and honeycomb shielding, which helps focus pressure on the bomb's inner fusion core, are made in Kansas City, Mo. by Bendix ("We speak technology"). The final assembly is conducted near Amarillo, Tex., at the Pantex plant operated by the Kentucky-based engineering firm of Mason &

Hanger-Silas Mason—the same people who brought New York the Lincoln Tunnel. Primary research and design for hydrogen bombs is conducted at the Los Alamos National Scientific Laboratory, thirty-five miles northwest of Santa Fe, New Mex., and the Lawrence Livermore National Laboratory, about an hour from downtown San Francisco. Both are funded by the Department of Energy—not the Department of Defense—and both are officially operated and sanctioned by the University of California ("Let there be light"). The major engineering arm for the non-nuclear aspects of nuclear weapons is Sandia Laboratories, operated by Western Electric, a subsidiary of AT&T ("The system is the solution") and headquartered at Kirtland Air Force Base, in Albuquerque, New Mex.

The nuclear fuel cycle is another saga, too complex to describe fully here, but nonetheless worthy of a nodding acquaintance. It begins with uranium mining—the major uranium producing region in the world is northwest New Mexico and southeast Wyoming, much of it Indian land. Kerr-McGee is the nation's largest uranium-mining company, followed by Continental, Anaconda, Gulf, Humble, Mobil, Phillips, and Exxon. According to the U.S. Public Health Service, lung cancer among uranium miners in the southwest (many of them Indians) was about five times that of the normal population.° The Department of Labor finally established safety standards in 1967, with vigorous opposition from the AEC, the Joint Committee on Atomic Energy, and of course, the mining companies. These standards were not enforced until ten years later, under the Carter Administration, in 1977. (We can confidently predict a vigorous policy of nonenforcement thanks to Ronald Reagan.)

The uranium ore known as yellowcake is combined with fluorine and converted to uranium hexafluoride gas at plants operated by the Kerr-McGee Corporation, at Sequoyah, Okla., and by Allied Chemical, at Metropolis, Ill. The gas is then trucked in 14-ton cylinders to a gaseous diffusion plant of which the U.S. has three: Oak Ridge, Tenn.; Paducah, Ky., and Piketon, Ohio. Union Carbide

---

°It is noteworthy that before uranium mining, lung cancer was essentially unknown among the Navaho and other Indians of this region.

runs the first two, and Goodyear Atomic Corporation operates the Piketon plant. Gaseous diffusion is an immensely expensive process—the three plants cost $13 billion to build, and they use enormous amounts of electricity: about 3 percent of all the electricity consumed in the entire country!

Since $U_{235}$ (the easily fissionable isotope of uranium) occurs naturally as only about three-fourths of 1 percent of natural uranium ore, it must be concentrated for use in either reactors or bombs. Typically, the Paducah plant enriches the $U_{235}$ up to about 2 percent—in the process, using more electricity than all of Kentucky's remaining industries combined. The uranium is then shipped to Oak Ridge, for enrichment up to 3 or 4 percent, for use in power reactors, or to Piketon, for enrichment up to 90–97 percent, for bombs. Cancer rates appear to be high, especially at the Piketon plant, and there have been numerous strikes by the Oil, Chemical and Atomic Workers Union. However, the Department of Energy, which has sole authority here (as at other nuclear weapons facilities) has refused to permit independent investigations of health and safety conditions.

There are other important links in the complex nuclear network. For example, two factories in Ohio reprocess low-enriched and "depleted" uranium from the enrichment plants. These factories are at Fernald (near Cincinnati), operated by National Lead of Ohio, and at Ashtabula (on Lake Erie), operated by Reactive Metals, Inc. These plants reprocess the uranium into pipe-like metal pieces called "slugs," which are shipped to Hanford, Wash., or to Savannah River, S.C. At Hanford, sprawling across 570 sq. miles along the Columbia River in eastern Washington, uranium is made into plutonium. United Nuclear and Rockwell International are the major private contractors here. The Savannah River plant, operated by Du Pont, also manufactures plutonium which, along with Hanford plutonium, is shipped to Rocky Flats, Colo., where the plutonium "triggers" for H-bombs are built. In addition, the Savannah River plant has sole responsibility for manufacturing the two isotopes of hydrogen—tritium and the so-called "heavy water" deuterium—for use in hydrogen bombs. The deuterium is then shipped to Oak Ridge, Tenn., where it is combined with the metal lithium to make lithium deuteride, a white powder, pressed into aspirin-like tablets and ready to provide the major hydrogen fuel of hydrogen bombs. Thin sheets of uranium are also carefully machined at Oak Ridge, providing the $U_{238}$ casing for each bomb.

Thus, building hydrogen bombs is not a trivial enterprise, and many different corporations have their fingers in the radioactive pie, as the various ingredients are shipped from place to place throughout the country, mined, combined, and refined according to a complex recipe. Serious questions have been raised—but never satisfactorily answered—regarding the public health risks at nearly every stage of the manufacturing process, since the materials are highly toxic, aside from their even more lethal potential as bombs.

✿ ✿ ✿

So much for the cross we all bear, and for those few who profit from it. Next, we shall briefly review efforts to lighten that load— the confusing, disappointing, occasionally helpful, and often contradictory record of negotiated arms control agreements.

# 12. Jaw, Jaw, Jaw:

## A Quick Review of Negotiated Agreements

What would you think about a meeting of a town council which is concerned because an increasing number of people are knifed to death each night in drunken brawls, and which proceeds to discuss just how long and how sharp shall be the knife that the inhabitants of the city may be permitted to carry?

> —ALBERT EINSTEIN, when asked his opinion of the Geneva disarmament conference, 1926

For the first time in a quarter of a century of working with the problems of the arms race and arms control, I am beginning to get scared.

> —WILLIAM EPSTEIN (1976)

Arms control agreements are easy to make—we have negotiated many of them. Mark Twain once commented similarly that it was easy to stop smoking—he had done it hundreds of times! The fact is, if we survey the nuclear weapons agreements of the past twenty years or so, we find a long but unimpressive list. We also find that we and the U.S.S.R. are more threatened, less secure and more grossly overarmed than ever before. This is partly because negotiated agreements are themselves two-edged swords, often carrying drawbacks as well as benefits. But it is also because the forces leading to military build-up and to war have, quite simply, been stronger than those leading to arms control, disarmament, and peace. Let us look at what has been done.

### The Fiasco of 1955

Ever since the failure of the Baruch Plan, both the U.S. and the U.S.S.R. have been floating various peace proposals, with the Soviets emphasizing "general and complete disarmament" but balking at detailed inspections, and the U.S. holding out for more restricted, system-by-system controls. The cynical observer might have concluded that neither side expected or even wanted the other to accept its proposals. Then, in 1955, an incident occurred which can only reinforce this view. Understandably, it received very little attention in the U.S., and even now is barely mentioned in reviews of arms control negotiations. On May 10, 1955, the Soviet Union made certain proposals to the U.N. Disarmament Subcommittee: manpower ceilings of 1.5 million; reductions in conventional arms; the abolition of three-fourths of all nuclear weapons; and an international control system with inspectors having complete access to all objects of control. It was almost exactly what the U.S. had been requesting.

The French delegate blurted out that this Soviet acceptance was "too good to be true." The British delegate commented "the Western proposals have now been largely and in some cases entirely, adopted by the Soviet Union and made into its own proposals." According to the U.S. delegate, "We have been gratified to find that the concepts we have put forward over a considerable length of time, and which we have repeated many times during this past two months, have been accepted in a large measure by the Soviet Union." But of course, no agreement was reached. On September 6, 1955, the U.S. delegate did a complete 180-degree turn and announced: "The United States does now place a reservation upon all of its pre-Geneva substantive positions taken in this Subcommittee or in the Disarmament Commission or in the UN on these questions in relations to levels of armaments." What had happened? Just this: the U.S.S.R. had accepted our disarmament offers, whereupon after hurried top-level consultations, we withdrew them! We had never expected them to accept, and were totally surprised when they did. This little episode did not enhance the credibility of disarmament efforts. If nothing else, it emphasizes that one must distinguish between *offers* to negotiate and any real desire to do so.

### The Limited Test-Ban

On August 5, 1963, the U.S. and U.S.S.R. signed the "Treaty Banning Nuclear Weapons Tests in the Atmosphere, in Outer

Space and Under Water," generally known as the Limited or Partial Test-Ban. It capped years of petitioning, demonstrations, and widespread lobbying about the worldwide radioactive contamination from atmospheric nuclear tests.

John F. Kennedy had assumed the presidency in 1961 determined to build up the U.S. military posture, even after the missile gap which helped elect him was revealed to be nonexistent. Following the Cuban missile crisis, however, there followed a period of reappraisal and worry, not only about the dangers of nuclear war—which had so narrowly been averted—but also the dangers of preparing for war, especially atmospheric testing. With the aid of GRIT, an agreement was finally reached. The limited test-ban was certainly a good thing, but unfortunately, there is a cloud or two surrounding even this well-known silver lining.

Because of the test-ban, radioactive pollution has been greatly reduced. Strontium-90, for example, is not nearly the danger that it used to be, and many thousands—perhaps millions—of cancers and genetic defects have been forestalled. In addition, the treaty established that the U.S. and the U.S.S.R. can reach important agreements, and that both sides can abide by them. The psychological power of this fact, and the value of establishing precedents of this sort, should never be forgotten.

In addition, the test-ban increases world security, paradoxically, by keeping both sides equally in the dark about some important information. Thus, uncertainty about some aspects of nuclear weapons is a major protection for us all, especially when scenarios for first-strike, counterforce attacks are developed. For example, uncertainty about EMP makes each side less willing to chance an initial attack. Similarly, uncertainty about the actual effectiveness of silo "hardening" against an attack by the opponent makes each more wary about whether, in fact, its missiles could destroy the other's missiles in a surprise attack. And as long as these answers are unclear, "worst-case" analyses by conservative military planners on both sides should give us a degree of safety. Finally, a successful counterforce attack would require firing two missiles at each silo; at present, there is uncertainty about the "fratricide" effect—that is, how one explosion would interfere with the accuracy of a second, incoming missile. There may be some optimum spacing between explosions, but unless both sides begin atmospheric testing again, no one will know. For this we should be grateful: as long as the atmospheric test ban treaty is observed, many things about nuclear war remain shrouded in doubt. For all of us, the more doubt the better.

That is the good news. Now the bad news.

The limited test-ban treaty did not halt the nuclear arms race; it simply moved underground. There have actually been more tests, not fewer, after the treaty than there were before it. During the period 1945 to 1963 there were 488 tests on both sides; from 1963 to 1979, with the treaty in effect, there were 733. We have averaged about 35 per year, and the Soviets about 10. Moreover, in return for their approval of the treaty, President Kennedy had to promise the Joint Chiefs of Staff that he would vigorously pursue military options not precluded by the treaty. In particular, JFK agreed to "the conduct of comprehensive, aggressive and continuing underground nuclear test programs designed to add to our knowledge and improve our weapons in all areas of significance to our military posture for the future." As we shall see, this is a continuing problem: as a carrot in return for military support, arms control agreements typically must include a guarantee to pursue other military avenues, some of which turn out to be worse than whatever is foresworn by the treaty itself. As George Rathjens has pointed out, arms control agreements are often like squeezing a balloon: push it in someplace and it pops out somewhere else.

Finally, and most seriously, the limited test-ban treaty gave most Americans the impression that the problem of nuclear weapons had somehow been "solved." Indeed, the problem of *fallout* had largely been solved, but the much greater problem—nuclear war—had scarcely been touched. Nonetheless, attention shifted to the civil rights movement and the war in Vietnam, while, the arms race went on, more strongly than ever: new and more accurate missiles, communication and control systems, and a testing and building problem that made or recycled from three to ten nuclear warheads per day. The problem had not gone away, only our worry about it. In a sense, then, the limited test-ban treaty was an opiate that dulled our senses, anesthetizing the outrage that all America should have felt.

## SALT I

The groundwork for SALT—Strategic Arms Limitation Talks— was laid during the Johnson administration. Initial overtures were rebuffed, however, largely because the U.S. enjoyed such an enormous lead in both missiles and warheads that any agreement seemed likely to freeze the Soviet Union in a permanently inferior position. By the end of the 1960s, however, even though the U.S. still had an enormous lead in warheads and in weapons technology, the U.S.S.R. had caught up sufficiently in gross number of missiles for meaningful discussions to take place. The Soviet invasion of Czechoslovakia, in August 1968, came one day after the opening of the SALT I negotiations had been set, and this delayed things by more than a year. Then at last, in November 1969, negotiations began in Helsinki under the Nixon administration, and were concluded with the signing of SALT I on May 26, 1972.

SALT I was actually two parts, a treaty and an "Interim Agreement." The treaty was the ABM Treaty, which limited ABM systems to two sites in each country, with no more than 100 ABMs at each. Two years later, on July 3, 1974, President Ford and President Brezhnev agreed to a "protocol" amending the 1972 ABM treaty by limiting ABM systems to one site with 100 ABMs in each country.

The "Interim Agreement Limiting Strategic Arms" set limits on the number of ICBMs and submarine-launched ballistic missiles (SLBMs) for each side. The U.S. was permitted 1,054 ICBMs; the U.S.S.R. 1,408. The U.S. was permitted 656 SLBMs; the U.S.S.R. 950. To some, these numbers seemed unfair. "They" were allowed to have more missiles than "we," and everyone knows that more is better. After all, no self-respecting child will permit his opponent to have more marbles. Consistent with this mature attitude, Senator Henry Jackson insisted upon an amendment, declaring that henceforth, the government would not agree to any arms limitation pact that gave the U.S. fewer of anything than its opponent.

In fact, at the time of SALT I, the U.S. had no plans for additional missiles, although the Soviet Union did. But we could—and did—MIRV those we had. We had about 4,000 strategic warheads and the Soviets about 1,300. Forgotten by SALT critics were the following additional U.S. advantages:

1. MIRVing was unaffected by the agreement; the U.S. began MIRVing in 1970—the U.S.S.R. not until 1975.

2. The U.S. had nearly a 3:1 lead in strategic bombers, and moreover, our B-52s were—and still are—technologically far superior to the Soviet Bear and Bison counterparts.

3. Because of U.S. foreign submarine bases, and superior maintenance and operational capabilities, nearly four times as many U.S. submarines are on constant launch-ready status as their Soviet counterparts, so that the apparent Soviet SLBM lead is actually a substantial lead in our favor.

4. Nuclear weapons in the hands of Britain and France were not counted against the U.S. total in SALT I; yet these weapons are clearly aimed at the U.S.S.R., not at us.

5. The U.S.S.R. had granted another major concession in the definition of "strategic" weapons. Thus the Soviets had argued that strategic weapons be considered as anything capable of hitting the other's territory—accordingly, this would include carrier-based aircraft (of which we have a virtual monopoly) as well as forward-based systems in Europe, all of which can reach the U.S.S.R., and for which the Russians have no counterpart capable of reaching the U.S. The U.S., on the other hand, argued that strategic weapons be defined only as ICBMs and SLBMs. We won.

The SALT I agreement also regulated the replacement of old ICBMs and SLBMs, and prohibited the substitution of new heavy ICBMs (a Soviet specialty) for lighter models then in existence. The Interim Agreement was for five years. Hence, it lapsed in May 1977, although by mutual understanding both sides continued to abide by its terms. Also implicit in SALT I was the agreement that too much secrecy can only impede arms control, and so "national technical means" of verification—that is, spy satellites— were deemed acceptable. The most important and potentially lasting legacy of SALT I, however, was the ABM Treaty, which saved both sides billions in further arms development. Although it did not make things better, at least the ABM Treaty has kept things from getting worse. It curtailed new competition for ABM development and for certain offensive "penetration aids."

## SALT II

Negotiations for SALT II began in November 1972. Two years later, a breakthrough was announced at the meeting between Presidents Ford and Brezhnev, at Vladivostock. The U.S.S.R. agreed, once again, to exclude American "forward-based" systems in Europe from the grand total of allowable strategic weapons. Both sides agreed to a limit in the number of strategic delivery vehicles (ICBMs, SLBMs and bombers), with each side free to reach the total by mixing as it wished among these three types—sort of a Chinese restaurant style of arms limitation, with choices from three columns. Many details remained to be ironed out, however.

Following Jimmy Carter's election victory, Secretary of State Cyrus Vance and chief SALT negotiator Paul Warnke brought a new proposal to Moscow. This "comprehensive proposal" was rejected vehemently by the Soviets. Their response is regrettable, but not at all surprising. Thus, the U.S. proposal had called for heavy cuts in land-based ICBMs—an area of particular Soviet strength—but no equivalent offer of cuts in areas where the U.S. had a lead: number of warheads, MIRV technology, cruise missiles. Specifically, the Carter/Vance/Warnke offer had called for a reduction in heavy ICBMs from 308 to 150 (only the Soviet Union has heavy ICBMs of this sort!) and a limit of 550 MIRVed ICBMs (conveniently, the number we had at the time!). It also banned cruise missiles of range greater than 1,550 miles (the U.S.S.R. had been arguing for a ban on such missiles with a range of greater than 375 miles). There were, in addition, some very useful limits on flight testing and modernization. If accepted, this offer would have stopped the MX missile and the deployment of Mark 12-A warheads, as well as the MIRVing of Soviet SS-17, SS-18 and SS-19 missiles. But it was not. It is important to emphasize that their response does not necessarily indicate gross Soviet intransigence;

after all, these proposals were heavily weighted in our favor. Unfortunately, this little episode fueled the American image of the U.S.S.R. as stubborn, untrustworthy and not really interested in arms control. It was also used by candidate Reagan as evidence that the Carter administration had not been "tough enough" with the Russians.

Finally, a SALT II agreement was nonetheless signed by Presidents Carter and Brezhnev, on June 18, 1979. However, because of vigorous lobbying by the "Committee on the Present Danger," various public relations blunders, the Soviet invasion of Afghanistan, and the pre-election distrust of the Russians (fueled by the Democrats' fear of Ronald Reagan), SALT II was withdrawn from Senate consideration and is now dead. It was a complex document, unnecessary to review in detail here. However, it is useful to consider its basic terms, to see the kind of agreements that can be reached. Our intent is not to beat a dead horse; just to learn how far it might have carried us.

Basically, SALT II formalized the agreements made five years earlier at Vladivostock. Each side was allowed 2,400 strategic delivery vehicles: ICBMs, SLBMs, and bombers. Their ceiling was to be lowered to 2,250 by December 31, 1981, with additional "subceilings": no more than a total of 1,320 MIRVed systems, and no more than 820 MIRVed ICBMs. Limits were also placed on the number of MIRVed warheads for each type of missile, on the total throw-weight allowed per missile, on testing or deployment of new ICBMs, on the number of Soviet heavy ICBMs, and on the number of long-range cruise missiles permitted to a bomber. It was also agreed that the Soviet Backfire bomber would not be outfitted for intercontinental ranges, and it permitted development and deployment of long-range cruise missiles (although the Soviets have none). Finally, SALT II prohibited any interference by one nation in the verification systems of the other.

We are now left without SALT, however, and in desperate need of a SALT substitute. The Reagan Administration has finally begun a new round of talks, dubbed START: Strategic Arms Reduction Talks. The auguries, however, are not promising. Thus, the chief negotiator is General Edward Rowny, retired from the U.S. Army. General Rowny was for years a military representative at the SALT negotiations, and much of the difficulty in reaching an agreement can, in fact, be laid at his door, testimony to his unflagging opposition and suspicion—both of the U.S.S.R. and of the whole negotiating process. Once the agreement was signed, General Rowny still did not give up; he resigned to campaign actively—and ultimately, successfully—for its defeat. In such hands a false START seems all too likely.

### Other Agreements

More than anything else, SALT has become a symbol of détente, although of course, it is more than a mere symbol. However, there have also been other agreements. Here is a brief list:

*The Non-Proliferation Treaty.* First proposed by Ireland in 1958, Sweden in 1961, and then India in 1962, the U.S. and U.S.S.R. saw merit in an agreement to halt the spread of nuclear weapons. The Non-Proliferation Treaty was signed in 1968 and ratified by the U.S. Senate in 1970. As NPT signers, the non-nuclear nations agree "not to receive . . . manufacture or otherwise acquire nuclear weapons or other nuclear explosive devices" (Article II). In return, the nuclear nations agree to provide advice and materials for peaceful nuclear technology (power and research), with safeguards to be administered by the International Atomic Energy Agency. In addition, the nuclear nations agree to "pursue negotiations in good faith on effective measures relating to cessation of the nuclear arms race at an early date and to nuclear disarmament and on a treaty on general and complete disarmament, under strict and effective international control" (Article VI).

The "non-proliferation regime" is critical to world security. Tragically, it is cracking at the seams. Many important nations are not signatories: Israel, France, Cuba, Argentina, Brazil, Pakistan, Spain, South Africa, China, and India. Moreover, IAEA safeguards are woefully inadequate. And perhaps most important, the U.S. and U.S.S.R. have clearly not lived up to their obligations under Article VI. As we stubbornly refuse even to limit (never mind to freeze or reduce) our own nuclear weapons, we make a mockery of non-proliferation efforts. Nuclear weapons, we seem to be saying, are good for us but bad for you. Without impressive controls on "vertical proliferation"—the piling of bomb upon bomb by the super-powers—we have little moral leverage in preventing "horizontal proliferation," the spreading of nuclear weapons to every tinhorn despot who wants them.

*The Treaty of Tlateloco* (1967). Named after a suburb of Mexico City, this treaty banned nuclear weapons in Latin America. Unfortunately, however, it has not yet been ratified by Brazil, Chile, or Argentina, the "Big Three" of South America, and has not even been signed by Cuba. Nevertheless, the formal establishment of "nuclear free zones" is an important idea, whose time may finally have come. Proposals have been made, and with increasing vehemence, for nuclear free zones in the Middle East, in Africa, and in southeast Asia. Advocacy of a European nuclear free zone, "from Poland to Portugal," has received growing attention from nearly all sides of the European political spectrum. Suggestions for a Scandinavian and a Balkan nuclear free zone seem especially feasible, and one of the best-known proposals still remains a possibility: the Rapacki Plan, first proposed in 1957, which would establish a nuclear free zone in central Europe, involving Poland, Czechoslovakia, East Germany, and West Germany. This plan has been consistently opposed by the NATO powers; with the growing antiwar sentiment in Europe, however, it's time may yet come.

*Conference on Security and Cooperation in Europe.* Agreed in 1975 and widely known as the "Helsinki accords," this called for each side warning the other of any military maneuvers of more than 25,000 troops, thereby avoiding misunderstanding. It also included declarations regarding human rights, freedom of travel and communication in Europe, and confirmation of the existing political boundaries.

*Mutual and Balanced Force Reduction* talks have been going on intermittently in Vienna since 1973, aimed at reducing military concentrations in central Europe. They have been notably unsuccessful, probably in part because the U.S.S.R. is not terribly interested in their success; thus the cold war in Europe permits them to garrison troops in Eastern Europe, the presence of which might otherwise be difficult to justify.

Other, lesser treaties have also been signed, including one banning nuclear weapons in outer space, on the ocean floor, in the Antarctic, and the Threshold Test-Ban Treaty, limiting underground tests to 150 kilotons.

### To Negotiate or Not To Negotiate?

*Some disadvantages of negotiating:*

Negotiations, even when they work, do not always make things better. Often, there are hidden costs to formal arms control treaties. For one thing, the negotiating process is typically slow, even ponderous, and often outrun by the newest developments in weapons. As a result, agreements are often out of date before the ink is even dry. It took seven years, for example, to reach an agreement on SALT II, during which time tremendous advances in MIRVs, MARVs, cruise missiles, and accuracy improvements also occurred.

Negotiations also proceed best when the two parties are symmetric; that is, when their strengths and weaknesses are equivalent. Although the U.S. and U.S.S.R. are, in fact, *roughly* equal in overall strength, they differ strikingly in details. Thus, for example, the U.S. has major nuclear allies in France and Great Britain; the U.S.S.R. has none. As a result, the Soviets characteristically argue that British and French forces should be counted against the U.S. tally, while the U.S. disagrees. In addition, the U.S. military style emphasizes innovations—we have always been at the cutting edge of the newest in weapons and delivery systems. The Soviets, by contrast, make up for their lack of innovation by the production of large numbers. Hence, the U.S.S.R. tends to argue for restrictions in new technology, whereas the U.S. typically argues for numerical ceilings combined with unrestricted opportunity for further weapons development and testing. In general, we develop something new—MIRVing, cruise missiles, the atomic bomb itself—and then we seek to prohibit it to the Soviets.

The decision to proceed with a new escalation of the arms race is taken unilaterally. By contrast, the decision to control or eliminate weapons must be taken *bilaterally*, and this is necessarily much more difficult to achieve. As a result, each side builds additional weapons much more readily than both can agree to control or reduce what they already have. The direction, then, is toward accumulation, like traffic on a one way street.

But these are really obstacles to agreements, not disadvantages of the agreements themselves, once they have been reached. And unfortunately, the negotiating process often carries some serious disadvantages as well. For one, arms control agreements typically set "ceilings" that are above those achieved at the time. These allowable ceilings then become production goals to be reached. For example, the Vladivostock accords, desirable as they were, allowed an increase of 1,808 MIRVed missiles, a 217 percent increase over levels at that time. In this way, such agreements can actually stimulate the arms race; only rarely do they inhibit it. In fact, we do not know of any case in which a weapons system that either side wanted was prohibited by a treaty. (The most successful agreement to date, the ABM Treaty, restricted a system only after both sides acknowledged that it didn't work and they didn't want it!) It is relatively easy to agree on banning something that no one wants anyhow: nuclear weapons in outer space, the Antarctic or the ocean floor, but virtually impossible to ban—or even restrict—such things as MIRVs or cruise missiles, which one side or the other really wants.

When, as often happens, two sides approach the bargaining table with different strengths, several outcomes are possible: they can settle for the lower of the two levels, they can choose some compromise between them, or they can choose a new, and lower level for both. (The last is almost unheard of.) All these options require that one side (or both) destroy some of their weapons, and the military and hardline advisors on the affected side(s) nearly always argue strenuously against this. What often happens, therefore, is that a fourth alternative is chosen: rather than the high side reduce its armaments, the low side is typically permitted to increase its. Most often, *both sides* are permitted to increase. The result may therefore be a mockery of arms control, made ever worse by the fact that the called-for increases are legitimized by the negotiating process. In such cases, negotiations do nothing to halt the arms race; rather, they provide guidelines, structure and a sense of legitimacy, while abetting the arms race, and sometimes even fanning it to a greater pace.

There are two other problems, about equally serious: 1) bargaining chips, ostensibly for use with the opponent, and 2) weapons payoffs, for the military at home. Many weapons have been justified as "bargaining chips," that is, things that are supposedly needed so that we will have something to bargain away during the negotiations. Indeed, this became the sole argument for the ABM, eventually bargained away in SALT I. Our admittedly useless ABMs cost nearly $6 billion, although one might argue that since they purchased a guarantee not to compete further in this arena, it actually was a bargain! Unfortunately, however, bargaining chips are useful only if they are truly desirable to the nation's military—and if they *are* truly desirable, then the military has a hard time agreeing to their elimination. As a new system originally justified as a bargaining chip reaches advanced development, it becomes less negotiable. We grow fond of it. Thousands of officers and a large group of contractors, sub-contractors and their congressional patrons begin pressing for the system, and as momentum for deployment increases, the former bargaining chip becomes "essential to our national security" and no longer a bargaining chip at all. Then, we are stuck with it, and the arms race has moved up one more notch. Early in the 1970s, the B-1 bomber and the Trident submarine were both justified as bargaining chips for the (then forthcoming) SALT II negotiations. Now, in the early 1980s, we have no SALT II, but we seem destined to have both the B-1 and the Trident!

Weapons payoffs for the military at home are essentially bargaining chips as well, but intended for distribution to domestic political forces, in return for their support. Since a two-thirds vote of the Senate is required for ratification of any foreign treaty, this means that one-third of the Senate (plus one) can insist on substantial weapons payoffs, or else no treaty. In short, treaties can be held hostage to the demands of a hawkish minority. Thus, as we have seen, in return for the partial test-ban treaty, JFK had to promise the Joint Chiefs of Staff that we would increase our underground testing and other weapons development programs. In return for hawkish support of SALT I, President Nixon had to promise vigorous exploitation of all weapons systems not explicitly prohibited by that treaty—notably cruise missiles and prompt MIRVing of

ICBMs and SLBMs. In return for hawkish support for SALT II, President Carter offered up the MX missile, with its bizarre shell-game basing scheme; now, in the 1980s and with SALT II dead and buried, we may nonetheless be stuck with the MX, in one ridiculous basing scheme or another.

In view of all this, even the most informed and dedicated opponent of nuclear war may have some reservations about arms control agreements.

## The Advantages of Negotiating

But we have little choice. Negotiated agreements are rarely perfect, and sometimes they are downright troublesome. However, they do offer real hope, especially if the pitfalls of negotiating can be recognized and avoided. Thus, all too often, negotiated arms agreements seem like deals between the military on each side, with the respective governments mere intermediaries or figureheads. This must change. Because of their expertise, military advisers deserve a prominent role in arms negotiations. But we must realize that they are hardly disinterested observers. Letting the military decide on military treaties is like letting the criminals decide on the enforcement of criminal law. Rather, let us learn from them, listen to them, but then do what is right for the country, not for their narrow constituencies.

Aside from the prospect of restricting and ultimately reducing weapons, arms negotiations are important as indications of peaceful intent, as statements of both sides' commitment to peaceful resolution of their differences. Or more accurately, negotiated settlements show mutual agreement to avoid war and the escalation to war. One of the important, and often unappreciated, advantages of negotiations is that they bring about dialogue and can prevent misunderstanding. Thus, for example, one of the most useful things to come out of the SALT I agreement was the establishment of a Standing Consultative Commission, with representatives from both the U.S. and U.S.S.R. The SCC serves as a forum in which suspected treaty violations are discussed and in the process, valuable information is exchanged.

Furthermore, the possibility of meaningful reductions via negotiations should never be ruled out. For example, both sides would profit by restricting the forthcoming generation of potential first-strike weaponry. The basic adage, "I won't do it if you won't" could easily apply to improvements in missile accuracy, which convey first-strike, silo-busting capacity, and which, as we have seen, would be dangerously destabilizing. Nonetheless, given the bureaucratic and political pressures within each country, it is difficult (but not impossible!) for either side to renounce such developments unilaterally. By mutual agreement, then, both sides can agree to do what each wants to do separately, but which might be politically awkward without a formal commitment of reciprocity from the other side.

In his Farewell Address, President Dwight Eisenhower said it best:

> The conference table, though scarred by many past frustrations, cannot be abandoned for the certain agony of the battlefield. Disarmament, with mutual honor and confidence, is a continuing imperative. Together we must learn how to compose differences, not with arms but with intellect and decent purpose.

Lasting peace cannot be built on a perpetual arms race. It's that simple. There are numerous measures for arms control and reduction by which both sides would come out ahead. Thus, nuclear disarmament is not what mathematicians call a "zero sum game," a situation in which the total profit remains fixed, so that as one side benefits, the other side loses. Rather, both sides can gain. There is nothing that we all need more than to reduce the threat of war and eventually, to achieve nuclear disarmament.

Finally, there are myriad possibilities for effective enforcement, verification and sanctions in the event of treaty violations. The crucial problems, however, lie not in this arena but in the social, economic, and political will to make such agreements in the first place. In fact, the ultimate guarantor of international treaties is the mutual self-interest of the nations involved, dictating adherence to the negotiated agreement. And we all have no more basic self-interest than survival. Out of our great need, then, comes our greatest hope—that from our mutual peril, mutually recognized, there will come a mutual commitment to a safe future.

As Bernard Baruch put it in 1946, we have a "choice between the quick and the dead." He went on:

> Behind the black portent of the new atomic age lies a hope which seized upon with faith, can work out salvation. If we fail, then we have damned every man to be the slave of fear. Let us not deceive ourselves: we must elect world peace or world destruction.

# 13. Some Conclusions to Live By

1. Nuclear weapons are wholly evil. They are medically, socially, biologically, morally, politically, and even militarily unacceptable; ultimately, they must be eliminated from the earth.

2. The first step should be a joint U.S.–Soviet freeze on the testing, production and deployment of nuclear weapons and their delivery systems, followed by negotiated reductions.

3. Nuclear war cannot be limited or won. Its consequences are death, death, and more death.

4. "Civil defense" is neither civil nor defense. It should be opposed.

5. Possessing more, or more accurate, nuclear weapons does not make a country more secure; rather, it increases the danger of nuclear war.

6. The U.S. has never been "behind" the U.S.S.R., and is not now.

7. Although the risk of nuclear war is high, it is a man-made problem, with man and woman-made solutions. It is *not* inevitable.

8. The movement to stop nuclear war should celebrate life, bringing people together in love, joy, hope, and nurturance.

9. Each of us has a profound moral obligation to help stop nuclear war.

10. Every person counts. We must work together to stop nuclear war.

# Appendix A

## Organizations to Join

There are many fine organizations, most of them with national subscription. Join several. The cost is usually low ($5 to $25 per year) and membership typically includes some sort of regular newsletter. By joining a good organization, you strengthen yourself by the information you receive; you also strengthen the organization, not only by the money they receive, but also because your membership adds to their political clout. Here is a list of some of the major ones; don't be overwhelmed by the number—they are positive resources, a buffet of goodies from which you can pick, choose, and feast.

*Scientists:*

Union of Concerned Scientists
1384 Mass. Av
Cambridge, Mass. 02138

Federation of American Scientists
307 Mass. Ave. NE
Washington, D.C. 20002

*Physicians and Health Care Professionals:*

Physicians for Social Responsibility
639 Mass. Avenue
Cambridge, Mass. 02139

International Physicians for the
   Prevention of Nuclear War
635 Huntington Avenue
Boston, Mass. 02115

Following the lead of the scientists and physicians, numerous other professional groups have begun springing up, most of them in the Boston area. Here is a partial list; write to them for more information, and to find out about starting a local chapter in your own community:

Artists for Survival
144 Moody Street
Waltham, Mass. 02154

Arts Alive!/Poets Against The End
   Of the World
490 Riverside Drive
New York, N.Y. 10027

Business Alert to Nuclear War
Box 7
Belmont, Mass. 02178

Children's Campaign for Nuclear
 Disarmament
Box 550
Plainfield, Vt. 0560 ¿

Communicators for Nuclear
 Disarmament
44 Hunt Street
Watertown, Mass. 02172

Educators for Social Responsibility
Box 1041
Brookline Village, Mass. 02147

Union of Concerned Educators
4534½ University Way, NE
Seattle, Wash. 98105

High-Technology Professionals
 for Peace
52 Walker Street
Newtonville, Mass. 02160

Lawyers' Alliance for Nuclear
 Arms Control
P. O. Box 9171
Boston, Mass. 02114

Musicians Against Nuclear Arms
57 Francis Avenue
Cambridge, Mass. 02138

Nurses' Alliance for the
 Prevention of Nuclear War
P. O. Box 319
Chestnut Hill, Mass. 02167

Performing Artists for
Nuclear Disarmament
P. O. Box 775, Cooper Station
New York, N.Y. 10276

United Campuses to Prevent Nuclear War
1346 Connecticut Ave., NW
Washington, D.C. 20036

*Antiwar and Pacifist Groups:*

War Resisters League
339 Lafayette Street
New York, N.Y. 10012

War Resisters League
85 Carl Street
San Francisco, Calif. 94117

Women's International League
 for Peace and Freedom
1213 Face Street
Philadelphia, Pa. 19167

Women Strike for Peace
145 South 13th St.
Philadelphia, Pa. 19107

American Friends Service Committee (AFSC)
1501 Cherry Street
Philadelphia, Pa. 19102

The AFSC won the Nobel Peace Prize in 1947. It has a longstanding and ongoing Disarmament Program, with abundant resources and an experienced staff. Although a Quaker group, its peace activities are nondenominational and open to all. Here are some regional offices:

AFSC
317 East 25th Street
Baltimore, Md. 21218

AFSC
92 Piedmont Avenue NE
Atlanta, Ga. 30303

AFSC
2161 Massachusetts Avenue
Cambridge, Mass. 02140

AFSC
15 Rutherford Place
New York, N. Y. 10003

AFSC
407 South Dearborn Street
Chicago, Il. 60605

AFSC
980 North Fair Oaks Avenue
Pasadena, Calif. 91103

AFSC
4211 Grand Avenue
Des Moines, Iowa 50312

AFSC
2160 Lake Street
San Francisco, Calif. 94121

AFSC
915 Salem Avenue
Dayton, Ohio 45406

AFSC
814 N.E. 40th Street
Seattle, Wash. 98105

AFSC
1022 West 6th Street
Austin, Tex. 78703

*Educational groups emphasizing military policy and disarmament:*

Arms Control Association
11 Dupont Circle NW
Washington, D.C. 20036

Council for a Livable World
11 Beacon Street
Boston, Mass. 02108

Coalition for a New Foreign
and Military Policy
120 Maryland Avenue, NE
Washington, D.C. 20002

Institute for Defense and
Disarmament Studies
251 Harvard St.
Brookline, Mass. 92146
(publishes "The American Peace
Directory," with names of most
local and national peace groups)

Center for Defense Information
122 Maryland Ave. NE
Washington, D.C. 20002

Ground Zero
506 15th St. NW
Washington, D.C. 20005

*Groups emphasizing global connectedness:*

Fund for Peace
1995 Broadway
New York, N.Y. 10023

World Federalists Association
1011 Arlington Blvd.
Arlington, Va. 22209

World Service Authority
National Press Bldg., Suite 440
529 14th St, NW
Washington, D.C. 20024

United Nations Association
300 East 42nd St.
New York, N.Y. 10017

The Committee on East-West Accord
227 Mass. Ave. NE
Washington, D.C. 20002

U.S. Peace Council
7 East 15th Street
New York, N.Y. 10003

*Antinuclear groups with information about nearest local contacts:*

Mobilization for Survival
3601 Locust Walk
Philadelphia, Pa. 19164

Nuclear Information and Resource
Center
1536 16th St. NW
Washington, D.C. 20036

*National groups emphasizing economic conversion:*

SANE
514 C Street NE
Washington, D. C. 20002

Council on Economic Priorities
84 Fifth Ave.
New York, N.Y. 10011

WILPF Nuclear Network
255 Grove Street
White Plains, N.Y. 10601

Plowshares Press
867 West Dana, #203
Mountainview, Calif. 94041

Employment Research Associates
105 East Washtenaw
Lansing, Mich. 48933

Interfaith Center on Corporate
Responsibility
475 Riverside Drive
New York, N.Y. 10027

Trade Union Committee for the
Transfer Amendment and
Economic Conversion
c/o Labor Research Associates
80 East 11th St.
New York, N.Y. 10003

Public Relations Department
International Association of
Machinists and Aerospace Workers
1300 Conn. Ave. NW
Washington, D.C. 20036

*Groups active in converting weapons, research, design, manufacturing and reprocessing plants:*

*National:*

American Friends Service
Committee/Nuclear Weapons Facilities
Project
1660 Lafayette Street, Suite D
Denver, Colo. 80218

Fellowship of Reconciliation/Nuclear
Weapons Facilities Project
Box 271
Nyack, N. Y. 10960

*Regional:*

*Livermore Lab*
University of California Nuclear
Weapons
Labs Conversion Project
944 Market Street
San Francisco, Calif. 94102

*Kansas City Plant*
Bendix Conversion Project
811 East 47th Street
Kansas City, Mo. 64110

Mid-Peninsula Conversion Project
867 W. Data #203
Mountain View, Calif. 94041

*Mound Laboratory*
Monsanto Conversion Project/
American Friends Service Committee
915 Salem Avenue
Dayton, Ohio 45406

*Canoga Park*
Bridge the Gap
10915 Strathmore Drive
Los Angeles, Calif. 90024

*Pinellas Plant*
Pinellas Conversion Project
242 10th Avenue NE
St. Petersburg, Fla. 33701

*Hanford*
Hanford Conversion Project/CALC
1414 Kincaid
Eugene, Ore. 97401

*Savannah River Plant*
Palmetto Alliance
2135 ½ Divine Street
Columbia, S. Carolina 29205

*Idaho National Engineering Lab*
Snake River Alliance
P.O. Box 1731
Boise, Idaho 83701

Savannah River Project
630 Shell Street
West Columbia, S. Carolina 29169

Nuclear Counterbalance
P.O. Box 100
Pocatello, Idaho 83201

Grass Roots Organizing Workshop
18 Bluff Road
Columbia, S. Carolina 29201

*Rocky Flats*
American Friends Service
Committee/Rocky Flats Project
1660 Lafayette Street, Suite D
Denver, Colo. 80281

*Los Alamos and Sandia Labs*
New Mexico Peace Conversion Project
2405 Meadow Road SW
Albuquerque, New Mex. 87105

Rocky Flats Coalition
1315 Broadway #1
Boulder, Colo. 80302

*Pantex*
Panhandle Environmental Awareness
Committee
1008 South Madison
Amarillo, Tex. 79101

Solidarity Peace Fund
Diocesan Pastoral Center
Box 5644
Amarillo, Tex. 79107

*Groups concerned with military bases:*

Seal Beach Naval Affinity Group
P.O. Box 14402
Long Beach, Calif. 90814

Concord Naval Weapons Station Group
65 Eckley Lane
Walnut Creek, Calif. 94598

Omaha Pax Christi
2104 Davenport Street
Omaha, Neb. 68102

Nebraskans for Peace
420 South 16th Street
Lincoln, Neb. 68508

Ella McDonald
9 Diane Drive
Little Rock, Ark. 72205

*Groups concerned with specific weapons systems:*

*Trident*

Armistice
P.O. Box 12007
Seattle, Wash. 98102

Knolls Action Coalition
41 State Street, Room 505
Albany, N. Y. 12207

Dorothy Day Community
P.O. Box 1093
Norwich, Conn. 06360

Stop ELF Committee
RR2 Box 1660
Ashland, Wis. 54806

Ground Zero Center for
   Nonviolent Action
16159 Clear Creek Road NW
Poulsbo, Wash. 98370

*MX Missile*

MX Information Coalition
232 ½ University Street
Salt Lake City, Utah 84102

Orange County Peace Conversion
   Project
331 N. Olive Street
Orange, Calif. 92666

San Fernando Alliance for Survival
(also Canoga Park)
13615 Victory Blvd.
Van Nuys, Calif. 91401

Great Basin MX Alliance
P.O. Box 27
Baker, Nev. 89311

Rockwell/MX Conversion Project
125 West Third
Tulsa, Okla. 74103

Southern California CALC
P.O. Box 32305
Los Angeles, Calif. 90032

*Cruise Missile*

Cruise Control Project/American
Friends Service Committee
821 Euclid Avenue
Syracuse, N. Y. 13210
and
141 Chafee Avenue
Syracuse, N. Y. 13207

Pacific Life Community
331 17th East
Seattle, Wash. 90811

St. Louis Economic Conversion Project
(General Dynamics)
P.O. Box 1693
St. Louis, Mo. 63188

Trident Conversion Campaign/
American Friends Service Committee
RD 1, Box 494
Voluntown, Conn. 06384

Electric Boat Trade Unions for
Democratic Action
P.O. Box 294, Boro Station
Groton, Conn. 06340

People for a Nuclear Free Future
7915 Empire Grade
Santa Cruz, Calif. 95060
and
P.O. Box 2324
Santa Cruz, Calif. 95063

*Environmental groups with a particular antinuclear orientation:*

Friends of the Earth
530 7th Street SE
Washington, D.C. 20003

Greenpeace
Building E, Fort Mason
San Francisco, Calif. 94123

Natural Resources Defense Council
1725 I Street NW
Washington, D.C. 20002

*Groups especially opposed to nuclear testing and favoring a comprehensive test-ban:*

Downwinders
1321 East 400 South
Salt Lake City, Utah 84102
and
126 South 1400 West
Cedar City, Utah 84720

Sagebrush Alliance
704 West McWilliams Avenue
Las Vegas, Nev. 89105

National Association of
  Atomic Veterans
1109 Franklin Street
Burlington, Iowa 52601

National Committee for Radiation
  Victims
317 Pennsylvania Avenue SE
Washington, D.C. 20003

Nevada Test Site Radiation
Victims Association
P.O. Box 18414-192
Las Vegas, Nev. 89114

*The nuclear freeze campaign (national coordinator):*

Nuclear Weapons Freeze Campaign
National Clearinghouse
4144 Lindell Blvd.
St. Louis, Mo. 63108
(314) 533-1169

As we have seen, the freeze campaign is one of the most exciting and important developments in the new anti-nuclear war movement. The national clearinghouse, in Saint Louis, coordinates local activities. However, the real power of this movement lies in the local organizations. Following is a list of regional and statewide contacts, updated as of spring 1982:

ALABAMA

Judy/Jack Cumbee
Rte. 3 Box 490
Tuskegee, Ala. 36083
(205) 727-6922

Judy Hand
Soutnern Org. Comm.
7715 A 7th Ave. South
Birmingham, Ala. 35206
(205) 838-1056

Roslyn Snider
AFSC Disarmament Program
560 Dauphine St.
Mobile, Ala. 36602
(205) 438-1603

ALASKA

John Havelozk
2024 Esquire Dr.
Anchorage, Alaska 99503
(903) 263-1810

ARIZONA

Edwina Vogan
Nuclear-Free State
1145 East 6th St.
Tucson, Ariz. 85719
(602) 792-3517

Elaine G. Schwartz
Women's Party for Survival
5516 E. Rosewood
Tucson, Ariz. 85711

Michael Stock
Box 338 Lake Mary Rd.
Flagstaff, Ariz. 86001

CALIFORNIA

Harold Willens
Californians for a Bilateral Nuclear
  Weapons Freeze
7250 Franklin Ave.
Los Angeles, Calif. 90046
(213) 876-5971

Pam Nichols
Northern California
Nuclear Weapons Freeze
944 Market St. Rm 513
San Francisco, Calif. 94102
(414) 981-8423

Anne Sutherland
Interfaith Center to
Reverse the Arms Race
132 N. Euclid Ave.
Pasadena, Calif. 91101
(213) 449-9430

Maria Faer
Montclair Presb. Church
Freeze Task Force 270 Mountain Ave.
Piedmont, Calif. 94611

Jo Seidita
Sepulveda UUA Freeze
Ballot Initiative
9601 Corbin Ave.
Northridge, Calif 91324
(213) 886-4489

Chris Stowell
5102 Towle Ct.
San Diego, Calif. 92105
(714) 282-4726

Gary Comer
WILPF
5725 N. Maroa #218
Fresno, Calif. 93704
(209) 435-3048

Chris Summerville
1075 Olive Dr., #7
Davis, Calif. 95616

San Jose Peace Center
520 S. 10th St.
San Jose, Calif. 95112
(408) 297-2299

COLORADO

Helen Henry
Nuclear Weapons
Facilities TF/AFSC
1660 Lafayette St.
Denver, Colo. 80218
(303) 832-4508

John D. Minear, Chair.
Interfaith Concerns and
Action Committee
Box 387
Laporte, Colo. 80535
(303) 482-0151

Sr. Mary Luke Tobin
Loretto Disarmament
2832 So. Vrain St.
Denver, Colo. 80236
(303) 922-7141

Citizens Calling for a
Nuclear Arms Freeze
1520 Euclid
Boulder, Colo. 90302
(303) 443-3680

Poudre Nuclear Freeze Camp.
629 S. Howes Street
Fort Collins, Colo. 90521

Boulder County Freeze Campaign
P.O. Box 1992
Boulder, Colo. 80306
(303) 444-8921

Aspen Peace Fellowship
720 E. Hyman
Aspen, Colo. 81699
(303) 925-5953

Pike's Peak Justice and Peace
Commission
235 E. Fountain Blvd.
Colorado Springs, Colo. 80903
(303) 632-6189

## CONNECTICUT

Connecticut Coal. for a
Nuclear Arms Freeze
c/o AFSC
RD #1, Box 494
Voluntown, Conn. 06384
(203) 376-4098

Health Professionals to Prevent
Nuclear War
165 Alden Avenue
New Haven, Conn.
06515

Paul Hodel
Peace Ed. & Action Ctr.
64 Edgewood Ave.
New Haven, Conn. 06511
(203) 633-0120

Rox Spier
Nuclear Freeze Camp.
111 Whapley
Glastonbury, Conn. 06033
(203) 633-0120

## DELAWARE

Charles Zoeller
Pacem in Terris/AFSC
1106 Adams Street
Wilmington, Dela. 19801
(302) 656-2721

David Nuttal
P.O. Box 91
Wilmington, Dela. 19899
(302) 654-3068

## DISTRICT OF COLUMBIA

William J. Price
World Peacemakers
2852 Ontario Rd. NW
Washington, D.C. 20009
(202) 265-7582

Edith Villastrigo
Women Strike for Peace
201 Mass. Ave. NE #102
Washington, D.C. 20002
(202 546-7397

Mernie King
Sojourners
1309 U St. NW
Washington, D.C. 20005
(202)737-2525

Government Relations Task Force
National Nuclear Weapons Freeze
Campaign
100 Maryland Ave. NE
Washington, D.C. 20002
(202) 547-0254

Barry Israel
Clifford and Warnke
815 Connecticut Ave. NW
Washington, D.C. 20006
(202) 828-4263

D.C. Campaign for a Nuclear
Weapons Freeze
1169 Columbia Rd. NW
Washington, D.C. 20009
(202) 265-6136

**FLORDIA**

Ethel Felts
Coalition for Arms Limitation and
Survival
Box 931
Miami, Fla. 33133
(305) 856-6373

Bob Brister
AFSC Tampa Bay Program
130 19th St. SE
St. Petersburg, Fla. 33705
(813) 822-5522

Dave McLintock
Peace Fellowship of
North Florida
2257 Dellwood Ave.
Jacksonville, Fla. 32204
(904) 354-7355

Tallahassee Peace Coalition
P.O. Box 20168
Tallahassee, Fla. 32304
(904) 222-5845

Lillian Jaros
Coalition for Survival
5860 Midnight Pass Rd. #20
Sarasota, Fla. 33581
(813) 349-3983

The Community Alliance for
Peace Ed.
Box 180F
Gainesville, Fla. 32606
(904) 462-3201

**GEORGIA**

Chip Reynolds
AFSC Regional Office
92 Peidmont Ave. NE
Atlanta, Ga. 30303
(404) 586-0460

Mark Reeve
Clergy and Laity Concerned
222 East Lake Drive
Decatur, Ga. 30030

**HAWAII**

Mike Cervice
General Delivery
Captain Cook, Hawaii 96704

**IDAHO**

Michael Jones
Snake River Alliance
Box 1731
Boise, Idaho 83701
(208) 345-4675

ILLINOIS

Ill. Nuclear Weapons
Freeze Campaign
22 E. Van Buren 5th Fl.
Chicago, Ill. 60605

Robert Cleland
NOMOR
407 S. Dearborn St. #935
Chicago, Ill. 60605
(312) 663-1246

Glenview Nuclear Weapons
Freeze Campaign
1321 Sleepy Hollow Rd.
Glenview, Ill. 60025
(312) 724-8957

Rose Mary Meyer
8th Day Center for Justice
22 E. Van Buren
Chicago, Ill. 60605
(312) 427-4351

Robert Dodaro
Pax Christi
3000 N. Mango Ave
Chicago, Ill. 60634
(312) 637-2555

North Shore Peace Initiative
723 Seward St.
Evanston, Ill. 60202
(312) 475-3692

Champagne/Urbana Peace
Initiative
405 W. Illinois
Urbana, Ill. 61801
(217) 328-5222

Wilmette Freeze Campaign
530 Knox
Wilmette, Ill. 60091
(312) 251-0830

Illinois Council of Churches
615 S. 5th St.
Springfield, Ill. 62703
(217) 522-4415

INDIANA

Br. William Mewes, CSC
Social Justice Commission
Holy Cross Brothers Center
Notre Dame, Ind. 46556
(219) 233-8273

Shirley Whiteside
FOR
P.O. Box 25
No. Manchester, Ind. 46962
(219) 982-4277

Don Nead
Presbytery of Wabasho Val.
P.O. Box 3024, 320 North St.
West Lafayette, Ind. 47906
(317) 743-3861

Howard Alexander
Friends Coordinating
Committee on Peace
Friends United Meeting
101 Quaker Hill Dr.
Richmond, Ind. 47374
(317) 962-7573

Helen Kennedy
2750 Two Worlds Drive
Columbus, Ind. 47201
(812) 379-2076

IOWA

Iowa Freeze Campaign
4211 Grand Ave.
Des Moines, Iowa 50312
(515) 274-4851

Ron Nelson
History Dept.
Northwestern College
Orange City, Iowa 50051
(712) 737-4821

Sally McMillan
1825 Vogt
Burlington, Iowa 52601
(319) 753-1142, 754-4807

Freeze Iowa
RR3 Box 229
Marion, Iowa 52302
(319) 377-2456

Rev. Charles Pullen
Prospect Hill Presby.
Box 1405
Storm Lake, Iowa 50588
(712) 732-2097

Theresa Caluori
Catholic Peace Fellowship
1100 Carmel Dr.
DuBuque, Iowa 52001
(319) 588-2351

Daniel Clark
Consortium of International
Peace and Reconciliation
317 E. 5th St. #8
Des Moines, Iowa 50309
(515) 244-2253

Freeze Iowa
2631 Knapp St.
Ames, Iowa 50010
(515) 292-4381

KANSAS

Annabell Haupt
1006 Amadon
Wichita, Kans. 67203
(316) 264-4197

Fred Loganhill
514 W. 12th
Newton, Kans. 67114
(316) 284-2452

KENTUCKY

Pat McCullough
Council of Peacemaking
and Religion
3940 Poplar Level Rd.
Louisville, Ky. 40213
(502) 458-0269

Sister Jane Luttrell
4331 Hazelwood Ave.
Louisville, Ky. 40215

CKFOR
812 Severey Lane
Lexington, Ky. 40503
(606) 278-2173

LOUISIANA

Lafayette Pax Christi
c/ Joe McCarthy
611 Taft St.
Lafayette, La. 70503
(318) 233-5970

Herbert Rothschild
Center for Disarmament Ed.
P.O. Box 23790
Baton Rouge, La. 70893
(504) 924-1519

MAINE

Deborah Hibbard
AFSC
P.O. Box 7097
Lewiston, Maine 04240
(207) 772-0680, 784-1278

Pat Jones
Womens Party for Survival
Box 126
Kennybunk, ME 04046
(207) 967-2375

Larry Dassinger
Maine CALC
RFD 1
Newport, ME 04953

MARYLAND

Barbara & Joseph Jensen
FOR
One York Court
Baltimore, Md. 21218
(301) 467-4611

Fran Donalan
Disarmament Program AFSC
317 East 25th St.
Baltimore, Md. 21218
(301) 366-7200

Daniel L. Jerrems
MD Freeze Campaign
2702 Maryland Ave.
Baltimore, Md. 21218
(301) 366-3758

Charles Maxwell
Cedar Lane Unitarians
Bd. of Social Concern
4510 Gretna St.
Bethesda, Md. 20014
(301) 530-1683

Sarah Reese
Nuclear Arms Freeze Task
Force of Maryland
9601 Cedar Lane
Bethesda, Md.
20814
(301) 593-4527

Dave Davis
1912 S. Fountain Green Rd.
Bel Air, Md. 21014
(301) 734-4148

MASSACHUSETTS

Traprock Peace Center
Woolman Hill, Keats Rd.
Deerfield, Mass. 01342
(413) 773-5188

Frances Crowe
3 Langworthy Rd.
Northampton, Mass. 01060
(413) 583-8975

Mark Niedergang
Melinda Fine
Institute for Defense
and Disarmament Studies
251 Harvard St.
Brookline, Mass. 02146
(617) 734-4216

Council for a Nuclear
Weapons Freeze
2161 Massachusetts Ave.
Cambridge, Mass. 02140
(617) 491-7809

Womens Action for Nuclear
Disarmament
56 North Beacon St.
Watertown, Mass. 02172
(617) 923-9542

Ellen Althouse
Cape Cod Chapter
Fellowship of Reconciliation
32 Landings Dr. RR 3
Brewster, Mass. 02631
(617) 896-3106

People for Peace
P.O. Box 537
Great Barrington, Mass. 01230
(413) 229-3457

Louise Bruyn
AFSC
2161 Massachusetts Ave.
Cambridge, Mass. 02140
(617) 661-6130

MICHIGAN

Interfaith Council for Peace
614 E. Huron
Ann Arbor, Mich. 48104
(313) 663-1870

Michigan Nuclear Weapons
Freeze Campaign
P.O. Box 2257
Detroit, Mich. 48226
(313) 962-0416

Institute for Global Ed.
25 Sheldon SE Suite 315
Grand Rapids, Mich. 49503
(616) 454-1642

Mary Curry
Peace & National Priorities
Ctr. of Oakland County
PO Box 5194
Orchard Lake, Mich. 48033
(313) 626-8396

Glen Rouse
PO Box 382
Traverse City, Mich. 49684
(616) 946-1638

MINNESOTA

Sr. Kathleen Shields CSJ
1884 Randolph Ave.
St. Paul, Minn. 55105
(612) 690-2481

Madge Michaels-Cyrus
People for Survival
1925 Nicollet, Suite 101
Minneapolis, Minn. 55403
(612) 870-1501, 874-1540

Dianne Wanner
CALC
122 W. Franklin St.
Minneapolis, Minn. 55404
(612) 871-8033

George E. Dizard
3925 London Rd.
Duluth, Minn. 55804
(218) 525-3617

Cherie Lozier
Rte. 2 Box 184
Frontenac, Minn. 55026

MISSISSIPPI

Carol Burnett
Rte. 4 Box 235
Hattiesburg, Miss. 39401
(601) 864-8715

MISSOURI

Mary Alice Guilfoil, OSB
Peace House
3741 Forest
Kansas City, Mo. 64109

Bill Ramsey
AFSC
438 N. Skinner Blvd.
St. Louis. Mo. 63130
(314) 862-5770

M. Francis Kenoyer, SL
Loretto Disarmament
2544 Cherry
Kansas City, Mo. 64108
(816) 842-5170

Yvonne Logan
WILPF
438 N. Skinner
St. Louis, Mo. 63130
(314) 862-5735

Kansas City Freeze Campaign
629 W. 39th Terr.
Kansas City, Mo. 64111
(816) 756-1904

Ned Stowe
1616 University
Columbus, Mo. 65201
(314) 449-5688

MONTANA

Melissa Kwasny
Womens Party for Survival
Box 464
Basin, Mon. 59631

Mike Kadas
Student Action Center
University Center 105
University of Montana
Missoula, Mon. 59812
(406) 243-5897

NEBRASKA

Nebraskans for Peace
420 South 16th St.
Lincoln, Neb. 68508
(402) 475-4620

Diane Schuette
Omaha Coal. to Freeze
the Arms Race
2104 Davenport
Omaha, Neb. 68102
(402) 345-0539

NEVADA

Great Basin MX Alliance
1650 South Rock Blvd.
Reno, Nev. 89502

Rosemary Lynch
Sagebrush Alliance
704 W. McWilliams Ave.
Las Vegas, Nev. 89106

Arnie Alpert
AFSC
Box 1081, 77 N. Main
Concord, N.H. 03301
(603) 224-2407

Harriet V. Allen
Coal. For Peoples
Rights and Survival
P.O. Box 1032
Dover, N.H. 03820
(603) 749-4076

Dorothy Eldrige
New Jersey SANE
324 Bloomfield Ave.
Montclair, N.J. 07042
(201) 744-3263

Rev. Bob Moore
Coalition for
Nuclear Disarmament
Room #501
20 Nassau St.
Princeton, N.J. 08540
(609) 924-5022

Frank Askin
Coal. For Human Prior.
23 Beaumont Terr.
West Orange, N.J. 07052
(201) 731-2355

Dorie Bunting
NM Peace Conversion
5021 Guadalupe Tr. NW
Albuquerque, N.M. 87107
(505) 344-1140

Ann Kirschner
Box 119
Corrales, N.M. 87048
(505) 842-9498

New Mexicans for a Bilateral
Freeze
2425 Alamo Ave. SE
Albuquerque, N.M. 87106
(505) 255-0381

Santa Fe Peace Coalition
128 Lugar de Oro
Santa Fe, N.M. 85701

Patsy Leake
AFSC New Manhattan Proj.
15 Rutherford Place
New York, N.Y. 10003
(212) 598-0971

James Mang
Western N.Y. Peace Center
440 Leroy Ave.
Buffalo, N.Y. 14215
(716) 835-4073

Rod Morris
Peace Associates
Box 386
Oxford, N.Y. 13830
(607) 843-9382

Nuclear Weapons Freeze
727 Madison Ave.
Albany, N.Y. 12208
(518) 477-4004 or
449-2985,-8673

Nuclear Weapons Freeze Campaign
Suffolk
12 Maple St.
Port Jefferson Station, N.Y. 11776
(516) 928-5555

Ruth Yarrow
Tompkins County
Freeze Campaign
407 Hancock
Itacha, N.Y. 14850
(607) 272-4943

Virden Seybold
AFSC-Upper N.Y. State Area
821 Euclid Ave.
Syracuse, N.Y. 13210

Robert Staley-Mays
Peace & Justice Ed. Ctr.
713 Monroe Ave.
Rochester, N.Y. 14607
(716) 244-7191

Rick Warner
23 University Drive
Clinton, N.Y. 13323
(313) 853-6843, 859-7404

Marty Bartlett
Central N.Y. Freeze Camp.
103 Rita Dr.
N. Syracuse, N.Y. 13212
(315) 458-6266

Cora Weiss
Riverside Church Disarmament
Program
490 Riverside Dr.
New York, N.Y. 10027
(212) 222-5900

NORTH CAROLINA

Mark Legerton/Donna Chavis
Robeson County CALC
P.O. Box 9
Pembroke, N.C. 28372
(919) 521-3269

Anne Welsh
AFSC
PO Box 2234
High Point, N.C. 27261
(919) 882-0109

Steve Summerford
WRL/Southeast
604 W. Chapel Hill St.
Durham, N.C. 27701
(919) 682-6374

Ellen Krebs & Rev. H. Lull
Franklin Peace Fellowship
Rte 3 Box 1164
Franklin, N.C. 28734

John Stevens
University of North Carolina
University Heights
Asheville, N.C. 28814
(704) 258-6600

Coastal Alliance for a Safe
Environment
105 Kenwood Ave.
Wilmington, N.C. 28405
(919) 762-8530

### NORTH DAKOTA

North Dakota Peace Network
Box 782
Mandan, N. D. 58554
(701) 663-6522

### OHIO

Saran Kirschenbaum
Reverse the Arms Race Fed. of Ohio
Ohio Nuclear Weapons Freeze
at the Holy Family Peace Center
584 West Broad
Columbus, Ohio 43215
(614) 221-3741

Columbus Area NWFC
c/o John Lonney AFSC
475 W. Market St.
Akron, Ohio 44303
H) (216) 335-1593
W) (216) 253-7151

Peter Shidemantle
Swords into Plowshares
14321 Detroit Ave.
Lakewood, Ohio 44107
(216) 221-7264

Reverse the Arms Race
Federation of Ohio
3800 Bridge Ave.
Cleveland, Ohio 44113
(216) 281-2600

### OKLAHOMA

Hugh Tribbey
Enid Arms Reduction
Task Force
1802 East Park
Enid, Okla. 73701

Jim Bowers
Oklahoma Peace Center
1829 Gatewood
Oklahoma City, Okla. 73106
(405) 524-1493, 632-7574

### OREGON

Citizens Action for
Lasting Security
Box 12763
Salem, Ore. 97303
(503) 371-8002

Citizens Action for Lasting
Security
P.O. Box 12229
Portland, Ore. 97212
(503) 243-2257

Nora Hallet
Oregon FOR
1838 SW Jefferson
Portland, Ore. 97201
(503) 222-7293

Citizens Action for a Lasting
Security
454 Willanette St.
Eugene, Ore. 97401
(503) 343-8548

Citizens Action for a Lasting
Security
221 Granite St.
Ashland, Ore., 97520
(503) 482-9787

PENNSYLVANIA

Billy Grassie
Penn. Camp. for a
Nuclear Weap. Freeze
1515 Cherry St.
Phila. Pa. 19102
(215) 241-7230

Marlene Bertke, OSB
Pax Center
345 E. 9th St.
Erie, Pa. 16503

Prolifers for Survival
252 E. 9th St.
Erie, Pa. 16503
(814) 456-1791

Nancy Strong
Bucks County WILPS
120 S. Chancellor St.
Newtown, Pa. 18940

Bob Ellenberg
Wayne Citizens for a
Nuclear Weap. Freeze
950 Maple Ave.
Homesdale, Pa. 18431
(717) 253-4051

RHODE ISLAND

Carol Bragg
AFSC
2 Stimson Ave.
Providence, R.I. 02906
(401) 751-4488

SOUTH DAKOTA

Tim Langley
South Dakota Peace
and Justice Center
Box 405
Watertown, S.D. 57201
(605) 882-2822

TENNESSEE

Joceline Lemaire
Nashville CALC
PO Box 90557
Nashville, Tenn. 37209
(615) 292-7607

Sam H. Franklin, Jr.
Oread for the World
513 Court St.
Maryville, Tenn. 37801
(615) 984-3908

Rev. Thomas Kirchberg
3867 Summer Ave.
Memphis, Tenn. 38122

Tenn. Freeze Campaign
3730 Westport Dr.
Nashville, Tenn. 37218
(615) 876-3114

TEXAS

Mary Peter Bruce
Loretto Disarm. Comm.
1300 Hardaway
El Paso, Tex. 79903
(915) 566-1628

Northwest Texas CALC
2500 S. Bowie
Amarillo, Tex. 79109

Mr. & Ms. William C. Hardt
Ecumenical Peace Force
4907 Caris
Houston, Tex. 77091
(713) 688-3803

Roxanne Elder
Texas Mobilization for Survival
1022 W. 6th St.
Austin, Tex. 78703
(512) 474-2399

Ann Wharton
Citizens Anti-Nuclear
Information Team (CAN-IT)
1401 Harold
Houston, Tex. 77006
(713) 528-0397

Diane Orr
2229 Winton Terrace W.
Fort Worth, Tex. 76109
(817) 926-3827

Nuclear Weapons Freeze Campaign
Box 4413
Austin, Tex. 78765
(512) 476-3294

UTAH

Janet Gordon
Citizens Call in Utah
126 S. 1400 West
Cedar City, Utah 84720
(801) 586-6674

MX Information Center
232 ½ University St.
Salt Lake City, Utah 84102
(801) 581-9027

VERMONT

David McCauley AFSC
RD 1
Putney, Vt. 05346
(802) 387-5732

Rev. Howard Stearns
Vermont Ecumenical
Peace Committee
PO Box 593
Burlington, Vt. 05402
(802) 658-2540

The Norwich Center
Main St.
Norwich, Vt. 05055
(802) 649-1000

VIRGINIA

Norman Jimerson
Plowshare Peace Center
P.O.Box 1623
Roanoke, Va. 24008
(703) 985-0808

Steve Hodges
Peace Ed. Center
14 N. Laurel St.
Richmond, Va. 23220
(804) 358-1958

Phyllis Conklin
WILPF
8429 Ben Nevis Dr.
Bel Air, Va. 23235
(804) 272-1851

Nan Rodney
Nuclear Weapon Freeze
6318 Rolling Rd.
Springfield, Va. 22162
(703) 451-5657

Scott Moore
947 Rock Creek Rd.
Charlottesville, Va. 22903
(804) 295-0033

WASHINGTON

Mark Plunkett
Nuclear Weapons Freeze Camp.
4534 ½ University Way NE
Seattle, Wash. 98105

Armistice
P.O. Box 12007
Seattle, Wash. 98102
(206) 324-1489

Nick Kassenbaum
FOR
224 E. Sharpe
Spokane, Wash. 99202

Alice Litton
Whatcom County Nuclear
Arms Freeze
520 17th St.
Bellingham, Wash. 98225

WEST VIRGINIA

AWARE
4030 Clark Graham Rd.
Huntington, W. Va. 25710
(304) 529-3643

Mike Kelly
Box 247
Charleston, W. Va. 25321
(304) 342-2395

WISCONSIN

Michael Trokan
c/o Justice and Peace Ctr.
1016 N. 9th St.
Milwaukee, Wis. 53233

John Stauber
Stop Sanguine ELF
Rt 2 Box 1660
Ashland, Wis. 54806
(715) 278-3758

Dick Bruesehoff
Ecumenical Partnership
for Peace & Justice
Rte. 2 Box 161
Turtle Lake, Wis. 54889
(715) 268-2816

Gary Houser
120 W. Vine St.
Milwaukee, Wis. 53212

Wisconsin Freeze Campaign
315 W. Gorham St.
Madison, Wis. 53703
(608) 256-4146

Lynette Biesamz
Rte. 1
Cochrane, Wis. 54722
(608) 626-3331

WYOMING

Mignon S. & John M. Hill
264 N. 9th
Laramie, Wyo. 82070
(307) 742-2259

Francis Russell, SCL
720 W. 25th St.
Cheyenne, Wyo. 82001

## Groups in Other Countries

**AUSTRALIA**
Australian Liaison Peace Committee
P.O. Box A243
Sydney, NSW 2000

**CANADA**
Canadian Coalition for Nuclear
Responsibility
2010 Mackay St.
Montreal, Quebec

Coalition for World Disarmament
1811 West 16th Ave.
Vancouver, B.C. V6J 2MS

**FRANCE**
Mouvement International De
La Reconciliation
99 Bd. Beaumarchais
75003 Paris

**GERMANY** *(Federal Republic)*
Aktionsgemeinshaft Dienst
Für Den Frieden
D533 Bonn 1, Blücherstr 14

**GREAT BRITAIN**
Campaign for Nuclear Disarmament
11 Goodwin St.
London N4 HQ

European Nuclear Disarmament
Campaign
6 Endsleigh
London WC1H ODX

**ITALY**
Lega International Feminile
Per La Pace E ha Liberta
Viale Glorioso 16
00153 Rome

**JAPAN**
Council Against A and H Bombs
6-19-23 Shimbashi, Minato-ku
Tokyo 105

**NETHERLANDS**
Interkerkelijk, Vrede Sheraad
P.O. Box 18747, Ana Paulownaplein 3
518 BK Den Haag

This is only a partial listing. For a more complete guide to international peace organizations, see the *Peace Diary*, available for $5.50 from Housman's, Publishers and Booksellers, 5 Calendonian Road, London, N. 1, Great Britain.

# Appendix B

## Sources of Information

Get information; it is the best way to arm yourself and disarm others. But on the other hand, don't be overwhelmed by the potential landslide of material available to you. Inform yourself, by all means, but don't get trapped into thinking that you must fully absorb and understand every detail of every argument before speaking out and becoming active; there simply isn't time. And besides, *all* the facts will never be in. Remember: information must be a tool for action, not an end in itself, and you must be sure that the pursuit of ever more information never prevents you from getting something done. Otherwise, you are in danger of suffering Hamlet's dilemma, in which:

> the native hue of resolution
> Is sicklied o'er with the pale cast of thought,
> And enterprises of great pith and moment
> With this regard their currents turn away,
> And lose the name of action.

The key, then, is not information, but action.

As the Red Queen pointed out to Alice, the world is moving so fast that we must run just to keep in place. To get anywhere, we must go twice as fast! So inform yourself but don't forget to start running also.

Most of the organizations in Appendix A provide valuable information, as regular newsletters. For example: "The Defense Monitor" from the Center for Defense Information, "Arms Control Today" from the Arms Control Association, "Sane World" from SANE, etc. They also typically have additional material on selected topics—ask for their list of available literature. For example, Physicians for Social Responsibility has extensive information and reading lists regarding the medical consequences of nuclear war and the nuclear fuel cycle, the AFSC has detailed accounts of nuclear weapons facilities, and the Center for Defense Information publishes a "Nuclear War Prevention Kit," complete with practical suggestions.

Here are some additional sources:

Disarmament Times
Room 7B
777 United Nations Plaza
New York, N.Y. 10001

Institute for Policy Studies
1910 Q St. NW
Washington, D.C. 20009

Sojourners Book Service
1309 L St. NW
Washington, D.C. 20005

"Nuclear Weapons Facilities
    Organizing Packet" available from
AFSC/FOR Nuclear Weapons
    Facilities Project
c/o Fellowship of Reconciliation
Box 271
Nyack, N.Y. 10960

"Resource Packet" containing reading
    lists, flyers, and possible classroom
    syllabus available from
Riverside Church Disarmament Program
490 Riverside Dr.
New York, N.Y. 10027

The following magazines are particularly useful:

The Bulletin of the Atomic Scientists
1029-24 East 58th St.
Chicago, Ill. 60637

Mother Jones
607 Market Street
San Francisco, Calif. 94105

WIN
326 Livingston St.
Brooklyn, N.Y. 11217

The Progressive
408.W. Gorham St.
Madison, Wis. 53703

The Nation
333 6th Ave.
New York, N.Y. 10014

You may also find it interesting to look through some of the many military and military contractor magazines. Although the articles are illuminating ("know your enemy"), the splashy advertisements for new weapons systems are equally thought-provoking. Most of the following can be found in libraries: *Air Force Magazine, Armed Forces Journal, Army Magazine, Aviation Week* and *Space Technology, DMS* (formerly Defense Marketing Service), and *Strategic Review.*

A useful guide through the labyrinth of antiwar magazines is "Periodicals of Public Interest Organizations—A citizen's guide," available for $5 from the Commission for the Advancement of Public Interest Organizations; 1875 Conn. Ave. NW, Suite 1013; Washington, D.C. 20009.

There are also many good books, a large number of which are quite recent, up-to-date. and nontechnical. Our special favorites are

*The Fate of the Earth,*
by Jonathan Schell.
Knopf, New York, 1982.

*Protest and Survive,* edited by
E. P. Thompson and Dan Smith.
Monthly Review Press, New York, 1981.

*Freeze!* by Edward Kennedy
and Mark Hatfield.
Bantam, New York, 1982.

*The Final Epidemic,* edited by
Ruth Adams and Susan Cullen.
Bulletin of the Atomic Scientists,
Chicago, 1981.

*Nuclear Madness,* by Helen Caldicott.
Bantam, New York, 1980.

*Indefensible Weapons: The Political
and Psychological Case Against
Nuclearism,* by Robert Jay Lifton and
Richard Falk. Basic, New York, 1982.

*Other good ones, by topic, include:*

GENERAL

*Nuclear War: What's in it for you?*
by Ground Zero.
Pocket Books, New York, 1982

*Nuclear Nightmares,*
by Nigel Calder.
Viking, New York, 1979.

*The Broken Connection,*
by Robert Jay Lifton.
Simon & Schuster, New York, 1979.

HISTORY

*The Winning Weapon: The Atomic
Bomb in the Cold War 1945-1950*
by Gregg Herken.
Knopf, New York, 1980.

*A World Destroyed: The Atomic
Bomb and the Grand Alliance,*
by Martin J. Sherwin.
Knopf, New York, 1975.

*The Bomb,* by Sidney Lens.
E. P. Dutton, New York, 1982.

*The Balance of Terror*
by Edgar Bottome.
Boston, Beacon, 1971.

CURRENT STATUS OF THE ARMS RACE

*World Armaments and Disarmaments:
The SIPRI Yearbook,*
published annually by the Stockholm
International Peace Research Institute.
Oelgeschlager, Gunn & Hain,
Cambridge, Mass.

*The Military Balance,* published
annually
by the International Institute
of Strategic Studies,
London.

*Dubious Specter: a skeptical look
at the Soviet nuclear threat,*
by Fred M. Kaplan.
Institute for Policy Studies,
Washingon, D.C., 1980.

*The Counterforce Syndrome: a guide
to U.S. nuclear weapons and strategic
doctrine,* by Robert C. Aldridge.
Institute for Policy Studies,
Washington, D.C., 1978

STRATEGIC DOCTRINE

*The Evolution of Nuclear Strategy,*
by Lawrence Freedman.
St. Martin's, New York, 1981.

*Nuclear Illusion and Reality,*
by Sir S. Zuckerman.
Viking, New York, 1982.

EFFECTS OF NUCLEAR WAR

*Hiroshima and Nagasaki,* translated by
E. Ishikawa and D. L. Swain.
Basic, New York, 1981.

*Life After Nuclear War,*
by Arthur M. Katz.
Ballinger, Cambridge, Mass., 1982.

*The Effects of Nuclear War,* by the
Office of Technology Assessment.
Allanheld, Osmun & Co.,
Montclair, N.J., 1980.

*Death In Life: Survivors of Hiroshima,*
by Robert Jay Lifton.
Random House, New York, 1967.

NUCLEAR POWER/NUCLEAR WAR

*Energy/War: Breaking the Nuclear
Link,*
by Amory B. and L. Hunter Lovins.
Harper & Row, New York, 1981.

*The Plutonium Culture,*
by Jim Garrison.
Continuum, New York, 1981.

ARMS CONTROL

*Russian Roulette: The Superpower
Game,* by Arthur Macy Cox.
Times Books, New York, 1982.

*Progress in Arms Control?
Readings from Scientific American,*
edited by Bruce M. Russett
and Bruce G. Blair. W. H. Freeman,
San Francisco, 1979.

*Apocalypse: Nuclear Catastrophe
in World Politics,* by Louis Rene Beres.
University of Chicago Press,
Chicago, 1980.

*The Arms Race and Arms Control,* by
Stockholm International Peace
Research Institute.
Oelgeschlager, Gunn & Hain,
Cambridge, Mass., 1982.

NON-PROLIFERATION

*The Last Chance,* by William Epstein.
Free Press, New York, 1976.

*Controlling the Bomb*,
by Lewis A. Dunn.
Yale University Press,
New Haven, Conn., 1982.

ECONOMICS OF THE ARMS RACE

*The Costs and Consequences of Reagan's Military Buildup*,
by Robert DeGrasse Jr.
with P. Murphy and W. Ragen.
Council on Economic Priorities,
New York, 1982.

*The Zero-Sum Society*,
by Lester Thurow.
Basic, New York, 1980.

*The Empty Pork Barrel: Unemployment and the Pentagon Budget*
by Marion Anderson.
Employment Research Associates,
Lansing, Michigan, 1982.

*World Military and Social Expenditures*, by Ruth Leger Sivard.
World Priorities, Leesburg, Va.,
published annually.

*The Permanent War Economy*,
by Seymour Melman.
Simon and Schuster,
New York, 1974.

RELIGIOUS PERSPECTIVES

*Rumors of War: A Moral and Theological Perspective on the Arms Race*
edited by C. A. Cesaretti
and Joseph T. Vitale.
Seabury Press, New York, 1982.

*Nuclear Disarmament: Key statements from the Vatican, Catholic leaders in North America and Ecumenical bodies*,
edited by Robert J. Heyer.
Paulist Press, Ramsey, N.J., 1982.

*Darkening Valley: A Biblical Perspective on Nuclear War*,
by Dale Aukerman.
Seabury, New York, 1981.

*The Nonviolent Alternative*,
by Thomas Merton.
Farrar, Straus & Giroux,
New York. 1980.

DISARMAMENT

*New Directions in Disarmament*,
edited by William Epstein
and Bernard Feld.
Praeger, New York, 1981.

*The Idea of Disarmament: Rethinking the Unthinkable*,
by Alan Geyer.
Caroline House, Ottawa, Ill., 1982.

*Dynamics of European Nuclear Disarmament* by R. Bahro et al.
Spokesman University Paperbacks
(Bertrand Russell Peace Foundation)
Nottingham, U.K., 1981.

MILITARY POLICY AND CURRENT ARMAMENTS

*The Baroque Arsenal*, by Mary Kaldor.
Farrar, Straus & Giroux,
New York, 1981.

*National Defense,* by James Fallows,
Random House, New York, 1981.

*Arsenal of Democracy II*
by Tom Gervasi.
Grove Press, New York. 1981.

NUCLEAR POLITICS

*The Day Before Doomsday,*
by Sidney Lens.
Beacon, Boston, 1978.

*The Nuclear Question,*
by Michael Mandelbaum.
Cambridge University Press,
New York, 1979.

*The Iron Triangle: The Politics
of Defense Contracting,*
by Gordon Adams.
Council on Economic Priorities,
New York, 1981.

*Real Security,* by Richard J. Barnet.
Simon & Schuster, New York, 1981.

NUCLEAR NEGOTIATIONS

*The Politics of Peace,* by John Barton.
Stanford University Press,
Stanford, 1981.

*Agreements for Arms Control,*
by Josef Goldblat.
Oelgeschlager, Gunn & Hain,
Cambridge, Mass., 1982.

# Appendix C

## Religious Organizations

National Council of Churches
110 Maryland Ave NE
Washington, D. C. 20002

Union of American Hebrew
Congregations
2027 Mass. Ave NW
Washington, D. C. 20036

Interfaith Center to Reverse
the Arms Race
132 North Euclid Ave.
Pasadena, Calif. 91101

Prolifers for Survival
345 East 9th St.
Erie, Pa. 16504

Pax Christi
3000 N. Mango
Chicago, Ill. 61634

National Interreligious Service Board
for Conscientious Objectors
550 Washington Bldg.
15th and New York Ave. NW
Washington, D.C. 20005

New Jewish Agenda
150 Fifth Avenue
New York, N.Y. 10011

Religious Task Force Mobilization
for Survival
Lafayette Avenue Presbyterian Church
85 S. Oxford Street
Brooklyn, N.Y. 11217

Jonah House
1933 Park Avenue
Baltimore, Md. 21217

U.S. Catholic Conference
1312 Mass. Ave NW
Washington, D. C. 20005

World Peacemakers
2852 Ontario Rd NW
Washington, D.C. 20009

Clergy and Laity Concerned
196 Broadway
New York, N.Y. 10038
(212) 964-6730

There are 40 local Clergy and Laity Concerned (CALC) offices, as
follows:

ARIZONA

Arizonians for Peace
c/o Nina Mohit &
Tom Broderson
919 E. Southern Ave.
Phoenix, AZ 85040
(602) 268-3952

CALIFORNIA

Ecumenical Peace
Institute/CALC
944 Market St., Rm. 509
San Francisco, CA 94102
(415) 391-5215

Southern California CALC
P.O. Box 3820
Rosebowl Station
Pasadena, CA 91103
(213) 794-6578

CONNECTICUT

Peace Education & Action
Center
64 Edgewood Ave.
New Haven, CT 06511
(203) 624-0339

DISTRICT OF COLUMBIA

Washington Area CALC
1322 18th St., NW
Washington, D.C. 20036
(202) 223-0527

FLORIDA

Peace Fellowship of North
Florida
P.O. Box 2763
Jacksonville, FL 32203
(904) 354-7355

GEORGIA

Atlantic CALC
222 East Lake Dr.
Decatur, GA 30030
(404) 377-6516

ILLINOIS

Chicago CALC
542 S. Dearborn, Rm. 510
Chicago, IL 60605
(312) 922-8234

Bloomington CALC
812 E. Front St.
Bloomington, IL 61701
(309) 829-5195

IOWA

Quad City CALC
c/o Fr. William Dawson
St. Ambrose College
Davenport, IA 52803
(319) 324-4519

LOUISIANA

Center for Disarmament
Education/CALC
P.O. Box 23790
Baton Rouge, LA 70893
(504) 344-8211 or
924-1519

## MARYLAND

Western Maryland CALC
c/o L. Richard Batzler
9333 Opossumtown Pike
Frederick, MD 21701
(301) 663-0032

Baltimore CALC
c/o Rev. Hope
Harle-Mould
1201 Maple Ave.
Baltimore, MD 21227
(301) 242-9029 (o)
(301) 756-2687 (h)

## MASSACHUSETTS

Central Massachusetts
CALC
14 Castle St.
Worcester, MA 01610
(617) 755-0523

## NEBRASKA

Nebraskans for Peace
430 South 16th St.
Lincoln, NE 68508
(402) 475-4620

## NEW HAMPSHIRE

New Hampshire CALC
c/o Lucille Gundersen
506A RD #2
Plaistow, NH 03865
(603) 382-8023
(617) 373-1284

## NEW YORK

Rochester Peace & Justice
Education Center/CALC
713 Monroe Avenue
Rochester, NY 14607
(716) 244-7191

Syracuse Peace Council
924 Burnett Ave.
Syracuse, NY 13203
(315) 472-5478

Western NY Peace Center
440 Leroy Avenue
Buffalo, NY 14215
(716) 835-4073

## NORTH CAROLINA

Robeson County CALC
c/o Mac Legerton &
Donna Chavis
P.O. Box 9
Pembroke, NC 28372
(919) 521-3269

## MICHIGAN

Detroit CALC
2640 Trumbull
Detroit, MI 48216
(313) 963-4539

Interfaith Council for
Peace/CALC
604 E. Huron
Ann Arbor, MI 48104
(313) 663-1870

Peace & National Priorities
Center of Oakland County
P.O. Box 5194
Orchard Lake, MI 48033
(313) 626-8396

**MINNESOTA**

Minnesota CALC
122 W. Franklin Ave.
Minneapolis, MN 55404
(612) 871-8033

Duluth CALC
First Unitarian Church
1802 E. First St.
Duluth, MN 55812
(218) 724-6084

Morrison County CALC
106 NE 4th Ave.
Little Falls, MN 56345
(612) 632-4384

**MISSOURI**

St. Louis CALC
3753 West Pine
St. Louis, MO 63108
(314) 533-3121 (o)
(314) 865-2093 (h)

**OHIO**

Cleveland CALC
3484 Fairmount Blvd.
Cleveland Hts., OH 44118
(216) 932-9919

Grand Valley CALC
c/o Marge Townsend
7490 Noble Rd.
Windson, OH 44099
(216) 272-5174

**OREGON**

Lane County CALC
1414 Kincaid
Eugene, OR 97401
(503) 485-1755

Mid-Valley Center for
Peace & Justice/CALC
1165 NW Monroe St.
Corvallis, OR 97330
(503) 752-2491

**PENNSYLVANIA**

Philadelphia CALC
300 West Apsley
Philadelphia, PA 19144
(215) 848-8860

Central Pennsylvania

CALC
1706 Maple St.
New Cumberland, PA
17070
(717) 774-6711

**SOUTH CAROLINA**

Columbia CALC
1401 Washington St.
Columbia, SC 29201
(803) 254-9348 (o)
(803) 782-9536 (h)

**TENNESSEE**

Nashville CALC
P.O. Box 90557
Nashville, TN 37209
(615) 292-7607

VERMONT

St. Johnsbury Peace
Team/CALC
P.O. Box 22
East St. Johnsbury, VT
05838
(802) 748-8644

WASHINGTON

Seattle Religious Peace
Action Coaliton/CALC
4759 15th Ave. NE
Seattle, WA 98105
(206) 525-1213

In addition to CALC, the other major interfaith organization is the Fellowship of Reconciliation, P. O. Box 271, Nyack, N. Y. 10960. Numerous denominations have offices affiliated with FOR. They can provide interested church members with literature and advice regarding their own particular denomination and its relationship to nuclear war and the nuclear arms race:

Baptist Peace Fellowship
115 N. Broadway
Nyack, N.Y. 10960

Brethren Peace Fellowship
Box 415
New Windsor, Md. 21776

Buddhist Peace Fellowship
Box 4650
Berkeley, Calif. 94704

Catholic Peace Fellowship
339 Lafayette St.
New York, N.Y. 10012

Church of God Peace Fellowship
1303 E. 5th St.
Anderson, Ind. 46011

Disciples Peace Fellowship
Box 1986
Indianapolis, Ind. 46206

Episcopal Peace Fellowship
Wisconsin Ave. & Woodley Rd. NW
Washington, D.C. 20016

Jewish Peace Fellowship
Box 271
Nyack, N.Y. 10960

Lutheran Peace Fellowship
168 West 100th St.
New York, N.Y. 10025

Southern Presbyterian Peace
Fellowship
1808 Stokes Lane
Nashville, Tenn. 37215

Unitarian-Universalist Peace
Fellowship
12861 Titian
Granada Hills, Calif. 91344

United Methodist Peace Fellowship
5123 Truman Rd.
Kansas City, Mo. 64127

United Presbyterian Peace Fellowship
Box 271
Nyack, N.Y. 10960

# Appendix D

## Tax Resistance Groups

This partial list was prepared originally by the Philadelphia War Tax Resistance League, 2208 South St., Philadelphia, Pa. 19146.

O = organizing and actions

C = counseling

F (L&G) = Alternative Fund (Loans and Grants)

L = living in community

NV = training in nonviolence

Bartimaeus Community
2118 8th St.
Berkeley, CA 94710
(415) 841-7121 C. L.

Teven Laxer
515 20th St.
Sacramento, CA 95814
(976) 442-5120

Berkeley Students for Peace
608 Eshelman Hall
UC Berkeley
Berkeley, CA 94720
(415) 642-7783

Monterey County WTR
251 Littleness Ave.
Monterey, CA 93940
(408) 375-1776 L

The Peacemaker (newsletter)
PO Box 627
Garberville, CA 95440

Eric Schell
1962 Railroad Ave.
Livermore, CA 94550
(415) 449-0494
C. L. Tax Revolt

Resource Center for Nonviolence
PO Box 2324
Santa Cruz, CA 95063
(408) 423-1626
O. C. NV, L

Sam Tyson
Modesto Peace/Life Center
631 15th Street
Modesto, CA 95354
(209) 529-5750 or 874-2498

Lonnie Valentine
25985 Via Pera
Mission Viejo, CA 92691
(714) 586-5190 O. C.

War Resisters League West
War Tax Resistance
1360 Howard St., 2nd fl.
San Francisco, CA 94103
(415) 626-6976
O. C. F(G), NV

Franklin Zahn
836 So. Hamilton Blvd.
Pomona, CA 91766
(714) 629-5675 O. C.

CONNECTICUT

Common Cents
Community for Nonviolent Action
R.D. 1, Box 430
Voluntown, CT
(203) 376-9970
O. C. F(G), NV. L

DISTRICT OF COLUMBIA

Washington Area Fund for Life
Norm & Gwen Strike
3142 19th St., NW
Washington, DC 20010
(202) 483-1168
F(G)

Washington WTR
c/o Bill Samuel
3417 Carlin Springs Rd. #202
Falls Church, VA 22041
(703) 578-0625 O. C.

GEORGIA

Kathy Johnson
1425 Miller Ave.
Atlanta, GA 30307
(404) 577-1498
O. NV, L

Robert G. Randall II
1714 Adolphus St., NE
Atlanta, GA 30307
(404) 377-5431
O. C. NV

Tax Conversion Fund for Peace
and Human Needs
1225 Cameron Court, NE
Atlanta, GA 30306
(404) 378-3237 or 377-5431
F(G&L)

ILLINOIS

Karl Meyer
1460 Carmen
Chicago, IL 60640
(312) 784-8065 C

KANSAS

Peace & Social Concerns
General Conference Mennonite
Church, Box 347
Newton, KS 67114
(316) 283-5100
C (and education)

Kaye Yoder
141 N. Charies
McPherson, KS 67460
(316) 241-2935

MAINE

Cushman D. Anthony
177 Commercial St.
Portland, ME 04111
(207) 775-6371 evenings 767-2419
C

Larry Dansinger, INVERT
RFD 1
Newport, ME 04953
(207) 938-2219 O. C. NV

MARYLAND

Eleanor B. Webb
5622 Alhambra Ave.
Baltimore, MD 21212
(301) 435-6928

MASSACHUSETTS

Dan Lawrence
138 Prescott St.
South Lancaster, MA 01561
(617) 368-0009

Jean & Jim Matlack
623 Main St.
Amherst, MA 01002
(413) 253-5390

Wally & Juanita Nelson
Woolman Hill
Deerfield, MA 01342
(413) 773-9065

New England War Tax Resistance
Box 174, MIT Branch PO
Cambridge, MA 02139
(617) 731-6139
O. C. F(L&G)

War Tax Resistance Group
Friends Meeting at Cambridge
5 Longfellow Park
Cambridge, MA 02138
(617) 876-6883 O. C.

MICHIGAN

Richard Chandler
448 Pleasant St., SE
Grand Rapids, MI 49503
(616) 452-8044
O. C. F(L&G), NV, L

Day House
2640 Trumbull
Detroit, MI 48216
(313) 963-4539
O. C. F(L&G), L

Detroit Fund for Life
c/o John Jones
5511 Three Mile Drive
Detroit, MI 48224
(313) 884-0583
O (as individuals), F

Bruce B. & Ruth K. Graves
1209 Roosevelt Blvd.
Ypsilanti, MI 48197
(313) 483-0058
court experience

Greenwood Community
254 E. Michigan
Battle Creek, MI 49017
(616) 963-0113

Jasiu Milanowski
Ammon Hennacy House
241 Charles, SE
Grand Rapids, MI 49503
(616) 454-8491
O. C. F(L&G), NV. L

Life Sharing Fund
320 MAC Ave.
East Lansing, MI 48823
(517) 337-2731
O. C.° F(L&G), NV, L

Noah's Raft Community
439 Park Place
Kalamazoo, MI 49001
(616) 343-3875
O. C.° F(L&G), NV, L

° all the same fund

MINNESOTA

Minnesota WTR
122 W. Franklin, Rm. 302
Minneapolis, MN 55404
(612) 871-8033
O. C. F(G)

MISSISSIPPI

Clarice Campbell
P.O. Box 792
Holly Springs, MS 38635
(601) 252-2534

NEW JERSEY

North Jersey WTR
c/o Community Store, Inc.
3716 Park Ave.
Weehawken, NJ 07087
(201) 539-6315

NEW MEXICO

Albuquerque War Resisters League
5021 Guadalupe Trail, NW
Albuquerque, NM 87106
(505) 243-6169
O. C. NV

NEW YORK

New York City WTR
339 Lafayette St.
New York, NY 10012
(212) 244-4270
O. C. F(L)

Rochester Peace & Justice
Education Center
713 Monroe Ave.
Rochester, NY 14607
(716) 244-7191
O. C. NV. L

Suffolk County Committee for a
World Peace Tax Fund
44 Bellhaven Road
Bellport, NY 11713
(516) 286-8824
O. C. WPTF escrow account

Syracuse Peace Council
924 Burnett Ave.
Syracuse, NY 13203
(315) 472-5478

War Resisters League
339 Lafayette St.
New York, NY 10012
(212) 228-0450

## NORTH CAROLINA

Lyle & Sue Snider
50 Albemarle Rd.
Asheville, NC 28801
(704) 254-3469
O (and education)

WRL Southeast
604 W. Chapel Hill St.
Durham, NC 27701
(919) 682-6374
O. NV

## OHIO

Rod Nippert/Peacemakers
Rt. #1, Box 90-B
Amesville, OH 45711
O. NV. L

Marty Zinn
Rt. 1, Box 475-A
Athens, OH 45701
(614) 696-7724
C. NV. L

## OREGON

Military Tax Resistance/Portland
Peace Investors
c/o Genny Barnhart
1809 SE Hawthorne # 103
Portland, OR 97214
(503) 231-9551
O. C. F(G), NV

## PENNSYLVANIA

Brandywine Peace Community and
Alternative Fund
51 Barron Rd.
Media, PA 19063
(215) 565-0247
O. C. F(L), NV. L

Center on Law and Pacifism
300 W. Apsley St.
Phila., PA 19144
(215) 844-0365
C. legal aid

Friends Peace Center
4836 Ellsworth Ave.
Pittsburgh, PA 15213
(412) 683-2669
C. F(L), NV, education

London Grove Friends Peace
Committee
Arthur P. Yeatman
RD 1
Cochranville, PA 19330
(215) 593-2346 C

Philadelphia WTR/WRL
2208 South St.
Phila., PA 19146
(215) 545-4626
O. C. F(L)

War Tax Concerns Support
Committee, Phila. Yearly Meeting
of Friends
1501 Cherry St.
Phila., PA 19102
(215) 241-7230

**RHODE ISLAND**

Rhode Island Alternative Fund
c/ AFSC
2 Stimson Ave.
Providence, RI 02906
(401) 751-4488
O. F(L&G)

**VERMONT**

Robert Zeuner
Dairy Hill Rd.
So. Royalton, VT 05068

**VIRGINIA**

(see DC or NC)

**WASHINGTON**

WR/PLC Newsletter
331 17 Ave., East
Seattle, WA 98112

**WISCONSIN**

Apple River Peace Fellowship/
Wisconsin WTR Alternative Fund
RR 2, Box 161
Turtle Lake, WI 54889
O. C. F(L&G), NV, L